CONTENTS

ILLUSTRATIONS

THREE RENAISSANCE TRAVEL PLAYS

This volume brings together three little-known plays that convey vividly the fascination in early seventeenth-century England with travel and exploration. In their different ways they are all dramas of wandering and adventure, and they explore the great diversity of responses in the period to the lures of tourism and colonial expansion, and to the challenges posed by the encounter with exotic places and peoples.

In *The Antipodes*, written in 1638, we encounter the first travel snob in English drama, who declares that 'Of Europe I'll not speak: 'tis too near home'; but the two earlier plays already reflect England's far-flung pursuit of trade and diplomacy in the Islamic world and settlement in North America. Both also give prominence to the hazards and opportunities regarded as typical of such ventures: piracy, shipwreck, cannibalism; untold wealth, foreign despots and glamorous women.

The first two plays appear for the first time in a modern edition, whilst Brome's masterpiece has not been available for some years. This collection presents modernised texts with an extensive commentary and a full introduction to set the plays in their historical and cultural context.

Anthony Parr is Senior Lecturer in English at the University of the Western Cape.

The Revels Plays
COMPANION
LIBRARY

E. A. J. HONIGMANN, J. R. MULRYNE,
R. L. SMALLWOOD and PETER CORBIN general editors

For over thirty years *The Revels Plays* have offered the most authoritative editions of Elizabethan and Jacobean plays by authors other than Shakespeare. The *Companion Library* provides a fuller background to the main series by publishing worthwhile dramatic and non-dramatic material that will be essential for the serious student of the period.

All titles distributed in the USA by St. Martin's Press

THE REVELS PLAYS COMPANION LIBRARY

Three Renaissance travel plays

THE TRAVELS OF
THE THREE ENGLISH BROTHERS

THE SEA VOYAGE

THE ANTIPODES

edited by Anthony Parr

Manchester University Press

Manchester and New York

distributed exclusively in the USA and Canada
by St. Martin's Press

COPYRIGHT © Anthony Parr 1995

published by MANCHESTER UNIVERSITY PRESS
Oxford Road, Manchester M13 9NR, UK
and Room 400, 175 Fifth Avenue
New York, NY 10010, USA

distributed exclusively in the USA and Canada
by ST. MARTIN'S PRESS, Inc.
175 Fifth Avenue, New York, NY 10010, USA

British Library Cataloguing-in-Publication data
A catalogue record for this book is available
from the British Library

Library of Congress Cataloging-in-Publication data applied for

ISBN 0 7190 3746 8 *hardback*

Typeset by Best-set Typesetter Ltd., Hong Kong

Printed in Great Britain
by Biddles Ltd, Guildford and King's Lynn

GENERAL EDITORS' PREFACE

Since the late 1950s the series known as the Revels Plays has provided for students of the English Renaissance drama carefully edited texts of the major Elizabethan and Jacobean plays. The series now includes some of the best known drama of the period and has continued to expand, both within its original field and, to a lesser extent, beyond it, to include some important plays from the earlier Tudor and from the Restoration periods. The Revels Plays Companion Library is intended to further this expansion and to allow for new developments.

The aim of the Companion Library is to provide students of the Elizabethan and Jacobean drama with a fuller sense of its background and context. The series includes volumes of a variety of kinds. Small collections of plays, by a single author or concerned with a single theme and edited in accordance with the principles of textual modernisation of the Revels Plays, offer a wider range of drama than the main series can include. Together with editions of masques, pageants, and the non-dramatic work of Elizabethan and Jacobean playwrights, these volumes make it possible, within the overall Revels enterprise, to examine the achievement of the major dramatists from a broader perspective. Other volumes provide a fuller context for the plays of the period by offering new collections of documentary evidence on Elizabethan theatrical conditions and on the performance of plays during that period and later. A third aim of the series is to offer modern critical interpretation, in the form of collections of essays or of monographs, of the dramatic achievement of the English Renaissance.

So wide a range of material necessarily precludes the standard format and uniform general editorial control which is possible in the original series of Revels Plays. To a considerable extent, therefore, treatment and approach is determined by the needs and intentions of individual volume editors. Within this rather ampler area, however, we hope that the Companion Library maintains the standards of scholarship which have for so long characterised the Revels Plays, and that it offers a useful enlargement of the work of the series in preserving, illuminating, and celebrating the drama of Elizabethan and Jacobean England.

E. A. J. HONIGMANN
J. R. MULRYNE
R. L. SMALLWOOD
PETER CORBIN

In memory of Philip Birkinshaw

ACKNOWLEDGEMENTS

Much of the research for this volume, and most of the writing, was done at the Huntington Library in San Marino, California, and like others before me I found there both the peace and the scholarly stimulus that make it virtually an ideal working environment. To Martin Ridge and Roy Ritchie, as successive Directors of Research, and to their courteous and efficient colleagues at the library, I owe my sincere thanks. I am also grateful for the material support offered by fellowships at the Huntington in 1990 and 1992, and to the British Academy for covering the cost of travel to California.

My own peregrinations during a sabbatical year also took me to Cape Town, where I was hospitably received by the English Department at UCT and given a place to work. I have incurred numerous other debts in the course of preparing this book. In London, Richard Proudfoot and Thomas Healy helped to clarify my early ideas about its shape, and Peter Holland supplied some timely hints when those ideas needed to be modified, as well as sharing with me his own thoughts about travel plays. Kevin Sharpe was consistently generous with advice and encouragement, and Lesley Marx helped to pull the book together after reminding me that travel can still yield fortunate discoveries. For other help and advice I am grateful to Bill Deverell, Barbara Donagan, Reg Foakes, Helga Galvan, Larry and Susan Green, Michael Hattaway, John Mortell, Wendy Piatt, Roy Ritchie, Eleanor Searle, Adrian Weiss and Peter Wright. I would also like to thank the staff of the British Library and the Bodleian Library, and those who assisted me at the libraries of the Victoria and Albert Museum, the Warburg Institute, and the California Institute of Technology.

Through their meticulous scrutiny of my travails, Peter Corbin and John Banks have saved me from stumbling at numerous points, though any remaining potholes must be my responsibility. Anita Roy and her team at Manchester University Press were unfailingly helpful and efficient.

Cape Town   A.P.
January 1995

ABBREVIATIONS AND REFERENCES

The collaborative authorship of the first two plays (a process which this edition does not explore) is usually reduced to the names Day and Fletcher respectively; and the title of the first play is generally shortened to *Travels*.

References to Shakespeare's plays are to the one-volume Oxford Shakespeare, ed. Stanley Wells & Gary Taylor, unless otherwise indicated. References to plays by other writers are to the Revels Plays series where applicable; otherwise, first editions or modern Complete Works are cited. Those of Jonson's plays not published in the Revels series are quoted from Herford and Simpson (HS). Proverbs are identified by their reference number in Tilley or, where specified, in Dent. All cited texts before 1900 were published in London unless otherwise indicated.

Quotations from early-modern sources in the Commentary and Introduction are given in the original spelling, unless taken from modernised editions; but I have silently normalised i/j, u/v, and the long 's' (except in the Collation). Archaic contractions have also been expanded without comment.

EDITIONS AND EDITORIAL

Travels

Q   John Day, William Rowley & George Wilkins, *The Travailes of the Three English Brothers*, 1607.

Bu.   *The Works of John Day*, ed. A. H. Bullen, 1887

The Sea Voyage

F   *Comedies and Tragedies Written by Francis Beaumont & John Fletcher Gentlemen. Never printed before, And now published by the Authours Originall Copies*, 1647.

F2   *Fifty Comedies and Tragedies. Written by Francis Beaumont & John Fletcher Gentlemen. All in one Volume*, 1679.

Mason   J. Monck Mason, *Comments on the Plays of Beaumont and Fletcher*, 1798.

Dyce   *The Works of Beaumont & Fletcher*, ed. Alexander Dyce, 1845, vol. 8.

The Antipodes

Q   Richard Brome, *The Antipodes*, 1640.

Works 1873   *The Dramatic Works of Richard Brome . . . in Three Volumes*, 1873.

Baker   *Representative English Comedies*, ed. C. M. Gayley, 1914 (vol. 3 includes G. P. Baker's ed. of *The Antipodes*).

Haaker   *The Antipodes*, ed. Ann Haaker, Regents series, 1966.

OTHER TEXTS

HS   Herford and Simpson, *Ben Jonson* (11 vols.), 1925–52.
Knight   Francis Beaumont, *The Knight of the Burning Pestle* (1607), ed. Sheldon Zitner, The Revels Plays, 1984.
conj.   conjectural emendation (not promoted by editor to text).
edd.   previous editors.
om.   omitted.
SD   Stage direction.
SP   Speech prefix.

GENERAL

Bentley   G. E. Bentley, *The Jacobean and Caroline Stage*, 7 vols., 1941–68.
Burton   Robert Burton, *The Anatomy of Melancholy*, ed. T. C. Faulkner *et al.*, 1989–.
Cartwright   John Cartwright, *The Preachers Travels . . . to . . . the East Indies . . . Containing a full servew of the Kingdom of Persia: and . . . a true relation of Sir Anthony Sherley's entertainment there*, 1611.
Cotgrave   Randle Cotgrave, *A Dictionarie of the French and English Tongues*, 1611.
CSP   Calendar of State Papers.
Davies   D. W. Davies, *Elizabethans Errant: The Strange Fortunes of Sir Thomas Sherley and his three sons*, 1967.
Dent   R. W. Dent, *Proverbial Language in English Drama Exclusive of Shakespeare, 1495–1616*, 1984.
Gurr   Andrew Gurr, *The Shakespearean Stage*, 3rd ed., 1992.
Hakluyt   Richard Hakluyt, *The Principall Navigations, Voyages & Discoveries of the English Nation* (1598), repr. 1903–5.
Linthicum   M. Channing Linthicum. *Costume in the Drama of Shakespeare and his Contemporaries*, 1936.
Mandeville   *The Voyages and Travailes of Sir John Mandeville Knight . . . Together with the many and strange Mervailes therein*, 1625.
Newes in the Antipodes   *Newes, True Newes, Laudable Newes . . . The World is mad . . . especially now when in the Antipodes these things are come to passe*, 1642.
Nixon   Anthony Nixon, *The Three English Brothers*, 1607.
Nungezer   E. Nungezer, *A Dictionary of Actors*, 1929.
Parry   William Parry, *A new and large discourse of the Travels of sir Anthony Sherley Knight . . . to the Persian Empire*, 1601.
Purchas   Samuel Purchas, *Hakluytus Posthumus or Purchas His Pilgrimes* (1625), repr. 1905–7.
Reynolds   G. F. Reynolds, *The Staging of Elizabethan Plays at the Red Bull Theater 1605–1625*, 1940.
Sandys, *Ovid*   George Sandys, *Ovid's Metamorphosis Englished, Mythologiz'd, and Represented in figures . . .*, 1632.

Sandys, *Relation*   George Sandys, *A Relation of a Journey*, 1615.

The Sherley Brothers   *The Sherley Brothers, an historical memoir . . . by one of the same house*, 1848.

Tilley   M. P. Tilley, *A Dictionary of the Proverbs in England in the Sixteenth and Seventeenth Centuries*, 1950.

Torquemeda   Antonio de Torquemeda (transl. L. Lewkenor), *The Spanish Mandeville of Miracles*, 2nd ed., 1618.

Warner   William Warner, *SYRINX, or A seavenfold Historie, handled with varietie of pleasant and profitable both commicall and tragicall Argument*, 2nd ed., 1597.

INTRODUCTION

And when, after the long trip, I arrived in Patagonia I felt I was nowhere. But the most surprising thing of all was that I was still in the world—I had been travelling south for months. The landscape had a gaunt expression, but I could not deny that it had readable features and that I existed in it. This was a discovery—the look of it. I thought: *Nowhere is a place.*

Paul Theroux, *Patagonia Revisited*

LEARNING AT HOME

In his account of a visit to England in 1599, the Swiss traveller Thomas Platter comments at some length on the variety of organised entertainment available in London, reporting visits to two plays and a bearbaiting, and concludes: 'With these and many more amusements the English pass their time, learning at the play what is happening abroad... since the English for the most part do not travel much, but prefer to learn foreign matters and take their pleasures at home.'[1] Platter's picture seems to suggest an important role for the travel play in Renaissance England. By 1599 Hakluyt's *Principall Navigations* and imported Dutch atlases were—at a price— available to armchair travellers, and some of the innovative work done on the Continent in geography and comparative history was beginning to be translated into English. But most people still relied for foreign information on the travellers' tales that abounded in port cities like London and Bristol and on much-reprinted compilations like the 'briefe collection... of strange and memorable thinges' made from Sebastian Munster's *Cosmographia* in 1572. Otherwise, popular conceptions of exotic experience were shaped by occasional journalism (pamphlets with titles like *Strange Newes out of Poland*) or by *Mandeville's Travels* and romance fiction, writing whose images of 'abroad', when they were not purely conventional, drew from the encyclopaedias and natural histories, with their catalogues of marvels and curiosities, that the Renaissance inherited from late antiquity and the Middle Ages.[2]

Platter's assertion that the English do not travel much conflicts with an old idea that they are naturally errant and curious, governed by the moon,[3] and it ignores their role in opening maritime trade routes and their robust legends of westward discovery.[4] Moreover, his picture of a people remaining in its island fastness can be qualified by pointing to aristocratic tourists in the sixteenth century—early exponents of what would evolve into the Grand Tour—and the pioneering forays of British merchants into Russia and the Middle East.[5] But despite the feats of its seamen and the determined efforts of the colonising lobby to settle North America in the 1570s and 1580s, England remained a deeply insular country. Fernand Braudel asserts, with telling hyperbole, that with the loss of its Angevin possessions in France and the subsequent break with Catholic Europe, England 'became . . . an island';[6] and Jeffrey Knapp has recently suggested that humanism merely emphasised the breach, since the rediscovery of the classics 'gave new life to an old image of England that uncannily reflected its modern plight—an island whose inhabitants were *penitus toto divisos orbe* (Virgil, *Eclogues* 1), wholly divided from all the world'.[7] In such a situation, a popular art-form like the theatre which undertook to deal with foreign subjects might find itself with a ready audience and an opportunity to shape its views.

Consciousness of their relative isolation led to much soul-searching by English humanists. The lure of European travel was considerable for those wanting to participate in the Renaissance movement: it offered opportunities to meet foreign intellectuals, visit famous cities and their universities, and learn about modern art and architecture, as well as to tour the ancient sites. But enthusiasm for this project was constantly hedged around by anxiety about the moral and physical dangers posed by foreign places—particularly the risk to Protestants travelling in the Catholic south—and checked by more fundamental doubts about the wisdom of being on the move. Moralists were fond of quoting classical admonitions on the subject, and this rendering of lines from Horace's second Epistle is one of many that reached a wide audience:

> Why fleest thou through the worlde? in hope to alter kinde:
> No forren soile, hath anie force to change the inward minde.
> Thou doste but alter aire, thou alterest not thy thoughte:
> No distance farre can wipe awaye, what Nature first hath wroughte.
> The foole, that farre is sente some wisdome to attaine:
> Returnes an Ideot, as he wente, and brings the foole againe.[8]

Parochial assurance of this sort will always find a voice, though inevitably it did not still the aspirations of most humanists. Their response to the perceived perils of travel was to turn it as far as possible into a controlled exercise, setting out itineraries and stipulating the conduct and agenda of the cultural tourist in guides which, despite their forbidding tone, were to be enormously influential, and in some ways have never been entirely superseded.[9]

The other major focus of humanist aspiration lay in the west, as the English pondered the Iberian achievement in Central and South

America (for many the consequence of the Tudor failure to back Columbus) and made the first tentative moves towards their own colonial effort. In 1519 the lawyer and printer John Rastell, who two years earlier had launched an abortive colonising voyage to North America, consoled himself with writing what might be called the first English travel play and lamented the opportunity lost in the New World:

> O what a thynge had be[en] than
> yf that they that bee Englyshe men
> Myght have ben the furst of all
> That there shulde have take possessyon
> And made furst buyldynge & habytacion . . .[10]

Other voyages followed, but more than half a century was to pass before plans for a colony were renewed, and none of the settlements planted in Elizabeth's reign managed to put down lasting roots.

At the end of the sixteenth century, then, interest in a wider world was vigorous but largely unfulfilled. For many Londoners it may have best been satisfied at the theatre. In 1599 Thomas Platter could have seen or heard of performances of *Sir John Mandeville*, *Jerusalem*, and *Muly Molloco* (all now lost plays); English military adventures abroad were portrayed in *Henry V* and their consequences for impressed soldiers shown in *The Shoemaker's Holiday*; Dekker's *Old Fortunatus* offered a lively and mildly topical version of the romantic 'journeying' play. Marlowe's plays still held the stage, recreating Tamburlaine's campaigns and more recent historical conflicts in Malta and Paris, and exposing in Dr Faustus' world tour the ultimate vanity of travel—a message that was being more satirically enforced in 1599 by Jonson's *Every Man out of his Humour*. More than one play, no doubt, portrayed Sir Philip Sidney's 'awry-transformed traveller' who brings home foreign fashions and affectations.[11] In 1595 the Admiral's Men had staged *The New World's Tragedy*, perhaps inspired by the lost colony on Roanoke Island in Virginia or by the much-trumpeted atrocities of the Spanish further south; and there must have been other plays which exploited the large chronicle of travel and adventure by then available in English.

Platter sees the London audience going to such plays for information, to get a window on the world. This appears to be too simple a view, reducing all foreign representations to a documentary function. But there is a sense in which the capacious category of 'travel writing', as defined by Hakluyt's great project, might have encouraged that audience to see foreign subjects on the stage as part of a current debate about England's place within and designs upon a larger world. Travel literature at this date means many things—various kinds of survey, historical geography, accounts of colonial conquest, as well as actual relations of a journey. Even for the more empirically-minded 'travel writing' meant almost any kind of enquiry into foreign matters, and the few accounts of a journey proper that exist from the sixteenth century were not recognised as belonging to a distinct genre. Hakluyt had included Mandeville in his first edition of 1589, and by the end of the century the empirical endeavour to describe the variousness of the world and its inhabitants was only just beginning to sort itself into distinct categories of study and writing. The travel play is an offshoot of this vigorous, confused and fluid project.

The question of drama as information raises another issue. Recently there has been a tendency to see travel writing in general as a discursive operation rather than as an historical record, dissolving the difference between real-life and fictional narratives and insisting upon the dependence of both on prior perspectives and established tropes. Philip Edwards has eloquently defended the factual accounts of travel and exploration against this levelling process, which effec-tively equates things that happened with things that are made up.[12] Where literary and dramatic fictions about travel are concerned the argument is more slippery. Even where they obviously owe something to recorded events, plays, stories and poems also operate by their own laws, and there is one kind of 'travel writing', the peripatetic romance in which the characters seek themselves and each other through an exotic landscape, which remains almost entirely untrau-matised by the specifics of Renaissance discovery: a good example is the recently discovered play *Tom o'Lincoln*, which puts Prester John and the Amazons on stage without a flicker of geographical or cultural curiosity.[13] But most travel fictions lack this kind of her-meneutic purity. All the plays in this volume originally appealed to their audiences' imaginative investment in a *developing* state of affairs, whether it was an on-going political story like the Sherley brothers' adventures, or the latest developments in Atlantic colon-isation, or the current exploration of the southern hemisphere. The crusade against Islam, the shipwreck on a desert isle, and the trope of the world upside-down are long-established motifs made subject to modification by the pressure of contemporary events and discoveries, and no dramatist dealing with such subjects could assume that the curiosity of the theatre spectator would automatically be satisfied by received ideas, or that his own *inventio*—his particular assembly of exotic themes and materials—had an authority independent of the reconstructions of the world that travel and exploration were them-selves effecting.

In other words, the travel play is implicated in the material pro-cesses of Europe's reconnaissance of the Old World and its 'fortunate discovery' of the New. In it traditional ideas become volatile, trendy and debatable, and it is potentially a very sensitive register of changing historical (and spacial) awareness. This is not to say that its function is usually a documentary one. There are few surviving plays which take a recorded journey as their subject, perhaps in part because the most prestigious English travels were those of sailors like Drake and Cavendish, whose adventures could scarcely be staged; and the awareness amongst dramatists of the technical difficulties of dramatising *any* journey may have inhibited them from using ones that already existed in written form. It is unfortunate that plays like the already-mentioned *New World's Tragedy* and *The Plantation of Virginia* (1623)—the latter presumably about the massacre of colonists by the Indians in 1622—have not survived, since these may well have been attempts to stage specific instances of cultural encounter in the Americas. But between such chronicle efforts and the wandering romance lies a body of writing whose contract with the realities of travel is complex and difficult to define. To take a well-known example: critics have worked hard to justify the conviction that *The Tempest* is a play about colonialism and New World discovery, despite its paucity of reference to such things; and without wanting to rely, as too much new-historicist writing has done, on the argument that 'absence is presence', it is clear that, when a dramatist declines to make his exotic setting conform exactly to one in Hakluyt, he is not necessarily discouraging us from making an imaginative connection with the navigations of his own or any other nation. *The Tempest* and *The Sea Voyage* in their very different ways depend on a lack of geographical specificity to create a world that seems full of the travails of contemporary voyaging.

Fletcher and Massinger's *The Sea Voyage* (acted 1622) is the most promiscuous of these three plays in exploiting a wide variety of travel reports for the purposes of a theatrical entertainment. As a consequence it manages to be modish and 'relevant' without having to make claims for its accuracy. It is preceded here by a drama as topical as anything which survives from the Renaissance stage—indeed, one which might easily have offended political sensibilities, given its advocacy of a clan whose activities continued to be suspect in government eyes even as the play was being performed. The praise of maverick adventurers in *The Travels of the Three English Brothers*, written by Day, Rowley and Wilkins and acted in 1607, was, however, probably designed to set them off against the eponymous hero in *Captain Thomas Stukely*, a 1590s play about a notorious Elizabethan pirate and traitor which was published in 1605 and probably revived at the rival Fortune theatre at about the same time. Anthony Nixon, whose pamphlet about the Sherleys was the principal source for *Travels*, explicitly invokes Stukely and points the contrast between 'the manner of their travels...The one having his desire upon a luxurious, and libidinous life: The other [i.e. Sir Anthony Sherley] having principally before him, the project of honour' (Gv); but it is a comparison which links as much as it distinguishes the two plays. At a time when some theatrical companies were poking fun at the vogue for travel and staging burlesques of the journeying play—the collaborative *Eastward Ho!* (1606) is a prime example—the more popular playhouses like the Red Bull and the Fortune were plotting the courses of contemporary knights-errant and assimilating their travels to an older species of quest. It is a kind of writing which may have helped to provoke the satirical mood on the other London stages, though (as I shall suggest) we should not assume too readily that it had only a naive appeal. *Travels* takes its task seriously, for it undertakes to portray diplomatic activity and cultural contact between England and both Catholic and non-European powers in a way that was impossible as long as the foreign was simply demonised or caricatured on the stage. Its topicality is part of a cultural process.

At the other end of the spectrum, seemingly, is Richard Brome's *The Antipodes* (acted 1638), in which the theatrical representation of a journey is designed to cure the obsession with foreign marvels and promote harmony at home. In many ways Brome's play, written when tourism was commonplace and colonial voyages had become routine, returns to old humanist anxieties about travel and its consequences for education and self-knowledge. Peregrine's disorientation sounds a note that is largely absent from the tribulations of the Sherley brothers and Fletcher's castaways, but recalls the warnings of earlier moralists on the perils of what the play calls 'extravagant thoughts' (I.i.147). Essentially this is because the issue of the efficacy of travel is built into the play, in a fantasy journey which is designed to discredit itself in the eyes of its protagonist. Is the only worthwhile journey the one that leads to disillusionment? Is the same true of representations of travel? In one sense we are not very far here from Ascham's jeremiad against Italy in *The Scholemaster* ('I was once in Italy myself, but I thank God my abode there was but nine days');[14] but whereas for the early humanists the argument was often conducted in terms of books versus experience, with the study being recommended as safer and more beneficial than actually venturing abroad, by the seventeenth century the issue had become more complicated. Peregrine after all has lost his wits not by travelling but because he was refused the opportunity to put his reading into practice. This is an interesting variant on the scenario drawn by Joseph Hall in one of his verse satires, where he describes 'the brainsicke youth that feeds his tickled eare' with 'whet-stone leasings of old *Maundevile*' and talks obsessively about mermaids, 'head-lesse men' and cannibals, until he is driven

> Of voyages and ventures to enquire.
> His land mortgag'd, He sea-beat in the way
> Wishes for home a thousand sithes a day:
> And now he deemes his home-bred fare as leefe
> As his parch't Bisket, or his barreld Beefe.[15]

It is unlikely that by 1598 *Mandeville's Travels* inspired many to follow in his footsteps, and it is doubtful whether Hall thought that it did. His collocation of reading and venturing is itself a kind of literary conceit which takes general aim at the frivolity of the age. But it leaves open the question of how travel accounts were to be regarded and used by his contemporaries. The quoted lines are also reminiscent of the gallants in *The Sea Voyage* as they complain about the sacrifices they have made and think nostalgically about home comforts; Hall would perhaps have read that play as a cautionary fable, warning the audience against the folly and danger of overseas ventures. Yet in his own terms it is also an incitement to travel, and even his scornful dismissal of Mandeville's tall tales recognises their appeal to the imagination. Hall went on to create his own antipodean fiction in *Mundus Alter et Idem* (1605), a scathing satire on social and intellectual trends which, like Brome's play, creates an exotic fantasy world designed to disturb the assumptions of its audience. The admonitory purpose of these fictions is realised not by putting up a No Entry sign but by taking the reader or viewer on a journey of discovery, one which (to invert the Horatian dictum quoted earlier) changes our minds despite not requiring us to tread on foreign soil.

BROTHERS AND OTHERS:
The Travels of the Three English Brothers

The circumstances in which *The Travels of the Three English Brothers* was written and performed in 1607 give us some insight into the commercial opportunities that well-documented foreign adventures offered to the professional stage. The play is fairly closely based on Anthony Nixon's pamphlet *The Three English Brothers*, but the exact relationship between the two works has never been properly stated. The three-week difference between their entries in the Stationers' Register has sometimes been taken as a measure of how quickly the play was written, but if it was a rush job it was done earlier in the year, since the results were evidently on the stage before Nixon's account went to press. The playwrights must have had access to Nixon's manuscript, or to the sources (written or oral) on which Nixon drew. It seems possible that there was extensive collusion. If, as is likely, Thomas Sherley commissioned Nixon soon after his return to England in December 1606, he may well have encouraged plans for a stage play as well, to give maximum publicity to the brothers' adventures. And Nixon might not have been averse to a theatrical trailer for his own efforts. But the decision to print the play seems to have caused a few ripples. Judging by the Stationers' Register entry, Nixon's original title was to have been the same as the play's, and the sub-title given there reflected his statement in the text that Robert Sherley married the Sophy's 'cousin Germaine'. When his book appeared, however, the title was abbreviated to *The Three English Brothers*, and the sub-title (though not the text) now agreed with the play that Robert's wife was the Sophy's niece. It looks as though the decision to publish the play was announced after Nixon's book had been registered but before it (or at any rate its title-page) was actually printed.

Why did the players decide to publish? The usual argument against doing so—that the company would lose exclusive control of the text—had particular force in 1607, for it was in that year that play-texts began to be registered under the hand of the Master of the Revels, in effect acknowledging that publication of a play was equivalent to licensing it for performance.[16] It had always been the case that a printed play was available to be acted by other companies; but the new practice of official registration seems to recognise that the conditions now existed for widespread production of plays that had done well in London. The provinces boasted a number of competent acting companies which toured widely, and one of these—known to have used printed quartos to make its own prompt-books—staged *Travels* in Yorkshire at Christmas in 1609.[17] Other plays in this company's repertory that season were *Pericles and King Lear*, so clearly they went for the most popular and up-to-date plays available. And since Queen Anne's Men (who performed *Travels* in London) also did a fair amount of touring, it had a strong incentive in these circumstances not to let its most successful plays escape into print.

The most likely explanation is that the company saw Nixon's book as about to capitalise on successful production of their play in the summer of 1607, and decided not to let it reap all the advantage to be had out of printing the Sherley story. A longish summer run of a highly topical play may have been thought to have exhausted its theatrical interest, and since parts of the saga it tells were unfinished it ran the risk of being overtaken by future events. Commercial judgements of this kind probably coincided with a desire on the part of Thomas Sherley to help his brothers, both of whom were effectively marooned abroad, by circulating their story as widely as possible. In the wake of Anthony Sherley's inconclusive embassy, the problem was how to keep the absent brothers in the public eye, and in the Epistle to the printed quarto edition the authors are careful to point out that a book can be a reassuringly solid 'picture' of absent friends and heroes. But we need to look more closely at the kind of impact this play was designed to have, and the effect it actually had, on audiences and readers in the early Jacobean period.

Thomas Fuller later described *Travels* as 'but a *friendly foe*' to the memory of the Sherleys, 'more accommodated to please the present spectators than inform posterity'.[18] But the dramatists felt able to claim that their treatment of the brothers was based on available knowledge, and would not be condemned by anyone in the audience who might 'better know their states than we' (Epilogue, 26—see note). We should be cautious about seeing the play only through the eyes of a rival dramatist like Francis Beaumont, whose *Knight of the Burning Pestle* (1608) is a thoroughgoing burlesque of 'adventuring' plays like *Travels* and Heywood's *Four Prentices of London*, mocking the pretensions of a patriotic drama which shows English heroes abroad in a series of implausible triumphs over foreign adversaries. That such plays appealed to popular taste at theatres like the Fortune and the Red Bull is unquestionable; but it is less clear that martial adventure on the stage found favour only with unsophisticated audiences. Recently William Hunt, discussing the fashion for military exercises amongst London's citizens, and Marion Lomax have each suggested that Beaumont's play may have failed at its first Blackfriars production because it underestimated the appeal of chivalric subjects to educated tastes.[19] Lomax points out that Shakespeare's *Pericles*, a play which is indebted in some ways to *Travels*, includes a visual quotation from *Don Quixote* by having Pericles appear at Simonides' court in rusty armour, but turns this potentially satirical moment into an affirmation of knightly virtue and endurance, one which 'defies ridicule and appears to support the current chivalric revival associated with James I's eldest son, Prince Henry'.[20] The dedication of the quarto of *Travels* to 'Honour's favourites' seems also to be aimed at the constituency around the prince which, in marked contrast to his father's court, was promoting an aggressive and interventionist foreign policy. It had been at the behest of the Earl of Essex that Anthony Sherley set out in 1598 on the travels which eventually took him to Persia, his initial brief being to defend the Italian city-state of Ferrara against the Pope; when this initiative collapsed, a visit to Venice yielded a commission to attack Portuguese bases in the Persian Gulf.[21] Many of Prince Henry's supporters were keen to espouse causes such as these, finding themselves 'cold and unactive' (as Sherley puts it in the play, i.144) in the cautious world of Jacobean diplomacy.

The appeal to militant Protestant opinion in *Travels* is not, however, allowed to exclude a broader vision of foreign relations. The play is remarkable for its sympathetic depiction of the Papacy in scene v, one that apparently helped to recommend *Travels* as suitable viewing for a Catholic family in 1609.[22] The dramatists were probably aware that at an early point in his travels Anthony Sherley had converted to Rome, and this may have influenced their decision to present the Pope as a dignified and credible spiritual leader, the 'mouth of heaven' and the 'stair of men's salvations' (v.39, 46). No such emphasis is to be found in the play's known sources; indeed, Nixon's way of promoting the Sherley mission was to contrast it with Thomas Stukeley's 'treacherous designes . . . in the behalfe of the *Pope*' (Gv). In 1607 anti-Catholic feeling was still rife in the wake of the Gunpowder Plot, and had contributed to the virulent polemic of a play like Dekker's *Whore of Babylon*, staged at the Fortune theatre in the previous year. But Day and his colleagues do not merely avoid anti-Papal propaganda: they actively counter it (and the prevailing public mood) by enlisting the Pope in a larger Christian cause. In their play Babylon is not Rome but the seat of the Ottoman empire, and the vaunt of Dekker's Empress that of 'this vast Globe Terrestriall . . . almost three parts [is] ours' (1607 ed., A4v) is transferred in *Travels* to the Great Turk who boasts that 'we . . . with our eagle's wings/Canopy o'er three quarters of the world' (viii.3−7).

This rephrasing in fact tightens the connection between the two plays, for that unexpected Ottoman eagle, and the Great Turk's reference to his 'petty kings' (viii.3), adapt Dekker's allusion to the apocryphal three-headed eagle that was taken to symbolise the tributary powers of the Roman Catholic Church.[23] The two plays give us very different and in effect mutually exclusive visions of how the outside world impinges on Europe's security. In one view, the power and wealth of the Iberian nations, fuelled by American conquest and East Indian trade, makes possible a Catholic crusade against the Protestant powers which needs to be resisted in every way; in the other, Europe must unite against her common enemy in the East. The fact that these two aims were in conflict did not prevent Anthony Sherley from switching between them, as he did when he abandoned the plan to attack the Portuguese base at Ormuz in the Gulf and took up the idea of a Perso-Christian alliance against the Turks—even though the latter project threatened trade routes used by English companies (passing overland from the East through Ottoman dominions) that the disruption of rival Portuguese seaways had been designed to promote. But the dramatists, even if they were aware of Sherley's change of heart, obey the logic of the situation as their sources presented it and omit any hostility towards the Catholic powers, making the vision of a pan-Christian contract with enlightened paganism the centre of their play.

It is a vision that relied heavily upon belief in the Turkish threat. Christian Europe generally overestimated the strength of the Ottoman empire in the early seventeenth century (see ii.6–7 note), but the Turkish stranglehold on the Near East was undeniable, and for purposes of trade several countries, including England, tried to retain cordial relations with Constantinople. Turkish customs and political organisation often aroused the grudging admiration of travellers, though few could overcome their resistance to what they perceived as a deeply alien culture, and the animus against Islam joined with the notorious cruelty of Ottoman sultans to create an immovable stereotype of the raging and expansionist Turk. Persia was a rather different case. Traditionally the land of wealth and luxury, with a glorious imperial past, it was for Western writers a genuinely exotic country, not a malign and unknowable neighbour but a fabulous resource. Like India or Japan, it was not so much Europe's Other as its opposite or foil; and while the fascination with the glamorous east was later to become a disabling orientalism, arguably it was during the early modern period a positive alternative to views of Asia either as the home of barbarian hordes or of the hellish doctrine of Islam— Western conceptions that Edward Said describes as 'a closed system' which 'no empirical material can either dislodge or alter'.[24] Of course, as an Islamic country itself Persia was capable of attracting opprobrium like its Ottoman neighbour, and some commentators were happy to contemplate the two infidel states being at war to their mutual disadvantage (an enmity 'very commodious and of great opportunitie to the Christian Commonweale', as John Cartwright put it (A2v)). But the long-cherished design of a league between Persia and Christian Europe, something which had been talked about for over three hundred years, was fed by more substantial ideas.

In a pamphlet published in 1609 to promote Robert Sherley's subsequent embassy to Europe, Thomas Middleton (as G. B. Shand has shown) carefully omits from the description of Persia any reference to Islam and almost all suggestion of hedonistic luxury. This is a spartan state in which Persians 'seem more like Protestants than like Turks in their religion'[25] and customs, and are thus a worthy ally against the Ottoman threat. The writers of Travels are altogether more eclectic in their portrayal of Europe's potential war partner. Like Middleton they make use of pre-Islamic descriptions of Persian society—many of which were reproduced in supposedly up-to-date geographies and ethnographies—but they also draw on first-hand travel accounts and do not avoid the tricky question of how a *rapprochement* between Christianity and Shia Islam is to be achieved. It is clear from contemporary references that Europeans were intrigued by the schism between Sunni Muslims (generally identified with the Turks) and the Shi'ites in Persia, and even when their interest was largely pragmatic—to drive a wedge between the followers of Mahomet—it forced them to look at, and seek correspondences with, the Islamic culture that they chose to support. Shi'ism, at least from the English perspective, was all about true succession and the legitimacy of a martyred prophet: 'Mortus Ali', as the son-in-law of Muhammad was known in the West, was regarded as the Prophet's nominated heir by Shi'ites who rejected the 'false' caliphs that had initially succeeded him. Later European translations of traditional Persian 'miracle' plays clearly find an analogy between 'Ali's messianic inheritance and the Christian ministry,[26] one that may also have been perceptible to sixteenth-century visitors attending performances of such plays. At the same time the claims of 'Ali could be seen to resemble those of dynastic monarchy, and both English and Persian sensitivity to the advantages of this is apparent in Sir Thomas Herbert's report that Shah Abbas I claimed to be '*of true Discent from* Mortys-Ally'.[27]

Although Abbas I tolerated some Christian minorities within his borders, it is doubtful that he spent any time thinking about ideological—as opposed to tactical—affinities with the Western powers. Similarly, as we have seen, Anthony Sherley was being thoroughly opportunistic in the way he took up the idea of a Perso-Christian alliance. But those whose job it was to write about Europe's new market-places and spheres of interest had the more considered task of placing them in an imaginative framework where their meaning, value and potential could be assessed. In travel accounts, geographies, promotional literature for trading and colonial companies, and fictional writing that takes up their concerns, the primary task is to provide a way of seeing the unfamiliar; and while this is almost by definition a matter of reconceiving the foreign in one's own terms, the process is not uniformly reductive. The Western demonisation of the Turk is a brutal travesty in a way that the attempt to accommodate Persian Shi'ism is not, even though the effect of the latter, and maybe part of its initial purpose, was to reinforce the prejudice against Ottoman power and beliefs. We should not be surprised that a play like *Travels* contains its fair share of crude caricature, for figures like The Great Turk and Zariph the Jew are theatrical stereotypes that keep the play anchored in a Renaissance audience's reality; but they co-exist with, and in a sense help to

Shah Abbas I. From Thomas Herbert,
A Relation of Some Yeares Travaile (1634)

support, a fairly complex dramatisation of cultural encounter.

Cultural difference is in fact the play's principal theme. The English negotiations at the Persian court, which span politics, religion, the ethics of war and mixed marriage, provide a sort of frame for arguments between Persians and Turks over Islamic doctrine,

Christian—Jewish antipathy in Venice, and an encounter between the two great acting traditions of the English stage and the Italian *commedia dell'arte*. Less an intricate fabric than a miscellany of related ideas, it is none the less rather carefully constructed, as Neville Davies has shown, so that a rough symmetry puts the encounter between Will Kemp and Harlequin (scene ix) at the centre of the play, sandwiched between the Zariph scenes which in turn are enclosed by the episodes featuring Thomas Sherley's adventures and his brother Robert's attempts to ransom him and vanquish his own enemies (scenes vi—vii and xi—xii).[28] As Davies points out, this symmetrical plan is somewhat obscured by other features, but the dramatists also endeavour to make it unobtrusive by not punctuating each episode with Chorus and dumb show, allowing the action 'to pass freely between narration, mime, and spoken drama'. Davies finds this 'mixing of media' to be 'unsettling',[29] but I would argue that it is a flexible and resourceful way of organising the material. The dramatists use the Chorus mainly to recount journeys which it is impracticable to stage, and accompanying mime to suggest key moments in the journeys like the events in Moscow in scenes iv and v. The Chorus's summary role in those scenes and at the beginning of scene vi, dispatching—with the aid of dumb show—a great deal of far-flung movement, offsets the lengthy opening sequence in Persia (i—iii), rapidly broadening the scene to prepare for the fluid interplay of geographically separated storylines in the remainder of the action. As a consequence the cross-cultural arguments about clemency, honour and religious belief which are raised in the first third of the play do not get lost in congested plot movements in its second half.

The debate that takes place between the Sophy and Anthony Sherley in scene i arises out of interpretation of the mock-battle that each side stages for the other: the Persians demonstrate a victory over the Turks by entering '*with heads on their swords*', while the Christian brothers conclude their show by having the winning side parade its prisoners (i.47—86). The episode reveals the dramatists' careful deployment of their source-material, coming as it does only a few lines after the entry direction for the Sophy '*from wars with drums and colours*' (i.32). All the contemporary accounts of the Sherley mission describe the Shah's return to Qasvin after his victory over the Uzbegs, and none omits the graphic detail that his army carried pikes surmounted by thousands of the heads of the defeated. I have tried to analyse these accounts elsewhere;[30] what is important now to note is the use made of this information in the play. The writers carefully avoid any suggestion that the heads on Persian swords are meant to be real: this is not a representation of an actual triumph, as it would have been if they had simply dramatised what they found in their sources, but a show of a show, a representation of courtly make-believe, a masque or pageant within a play. And it is clear that such a strategy is necessary to keep the Persian triumph within the same discursive arena as its Christian counterpart—as if the dramatists recognised that to *show* the procession of severed heads as part of the main action (and so early in the play) is a strong visual statement that might generate unwanted responses. As it is, the pageant of mock-battles establishes the context for a debate, initiated by the Sophy's puzzlement about one element in the Christian charade:

> *Sophy.* But what means those in bondage so?
> *Sir Anthony.* These are our prisoners.
> *Sophy.*   Why do they live?   (i.100−1)

To which Anthony replies that it is Christian practice to show clemency to a yielding foe. A significant portion of the later action is shaped by this issue: in the third scene Robert Sherley, Hotspur-like, refuses to yield up his Turkish prisoner to Halibeck, who relishes the prospect of putting him to death—a fate which his victim accepts as part of the 'custom of tyranny' between the two nations (ii.105). Later in the play Robert orders that the captains of the defeated Turkish army be put to death, on the grounds that as commander he is 'the Persian substitute/And cannot use our Christian clemency' (vii.14−15), though he halts the executions when he sees the chance to ransom his brother with those that remain alive. In his version of this episode Nixon reports that Robert cut off the heads of the captains 'and (according to the custome of Persia) caused them to bee carried in triumph about the Market place' (K3); but the dramatists avoid the implication either that Robert has gone native or that his action legitimises Persian military custom.

Any suggestion, however, that Persia is the acme of pagan cruelty is carefully qualified by other elements in the play. For instance, the dramatists pass over Nixon's story of a benevolent Jew who helped Thomas Sherley in prison in favour of their invented figure of Zariph, who in scene x proves himself a savage lurking in Christian society by his ambition to make Anthony's heart 'the sweetest part/Of a Jew's feast' (19−20). Even this melodramatic portrayal, though, is obedient to the play's interest in cultural encounter by interspersing Zariph's taunts and gloating with a certain amount of theological disputation. Sunni Islam, on the other hand, never succeeds in getting a hearing in the play, and the violent episode (xii.81−107) of Thomas Sherley's torture by the Ottoman Turks proves to be the play's starkest opposition of Christian fortitude and pagan tyranny. In the end The Great Turk is confounded by Thomas' inexplicable constancy, and returns his captive to King James with a pompous formality that on the Renaissance stage no doubt reflected the niceties of contemporary diplomacy—and leaves us clear about who is the moral victor. When we return after these episodes to Halibeck's hearing before the Persian court in scene xiii, the grounds for a *rapprochement* between England and Persia have been laid. Already the Sophy has shown a ludic sensitivity to the truth by his device of mock-execution in scene ix; and in the final scene his instinctive recognition of Halibeck's guilt is matched by a sure judgement of how it must be punished. Robert's plea for mercy on Halibeck's behalf (more substantial than it was in Nixon) is seen as honourable but unrealistic, and the condemnation of the traitor is the point at which Persian rigour and Jacobean security are seen to coincide: the Sophy makes a proper distinction between Halibeck's personal injury to the Sherleys and his offence against the state, one which an English audience would have been bound to endorse. In what follows the compliment is returned, as the granting of Robert's petition confirms the openness of Shi'ite Islam to the beneficial example of Christianity.

The diplomatic fiction created here is not entirely illusory. James I's officers of state may not have been interested in building the particular alliance adumbrated here, and indeed saw the Sherleys as a threat to their links with the Ottoman court and the interests of the Levant Company; but the vision of reciprocity conjured by Anthony in praising his homeland to the Sophy—

> There lives a princess
> Royal as yourself, whose subject I am
> As these are to you.   (i.136–8)

—is precisely the kind of gesture that was being made in numerous cultural encounters in the Americas and the Far East, where recognition of an analogous structure of authority was the easiest (and often the only) way of creating confidence on both sides. That such affirmations were often preludes to and even strategies for obtaining dominion over native peoples has, oddly, just been acknowledged in the Sophy's reaction to a demonstration of the English guns:

> *Chambers go off.*
>
> *Halibeck.*   Mahomet! It thunders.
> *Sophy.* Sure this is a god ...
>   First teach me how to call thee ere I speak.
>   I more and more doubt thy mortality.
>   Those tongues do imitate the voice of heaven
>   When the gods speak in thunder; your honours
>   And your qualities of war more than human.
>   If thou hast godhead, and disguised art come

To teach us unknown rudiments of war,
Tell us thy precepts and we'll adore thee. (i.117–27)

This speech, so reminiscent of reported first encounters in the New World, is hardly appropriate to the present context, though it is certainly revealing of the potential for misunderstanding and self-betrayal in any dialogue between widely dissimilar cultures. Anthony's response is in effect a tactful corrective, and the means by which the play recovers its balance: 'No stranger are the deeds I show to you/Than yours to me' (130–1). For the remainder of *Travels* Persia is shown neither as a primitive society nor as a luxurious and hedonistic one, and its political dignity and standards of honour (despite the Sophy's professed ignorance of the latter) are betrayed only by the provincial small-mindedness of courtiers like Halibeck and Calimath. It is such men, not problems of cultural difference, that jeopardise the prospect of real alliance, which Anthony enthusiastically perceives as resting on a fundamental human oneness:

> All that makes up this earthly edifice
> By which we are called men is all alike.
> Each may be the other's anatomy;
> Our nerves, our arteries, our pipes of life,
> The motives of our senses all do move
> As of one axletree, our shapes alike. (164–9)

We have already noted that this ecumenical vision has its human limits in the play—no room in it for Turk or Jew—and its rhetorical purpose of building political kinship is what emerges most clearly here. The dramatists shape their material with a similar end in mind, as for instance when they make Halibeck the sole cause of Anthony's subsequent problems in Moscow and Rome: in his account William Parry attributes some of the blame to a quarrelsome Dominican friar who was part of the embassy, but it is essential to the play's design for a seamless Christianity to underwrite the new alliance against the infidel. This artistic decision recognises the diplomatic truth that unity always depends to some extent on tactical exclusion.

How seriously, then, does the play take its own affirmations? It is tempting now to dismiss its ending (which attracted some contemporary ridicule) as a Eurocentric vanity, incorrigibly naive about the realities of cultural exchange. But Renaissance people were not modern multiculturalists, nor did the majority espouse the relativism of Montaigne. As J. H. Elliott has lately remarked, it is

> currently fashionable to denounce the observers of earlier ages for their insensitivity to the otherness of the Other. But . . . some of those observers . . . had quite a different set of goals from our own, and were strug-

gling to discover resemblances, not differences ... It was brothers, not others, whom they wished to find. Ironically, it is the otherness of these early European observers and ethnographers which now tends to be overlooked.[31]

What is true of explorers and missionaries is also true of those who use their findings, and in this play Day and his colleagues dramatise the Persian mission with some uncertainty of tone but with a sound sense of what is politically feasible. The final scene of *Travels* is a finely judged resolution, in which the Sophy grants a series of requests with a crisp urbanity that gives away nothing of importance: he shows no personal interest in Christianity, and the offer to stand godfather is the indulgent gesture of a self-confident ruler. In the dying moments of the play the barriers begin to go up again: Robert's last petition is for a Christian enclave or ghetto where children will be kept in ignorance of the surrounding culture, and the Epilogue confirms that he and Anthony Sherley, for all their status in foreign courts, have paid the price of estrangement for their travels:

> Unhappy they (and hapless in our scenes)
> That in the period of so many years
> Their destinies' mutable commandress
> Hath never suffered their regreeting eyes
> To kiss each other at an interview.   (3–7)

The final dumb show offers to rectify the situation:

> *Enter three several ways the three brothers: ...* Fame *gives to each a prospective glass: they seem to see one another and offer to embrace*

—but at this point 'Fame *parts them*', in a poignant acknowledgement that actual reconciliation is the one 'ornament' that poesy cannot add to the brothers' history (Prologue, 6–7).

The dangers passed by the Sherley brothers are meant to evoke admiration, approval and pity, but we might ask whether the dramatists altogether exclude the possibility of a contrary response. In scene vi, for instance, where Thomas Sherley invades the Greek island of Kea, it seems at first that they are trying to make the best of a sordid and ignominious episode, for the tone is heroic and there is no acknowledgement of who his antagonists really are. The play registers some of the logical objections to the raid (presenting them as his followers' disloyal sentiments), but suppresses the most obvious—that Sherley was not attacking Turks but killing and plundering their Greek subjects, whom Western Europe wanted to see freed from the Ottoman yoke. Anthony Nixon is uneasily aware of this, making sporadic references to 'Greeks' and having Thomas order that no Christians are to be harmed, but he leaves the issue

The prospective glass affords a glimpse of the antipodes (see Introduction, note 59). From title page of *Newes, True Newes* (1642)

unresolved. The playwrights cut the Gordian knot: committed overall to a design in which the Turk (here the occupying power) is the common enemy, they do not permit the question of the raid's morality (as opposed to its tactical wisdom) to complicate the issue. The Greeks are simply erased from the scene. But this economical account is managed in a heavily inflated register, so that the scene teeters on the edge of burlesque.

In his previous play, *The Ile of Gulls* (1606), John Day had aired the much-discussed issue of dramatic style on London's stages where, the Prologue complains, if the poet 'compose a Sceane/Of high writ Poesie, fitting a true stage,/Tis counted fustian'.[32] This suggests that he and his fellow-dramatists were well aware of the potential effect on an audience of Thomas' epic calls to arms, and of how cogent his followers' rejection of them might sound. The possible presence of the real Sir Thomas in the audience (perhaps as a sponsor of the play—see pp. 8–9 above) would have constrained the writers from

open criticism of his reckless aggression, but it might also have
encouraged the thought that he was one of those travellers who 'like
the industrious bee, having sucked the juice of foreign gardens, they
make wing to their own homes and there make merry with the
fraught of their adventures' (iii.126–9). (Nixon refers unsatirically
to 'the pleasure that he [Sir Thomas] now conceives in the remembrance of his forepassed miseries' (E3v).) The fact that this caveat
about adventurers is entered early in the play certainly renders the
brothers' exploits more subject to the audience's judgement. And if,
as suggested earlier, plays about knights-errant were popular at this
time and not simply considered low fare, this makes it all the more
likely that the substance and quality of the Sherleys' adventures
would have been a matter for general debate.

PIRACY AND SETTLEMENT:
The Sea Voyage

The hapless islanders of Zea, like the inhabitants of Iberian coastal
towns pillaged by Anthony and Thomas Sherley in the 1590s, had
good reason to agree with the Sophy's Niece that 'strangers' could
'prove dangerous' (iii.125–6). Her remark no doubt appealed to the
xenophobia of a Jacobean audience, but since she is talking about the
newly-arrived Englishmen it also posed a certain challenge to it. Not
many were yet ready to question the morality of overseas ventures
which imposed upon the lives of foreign peoples, but in other ways
English actions abroad were a source of considerable anxiety, and
easily fed the old suspicion that travel fosters an irregular and
renegade spirit. As we have seen, the exploits of the Sherley brothers
were an off-shoot of the bellicose and semi-official foreign policy
pursued by the Earl of Essex in the 1590s. A similar opportunism
was apparent in many colonial ventures: in 1573 Sir Thomas Smith
sternly admonished prospective Irish settlers that their task was 'to
laye the foundacion of a good and... an eternall colony for your
posteritie, not a may game or stage playe';[33] but even after the
establishment of joint-stock companies to direct foreign enterprise
there were plenty of freelance speculators looking for a share of the
overseas action. Discomforting the Spanish and the search for quick
riches were the sole motives behind Roger North's colony established
on the Amazon in 1620 in clear defiance of the orders of the Privy
Council;[34] and the difficulty of finding reliable colonists was also to
plague approved ventures like the early settlement of North America.
Fletcher's feckless gallants in *The Sea Voyage*, drawn by the prospect
of 'happy places and most fertile islands/Where we had constant

promises of all things' (SV, III.83–4), are modelled on the younger sons of minor gentry who hoped to find in the colonies the wealth and status denied them at home, and who proved in many cases to be maladjusted and work-shy. The ambitions of such men received a boost after 1617, when changes in the government of Virginia led to deregulation of previously tight controls on landholding and created opportunities for emigrants to establish large estates.[35]

The fact that the gallants are on board a pirate vessel is also significant. There was an unholy alliance between privateering and colonial voyages throughout the period: the early Virginia settlements had been financed out of attacks on the Spanish treasure fleet, and these did not cease even when peace with Spain in 1604 ended the issuing of letters of marque. In 1606 an independent syndicate set up a colonising mission to Virginia, but when the project disintegrated in July before leaving Ireland, one ship went instead to plunder merchant vessels in the Straits of Gibraltar (as Thomas Sherley had done in 1602), and others resorted to piracy off the Spanish coast. The hijacking of American voyages for such purposes was not uncommon, as two governors of Virginia, John White and John Smith, both learned to their cost;[36] and in 1609 Sir Richard Moryson proposed, as a solution to the growing problem of pirates on the south coast of Ireland, that since they were mainly interested in plundering Iberian shipping they should be deployed as a defence force for Virginia and supply the colony with spoil from raids on the Spanish West Indies.[37]

Thus when various characters in The Sea Voyage give contradictory reasons for the expedition, this is not the result of confused plotting on Fletcher's part but a reflection of contemporary maritime practices. The gallants complain that Albert, rather than fulfilling his commission to sail straight to the 'happy places', has been prevailed upon by Aminta to 'put in everywhere' (III.89) in search of her brother; but Albert's claim that this was his sole intention all along ('For you I put to sea to seek your brother', I.i.102) sounds like a romantic version of the priorities ascribed to the privateers taking John White to Virginia in 1590: 'Thus both Governors, Masters, and sailers, regarding very smally the good of their countreymen in Virginia; determined nothing lesse then to touch at those places, but wholly disposed themselves to seeke after purchase & spoiles, spending so much time therein, that Sommer was spent before we arrived at Virginia.'[38] The play was no doubt meant to remind an English audience of the French corsairs that for a century had harried Portuguese settlements in the Azores and Brazil, but merchants and officials in the Blackfriars audience also knew that by 1620 pirate ships had an important (and popular) function in supplying the

Atlantic colonies with commodities, often undercutting the prices set by the official companies. The scale of such operations is suggested by the fact that in 1616 the pirate captain Henry Mainwaring was reported as having six hundred men sailing under his banner in American waters.[39]

Fletcher does not set out to dramatise recent events with the same directness as *Travels*, but he is alert to a whole range of documentary reference which modernises and complicates his island story. The play cunningly exploits the Jacobean audience's dual desire for topicality and timeless adventure. Sea stories, whether on the page or in the theatre, usually derived from the Alexandrian romances and similar sources rather than from contemporary voyage accounts, and in obedience to this tradition Fletcher loosely bases the action of his play on William Warner's *Syrinx*, a euphuistic prose romance written in the 1580s. This tale of Medes and Assyrians occasionally uses an up-to-date travel idiom, and Fletcher may have been alerted to it by Warner's more famous work *Albions England*, which is full of references to the voyage literature; but for his purposes *Syrinx* is no more than a frame to catch and hold a number of echoes from the contemporary record.[40] It is in the same spirit that Fletcher 'overgoes' *The Tempest*. When it is discussed at all, *The Sea Voyage* is usually said to be largely derivative of that play, but this gives a misleading impression. The device of opening with a storm at sea is obviously inspired by Shakespeare's example, but in content and tone the two scenes are very different. Fletcher goes for pathos and satire and a joky decorousness: when a sailor gives offence it is for praying rather than swearing, and the keen bawdy of a ship 'leaky as an unstanched wench' (*Temp.*, I.i.45–6) is replaced by routine superstition about the presence of women on board. Similarly, Fletcher borrows from *The Tempest* the idea of the woman who has never seen a man, but puts it to quite different use. He follows Shakespeare, though, in making the island setting teasingly elusive. Because it uses a more circumstantial language than *The Tempest*, we seem to catch glimpses in *The Sea Voyage* of numerous places and situations that seventeenth-century readers would find in the voyage literature: the hot, swampy coastline of Guinea with its Portuguese outcasts, the great river estuaries of Brazil, the island chains of Cape Verde and the Canaries; and see reflected in the motley castaways and their dialogue some of the tensions and ambitions running through the English colonial effort in North America. But the very abundance of analogy tends to suggest that, like *The Tempest*, this play refutes any attempt to tie it exclusively to a particular place or venture.

Fletcher's substitution of French and Portuguese characters for the classical adventurers of *Syrinx* reflects the Atlantic struggles between

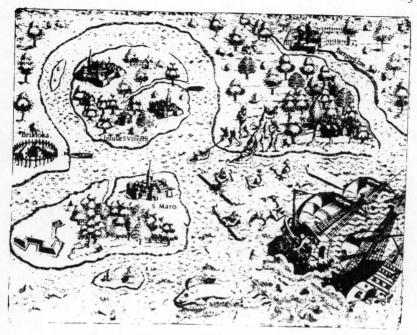

A Portuguese settlement off the Brazilian coast. Well known
images like this one probably shaped the play's island topography.
From T. de Bry, *America*, Part II (1592)

the two nations in the sixteenth century, of which many tales recur in
the voyage literature. One such is in André Thevet's *The New Found
Worlde* (1568), where he describes the 'Iland of Rats' off the Brazilian
coast, on which a Portuguese ship was wrecked and all but two of
the survivors died in the course of two years, 'which in the meane
time lived with Rattes, Birdes, and other beastes. And as on a time
there passed by a ship of *Normandie*, that returned from *America*,
they set their skiffe out for to rest in that Ilande, whereas they found
these two poore *Portingalls* ... the which they brought away with
them.'[41] These benevolent French voyagers find a place in Act IV
when Raymond rescues Sebastian and Nicusa, but a English audience
used to Dunkirk pirates would no doubt regard them as untypical,
and Fletcher models the rest of his French adventurers on the
Assyrians in *Syrinx*, described by Warner as 'these Rovers and
Robbers of the whole world' (S3). Looking into Hakluyt for further
French material, he would have read the account by René Laudonnière of the colonists planted in Florida in 1562 by Jean Ribault

under the leadership of a Captain Albert. The Indians give them pearls and silver, and tell them where to find more, but the French 'entred...into partialities and dissentions', and when these are settled look for means to escape. They build a pinnace, but get becalmed and run out of food: 'their victuals failed them altogether at once: and they had nothing for their more assured refuge but their shooes and leather jerkins which they did eat.'[42] Eventually they resort to cannibalism. This kind of story appealed to English chauvinism, but Fletcher may have wanted to make a less comfortable point. Hakluyt, in printing Laudonnière, pointed out the lessons to be learned by future English colonists from the 'disorders, and mutinies that fell out among the French',[43] lessons that had not always been heeded in Virginia, where dissension, food shortages and cannibalism were all reported around 1620. It is just possible that in his satirical portrait of the gallants Fletcher is renewing Hakluyt's plea for discipline and moderation in the colony; but more likely it reflects an antipathy to the entire enterprise—a feeling that was, incidentally, widespread in London's mercantile community when he wrote the play.[44]

In the opening scene of Act II, Albert calms Aminta's fears of being left alone on a barren island while he looks for food on a neighbouring one:

> Think you have sent me for discovery
> Of some most fortunate continent, yet unknown,
> Which you are to be queen of. (II.i.91−3)

Albert is one of several characters in the play who express the impulse to 'seek new fortunes in an unknown world'; but Rosellia, who speaks these words in the final scene, emphasises the adverse conditions that usually compel the search: referring to the French pirates who destroyed her happiness, she reminds their sons Albert and Raymond that

>   we were forced
> From that sweet air we breathed in by their rapine,
> And sought a place of being. (V.iv.25−7)

Another kind of enforced emigration is disclosed in Lamure's attempt to save his luggage:

>   Must my goods over too?
> Why, honest master, here lies all my money,
> The money I ha' racked by usury
> To buy new lands and lordships in new countries
> 'Cause I was banished from mine own. (I.i.115−19)

The facile optimism of the gallants that a brave new world awaits them is immediately belied by their inability to subsist and their futile appetite for gold—two key failings amongst the early Virginia colonists. It is also contradicted by the disillusionment of those who have already migrated: Crocale speaks for most of her companions when she says despairingly that 'if I have any pleasure/In this life but when I sleep, I am a pagan' (II.ii.43−4). The colonial dream has gone sour, and the past is a distant country which it proves convenient to idealise. Raymond acknowledges the fault of expelling 'the industrious Portugals/From their plantations in the happy islands'; but the Canary Isles to which this appellation commonly referred were known to English readers as a place of exile: 'True it is that that place is the refuge of all the banished of *Spaine* [which includes 'the *Portingals*'] the which for punishement are sent thither into exile'; the same was true of the Cape Verde islands, where an English expedition 'found 12 Portugals . . . which were banished men for a time'.[45] The play creates a vision of wandering and displacement, and these Europeans are seen as the descendants of Cain, preying on each other in alien lands and driven to lawlessness and cruelty by the primitive conditions imposed on them.

This dispiriting view of colonial enterprise is partly founded, ironically, in some of the arguments that were used to justify that enterprise. By creating a landscape empty of natives, *The Sea Voyage* sustains the common myth that what was discovered in the New World was virgin land, and that the only question to be decided was which colonising power held legitimate title to it. Where this led to conflict between the European powers, it created a drama in which colonists became natives, oppressed by an invading outsider. In Fletcher's play the 'industrious Portugals' are driven from their settlement, but the adjective describing them perhaps registers a vestigial awareness that in most colonial territories (including the Canaries) there was a prior displacement of peoples who were seen as *not* industrious but leading a carefree existence in a more or less Arcadian world. A principal justification for colonising such places was that it put idle land to work, an argument strong enough to fend off unease at destroying the Golden Age conditions (as some saw them) of aboriginal peoples. But the argument also reminded European colonists that they themselves laboured under Adam's curse, and that rather than enjoying Edenic peace and simplicity they were part of a scramble for new-found land that usually involved great hardship and insecurity. Fletcher underlines the point in his depiction of the neo-Amazonian colony established by Rosellia and her fellow-exiles.

The only hint in *The Sea Voyage* that any inhabitants have preceded these characters in their islands comes in Rosellia's insistence to her daughter that she should keep the faith:

> Did fortune guide—
> Or rather destiny—our bark, to which
> We could appoint no port, to this blest place,
> Inhabited heretofore by warlike women
> That kept men in subjection? Did we then,
> By their example, after we had lost
> All we could love in man, here plant ourselves
> With execrable oaths never to look
> On man but as a monster? And wilt thou
> Be the first precedent to infringe those vows
> We made to heaven?   (II.ii.194–204)

Rosellia has no sense of improving on the Amazons who went before them; rather they are an example to be followed. The Portuguese ladies have apparently gone native, although they have done so in a more positive way than the renegade Englishmen in Virginia whose notorious ambition was 'to live Idle among the Salvages'.[46] As Rosellia later points out, she and her companions have remained industrious, learning 'arts' to till the fertile earth (V.iv.42–3); and they first appear (II.ii) in bucolic guise like Diana and her nymphs, making a graceful and striking entrance. Albert is entranced, thinking they are goddesses. But it soon becomes clear that all is not well in the female commonwealth. The three women we meet first (who in rudimentary fashion balance the three disaffected gallants on the ship) are past their youth and deeply frustrated with the single life; and Fletcher makes diverting sexual comedy out of their encounter with the castaways, comedy that with a light touch exploits the traditional image of the Amazons as lustful and unscrupulous. His portrait of assertive women would also have recalled for a Jacobean audience the recent *Hic Mulier* controversy about female cross-dressing in 1620,[47] and no doubt prompted the thought in some quarters that consignment to foreign parts was as appropriate for such women as it was for the religious separatists who in the same year sailed for New England. But Fletcher is doing more than pander to such opinions.

Simon Shepherd has suggested that the play ridicules women's aspirations by portraying their bondage to natural instincts: any attempt 'to re-organise the existing state of relations between men and women is shown doomed to failure'.[48] However, Fletcher is presenting a very different situation from the one that prevailed in 1620s London society. No doubt his audience is invited to approve the spectacle of women in the end giving up their power and independence as 'too burdensome' (V.iv.98); but the fundamental issue that confronts Rosellia's commonwealth is not one of rights and status but one of survival. It was not just a female problem, as anyone who knew the recent history of Jamestown could attest. Just as the women need men to perpetuate their colony, so in Virginia there was an acute shortage of women until the Company, recognising the need for partners to 'make the men more setled & lesse moveable',[49] recruited and sent 140 'maids for wives' to the colony in 1620–2. (Single men were liable to be interested only in short-term gain, and could be tempted to join the Indians in order to satisfy sexual needs.) That some such parallel was in Fletcher's mind is indicated by Rosellia's appalled reaction when she sees the men her companions propose to have:

> Are these the jewels you run mad for?
> What can you see in one of these
> To whom you would vouchsafe a gentle touch?
> Can nothing persuade you to love yourselves
> And place your happiness in cold and chaste
> Embraces of each other? (III.217–22)

The ironic query in the first line allows the audience to equate the women's pursuit of the men with the latter's frantic scramble for wealth in Act I, and implies that their exclusive utopia is in danger of functioning as a parody of what it claims to shun—the world of predatory male venturers. In both situations the search for immediate gratification is seen as an inadequate response to the demands of survival.

The central imperative in isolated settlements was to achieve stable continuity, by making colonists 'more setled & lesse moveable'. The Amazons were renowned for their strength and resourcefulness, but they were also a famous example of a colony founded in adversity which lacked the proper means to secure its future. Regarded by many authorities as an historical reality, there was disagreement about where they lived, and when sixteenth-century explorers claim to find them (or good imitations) in remote corners of the world, their fame as a vigorous colonising power begins to look more like a reputation for nomadism.[50] The Amazons are the vagrants of sixteenth-century travel writing, turning up far from home in America like (on one argument) the Indians themselves: to maintain the dogma of a single Creation some authorities identified native Americans as one of the lost tribes of Israel and explained their primitive state as the result of massive migration. To Renaissance thinkers wandering meant degeneration, and was deemed inimical to social development. In The Sea Voyage Rosellia implies that the 'warlike women' have moved on (or died out) soon after she and her companions arrived, leaving behind only their example—and their problem. The Amazons' widely-reported solution to the problem (to consort for breeding purposes only with neighbouring males, and to keep only the female children) seems to be something that Rosellia has been keeping up her sleeve for the inevitable moment when she faces rebellion on the issue. It is a palliative rather than a principled move, and it seems to reveal their colony as a sort of apartheid fantasy, one whose survival actually relies on the equivalent of miscegenation. It is one of the minor ironies of this play that the Portuguese were in fact the colonising nation which most enthusiastically embraced a policy of interbreeding with the natives.

Such a policy was anathema to the English (except in isolated cases like that of John Rolfe, who married the Indian princess Pocahontas), leaving only the option of creating integrated communities which would seek a *modus vivendi* with the indigenous population. Fletcher's play seems to invite doubts about whether all this is possible. At a time when the Virginia Company was reporting that the Jamestown settlement 'beginneth now to have the face and fashion of an orderly State',[51] *The Sea Voyage* leaves the impression that, at best, colonisation exports the undesirable elements of a country to new lands where they will probably not survive; at worst, the colonists are likely to fall into depravity and barbarism. In Act III extremity drives the gallants into ecstasies of bad taste, longing for a suppository or a used bandage to chew, and removes the ultimate taboo when they propose to kill and eat the heroine. This foreshadows the final scene where Rosellia prepares to enact her 'horrid rites' of vengeance, recalling the ghastly images of human sacrifice in the Americas that were popularised by Theodore de Bry's engravings. Rosellia's priestly robes, altar and knife, with the hieratic effect probably heightened by masks for all the women, create an exotic version of the revenge charade that closes so many Jacobean tragedies, and perhaps induce a tremor of doubt in the audience as to whether comedy will be able to tame its barbaric energies. Published engravings had already shown Amazonian native women as cannibals dismembering their victims; this scene suggests a further adaptation of the legendary warrior-woman to the New World theatre of cruelty.

There has been a tendency of late to emphasise the dark and equivocal side of European voyaging, and my account so far of *The Sea Voyage* certainly reflects this, though it also shows, I hope, that the impulse to interrogate the whole colonial project is not confined to modern cultural critics. However, the ending of the play also brings reconciliation and renewal, and like its companions in this volume turns the act of travel into one of auspicious discovery. It can do so because the nomadic impulse is represented not only as a sign of estrangement—the mark of Cain—but also as a means of healing human divisions. Fletcher's comic art authorises the transformation of restless wandering into quest. It remains to ask how far, and in

[*above*] Brazilian women preparing a cannibal feast
[*below*] Aztec human sacrifice
From T. de Bry, *America*, Part III (1592)

what ways, the concluding affirmations resolve the difficult issues raised in the course of the play.

Divided brothers are a *leitmotif* in *The Sea Voyage*, as they were in *Travels*. In the earlier play, Anthony's reported dealings in Venice help fuel the Sophy's anger against Robert, whilst the latter's reputation threatens to destroy the imprisoned Thomas if he admits the family connection. As we saw, the geographical sundering of the brothers is emphasised in dumb show at the end of the play, not to suggest any disaffection but to underline the pathos of their inevitable separation. In Fletcher's play, on the other hand, alienation is explicitly linked to a kind of fraternal blood-guiltiness, for, as Raymond acknowledges to Albert in the closing scene, they have inherited a feud begun in the violent aftermath of their fathers' joint attack on the happy islands. The original expulsion of Sebastian and his colony led to dissension amongst the victorious French, who became 'fatal enemies to each other' (V.ii.107) and left Albert and Raymond in opposed camps. Albert's kidnapping of Aminta, whether or not motivated by star-crossed love for her, was also retaliation for old injuries to his family or faction, and was accompanied by the killing of some of her companions and the expulsion of the rest. Thus before the play opens, the civil strife that Hakluyt described in Ribault's Florida has already been repeated twice by French colonial adventurers, and a similar conflict is reported by Sebastian among his own exiled party (I.iii.177ff). When strife breaks out yet again in Act I the point seems to have been well made. Now, however, repetition offers an opportunity for restoration: just as in *The Antipodes* Peregrine must travel further into absurdity to understand his own folly (and be united with his wife), so this journey into starvation and gold-hunger is a means of confronting the murderous implications of the long colonial saga. The Ulyssean voyage, which in Dante's version ends with the hero veering southward to his death (*Inferno* 26) is redeemed only by the reuniting of hearts: before it can realise the aspiration after a brave new world it must heal the divisions of kin and community from which wandering and estrangement originally sprang. Others, once again, must be turned into brothers.

Fletcher facilitates this *rapprochement* by keeping the action within the European family, though the political resolution of old colonial rivalries remains in doubt: Raymond may acknowledge that his father's crimes left him with a poisoned inheritance, but Aminta has already described how he lost it to the equally guilty Albert, who at the end says nothing about yielding to Sebastian his former possessions. Sebastian's reference in the closing lines to the 'several homes' to which they will all repair conveniently glosses over the problem, and his description of the voyage as auspicious because it has brought people together stands in ambiguous relation to the play's earlier critique of seedy venturers and piracy. The half-truth of his statement might be compared with Gonzalo's enthusiastic tribute in *The Tempest* ('Was Milan thrust from Milan . . . ?', V.i.205ff), a speech whose trite rejoicing is mutely qualified by the charged situation in which it is delivered. The ending of *The Sea Voyage*, however, has none of the tense, calculated ambivalence of Shakespeare's resolution, and one is tempted to interpret this not only as reflecting differences in individual method and vision, but also as a sign of changes in the nature and reception of the travel play as the seventeenth century advanced.

Whereas Shakespeare indicates that Prospero's power to make everyone conform to Gonzalo's ideal scenario is limited, Fletcher calls on a blander theatrical magic to persuade us that all is well. We have seen the effects of this earlier in the final scene, where the lurid prospect of human sacrifice momentarily pushes the play in a tragicomic (or comi-tragic) direction, until the savage sight loses its enigmatic power in Rosellia's rational explication of her motives, and we are reassured that this is danger, not death. By such means, arguably, the exotic is harnessed and turned into a literary and theatrical resource, providing fare for sophisticated audiences or the armchair traveller. For all its sensationalism, the final scene of this play also anticipates the mock-Indians in Massinger's *City Madam* (1632) and the obligatory episodes of exotic disguise in so much English and French drama later in the century. Fletcher's travel play is recognisably the product of a different climate from the one that produced Hakluyt's promotional writings and the first voyages of the East India Company (and a play like *The Tempest*). It has more in common with a work like *Purchas His Pilgrimes* (1625), which builds on Hakluyt not just in adding to the travel chronicle but also by turning it into a different kind of reading experience. Purchas continues to hector and inform and encourage enterprise, and indeed does so with more editorial bustle than the disciplined Hakluyt, but one feels that by now readers are assumed to possess their own interior map to the world of travel literature, not one that tells them where everything is (the narratives themselves do that) but one that has prepared them for the kinds of discovery that are there to be made. It was some such understanding, I think, that the Blackfriars audience in 1622 took to *The Sea Voyage*, a sense of familiarity with the issues that a play about voyaging would be likely to raise, and an expectation that the standard *topoi* of 'colonial' writing—wilderness, promised land, cannibalism, gold hunger, savage customs—will be deployed to create a deft and topical entertainment.

PARENTHESIS: FREE OF THE COMPANY OF VENTURERS

A play about travel is a natural vehicle for a number of common fears and phobias in the period, and some of them are sufficiently recurrent and intertwined in these three examples to be worth a brief summary. To represent a journey on stage is to bring out the incipient analogy between the traveller and the 'vagabond' actor, each potentially discrediting the other; and the female characters become vulnerable to the widespread belief, as expressed in Jerome Turler's oft-quoted statement, that 'the wide wandering of Weemen cannot want suspition, & bringing some token of dishonestie'. Turler added that 'the Tragicall and Comicall Poets, when they bringe in any far traveiling Woman, for the most parte they feine her to be incontinent';[52] though he was writing before Shakespeare's questing comic heroines took the stage. Jonson's Lady Politic Would-Be and Fletcher's Amazon ladies are in the satirical tradition, but for the most part the plays in this volume seek to resolve, however partially, the anxieties and conflicts created by this troubled association of ideas.

In scene iii of *Travels* the Sophy's Niece discusses two of the Sherley brothers with her maid and dismisses Dalibra's prurient interest in them by declaring that 'I'd not be free of [i.e. a member of] that company of venturers'. But the assertion turns out to be double-edged, for despite being wary of involvement the Niece is drawn irresistibly to Robert Sherley and the world he represents; and when in scene xi both brothers are in disfavour with the Sophy, her refusal to abandon the venturers, to be free of them in that sense, is a vital factor in healing the rift. Ultimately her full-fledged commitment to Robert's company yields the most palpable evidence of Anglo-Persian accord in the 'show of the christening' at the end of the play, and provides the means by which her society is seen to diversify and replenish itself, averting the perils of endogamy. Yet her assertiveness puts her at considerable personal risk: the woman's biological role as the vehicle of change and diversity, however vital it is to social development, also makes her a potential threat to the integrity and self-definition of the community—a thought which no doubt lay behind Jerome Turler's words quoted above. It is on women in all three of our plays that the burden of being free (in every sense) of the company of venturers falls most heavily.

In the opening storm scene of *The Sea Voyage*, Aminta—as the only woman on board—is immediately blamed by the ship's master for their plight:

> We have ne'er better luck
> When we ha' such stowage as these trinkets with us,
> These sweet sin-breeders. (I.i.65–7)

Subsequently the gallants see her as having perverted the course of their voyage to the 'happy places' where they hoped to improve their lot, and so decide to incorporate her with a vengeance:

> *Morillat.* We are starved too, famished, all our hopes deluded.
>   Yet ere we die thus, we'll have one dainty meal.
> *Aminta.* Shall I be with ye, gentlemen?
> *Lamure.* Yes, marry shall ye! In our bellies, lady.   (III.123–6)

The cannibalism of which the Niece accused the salacious Dalibra in *Travels* ('Wouldst eat men?', iii.7) is now turned against the heroine of Fletcher's play, and although the treatment of the idea remains comic it has become more than a figure of speech. Aminta's predicament is of course a common romance motif—the gentle maid lost among rude savages—reminding us that cannibals or anthropophagi are part of European folk-lore; but in a play about modern voyaging it also capitalises on the interest generated by reports of their existence in the New World. The comedy, however, depends upon the sardonic perception that the wild man is not a colonial native but a European adventurer. It is the same point that Shakespeare makes more subtly in *The Tempest* when Gonzalo favourably compares the 'gentle' islanders with his own kind, and Prospero confirms that 'some of you there present/Are worse than devils' (III.iii.30, 36–7). Fletcher plays this scenario as black farce—his gallants are more like Trinculo and Stephano than Antonio and Sebastian—confining its negative resonances to the immediate context: they do not, for instance, extend to Albert, who kidnapped Aminta in the first place but who has permitted her to turn the journey into a quest for her brother which lifts it above the sordid self-seeking of the gallants. Aminta's participation in this enterprise is another high-risk strategy (like the Niece's in *Travels*) that is finally vindicated, but for much of the play her role as scapegoat and potential victim foregrounds what was thought to be dangerous and problematic in Renaissance venturing.

Even the lunatic distraction of poor Martha in *The Antipodes*, who finds herself all too free of her husband's company, becomes a measure of the disruption of settled life by 'extravagant' ideas, although by joining the fantasy voyage to the Antipodes she ultimately wins a new identity in Peregrine's eyes. But this and other kinds of theatrical journey in the plays open up some particularly sharp questions about female roles. Two further examples must suffice. In scene ix of *Travels*, Harlequin and Will Kemp discuss putting on a play and argue about the role to be taken by Harlequin's wife: both agree that, by playing the courtesan on public stages in Italy, she epitomises 'the custom of the country' (93) and, Kemp suggests in the scene's punchline, hastens her unfortunate husband on his 'Way to

Cuckold's-Haven' (144). Kemp, defending his native theatrical tradition, is made to glance satirically here at the frequent Puritan
charge that plays encourage women to deceive their husbands, and
he implicitly denies it by reminding the audience that the English
stage has shunned the foreign practice of using women actors. This is
a *safe* representation of unfamiliar experience, from which we can
learn without being contaminated. The same issue is addressed more
boldly in *The Antipodes*. Diana's delight at a trip to the theatre, one
that is coterminous with her visit to London but ends up transporting
her to a world where women rule men and young wives enjoy sexual
freedom, prompts her to intervene in the play, whereupon her frantic
husband demands:

> will you turn actor, too?
> Pray do, be put in for a share amongst 'em!
> *Diana.* How must I be put in?
> *Joyless.*   The players will quickly
> Show you, if you perform your part; perhaps
> They may want one to act the whore amongst 'em.   (III.242—6)

The mere representation of a journey may tempt her to become free
of the company, in a disturbing recapitulation of Peregrine's impulse
after reading travel narratives to 'be made one' of every foreign
expedition (I.i.143). But as we shall see in discussing *The Antipodes*,
Diana's handling of the venture in which she becomes involved
eventually discredits these male fears and helps to ensure that the
'wide wandering' of all the characters, male and female, is a journey
toward enlarged understanding.

NOWHERE IS A PLACE:
The Antipodes

The three plays in this volume, written over a period of some thirty
years, register an increasingly sophisticated response to the act
of travel, both in the attitudes and behaviour they attribute to
characters and in the methods they use to represent it. The gritty
earnestness of the Sherley brothers as they negotiate their way through
unfamiliar territory gives way in *The Sea Voyage* to the gallants' racy
expectations of pastures new, and in *The Antipodes* we encounter
our first travel snob, in the person of the doctor who declares
'Of Europe I'll not speak; 'tis too near home', and then carelessly
insinuates that he has seen most of Asia as well (I.iii.63—70). We
would expect to find these changing nuances in a period which saw
so much colonial activity and the consolidation of the Grand Tour,[53]
and the increasing refinement of English drama during these years

provided ready vehicles for more worldly and stylish ways of addressing exotic opportunities. The plays also illustrate the developing response of the professional theatre to the problem of representing travel on the stage. Renaissance dramatists regularly protest the inadequacy of their medium when it comes to portraying a journey. The Chorus to *Henry V* is only the most famous example; it is echoed by presenter-figures in several plays by Thomas Heywood and others, and of course by the Chorus in *Travels*. *The Sea Voyage* solves the problem by, in effect, breaking the promise of its title, for the play's action, set on two adjacent islands, brings together the consequences of three separate sea journeys (four if we count the original French expedition against the happy islands) but apart from the opening storm scene does not represent any of them. This imparts some unity and concentration to the play, however, and while its use of narrative speeches to relate the earlier voyages is dramaturgically not much of an advance on the choruses in *Travels*, Fletcher is quite successful in plotting for us the complicated topography of his island story, mainly through the use of the gallery to create imaginary sightlines at crucial moments in the action. But it is *The Antipodes* which provides the most ingenious answer to the difficulty of representing a journey, by making the implausible leap over space and time not a challenge to our credulity but an explicit device which we will Peregrine to accept, and by exploiting our sense of a *lack* of distance between London and the Antipodes for thematic purposes.

In giving meaning to this symbolic destination, Brome is assisted by the way in which the discourse of the marvellous has by the seventeenth century been drawn into and helped to shape a kind of informal self-analysis within urban popular culture. In Dekker's play *Patient Grissil* (1600), for instance, a former traveller who claims to have seen Mandevillian creatures like headless men and one-legged runners is told that they are surpassed by English drunkards with 'brainless scalps' and bankrupts who 'Scarse having one good leg, or one good limbe,/Out run their creditors, and those they wrong' (I4v). Other writers make similar use of the idea of the antipodes. Ian Donaldson has shown[54] that the trope of the world upside-down was an ancient and familiar one, based upon traditional scorn for the very idea of an inhabited nether world, as expressed here by John Melton, writing in 1620:

> Is it not . . . grosse in many Geographers & Astronomers, to argue with forcible reasons, that just underneath this habitable world there is another beyond the Ocean, in which people live whose feet are opposit to ours?

By the seventeenth century practical discovery had disposed of this controversy (as it had of such questions as whether life was possible

Amazons, woolly hens and other exotica.
From *The Voiage and Travayle of Sir John Maundeville Knight* (1568),
ed. J. Ashton, 1887

at the Equator); and when he restates it like this Melton is really preparing the ground for satire:

> No sure, these Geographers were deceived, for whereas they say the Antipodes were in a world under us, they should have affirmed that they were, and are, here with us; and then I should have agreed with them, for there are many, that seldome or never see the Light, the Sunne rise, or set: For what are Drunken-Alehouses, Wine tavernes, Bousing-kens, and Victualing-houses, where men drinke and swill, and never see any light, but that of a Candle to kindle their Tobacco, or that of the fire which burnes their Pipes, but the Antipodes? And doe not those that in a perverse order, and quite retrograde from Nature, making the Day Night, and deprive themselves not onely of the Common light, but the light of the Minde, by involving themelves in the thicke clouds of Ignorance and Heresie, live like true Antipodites?[55]

What is implied here and in *Patient Grissil* is still the inversion of agreed norms of behaviour, but the collapse of any spacial distinction between domestic sanity and exotic monstrosity threatens to dissolve confidence in a stable culture that can hold its own against competing values and standards. That, after all, is what the Other, opposites, monsters on the fringe of civilisation are for: to define by contrast what we are and fix the bounds of normality. The appropriation of such images to describe what is happening to European society is a sophisticated move, aided by the growing acceptance that people with heads in their breasts or walking upside down are simply beautiful fictions and therefore belong to the world of metaphor. But as they are gathered into the vernacular we become aware of an incipient relativism. One result of this process might indeed be simply to invert the categories—as happened in the primitivist argument contrasting the healthy virtue of Stone Age peoples with the distortions of the Old World. But a more radical effect is to suggest that polarity is breaking down into resemblance.

At the start of *The Antipodes*, so many of the characters are shown to be emotionally disordered or obsessive that we seem already to be cut adrift from normative standards of behaviour.[56] London itself is only just delivered from the plague (it is feared that the players, long out of work, are 'sunk past rising', in an early use of the play's central image), and the visit of the Joyless family brings to the city not only Peregrine with his travel mania but his wife's consequent derangement and his father's irrational jealousy of Diana. For his part Dr Hughball, driven by professional zeal, is determined to see mental disorder everywhere, while Lord Letoy has turned dress codes upside down and cultivates an eccentric image. All this must cast doubt on Ian Donaldson's conclusion that the play maintains a rock-solid opposition between the comfortable familiarity of the everyday world and the absurd customs of the antipodes, and that it 'never lets us feel ... the disturbance of a moral cross-current or paradox'.[57] Donaldson argues that the device of the fantastic journey is a simple therapy in which Peregrine and others are exposed to such patent absurdities that they are driven 'steadily back to normality' and the status quo is reaffirmed; he sees the play as being 'in touch with a kind of mid-seventeenth-century folk humour'.[58] Martin Butler also assumes that Brome has created the antipodes as a fixed pole to the England of 1638, but he sees many of the inner play's inversions as satire on contemporary manners and government, and deduces from it 'a political moral, that Charles [I] will rule better by turning his government upside-down'[59] and abandoning the autocratic regime that he had maintained since 1629. This is certainly a dimension of the play that Donaldson misses, perhaps because he sees *The Antipodes* as the product of 'a secure, pre-Civil War society'; and we might say that the inner play is designed by the doctor as a traditional cure to restore Peregrine's wits but is directed by the non-conformist Lord Letoy (whom Butler aligns with 'opposition' courtiers like the play's dedicatee William Seymour) as a critique of establishment values. But even if conservative and radical readings of *The Antipodes* can be reconciled in this way, we are left with a number of questions. If Peregrine is restored to a society which in the play at large is satirised as aberrant, is the disappearance of his wanderlust a good thing? Is his obsession with Mandeville an example of that society's muddled priorities (along the lines of Melton's satire)? Are we to infer that Peregrine would have avoided derangement if he had been allowed to travel and get it out of his system, as young men in Caroline England increasingly were doing? Or is his Mandeville madness simply a metaphor for the perils of such distraction?

These are all questions specific to the travel theme, but they help to focus others which are important for our understanding of the play as a whole. Peregrine's therapeutic journey snaps him out of his day-dream and confronts him with a world that is both like and unlike his own. The inner play of 'The Antipodes' reflects the madness of the 'real' world of the on-stage spectators, but like all mirror-images it reverses it, and the complex interaction of these two scenarios is the theatre audience's experience of the play. And what we discover—for we too are taken on a journey—involves confronting the literary and geographical meanings that cluster at this date around the concept of the antipodes.

In the 'Digression of the Ayre' in Part II of his *Anatomy of Melancholy*, Robert Burton embarks on a mental voyage 'round about the world' during which he muses upon the state of geographical knowledge: 'whether ... *China and Cataia* be all one, the great

Cham of *Tartary*, and the King of *China* bee the same . . . whether *Presbyter John* be in *Asia* or *Africk* . . . Whether . . . that hungry Spaniards discovery of *Terra Australis Incognita*, or *Magellicana*, be as true as that of *Mercurius Britannicus*, or his of *Utopia*' (II.33–4). His first three questions are ones that any enquiring reader of Mandeville who also had some knowledge of the geographical literature might ask. They would have been Peregrine's questions before he went mad, as he immersed himself in 'such books/As might convey his fancy round the world' (I.i.136–7): it is notable that Burton, whose account of melancholy symptoms is exploited by Brome elsewhere in this play, presents his very similar mental trip as anything but a distressing aberration. The last question is more recondite and complicated, requiring a knowledge both of contemporary exploration and of a tradition of learned satire. Burton wonders if the recently published (1617) account of Ferdinand de Quiros' search for the great southern continent in 1605, which found several south Pacific islands,[60] is 'as true' as antipodean fictions by writers like Thomas More and Joseph Hall (Mercurius Britannicus is the narrator of Hall's dystopic *Mundus Alter et Idem*, also 1605); and his enquiry seems to recognise that exploration and discovery can leave their mark not only on the factual record but also on literary *topoi*. Burton's question also draws attention to the paradoxical status in knowledge of the fifth continent, as described here by one of Hall's characters:

> It has always disturbed me to meet constantly with *Terra Australis Incognita* on geographical maps, and indeed, is there anyone who is not completely senseless who would read this without some indignation? For if they know it to be a *continent*, and a *southern* one, how can they then call it *unknown*?[61]

The paradox was an open invitation to create fictional landscapes based on the idea of *mundus inversus*, to make the empty space on the map speak to European concerns. (Other fantastic locations including outer space had been exploited in imaginative writing since Lucian's *True History*, and in the same year that *The Antipodes* was staged, William Godwin published his *Man in the Moone*.) And the literary result was not just a popular image of topsy-turvydom but— particularly in More's massively influential *Utopia*—a complex analogical design, setting the Old and New Worlds in apposition. As Burton guesses, it will be a long time before geographers know enough about the far south to redraw this imaginative map of the antipodes; and it is the 'truth' of the literary tradition, sometimes darkly satirical (as in Hall), sometimes idealistic, as in Bacon's *New Atlantis*, that is Brome's chief guiding principle in writing his play.

This does not mean that Brome's portrayal of the fantastic journey has no use for the methods and concerns of contemporary travel. Peregrine has read the advice manuals for prospective tourists, and after he awakes from his 'sleeping fit', believing himself transported to the antipodes, he exclaims at the missed opportunity:

> What worlds of lands and seas have I passed over,
> Neglecting to set down my observations!
> A thousand thousand things remarkable
> Have slipped my memory, as if all had been
> Mere shadowy phantasms, or fantastic dreams.   (II.ii.7–11)

The purpose of the journey is of course to persuade Peregrine that his travel enthusiasms really are no more than delusions; and yet, although he mistakes the trackings of his imagination for objective observation (an error he shares with many Renaissance travellers), his desire to register what he sees is crucial both to his own cure and to the play's larger commentary on social affairs. Dr Hughball reassures him that he can keep a diary of the return journey, and prompts his patient to recall at least one significant detail:

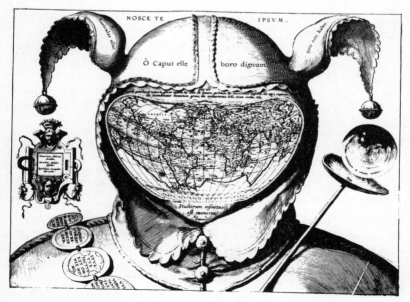

The folly of travel (anonymous engraving, 1580s). The inset world map shows the great 'unknown' southern continent

> But what chief thing of note now in our travels
> Can you call presently to mind? Speak like a traveller.
> *Peregrine.* I do remember, as we passed the verge
> O'th' upper world, coming down, downhill,
> The setting sun, then bidding them good night,
> Came gliding easily down by us and struck
> New day before us, lighting us our way,
> But with such heat that till he was got far
> Before us, we even melted. (23–31)

The crucial passage through the torrid zone, where life was traditionally thought to be impossible, is described in modern empirical
terms; but Peregrine's colloquial reference to the heat ('we even
melted') alludes also to ancient superstition about the 'burning
line' (the equator) and becomes a metaphor for the transformative
experience he is about to undergo. The moment is central to the
whole antipodean concept, as a comparison with More's *Utopia*
makes clear. After they pass through the torrid zone, the travellers in
the play 'come into a temperate clime/Of equal composition of
elements/With that of London' (II.ii.33–5), just as Hythloday and
his companions endure parched equatorial regions in order to reach
'temperate, and gentle' lands on the other side, where they find
'people, Cities and Townes'[62] with unfamiliar but highly developed
cultures. Both parties travel as it were through the looking-glass to a
world that reflects quixotically upon the practices and assumptions
prevailing at home.

In *Utopia* More was responding to the accounts of Vespucci's
voyages that swept Europe in the early 1500s, and he saw the
availability of new information about distant parts as an opportunity
to think seriously about the prospects for better human government.
In Part I More and his companions ask Hythloday many eager
questions about his travels, but

> as for Monsters, because they be no newes, of them we were nothing
> inquisitive: For nothing is more easie to be found, then be barking *Scillaes*,
> ravening *Celenos*, amd *Lestrigones* . . . and such like great and incredible
> monsters. But to find Citizens ruled by good and wholesome Lawes, that
> is an exceeding rare, & hard thing.[63]

In Brome's play, similarly, Barbara begs Dr Hughball to 'deliver'
Peregrine of 'his huge tympany of news—of monsters,/Pygmies and
giants . . . the strangest doings' (I.i.177–81) in order to focus his
mind on more important things. The antipodes conjured up by
Letoy's actors could not, of course, be mistaken as a prescription for
the perfect commonwealth, as More's imaginary state repeatedly
was. But Brome's method shares something with More's conception
and draws on the same tradition of *serio jocum*, though its ironies

are less enigmatic and the estates satire more direct. In both works the relation of the 'antipodes' to the real world is complex and unstable, toying with our everyday assumptions and testing the limits of possibility. And the literary methods at work here are also a way of confronting what was being disclosed by contemporary exploration. No writer of utopian or antipodean fictions in the period can ignore the discoveries and their actual or potential consequences for Europe. Joseph Hall's *Mundus Alter et Idem*, for instance, bears all the marks of his lifelong opposition to travel, depicting a southern continent which is quintessentially unfortunate, new lands that turn out to be the fitting harvest of shallow expansionism and greed. But for More and Brome, whatever their work finally implies about the viability of new worlds and the wisdom of those who dream about them, the idea of exploration held out greater possibilities.

It is clear that for several of Brome's characters a journey of discovery is needed, and the trip to London by the Joyless family is just a necessary preliminary to the more disorienting trip that is to follow. But the journey can be planned only up to a point, since discovery brings its own surprises and revelations. The playlet of 'The Antipodes' may offer an exemplary parade of absurdity, but the world it depicts has to be *encountered* for all its meanings to be made clear, which is why the line between the inner action and that of the on-stage spectators is repeatedly breached. Much of the play's intricacy of effect comes from the frequent interruptions of the inner play by the various members of the Joyless family and the responses that they draw from Letoy and Dr Hughball. Between them, these two have virtually scripted many of Diana's interventions (and her husband's reactions to them) by instructing her to 'spur his jealousy off o'the legs' (II.i.38)—a calculation made evident in performance by Letoy's device of making his actors freeze and 'lengthen time in silence' (III.9) while an episode is debated. Moreover, since it is also Diana's first play-going (as it is Peregrine's) she can be relied on to express her bemusement at the unlikely action. Her naive reaction to much of what she sees ('How contrary still to us!') underlines the trope of inversion even where she does not grasp its significance, and she can be unintentionally penetrating, as when she observes that 'courtiers are best beggars' (III.215) in the antipodes: at moments like these she is a vehicle for satire, reading antipodean customs in a way that brings out their ironic relationship to Caroline society.

But Diana is not just a puppet in Letoy's show. Encouraged to flirt and provoke her husband, she begins to find the challenge intoxicating, and in improvising a role she acquires a vitality and perceptiveness of her own. This can seem ambiguous: some critics overlook (or discount) the reference to a compact between her and

Dr Hughball to cure Joyless' jealousy, and view her risqué comments and flighty behaviour as clear evidence of promiscuous intentions, of which she is cured only when Letoy stages his seduction scene in Act V. But it is difficult to see her as a candidate for dramatic therapy like Peregrine, Martha and Joyless. Her flirtation with provocative ideas is capable of generating insights not dreamt of in Letoy's scheme, as when she asks Dr Hughball about marital relations in Anti-London:

> But pray, sir, is't by nature or by art
> That wives o'ersway their husbands there?
> *Doctor.*   By nature.
> *Diana.* Then art's above nature, as they are under us.   (I.iii.127–9)

Hughball's answer affirms that the situation in the antipodes is a total inversion, because husbands in England are *naturally* in authority; dominant and disobedient wives are a cultural aberration. But Diana's answering quip meets his satirical inference head on: London wives have shown themselves superior to their antipodean counterparts because (through 'art') they have created their own freedoms—her 'they' alludes also to husbands, of course, with a bawdy implication anticipating line 141. Diana then muses innocently about what women's freedom in the antipodes might mean:

> Why then, the women
> Do get the men with child, and put the poor fools
> To grievous pain, I warrant you, in bearing.   (133–5)

This is a Mandevillian fantasy, however, the sort that the inner play is designed to explode, and Hughball will have no truck with it ('that were to make men women,/And women men'). His original paradox recalls the conundrum posed by those who rejected the idea of an inhabited antipodes: that it implied a dual Creation, two separate orders of nature.[64] But Diana's previous insistence that 'art's above nature' cuts through this famous heresy, simply claiming that northern civilisation—or at any rate London society—has rectified the imbalances of nature as they are found everywhere. ('The air of London/Hath tainted her obedience already', as Joyless gloomily puts it, II.i.161–2). It is a witty analysis that must have gone down well with the women in a Caroline audience; and we can also see it as a kind of answer to the 'Amazonian Portugals' in *The Sea Voyage*, whose claim to independence and self-respect is based exclusively on a rejection of conventional society.

If Diana is an ambiguous figure it is not because her own morality is in doubt but because she focuses a tension at the heart of Letoy's design. She fits uneasily into his moral script, and her situation, as much as Peregrine's, makes us question the compatibility of Letoy's commitment to free play and personal discovery with his equally powerful desire to control the action and determine its outcome. In many ways Letoy is the Prospero figure who is missing from *The Sea Voyage*. He creates a kind of social experiment in fantasyland which promises to rescue people from their delusions, but when the characters have been reconciled and returned to normal life we are left wondering how far they have been enabled to see the world in new ways. This is of course the question that sceptics asked (and still ask) of travel experience, and in the journey of discovery that constitutes Letoy's play the issue of what is being apprehended, and how, and to what purpose, becomes crucial. In the end it is the function of dramatic comedy itself, ramifying from Letoy's play to Brome's own, that comes under inspection.

The methods and purpose of drama are made an issue right at the start of *The Antipodes*, when Brome distinguishes in the prologue between 'the old way of plays' (now, he claims, 'the weakest branch o'th' stage') from the current fashion for empty high-sounding spectacle. Letoy echoes this preference for a traditional drama whose purpose is to give delight (and by implication also to instruct), when he tells Blaze about an actor in his troupe who 'never will be perfect in a thing/He studies' but specialises in 'shifts extempore' (II.i.16–17), and confesses his partiality for this versatile clown. When Byplay is subsequently taxed about his improvising habits he asserts, echoing Letoy, that they are 'a way, my lord, has been allowed/On elder stages to move mirth and laughter' (II.i.100–1); though his employer now retorts:

> Yes, in the days of Tarlton and Kemp,
> Before the stage was purged from barbarism,
> And brought to the perfection it now shines with. (102–4)

This piece of Caroline triumphalism is uttered ironically—it is intended to restrain Byplay's wilder impulses—and yet it sounds a contrary note. Letoy's way with his actors is thoroughly autocratic and even bullying, and we are constantly reminded that this is a private troupe which exists to serve his particular tastes, not a theatre of mass appeal. His exchange with Byplay about the Elizabethan stage inevitably calls to mind the bawdy knockabout routine between Kemp and Harlequin in *Travels* (scene ix), where two traditions of clowning play off one another, and it is immediately apparent that the spontaneous feeling of cultural encounter in the earlier play has given way to a more calculated use of improvisation, one that will expose Peregrine and others to new experiences within a strictly controlled framework. Of course, the 'improvisation' in both plays is carefully scripted by the respective dramatists, and in both, I would argue, it consciously acknowledges the power of theatre to create new kinds of dialogue. The portrayal of Kemp in *Travels* is itself a nostalgic tribute in 1607 to the clown of 'our elder stages'; and the inventive freedom that he embodied is a vital part also of Brome's conception. But its function within Letoy's reflexive structure is shown ultimately to be more circumscribed.

For much of *The Antipodes* Letoy's on-stage direction looks like a skilful balancing-act, letting interruption and Byplay's mercurial acting bring out the satirical import of the inner play: in Act II, for instance, the vignettes of antipodean life are quickly turned from static paradoxes into elements within a fluid dialectic, when Diana intervenes on behalf of the geriatric schoolboys whom Byplay is chastising:

> Alas, will nobody beg pardon for
> The poor old boys?
> *Doctor.*   Sir, gentle sir, a word with you.
> *Byplay.* To strangers, sir, I can be gentle.
> *Letoy.*   Good!
> Now mark that fellow; he speaks extempore.
> *Diana.* Extempore call you him? He's a dogged fellow
> To the three poor old things there. Fie upon him!
> *Peregrine.* Do men of such fair years here go to school?
> *Byplay.* They would die dunces else.
> *Peregrine.* Have you no young men scholars, sir, I pray,
> When we have beardless doctors?
> *Doctor.* [*Aside*]   He has wiped
> My lips.—You question very wisely, sir.   (II.ii.195–205)

We are suddenly in the thick of debate. Letoy's design seems able also to accommodate Peregrine's most radical departure from the script—and possibly even predicts it. At the end of Act II Peregrine is taken off for refreshments, and does not reappear after the interval; the next we hear of him is in Byplay's virtuoso description of his actions behind the scenes:

> He has got into our tiring-house amongst us,
> And ta'en a strict survey of all our properties:
> Our statues and our images of gods,
> Our planets and our constellations,
> Our giants, monsters, furies, beasts, and bugbears,
> Our helmets, shields, and vizors, hairs, and beards,
> Our pasteboard marchpanes, and our wooden pies.   (III.288–94)

Peregrine has made up for not keeping a journal on the outward journey by noting everything in the prescribed fashion, and uses the occasion to live out every kind of travel experience he has ever read about. In Byplay's account the Grand Tourist admiring classical statuary, the Godwinian space traveller and the explorer of exotic lands full of marvels each flashes briefly into view, in what could have been a perfect theatrical catharsis: an opportunity to realise that the universe of travel is mere dross, an insubstantial pageant. But Peregrine does not turn his back on it; instead, Byplay relates,

> on the sudden, with thrice knightly force,
> And thrice thrice puissant arm he snatcheth down
> The sword and shield that I played Bevis with,
> Rusheth amongst the foresaid properties,
> Kills monster after monster, takes the puppets
> Prisoners, knocks down the Cyclops, tumbles all
> Our jigambobs and trinkets to the wall.
> Spying at last the crown and royal robes
> I'th' upper wardrobe, next to which by chance
> The devils' vizors hung, and their flame-painted
> Skin coats, those he removed with greater fury;
> And, having cut the infernal ugly faces
> All into mammocks, with a reverend hand
> He takes the imperial diadem and crowns
> Himself King of the Antipodes, and believes
> He has justly gained the kingdom by his conquest.   (302–17)

Modern critics are inevitably reminded by this speech of the apprentice riots on Shrove Tuesday which vandalised theatres and their stock; and it is possible to see this enactment of the antitheatrical impulse as Peregrine's literal destruction of the grounds of his own delusion. 'Let him enjoy his fancy' says Letoy on hearing of the rampage, secure in the expectation that it will lead inevitably to disillusionment with exotic distractions. But those frail props have in fact proved sufficient—as they did for Don Quixote—to permit an imaginative leap that cannot be contained by therapeutic imperatives.

When the inner play resumes, Byplay launches his next scheduled role—that of magistrate—with a verve to match these developments, subjecting antipodean justice to the critical scrutiny of the new monarch. Most of the on-stage audience is simply confused: Diana thinks Byplay is a king until Peregrine enters with the crown on his head; but the active participants co-operate in a splendid charade (III.403–77) that plays suggestively with the relationship between law and custom. 'Most admirable justice', says Peregrine of Byplay's unorthodox verdict (which closely anticipates one of Azdak's in Brecht's *Caucasian Chalk Circle*), a response which is in tune with the spirit of wise fooling that rules over the scene. When Byplay removes his robes Diana suddenly, finally gets the point:

> Protest, Extempore played the judge! And I
> Knew him not all this while.

> *Joyless.*   What oversight
>   Was there!
> *Diana.*   He is a properer man, methinks
>   Now, than he was before; sure I shall love him.   (III.486—9)

The social and intellectual implications of the episode have passed
her by, but Diana knows a convincing performance when she sees
one, and all her puzzlement at antipodean paradoxes gives way to
the irresistible logic of good theatre. She is responding to an energy
and a playfulness in the scene that fuse the high fantasy of Peregrine's
rule with the sustaining fictions of political ritual in the real world, as
when he decides to knight Byplay:

> [*Throws down Letoy's sword.*] I'll none o' this;
>   Give me that princely weapon.   [*Points at sword of office.*]
> *Letoy.*   Give it him.
> *Swordbearer.* [*Aside to Letoy*] It is a property, you know, my lord,
>   No blade, but a rich scabbard with a lath in't.
> *Letoy.* So is the sword of justice, for aught he knows.   (III.515—19)

We can read this as satire on authority—like the later moment when
Peregrine proposes to ask 'a counsel from New England' because the
old country without parliaments 'will spare me none' (IV.265—6), an
observation which Hughball takes as a sign of Peregrine's returning
sanity. But we do not need that inference to validate Peregrine's
quixotic assumption of power, which at this point resists attempts to
equate the travails of the imagination with a madness in need of cure.

Letoy and Hughball, however, have their own ideas about how to
use this fantasy of rule, and in Act IV they improvise the familiar
trope of the disguised prince. Peregrine is given a cloak and hat so
that he can 'make discovery of passages/Among the people' (IV.3—4),
and gradually the assumed role does its job, taming Peregrine's
extravagance and pushing him towards a conventional assessment of
antipodean life and customs. 'Sure these are dreams,/Nothing but
dreams' (IV.158—9) he exclaims at the sight of the man-scold being
ducked by angry women; and when Byplay mounts another of his
travesties of authority, as the statesman who grants benefits to
'cheaters, bawds, and thieves', Peregrine can stand no more and
unmasks himself. This is the cue for Letoy and Hughball to abandon
their script and 'do all by extempore' to bring Peregrine and Martha
together in matrimony, though it is worth noting that in giving
directions to start the wedding scene Letoy is actually trying to stop
improvisation from getting out of hand, as Byplay wildly overacts
and is applauded by Diana, who appeals for more of the same
(IV.382—402). Her attention is all on Byplay ('Never was such an
actor as Extempore!'), whereas we are aware of how his subversive

mumming has been deliberately subjugated to a decorous formal show.

After the wedding scene Letoy explains to Joyless the principle behind Hughball's theatrical cure:

> ...he has shifted your son's known disease
> Of madness into folly, and has wrought him
> As far short of a competent reason as
> He was of late beyond it... (IV.496–9)

But there is a sense in which Peregrine has been *deprived* of his folly, or at any rate of the kind which permits an unorthodox perception of reality. The 'disguised prince' motif in Renaissance drama rarely endorses altogether the perspective of the observing figure: it often satirises his pretensions or questions his ability to assess and influence human affairs. And when Peregrine is led to reject antipodean customs he is a little like More's persona in *Utopia*, who concludes the story by shaking his head over utopian practices which to him 'seemed to be instituted and founded of no good reason'.[65] Letoy's plot bears the same relation to Brome's overall conception as that statement has to the larger strategy of More's fiction. In the last act of *The Antipodes* a situation full of chaotic possibilities is normalised in a highly factitious way. The extraordinary scene of Diana's temptation by Letoy (V.ii.1–128), modelled on Volpone's attempted seduction of Celia, is obviously not a test of anything except Letoy's capacity to turn his inchoate fears (and possibly illicit desires) regarding women into a plausible plot; and following this there is a richly satirical moment (V.ii.320) when Hughball expresses the fear that telling Peregrine of Diana's newly-revealed relationship to Letoy will send him back into madness, the implication being that the last thing his patient needs now is more tall tales. The overt theatricality of these final-act disclosures leaves us in doubt about their value both as truth-claims and as therapeutic fictions.

The same is not true, finally, of Peregrine's adventures. It is in fact only in the antipodes that Peregrine can find himself, and then only by grasping their relationship to a larger reality. In the wedding scene his acceptance of Martha is a choice made *within* the fantasy world, but it depends upon being able to accommodate 'real' objections like the one that Peregrine himself unexpectedly makes when Martha is offered to him in the guise of an antipodean princess: 'A crown secures not an unlawful marriage./I have a wife already (IV.445–6). Hughball's improvised reply, 'No, you had, sir;/But she's deceased' saves the day, and confirms the demise of Peregrine's old inability to reconcile dream and reality. And when he reverts to Mandeville in a last attempt to resist Martha and stave off reality ('She may be of that serpentine generation/That stings oft-times to death'), Hughball appeals—like the authors of *Travels*—to a more humane vision of international relations:

> She's no Gadlibrien, sir, upon my knowledge.
> You may as safely lodge with her as with
> A maid of our own nation.   (IV.469–71)

In the final scene Peregrine enters, like many a spiritual voyager, disoriented and vulnerable, and

> so ignorant of mine own condition—
> Whether I sleep, or wake, or talk, or dream;
> Whether I be, or be not; or if I am,
> Whether I do, or do not anything.
> For I have had (if now I wake) such dreams . . .   (V.ii.308–12)

But beyond the echoes of Pericles and Lear there is one of a more robust Shakespearean character, who refuses to let go of the other worlds that have seized his imagination, and whose example serves to remind us that even when discoveries have given us an exact relation of the great globe's underside, our dream of what it contains still has no bottom.

A NOTE ON THE TEXTS

The Travels of the Three English Brothers was first published in a quarto edition of 1607, of which four copies have been collated to establish the present text. The play's only other appearance in print was in A. H. Bullen's makeshift edition of John Day's *Works* (1887). The quarto may have gone to press while the play was still on the stage in the summer of 1607: if its run were over we might expect the prompt-book to be available to the printer, but certain features of the text suggest that what he was faced with were authorial papers (or a copy thereof).[66] The play is a short one, but shows no obvious signs of having been cut: it was clearly written at speed, and would have been elongated in performance by its numerous dumb shows, processions and battle-scenes.

The Sea Voyage, first acted in 1622, had to wait for publication until the 1647 Folio (F) of Beaumont and Fletcher's *Works*, and was reprinted with a title-page in the 1679 Folio (F2).[67] The latter was advertised by its publishers as having been printed from a marked-up copy of F with authoritative corrections and additional information (like the list of Jacobean players of principal roles that appears on the title-page). Many of the 1679 changes to the text itself are in fact maladroit, but some are clearly due to intelligent emendation or are the result of privileged knowledge. They do not include, however, any additional lines: both texts give us what appears to be a shortened performing version of the play, signs of which are its brevity, the high incidence of half-lines, the re-entry of characters who have just left the stage and some abrupt transitions. For the purposes of this edition three copies of *F* and one of *F2* have been collated, and compared with the editions of Dyce and Waller (1910). No variants were discovered in *F*.

Lineation poses a considerable problem in *The Sea Voyage*: cramped type-setting in double columns in *F* frequently obscures Fletcher's intentions, and the resulting confusion is exacerbated by the cuts already mentioned. At times too the writing is rough and irregular, relying on accentual rhythms which produce a high proportion of hypermetrical lines (for example, see V.ii.10–45): there are limits to the metrical order that can be expected of such verse, and at times one can do no better than reproduce *F*; elsewhere, some lineations are no more than my own best guess. I have not attempted to collate the many changes made to *F*'s lineation, nor the solutions proposed by previous editors (some of which—notably Dyce's—I have adopted).

The Antipodes was first published in 1640, in a quarto edition of which twenty-two copies were collated by Ann Haaker for her 1966 Regents edition. My own collation of the two Huntington Library copies, checked against one in the British Library, confirms her findings and has resolved a few trivial queries.

This edition follows the act divisions in copytext for *The Sea Voyage* and *The Antipodes*; *Travels*, which has no formal divisions at all in *Q*, is here divided into scenes based upon the clearing of the stage. The same principle is followed to establish scene breaks in *The Sea Voyage*, which merely announces *Scoena Prima* in some Act headings, and in *The Antipodes*, where Brome's Jonsonian practice of beginning a fresh scene whenever a new character enters has been abandoned. I have collated these obsolete scene-divisions, but not the new ones introduced into the other two plays.

On nomenclature, I have retained archaic titles such as 'Sophy' and 'Portugals', and heavily anglicised names like 'Cushan Halibeck', but not old spellings like 'Casbin' or 'Basha', which are given in their accepted modern forms. There can be no absolute rule here, for English perceptions of the foreign are sometimes epitomised by the old form of a name (Mahomet, for instance), and Elizabethan names like Candish and Furbisher (*Antipodes*, I.iii.31) are arguably more 'authentic' than the polite versions that have come down to us.

I have tried in this edition to modernise as consistently as possible, and in doing so I have departed from recent practice in presenting stage directions. These I have added or expanded wherever this seems helpful to a reader, and such changes are usually recorded in the same way as are emendations to the spoken text, by collating them. New and altered stage directions, therefore, are not placed in square brackets unless they are incorporated into a line of spoken text. (Directions within a line need a bracket anyway to distinguish them from speech, and it seems pointless not to make use there of the distinction between square brackets to indicate an editorial addition and parentheses to indicate a direction found in copytext.) All other substantive alterations are collated. I have treated as non-substantive all changes which merely systematise the text or make it conform to consistent practice, such as standardising speech prefixes or expanding abbreviations. In the same category, for instance, are the insertion of a definite article before SOPHY in *Travels*, i.32.1 and the added conjunction *and* in the next line; or the addition of the word *Enter* to many directions in *The Antipodes*. Errors like *Exit* for *Exeunt* are silently corrected unless there is ambiguity about who is leaving the stage. Similarly, *Travels*, i.29 has the SD *Exit Rober.* on the same line as the character's departing speech; this edition tidies up Q by printing *Exit*. Such changes are collated only when they are of interest, in the same way that original spellings are sometimes (but usually not) recorded.

NOTES

1 *Thomas Platter's Travels in England 1599*, tr. Clare Williams, 1937, p. 170.
2 The fourteenth-century account of Sir John Mandeville's *Travels* was reprinted in 1568 and 1582. An influential example of exotic romance fiction is the *Primaleon of Greece*, translated into English by Anthony Munday in 1596 (see the illuminating discussion by Bruce Chatwin in *In Patagonia*, 1979, chapter 49). On the encyclopaedists, see Margaret Hodgen, *Early Anthropology in the 16th and 17th Centuries*, 1964.
3 *Mandeville's Travels*, ed. M. C. Seymour, 1967, pp. 119–20.
4 K. R. Andrews, *Trade, Plunder and Settlement*, 1984, p. 356; D. B. Quinn, *England and the Discovery of America, 1481–1620*, 1973, chapter 1.
5 Men like Sir Thomas Hoby and Sir Richard Moryson set the trend in Europe, followed by the generation of Sir Philip Sidney (see his and others' *Profitable Instructions*, published only in 1633). Boies Penrose, *Travel and Discovery in the Renaissance 1420–1620*, 1967, Ch. 13 deals with early trade missions to The Middle East. George B. Parks provides a useful overview of the literature generated by these various enterprises in D. B. Quinn (ed.), *The Hakluyt Handbook*, 1974, I.97–132.
6 Fernand Braudel, *The Perspective of the World*, 1984, p. 353.
7 Jeffrey Knapp, *An Empire Nowhere*, 1992, p. 7. See note to *Travels*, i.131–6.
8 G. Whitney, *A Choice of Emblemes*, 1586, p. 178.
9 Perhaps the most heavily used were Jerome Turler, *The Traveiler*, 1575; William Bourne, *A Treasure for Traveilers*, 1578; Justus Lipsius, *A Direction for Travailers*, 1592.

10 *A new interlude and a mery of the iiij elementes* (c. 1519), reprinted in Quinn, *England and the Discovery of America*, p. 168.

11 Philip Sidney, *The Defence of Poesy*, line 1370 (ed. K. Duncan-Jones, 1989, p. 245).

12 Philip Edwards, *Last Voyages*, 1988, pp. 7–14.

13 *Tom o'Lincoln*, ed. G. R. Proudfoot, Malone Soc., 1991.

14 Roger Ascham, *The Scholemaster*, 1570, fol. 29.

15 Joseph Hall, *Virgidemiarum* (1599), IV.6 (p. 48).

16 See Richard Dutton, *Mastering the Revels*, 1991, p. 149.

17 C. J. Sisson, 'Shakespeare Quartos as Prompt-Copies', *Review of English Studies* 18 (1942), 136–8.

18 Thomas Fuller, *The Worthies of England*, 1662, p. 108.

19 William Hunt, 'Civic Chivalry and the English Civil War', in A. Grafton & A. Blair (eds.), *The Transmission of Culture in Early Modern Europe*, 1990, pp. 206–17; Marion Lomax, *Stage Images and Traditions*, 1987, p. 74.

20 Lomax, p. 75.

21 The fullest account of the Sherleys' adventures is D. W. Davies, *Elizabethans Errant*, 1967.

22 W. Schrickx, '*Pericles* in a Book-list of 1619', *Shakespeare Survey* 29 (1976), 22–4.

23 See C. Hoy's note to I.i.0.3 of the play, in his *Introductions . . . to 'The Dramatic Works of Thomas Dekker'*, 1979, II.314. The shift of reference may also glance ironically at the treaty between the Ottomans and the Holy Roman Empire signed only a few months earlier, on 11 November 1606.

24 Edward Said, *Orientalism*, 1978, p. 70. See also Mary W. Helms, *Ulysses' Sail*, 1988, pp. 220–2, on the shaping of Renaissance views of the East.

25 G. B. Shand, 'Source and Intent in Middleton's *Sir Robert Sherley*', *Renaissance and Reformation* 19 (1983), 261.

26 In *The Miracle Play of Hasan and Husain*, ed. Sir L. Pelly, 1879, scene 5, the Prophet on his deathbed predicts to 'Ali that 'thy martyrdom will be the means of salvation to my people, in raising thee to the high office of intercessor for them' (I.87).

27 Thomas Herbert, *A Relation of some yeares travaile* (1634), p. 129.

28 H. Neville Davies, '*Pericles* and the Sherley brothers', in E. A. J. Honigmann (ed.), *Shakespeare and his Contemporaries: Essays in Comparison*, 1986, pp. 106–7.

29 *Ibid.*, p. 104.

30 See my 'Foreign Relations in Jacobean England', forthcoming in M. Willems & J.-P. Maquerlot (eds.), *Travel and Drama in Shakespeare's Time* (1995). Several first-hand accounts of the mission are collected in E. Denison Ross, *Sir Anthony Sherley and his Persian Adventure* (1933).

31 'The Rediscovery of America' (review of Anthony Pagden, *European Encounters with the New World*, 1993), *New York Review of Books*, XL. 12 (24 June 1993), p. 38. See also Pagden's 'Afterword' on the current tendency to sentimentalise the Other.

32 *The Ile of Gulls* (1606), A3v; E. A. J. Honigmann, *Shakespeare's Impact on his Contemporaries*, 1982, pp. 92–3.

33 Quoted in K. R. Andrews *et al.*, *The Westward Enterprise*, 1978, p. 37.

34 K. R. Andrews, *Trade, Plunder and Settlement*, 1984, p. 299.

35 Andrews, *Westward Enterprise*, p. 40; Robert Brenner, *Merchants and Revolution*, 1993, pp. 95–9.

36 Hakluyt VIII.405; *A description of New England*, 1616, pp. 50–3.

37 D. B. Quinn, 'The Voyage of *Triall* 1606–7: An Abortive Virginia Venture', *The American Neptune* 31 (1971), 85–103.

38 Hakluyt VIII.405.

39 R. Moore, *Some Aspects of the Origin and Nature of English Piracy, 1603–1625* (unpublished dissertation, University of Virginia, 1960), p. 238.

40 G. A. Jacobi discusses Fletcher's adaptation of Warner's tale in 'Zur Quellenfrage von Fletchers "The Sea Voyage"', *Anglia* 33 (1910), pp. 332–43.

41 André Thevet, *The New Found Worlde*, 1568, Ch. 67, fol. 107r–v.

42 *A Notable Historie*, transl. Hakluyt VIII.482–5.

43 *Ibid.*, p. 440.

44 Two John Fletchers appear in the 1620 list of 'Adventurers' on behalf of the Jamestown settlement, but the name was of course a common one. On the reluctance of London merchants to invest in the Virginia Company, and the withdrawal of many of them from its affairs between 1619 and 1623, see Brenner, *Merchants and Revolution*, pp. 96–101.

45 Thevet, fol. 8; Hakluyt VI.275.

46 *A Map of Virginia*, 1612, Pt. 2, p. 89.

47 See Linda Woodbridge, *Women and the English Renaissance*, 1984, Ch. 6, and note to *SV*, II.ii.o.1–2. On the Amazons, see C. T. Wright, 'The Amazons in Elizabethan Literature', *Studies in Philology* 37 (1940), 433–56.

48 Simon Shepherd, *Amazons and Warrior Women*, 1981, p. 135.

49 J. C. Spruill, *Women's Life and Work in the Southern Colonies*, 1972, p. 9.

50 The 1612 edition of Peter Martyr's *De Novo Orbe* describes a Caribbean island 'inhabited only with women, to whom the *Canibales* have accesse at certaine times of the yeere, as in old time the *Thracians* hadde to the *Amazones* in the Ilande of *Lesbos*' (p. 13). Fletcher's scenario is a sardonic version of this report.

51 *A Declaration of the State of the Colony and Affaires in Virginia*, 1620, p. 4.

52 Jerome Turler, *The Traveiler*, 1575, p. 9.

53 See Edward Chaney, *The Grand Tour and the Great Rebellion*, 1985.

54 Ian Donaldson, *The World Upside Down*, 1970.

55 J. Melton, *Astrologaster, or The Figure-Caster*, 1620, pp. 27–8.

56 For a stimulating analysis of the play along these lines, see Jackson I. Cope, *The Theatre and the Dream*, 1973, pp. 147–59.

57 Donaldson, p. 97.

58 *Ibid.*, pp. 94, 86.

59 Martin Butler, *Theatre and Crisis 1632–42*, 1984, p. 218. The play was extensively plagiarised in 1642 by the author of a satirical pamphlet, *Newes from the Antipodes* (see Abbreviations), which paints the antipodes as a puritan paradise.

60 Ferdinand de Quiros, *Terra Australis incognita, or a new Southerne Discoverie, containing a fifth part of the World*, 1617.

61 Joseph Hall, *Mundus Alter et Idem* [Another world and yet the same], ed. J. M. Wands, 1981, p. 12.

62 Thomas More, *Utopia* (1639 ed.), p. 11.

63 *Ibid.*, p. 14.

64 In *The Naturall and Morall Historie of the East and West Indies*, 1604, J. de Acosta quotes Augustine on the dogma that all men are descended from Adam, and poses the problem: 'it is a thing voide of all sense, to say, that men could passe from this continent to the new found world & cut through the Vast Ocean, seeing it were impossible for men to passe into those parts any other way' (p. 26).

65 *Utopia*, p. 303.

66 See notes to v.19–25 and vi.139.

67 The play was in fact the work of Fletcher and Massinger, the latter working either as collaborator or reviser, though Cyrus Hoy concludes that 'Fletcher was responsible for the play's final form' ('Shares', *Studies in Bibliography* 9 (1957), 153).

THE TRAVELS OF THE
THREE ENGLISH BROTHERS

To Honour's favourites, and the
entire friends to the family
of the Sherleys,
health.

It is a custom among friends, and sure a friendly custom: if the   5
obstacles of Fortune, the impediments of Nature, the bar of
time, the distance of place do hinder, nay if death itself doth
make that long separation amongst friends, the shadow or
picture of a friend is kept as a devoted ceremony. In that kind,
to all well-willers to those worthy subjects of our worthless   10
pens, we dedicate this idea and shape of honour. Being unable
to present the substances, we have epitomised their large volume
in a compendious abstract, which we wish all to peruse—and
yet none but friends, because we wish that all should be friends
to desert, and we ourselves could have a safe harbour and   15
umbrage for our well-willing yet weak labours. If we have not

---

The title-page of Q advertises Travels 'As it is now play'd by her Majesties Servants.'
The play was first staged in the first half of 1607: the entry on the Stationer's Register
for 29 June 1607 reads 'as yt was played at the Curten'; and the title-page of Anthony
Nixon's pamphlet The Three English Brothers (entered three weeks earlier) displays
the influence of the play in its reference to 'the Emperour of Persia his Neece'. Travels
is disparaged as 'stale' in Beaumont's Knight of the Burning Pestle, IV.29–32, which
was almost certainly staged towards the end of the year; but the present ascription
suggests that the play stayed in the repertory through much of the summer of 1607.
    The company was Queen Anne's Men, who acted at the Curtain and Red Bull
theatres. Travels was performed at both.

    1–3. To . . . Sherleys] See notes on Characters below, and Intro., pp. 9–10.
    8. shadow] representation; often applied to an actor or play.
    11. idea] perfect conception or standard.
    12. volume] record. Four pamphlets about the adventures of the Sherley brothers
had appeared by 1607, and the 'memorable exploytes' of Anthony Sherley in the West
Indies had been recorded by Richard Hakluyt (X.266–76).
    15. desert] deserving deeds.
    16. umbrage] protection.

limned to the life the true portrait of their deserts (our wills being sealed with our endeavours, and peized by an able censurer) we go (with the proverb) to a willing execution, *Leniter ex merito quicquid patiare ferendum est.*   20

Coelo beat Musa.

In our best endeavours,
YOURS,
JOHN DAY.
WILLIAM ROWLEY.
GEORGE WILKINS.   25

---

17. *limned*] depicted.
18. *peized*] weighed, assessed.
18–19. *able censurer*] possibly Anthony Nixon, whose narrative of the brothers' travels must have been available in MS to the playwrights; or Thomas Sherley who (*pace* 8) had been back in England since December 1606 and probably commissioned Nixon's pamphlet. See Intro., pp. 8–9.
19. *with ... execution*] not recorded as an English proverb.
19–20. Leniter ... est] from Ovid, *Heroides* V.7: 'Softly must we bear whatever suffering is our desert.'
23. Coelo ... Musa] Horace, *Odes* IV.8.29: 'the Muse bestows the boon of heaven.'

CHARACTERS

Chorus.
Sir Thomas Sherley, *the elder.*
SIR THOMAS SHERLEY, *the younger.*
SIR ANTHONY SHERLEY.
ROBERT SHERLEY.

5

THE SOPHY *of Persia.*
Governor *of Qasvin.*
CUSHAN HALIBECK.
CALIMATH.
NIECE *to the Sophy.*
DALIBRA, *her maid.*
Dalibra's Boy.

10

Scene-divisions and the list of characters' names are not given in Q; the Epistle is untitled and is found only in some copies.

---

2. *Sir . . . elder*] Head of the Sussex branch of a old family, Sir Thomas held high office under Elizabeth I but fell on hard times in the Jacobean period. He died in 1612, and the debts he left behind led to the loss of the family seat of Wiston in 1622.

3–5.] Thomas, the eldest son, was born about 1564, Anthony probably in the following year, and Robert in about 1581.

4. *SIR ANTHONY*] His knighthood was not English but a minor order conferred on him by Henri IV of France during a diplomatic mission in 1593. Elizabeth I's displeasure at this award forced him to return the insignia and forswear any allegiance to the French monarch, but he continued to be known by the title.

6. *SOPHY*] Shah. The English title is probably a corruption of 'Safi', from the Safavid dynasty which came to power in Iran in the early sixteenth century. Cartwright gives a representative view of the reign of Abbas I (1587–1629): 'since king *Abas* came unto the crowne, ful twenty yeares & upwards, the *Persian* Empire hath florished in sacred and redoubted laws . . . armes, artes, and sciences doe wonderfully prosper, and are very highly esteemed' (p. 67).

7. *Qasvin*] See note to Prologue, 40.

8. *CUSHAN HALIBECK*] English rendering of Husain 'Ali Beg, an elderly nobleman at the Persian court.

9. *CALIMATH*] Not a Persian name, and probably borrowed from the Turk Selim-Calymath in Marlowe's *Jew of Malta*, a play which enjoyed regular revivals and may have been owned and performed by Queen Anne's Men. The character's partnership with Halibeck could have been suggested by the Turkish brothers Hali and Cali in the anonymous *Selimus* (1594).

10. *NIECE*] Cartwright calls Robert Sherley's bride 'a *Cir[c]assian Lady* of great esteeme and regard' (p. 70), thereby emphasising that she was a Christian; and Nixon describes her as 'the cousin Germaine to the King of *Persia* (beeing the widowe of a Duke in that country)' (K4). The story that she was the Shah's niece apparently had its origins in the play, and was still current in 1625 when it helped to create a diplomatic incident at the English court. See Davies, pp. 263–4, and note to xi.57.

THE GREAT TURK.
A Pasha.
The Emperor of Russia. 15
THE POPE.
The King of Spain.

ZARIPH, *a Jew.*
WILL KEMP.
Kemp's Boy. 20
Harlequin.
Harlequin's Wife.

Gunner.
Captain.
Servant *to Sir Thomas Sherley.* 25
Jailer.
Christian prisoner.
Hermit.
English Agent.

Venetian citizens, Cardinals, Persian and Turkish soldiers, 30
Pashas, Attendants, Lords, Followers, Sailors, Sergeants,
Islanders, Messengers, Servants.

---

13. *GREAT TURK*] The usual English designation of the Ottoman Sultan; at the time of these events, Mehmet III (1595–1603). He was the first Turkish sovereign since Suleiman to lead his troops into battle.

14. *Pasha*] A provincial governor or military commander in the Ottoman empire; variously spelt 'basha' or 'bassa' in Q.

15. *Emperor*] Czar Boris Godunov (1552–1605).

16. *POPE*] Clement VIII.

17. *King of Spain*] Philip III (1598–1621). He appears only in the concluding dumb show.

19. *WILL KEMP*] Celebrated Elizabethan actor and jig-maker. He was a member of the King's Men in the 1590s and created a number of Shakespeare's earlier clown roles. After a Continental tour in 1601 he joined Worcester's (later Queen Anne's) Men, and died probably in 1603.

21. *Harlequin*] Clown-actor in the *commedia dell'arte.*

PROLOGUE

Enter Chorus *as a Prologue, attired like Fame.*

Chorus. The tranquil silence of a propitious hour
    Charm your attentions in a gentle spell,
    Whilst our endeavours get a vocal tongue
    To fill the pleasing roundure of your ears.
    Our scene is mantled in the robe of truth;   5
    Yet must we crave, by law of poesy,
    To give our history an ornament
    But equalling this definition, thus:
    Who gives a fowl unto his cook to dress
    Likewise expects to have a fowl again.   10
    Though in the cook's laborious workmanship
    Much may be diminished, somewhat added—
    The loss of feathers and the gain of sauce—
    Yet in the back surrender of this dish
    It is, and may be truly called, the same.   15
    Such are our acts. Should our tedious muse
    Pace the particulars of our travellers,
    Five days would break the limits of our scenes
    But to express the shadows. Therefore we
    (Leaving the feathers and some needless stuff)   20
    Present you with the fairest of our feast,
    Clothing our truth within an argument
    Fitting the stage and your attention.
    Yet not so hid but that she may appear
    To be herself, even truth. Now your assists   25
    To help the entrance of our history.
    First see a father parting with his sons;
    Then, in a moment, on the full sails of thought

0.1. *Enter* Chorus *as a*] *not in* Q.

0.1. like Fame] The figure of *Fama Bona* was conventionally represented in pageants and emblem literature as a winged female with a trumpet (cf. the title-page of Raleigh's *History of the World*). In Dekker's *Magnificent Entertainment* (1604) she wears a robe 'thickly set with open Eyes, and Tongues' (E3v), and she seems to have appeared thus on the public stage. Cf. Epilogue, 1.

7. *ornament*] a little dressing up. The claim is not that the narrative of events will be embroidered but that it needs reshaping for dramatic purposes.

16. *acts*] dramatic episodes or scenes. There is no implication that the play divides into five acts; but the Chorus goes on to insist that its action is carefully shaped.

We will divide them many hundred leagues.
Our scene lies speechless, active but yet dumb,   30
Till your expressing thoughts give it a tongue.

Enter Sir Thomas Sherley *the elder with his three sons,*
SIR THOMAS, SIR ANTHONY *and* MASTER ROBERT. SIR THOMAS
goes back with his father, the other take their leaves.

Imagine now the gentle breath of heaven
Hath on the liquid highway of the waves
Conveyed him many thousand leagues from us.
Think you have seen him sail by many lands;   35
And now at last, arrived in Persia,
Within the confines of the great Sophy,
Think you have heard his courteous salute
Speak in a peal of shot, the like till now
Ne'er heard at Qasvin, which town's governor   40
Doth kindly entertain our English knight—
With him expect him first. The rest observe:
If foreign strangers to him be so kind,
We hope his native country we shall find
More courteous. To your just censures then   45
We offer up their travels and our pen.   *Exit.*

SCENE i

Enter the Governor *of Qasvin,* SIR ANTHONY,
ROBERT *and others.*

Governor. Sir, yet your entertain hath been but weak,
But now assure ye 't shall be strengthened.

31.1. Sherley...*with*] not in Q.   31.3.] Q *prints at end of* SD: *Exeunt.*   40.
Qasvin] *Casbin* Q *(passim)*.

31.3] The two groups presumably leave the stage by separate doors (though the
travellers could remain to mime some of the action described in the speech that
follows). The modern theatre is more likely to synchronise words and spectacle, but
for Jacobean dramatists the use of the Chorus is an admission of the difficulty of
representing travel on the stage, and a way of appealing to the audience's imaginative
capacity rather than to its visual sense.
32–5.] A smooth passage glossing over the lengthy and complicated journey which
took two of the Sherley brothers to Persia in 1598. See Intro., p. 9.
34. *him*] i.e. Sir Anthony, whose leading role is presumably made clear in dumb
show.
40. *Qasvin*] The Persian capital under the Safavid Shahs until 1598, when Abbas
transferred his court to the new imperial city of Isfahan. Qasvin remained an important
centre, noted by travellers for its refinement and sophistication.
45. *censures*] evaluations.

A prince's absence clothes his public weal
In mourning garments; now our widowhood
In a conquering return shall be made good.   5
This day my royal master, the Persian Sophy,
Accompanied with a glorious tribute
Which forty thousand Turkish lives have paid,
Is hitherwards in march, to whom I have
Delivered your arrival here in Persia,   10
Your state, your habit, your fair demeanour;
And so well as my weak oratory could recite
Spoke of those worths I have observed in you.
Sir Anthony. Sir, nothing I fear so much
   Lest that the merit you have laid on me   15
   Should not go even with your report.
Governor.   It will.
   Yet (if I may) I'll thus far counsel ye:
   It is the Sophy's high will and pleasure
   That you be seated here in the market-place
   To view the manner of his victories;   20
   Which, would you greet with your high tongues of war
   Whose thunder ne'er was heard in Persia
   Till you gave voice to them at Qasvin first,
   In what his kingdom best can furnish ye
   It is his pleasure and command you want not.   25
Sir Anthony. It was my purpose so to salute him.
   Brother, pray ye see our directions falter not,
   See all in order as we did determine.
Robert. I shall, sir.   *Exit.*
Sir Anthony. With such a train as many casualties   30
   (A traveller's mishaps) have left with me,
   I'll greet his highness in the best I may.

   Enter from wars with drums and colours THE SOPHY,
   CUSHAN HALIBECK *and* CALIMATH *with soldiers.* THE SOPHY
   gives SIR ANTHONY *his hand as he offers to stoop to his foot.*

8.] In fact Abbas I was returning from a decisive victory over the Uzbegs which
secured Persia's eastern frontier and made possible a fresh initiative against the Turks,
with whom he had been forced to conclude a humiliating peace shortly after his
accession in 1587.

18–20.] Cartwright provides a vivid account of 'the great market place or high
streete' at Isfahan, in which 'are erected certain high scaffolds, where the multitude do
sit to behold the warlike exercises performed by the King and his courtiers ... In this
place also is to be seene severall times in the yeare, the pleasant sight of fireworks, of
banquets, of musickes, of wrastlings, and of whatsoever triumphes else is there to be
shewed, for the declaration of the joy of this people' (p. 66).

Sophy. Christian or howsoever, courteous thou seemest;
    We bid thee welcome in unusèd phrase.
    No gentle stranger greets our continent   35
    But our arms fold him in a soft embrace.
    Yet must his gratulation first be paid
    Upon our foot: you stoop but to our hand,
    This for your followers. Welcome, welcome!

        ROBERT *and the rest kiss his foot.*

    Our governor of Qasvin, see these strangers placed,   40
    Be it your care and charge. Since they have met
    Their welcome first in weatherbeaten steel
    We'll show the manner of our Persian wars,
    Our music and our conquests. [*To the soldiers*] Divide ye:
    The one half are Persians, the rest are Turks.   45
    Strike! A conqueror that still retains his name,
    To tell his conquests is not pride but fame.

   A battle presented. Excursion; the one half drive out the
      other, then enter with heads on their swords.

    These are our victories, to see those tongues
    That lately threw defiance in our teeth
    Quite put to silence in the caves of earth.   50
    Then are we sure our enemy is dead
    When from the body we divide the head.
    How likes the Christian of our Persian wars?
Sir Anthony. As themselves deserve, renownèd Sophy.
    Your wars are manly, stout and honourable,   55
    Your arms have no employment for a coward.

---

34. *unusèd*] i.e. reserved for the most privileged guests.
35. *continent*] domain.
40. *see . . . placed*] The brothers are presumably provided with stools, while the Sophy sits on a throne which might be carried in during his processional entry and placed on a dais which is permanently on stage.
47.1. Excursion] military action which moves on and off the stage.
47.2. with . . . swords] Cf. Anthony Sherley's *Relation* (1613), describing Abbas' preparations for a triumphal entry into Qasvin: 'there were 30000 men, sent out of the Towne on foote with horse-mens staves, upon which were fastened vizards of so many heads: All those in the morning, when we were commanded to meet him . . . wee found marching in battell aray towards the Towne' (p. 63; also in Purchas VIII.413).
50. *caves of earth*] graves. The phrase seems to have been synonymous with oblivion: cf. the melancholy epitaph on Almansor, the Muslim scourge of Spain, who 'as yesterday was . . . beloved of his people, and is now forgotten and forsaken of them all, and remaineth solitarie in the darke Caves of the earth' (Purchas X.387); and Bolingbroke's determination to heed the mute appeal of the murdered Woodstock from 'the tongueless caverns of the earth' (*Richard II*, I.i.105).

Who dares not charge his courage in the field
In hardy strokes 'gainst his opposèd foe,
May be your subject, not your soldier.
Your grace in this hath done me too much honour,   60
Which would you license me but in part to pay
With sight of such wars as Christians use—
So far as my small retinue will serve—
I'll shadow forth my country's hardiment.
Think it a picture which may seem as great   65
As the substantial self: when laid unto it
The compass of the hand would cover it.
Your favour and 'tis done, so that your eyes
Will deign to grace our seeming victories.
Sophy. You have prevented us in proffering it;   70
We had requested else. Our self will sit
And so justly censure of your state in field
That if yours best deserve, then ours shall yield.
                    Exeunt SIR ANTHONY, ROBERT *and the rest.*
What powers do wrap me in amazement thus?
Methinks this Christian's more than mortal.   75
Sure he conceals himself! Within my thoughts
Never was man so deeply registered.
But God or Christian, or whate'er he be,
I wish to be no other but as he.
Halibeck. The Sophy dotes upon this fellow already.   80
Calimath. Most devoutly; we shall have his statue erected in
    our temple shortly.
Halibeck. I'll ne'er pray again if it be.
Calimath. Hark, they come. We'll note how the Sophy will
    grace them.   85

---

66. self:] selfe, *Q.*

---

64. *hardiment*] valour.

66–7. *when . . . it*] i.e. since the real thing can be blocked from view as easily as our representation of it. Cf. Marlowe, *Dr. Faustus*, viii.72–3 (B text): 'looking down the earth appeared to me, /No bigger than my hand in quantity.'

70. *prevented*] forestalled.

76. *Sure . . . himself!*] Like Jove. The dramatists may have thought the allusion congruent with Persian beliefs (see ii.190–3 note), but such references are loosely used in the play (cf. **151**).

80. *already*] Abbas I was noted for his tolerance of non-Islamic minorities in Persia, and also for his patronage of European artists and craftsmen.

81–2. *statue . . . temple*] In fact Islam never represents the human form. The inspiration here is Roman and theatrical, as in the comparable sense of outrage amongst the Germanicans in Jonson's *Sejanus* (1605): 'Great Pompey's theatre was never ruined/Till now, that proud Sejanus hath a statue/Reared on his ashes' (I.542–4).

Halibeck. It shall not please me be it ne'er so good.

> *A Christian battle shown between the two brothers.*
> ROBERT *driven out, then enter* SIR ANTHONY *and the*
> *rest with the other part prisoners.*

Sophy. Next Mortus Ali, and those deities
    To whom we Persians pay devotion,
    We do adore thee. Your wars are royal,
    So joined with music that even death itself   90
    Would seem a dream; your instruments dissolve
    A body into spirit but to hear
    Their cheerful clamours; and those your engines—
    We cannot give their proper character—
    Those loud tongues that spit their spleen in fire,   95
    Drowning the groans of your then-dying friends
    And with the smoke hiding the gasp of life
    That you ne'er think of aught but victory
    Till all be won or lost. We cannot praise
    It well. But what means those in bondage so?   100
Sir Anthony. These are our prisoners.
Sophy.   Why do they live?
Sir Anthony. In this I show the nature of our wars.
    It is our clemency in victory
    To shed no blood upon a yielding foe.
    Sometimes we buy our friend's life with our foe's;   105
    Sometimes for gold, and that hardens valour
    When he that wins the honour gets the spoil.
    Sometimes for torment we give weary life:
    Our foes are such that they had rather die
    Than to have life in our captivity.   110
Sophy. We never heard of honour until now.
Sir Anthony. Yet have we engines of more force than these.
    When our o'er-heated bloods would massacre
    We can lay cities level with the pavement,

87.SP] *om. Q.*

87. *Next*] second only to.
Mortus Ali] 'Ali Ibn Abi Talib, son-in-law of the Prophet Muhammad and regarded by adherents of Shia Islam as his true successor. The Shi'ite faith was imposed on Persia by Ismail I, founder of the Safavid dynasty. *Mortus* is a corruption of the Persian 'murtaza' meaning chosen or approved, and may reflect a Western perception of 'Ali as a martyr. See Intro., p. 12.
91. *instruments*] drums and trumpets.
100. *But ... so?*] The mock-battle introduces one of the play's major subjects of debate.

Bandy up towers and turrets in the air   115
And on the seas o'erwhelm an argosy.
These are those warriors.

                          Chambers go off.

Halibeck.   Mahomet! It thunders.
Sophy. Sure this is a god.
Halibeck. [*Aside to Calimath*] Sure 'tis a devil,
    And I'm tormented to see him graced thus.
Sophy. First teach me how to call thee ere I speak.   120
    I more and more doubt thy mortality.
    Those tongues do imitate the voice of heaven
    When the gods speak in thunder; your honours
    And your qualities of war more than human.
    If thou hast godhead, and disguised art come   125
    To teach us unknown rudiments of war,
    Tell us thy precepts and we'll adore thee.
Sir Anthony. O, let your princely thoughts descend so low
    As my being's worth, think me as I am.
    No stranger are the deeds I show to you   130
    Than yours to me. My country's far remote,
    An island, but a handful to the world;

117–19.] *prose in* Q.

---

115. *Bandy up*] Toss. Bandy was a form of tennis.

117. SD] Cannon were used in public playhouse performances, and were part of the noisy and spectacular ambience of the Red Bull.

121–7.] An odd echo—given Persia's reputation as an ancient and sophisticated land—of the reported reactions of New World natives to European explorers. But the alignment is explicable in the light of some traditional accounts of Persia (see note to ii.190–3), and also in view of the widespread but erroneous belief that its army was without heavy guns until the Sherleys arrived. In *The History of the Warres between the Turkes and the Persians* (1595), J.–T. Minadoi (tr. A. Hartwell) averred that 'The people of *Persia* are afrayde of Artillery beyond measure ... And although they be so timorous and fearefull of that Engine, and know of what moment it is in a battell: yet have they not hetherto received the use thereof, being rather obstinate in their blind ambitious conceite, that it is a sinne and shame to exercise so cruell a weapon against mankinde' (pp. 74–5).

131–6. *My ... speak*] England's political and cultural isolation in the sixteenth century was often reconceived in terms of the classical *locus amoenus* by citing the famous line from Virgil's *Eclogues*, I.66: 'penitus toto divisos orbe Britannos'—translated by George Sandys in the passionate encomion that opens the last chapter of his *Relation*: 'Beloved soile: as in site—*Wholly from all the world disjoyned*: so in thy felicities. The Sommer burnes thee not, nor the Winter benums thee: defended by the Sea from wastfull incursions, and by the valour of thy sonnes from hostile invasions' (p. 218).

132. *but a handful*] i.e. a mere speck; see note to 66–7, and cf. Thomas Middleton, *Sir Robert Sherley Sent Ambassador* (1609), ' "England's complaint to Persia for her

Yet fruitful as the meads of paradise;
Defenced with streams such as from Eden run;
Each port and entrance kept with such a guard   135
As those you last heard speak. There lives a princess
Royal as yourself, whose subject I am
As these are to you.
Halibeck.   As we? Comparisons?
Sir Anthony. So long as war attempted our decay,
So ill repaid, we so by heaven preserved,   140
That war no more dares look upon our land.
All princes league with us, which causeth us
That wont to write our honours down in blood,
Cold and unactive. To seek for employment
Hither am I come, renownèd Persian.   145
My force and power is yours, say but the word,
So against Christians I may draw no sword.
Sophy. With arms of love and adoration
I entertain thee, worthy Christian,
And think me happier in thy embrace   150
Than if the god of battles fought for me.
Thou shalt be general against the Turks.
Calimath. He'll make him his heir next.
Halibeck.   I'll lose my head first.
Sophy. A camp of equal spirits to thyself
Would turn all Turkey into Persia.   155
Let me feast upon thy tongue. I delight to hear thee speak.
Halibeck. [*Aside*] I'll interrupt ye! Ye Persian gods, look on:
The Sophy will profane your deities,
And make an idol of a fugitive.—
My liege!
Sophy.   You describe wonders.   160

Sherley": though to the eye of the world I may perhaps appear beautiful and great, yet
in his eye I show no bigger than a small corner of the world' (*Works*, ed. Gary Taylor,
forthcoming).

140. *So ill repaid*] i.e. enemy hostilities met with such a fierce response.

144. *Cold*] i.e. to be denied the heat of battle. Sherley's terse statement expresses
not just national pride but the frustration of the Essex faction at the pacific foreign
policy of Elizabeth I, one that was continued by her successor.

146. *My . . . yours*] The frank admission of his mercenary status may be more
revealing than the dramatists intend. Sherley originally went to the Middle East to
attack the Portuguese presence in the Persian Gulf, but after his arrival in Persia turned
his attention to promoting an anti-Turkish alliance. He probably did so at the behest
of Shah Abbas, but his apologists were quick to present it as his own idea.

159. *fugitive*] An exaggeration, but Sherley had left England without permission in
1598, and after Elizabeth's death, despite being on reasonable terms with James I, he
was widely mistrusted in official circles. He was never to return home.

Halibeck. He minds me not.—My liege!
Sophy.   You trouble us.—
   And what's the difference 'twixt us and you?
Sir Anthony. None but the greatest, mighty Persian.
   All that makes up this earthly edifice
   By which we are called men is all alike.   165
   Each may be the other's anatomy;
   Our nerves, our arteries, our pipes of life,
   The motives of our senses all do move
   As of one axletree, our shapes alike.
   One workman made us all, and all offend   170
   That maker, all taste of interdicted sin.
   Only art in a peculiar change
   Each country shapes as she best can piece them.
   But that's not all: our inward offices
   Are most at jar—would they were not, great prince!   175
   Your favour here if I outstrip my bounds.
   We live and die, suffer calamities,
   Are underlings to sickness, fire, famine, sword.
   We all are punished by the same hand and rod,
   Our sins are all alike; why not our God?   180

              Enter Messenger.

Messenger. My liege.
Sophy. What makes these slaves so bold to trouble me?
   Well, sir, now your sweating message.
Messenger. The Turks have gathered power.
Sophy.   So have we.
Messenger. Those that retired from your last victory have met   185
   fresh supply, and all turn head upon your confines.
Sophy. So have we fresh supply;
   We'll meet half-way. Welcome again, brave Englishman.
   Our best employment in this war is thine.
   For thy sake do I love all Christians;   190
   We give thee liberty of conscience.

---

173. piece] *conj.Bu.;* please *Q.*

---

167. *pipes*] veins.
168. *motives*] promptings.
169. *axletree*] the imaginary line round which the Ptolemaic universe revolves.
172. *peculiar change*] particular fashion.
174. *But . . . all*] Yet there's one fundamental difference between us.
inward offices] modes of religious observance.
176. *outstrip my bounds*] presume too far.
178. *underlings*] subject.

Walk in our hand, thou hast possessed our heart.
Away for wars; we must cut short our feasts,
Lest that our foes prove our unwelcome guests.   *Exeunt.*

SCENE ii

Enter THE GREAT TURK, *with followers and a* Pasha.

Great Turk. Stand, stand! Our fury swells so high
     We cannot march a foot ere it break forth.
     O thou inconstant fate whose deadly wings
     Lifts thee like falcons up to fall on kings—
     On greater than on kings, for it strikes us   5
     To whom kings kneel. Our potent power,
     Whom judgement holds to be invincible,
     By but a handful of our enemies,
     The Sophy and his troops, are forced to fly,
     Not daring to resist, fearing to die!   10
Pasha. Yet let the Sun of Ottoman take strength,
     Call up his forces and join war again.

Soft march.

---

8. By] *conj.Bu.;* Be *Q.*

1–2.] At least since Marlowe's *Tamburlaine* Turkish sultans in plays could be expected to rant: witness the title of Thomas Goffe's play *The Raging Turk* (acted c.1618). The convention was well suited to the Red Bull, whose actors 'were terrible teare-throats' according to Edmund Gayton in his *Festivous Notes upon Don Quixote* (1654; quoted by Reynolds, p. 54). Gayton wrote about the 1630s, but was observing an acting style long established at that theatre.

6. *power*] army.

6–7.] 'The Turkes of all kinde of people, are sayde at these dayes to use moste lawfull fightinge, so that it is no marvayle whye their common wealth continueth so longe, and encreaseth so much that their Nation is almost invincible, excepte they be destroyed by some plague or pestilence, or civill discorde' (*A Briefe Collection . . . gathered out of the Cosmographye of Sebastian Munster*, 1574, fol. 34v). In the preface to *The History of the Warres between the Turkes and the Persians* (1595), Abraham Hartwell records an old prophecy that the Ottoman Empire would collapse in the mid-1590s and comments that 'we see all thinges go so quite contrarie to this prognosticon, and the power of the Turkes growe so huge and infinite . . . that . . . I feare greatly that the halfe Moone which now ruleth & raigneth almost over all the East, wil grow to the full, and breede such an Inundation as will utterly drowne al Christendome in the West' (A3v–4). In fact the Ottoman empire was in serious decline by the early seventeenth century.

11. *Sun of Ottoman*] The Turkish empire was identified more commonly with the crescent (the 'halfe Moone' of the previous quotation).

12.1. Soft march] This seems to call for a distant sound of drums (as in Heywood's *Four Prentises of London*, Hv) to signify an approaching army. The stage direction 'A

Great Turk. Join war again we may, to show our will,
　　But prove like those resist to their own ill.
　　Hark, Pasha, how their voice of coming on   15
　　Speaks like the tongue of heaven, threatening
　　Destruction to mankind when it please.
Pasha. Yet let your blood
　　Be like the ocean troubled with the wind,
　　Rise till it dim the stars; such your high mind.   20
Great Turk. It shall, it shall; we will hold calm no longer.
　　Swell, sea of fury, till these Persians
　　Standing like trees upon our circling banks
　　Be over-flown. Men, wrath and blood,
　　Meet like earth, fire and air that's not withstood.   25

Enter THE SOPHY, SIR ANTHONY SHERLEY, CUSHAN HALIBECK,
　　MASTER ROBERT SHERLEY *and* CALIMATH *in arms.*

Sophy. We thus confront thee.
Great Turk.　　　　　　　　　We thus answer thee.
Sophy. Know, thou that callst thyself a god on earth
　　And wouldst have nations stoop to thee as men to heaven,
　　We are thus armed—ay, and for this defence,
　　'Twixt God and man to approve a difference.   30
Great Turk. Know, thou whose power is but a wart to mine,
　　If earth have good from heaven, hell power by sinners,
　　If death be due to men as bliss to angels,
　　This sun at Christian's west shall not set true

---

15. Pasha] *Bassa Q.*　18–19.] *one line in Q.*

---

march afar off' is common in the period (e.g. *Hamlet*, V.ii.301). There is presumably a steady crescendo hereafter until the Persian entry, perhaps interrupted by a Turkish trumpet call to arms which is the *answer* of 26.

13–14.] i.e. we'll succeed only if we fight like men prepared to defy the worst (or perhaps: who are indifferent to what befalls them).

24. *over-flown*] submerged.

24–5. *Men ... withstood*] Clumsily expressed: the implied subject of *that's* is the force or energy generated by conflict between the elements.

26. *We ... thee*] The contrast between the two camps was probably evident in their costumes, and the acting company may have followed available information that in general the Turks wore green turbans and the Persians red. Both sides agree 'that it were not reasonable to cover the dishonest partes of the body, with the colour which the Prophetes did weare on their heads ... therefore is no more permitted unto the Turkes to weare green hose, then unto the Sophians to weare red hosen' (*The Navigations ... into Turkie by Nicholas Nicholay*, 1585, p. 108). Perhaps on stage one side was the reverse image of the other.

33.] This looks like a pointed correction of what Christian writers often took to be an erroneous Muslim belief, 'that at the winding of a horne not only all flesh shall die, but the Angells themselves' (Sandys, *Relation*, p. 58).

Before thy life meet death, hell have her due. 35
Sir Anthony. Endure him not, great emperor.
Sophy. Patience.
    Know thou again in this just war I'm knit
    With Christians and with subjects whose warlike arms
    Like steel rebates not, but like fire shall fly
    To burn thee down whose pride's above the sky. 40
Great Turk. Thy Christians I contemn like to their god.
Sir Anthony. O!
Great Turk. They shall have graves like thee dishonourèd,
    Unfit for heaven or earth. This we prepare:
    Betwixt them both we'll seat you in the air. 45
Sir Anthony. Turk, infidel, thou that talkst of angels,
    The chroniclers of heaven who in their register
    Record thee living as a soul for hell,
    By Him that died for me, my pains shall sweat
    These pores to open but I will pay this debt. 50
    I'll vex them with my sword, and being panged
    With earthly torments send them to be damned.
Great Turk. Wilt, Christian?
Sir Anthony. If I live I will,
    As sure as day doth progress toward night.
    In death of pagans all Christ's sons delight 55
    And I am one of them.
Great Turk. Alarum then!
Sir Anthony. To fight with devils loathed of virtuous men.

    Alarum; retreat. Then enter SIR ANTHONY *with his
    brother* ROBERT, *having taken the* Pasha *prisoner.*

Sir Anthony. Our patron the great Sophy hath the worst!
    Yet I have ta'en this pasha from the Turks.
    Stir not, thou son of Ismael, or thou diest. 60
    [*To Robert*] Young Robin and my brother, though as yet

39. *rebates*] blunts.
41. *contemn*] despise.
45. *in the air*] i.e. bearing their heads on swords (cf. 110–11), but also referring to the fact that their bodies will not receive proper burial (cf. 118–19); the implication is that their souls are lost as a result. Dramatists of the period assume that Christian ideas are universal when it suits them to do so.
51. *them*] i.e. the Turks. Perhaps Anthony threatens some of the Great Turk's retinue.
56. *Alarum*] To arms! In the theatre the term was a cue for drums, sometimes accompanied by trumpets.
60. *son of Ismael*] Abraham's son Ishmael (Genesis 16) was adopted by Islam as a prophet and holy man of antiquity.

Th' art but a novice in this school of death
And scarcely read in martial discipline,
As thou hast a great spirit or wouldst show
That thou art sprung from agèd Sherley's loins,　　65
Approve it now: keep this prisoner for me,
Lose rather life than leave him; if he 'scape
'Tis not by cowardice but by mishap.
Robert. And if I do not,
From all our ancestors' most worthy roll　　70
Be my name blotted, and from heaven my soul.
Sir Anthony. I thank thee, by my troth. I'll to the battle
To save the Sophy pressed with multitudes
And rescue him or die. Sure without doubt,
Our lives are lighted tapers that must out.　　*Exit.*　75
Robert. Come, Turk, I am made your jailer, and in these chains
To which thou art bondman, who dares fetch thee out?
I could have wished myself in thick of danger
When men drop down for graves like rain from heaven,
But that my brother counselled otherwise　　80
Who is my schoolmaster in these designs.
He sweats for honour like a Christian
Against Christ's foes, leaving me here
To keep thee prisoner, purchase of his sword.
And come thy father—that's the devil, Turk—　　85
To be thy rescue, though he fight in fire,
Rather than loose thee, by the king of stars
I'll part with life, make this a pile of scars.

Enter HALIBECK.

Halibeck. Resign thy prisoner, youthful Englishman.
His life, thy victory is due to us,　　90
By the custom of our nation.
Robert. Is it so, my lord?
Halibeck.　　　　It is:
Let it suffice thee that I say it is.
'Tis grace enough that thou hast made him captive.
His head shall be the honour of our sword;　　95
And thus I cease on it.
Robert.　　　　You may, my lord.

92–3. It . . . is] *one line in* Q.

87. *loose thee*] let you escape.
88. *this*] i.e. his own body.

Halibeck. Thou shalt have soldier's pay, good words for deeds;
　　Not have the honour to present his head.
　　That trophy's due to Cushan Halibeck.
Robert. Then Cushan Halibeck must have this prisoner?   100
Halibeck. I must, I will; who dare deny him me?
Robert. Not I, a Sherley dare not to deny a Persian.
Halibeck. [*Drawing his sword*] Pasha.
Pasha.   What sayst thou, Halibeck?
Halibeck. Seest thou this blade?
Pasha.   I do, but fear it not.
　　Custom of tyranny betwixt our nations   105
　　Hath made me not so much amazed of thee
　　As by a stranger which did conquer me.
Halibeck. This steel shall glaze itself within thy blood
　　And blunt his keen edge with thy Turkish bones.
　　This point shall tilt itself within thy skull   110
　　And bear it as birds fly 'twixt us and heaven;
　　And as thy blood shall stream along this blade
　　I'll laugh and say, 'for this our foes were made'.
Robert. Will the great Hali be so tyrannous?
Halibeck. What boots it thee to ask, or fit to know?   115
Robert. He was my prisoner; I had charge of him.
Halibeck. But now my prisoner, whoe'er conquered him,
　　Whose life shall pay his ransom, and his grave
　　Shall be i' the breast of fowls as 'fits a slave.
Robert. 'Twere good I see't not then.
Halibeck.   Ha!
Robert.   So.
Halibeck.   How?   120
Robert. Thus: 'twere good I see 't not then.
　　These hands were made his keeper by my brother,
　　Whose sword subdued him, gave him prisoner
　　To me.
Halibeck. To thee?
Robert.   To me, Persian, to me.
Halibeck. Thus eagle's wings shake off a buzzing fly.   125
　　Pray, Turk, let thy heart sigh and thine eyes weep
　　That thus they go to their eternal sleep.
Robert. Thou art better go down quick unto thy grave

---

107. *As . . . which*] as by the fact that a stranger.
119. *breast*] i.e. stomachs.
121.] Robert might make to leave or, more likely, turns his back in protest, then using this inscrutable posture to dominate his opponent.

Than touch him; better abuse thy parents,
Be thine own murderer, let thine own blood out   130
And seal therewith thine own damnation;
Better do all may tumble thee to hell
Than wrong him.
Halibeck.   How, Christian?
Robert. Thus, pagan: he's my prisoner,
    And here's the key that locks him in these chains.   135
    Rescue, release or hurt him if thou darest.
Halibeck. Dare?
Robert.   Dare:
    Stare out thine eye-balls, I outdare thee to 't!
    Or let thy hand wrong but a hair on's head,
    This hand metes out thy grave where thou dost tread.   140
Halibeck. Your will shall be our master; we'll obey you, sir.
Robert. Your sword's not tilted then within his skull?
Halibeck. Our nation's custom shall be awed by you.
Robert. Nor borne as birds do fly 'twixt us and heaven?
Halibeck. We will become your slaves and kneel to you.   145
Robert. He's not your prisoner then, whoever conquered him?
Halibeck. We'll be your dogs, and fawn, and curse our fate.
    When upstarts nobles brave, wretched's the state.
Robert. But 'tis more woe in realms when men's deserts
    Are spurned or stol'n, then worn in cowards' hearts.   150
Halibeck. Yet, English Christian, this be sure I'll keep.
    The sun's heat's waking when 'tis thought asleep.

          A flourish. Enter THE SOPHY, SIR ANTHONY *and*
                    CALIMATH *with* Attendants.

Sophy. Thy valour hath commanded us the day,
    Brave Englishman, we thank thee; and by a peace concluded,
    Pasha, we ransomless return thee to thy master.   155
    His valour that subdued thee we'll reward
    With favour and with bounty.   *Exit* ROBERT *with* Pasha.
                    And now to council,
    Where we'll determine of your motion
    Made of a league 'twixt us and Christendom.

---

152. heat's] heates Q.   152.2. *with* Attendants] *not in Q.*   157.SD] *not in Q.*

---

    139. *Or*] if you.
    140. *metes*] measures.
    143. *be awed by*] defer to.
    159. *a league*] 'Certaine Townes and Provinces, belonging to the *Persian*, bordering upon the Turkes, were lost by this Kings predecessors, which he hopeth to

Halibeck. A league with Christendom!   160
Calimath. He hath advised him to't: ha' patience, brother.
Sophy. I'the eye of heaven we swear, without offence
    We'll hear what instances you can produce
    How such a league may be advantage to us.
    Sit, sit, to hear and speak as free;   165
    Without control 'tis we give liberty.
    Concerning then our peace with Christian princes?
Sir Anthony. To join with them, great emperor, you shall be
    A captain for the highest, and in your war
    Have angels' hands to guard and fight for you.   170
    Religious men shall wear their bended knees
    Even to the bone, in ceaseless prayers for you;
    To whose continual kneelings, tears and sighs
    Heaven's ears be never shut but do receive
    Their souls' devotion; makes the clouds to clear,   175
    And thus dispatcheth each petitioner:
    'Who fights for us I'll be their comforter'.
    White-headed age then, with their hearts like youth,
    Go boldly to the field; infants at suck
    Cry as they thought it long ere they were men;   180
    Then Christian princes join their hands with yours
    And sweep their several nations to a heap
    With one desire to number out their men,
    Knowing who fight for heaven each soldier's ten,
    And every hand is free in shedding blood   185
    Since 'tis to wash the evil from the good.
Sophy. What profit may this war accrue to us?
Sir Anthony. Honour to your name, bliss to your soul.
Halibeck. Dishonour unto both, my sovereign.
    Shall you, whose empire for these thousand years   190
    Have given their adoration to the sun,
    The silver moon and those her countless eyes
    That like so many servants wait on her,

---

recover . . . For the undertaking whereof, Sir *Anthony* ceased not, during the time he
lay in the Cittie, by all importune meanes, and forcible reasons, to animate and incense
the *Persian*: alleaging how easie a matter it were for him, by his meanes, being a
Christian, to joyne many of the Christian Princes, his borderers, in League and
friendship with him' (Nixon, H2v–3). The idea of a Persian–Christian alliance against
the Turks had been mooted as early as the thirteenth century, and was frequently
explored in the sixteenth.
    190–3.] The Portuguese traveller Pedro Teixeira, who was in Persia at much the
same time as the Sherleys, noted that its 'ancient national religion' of Zoroastrianism
still survived in pockets (*Travels*, ed. W. F. Sinclair, 1902, p. 196). But the dramatists
rely on digests that derive ultimately from Herodotus (reprinted as *The Famous*

Forsake those lights? Perpetually abide
And kneel to one that lived a man and died?   195
Calimath. Or shall our sacred sovereign forget
Yon means by which his ancestors did rise
And had the name of Persian emperors?
Halibeck. What can this English Christian say that they receive
Of gift, of comfort, riches or of life   200
Unto the deity that he adores,
That we enjoy not from that glorious lamp?
Sir Anthony. Enough to make a pagan, if a man
Of understanding soul, turn Christian.
Halibeck. Our God gives us this light by which we see.   205
Sir Anthony. And our God made that light by which you see.
Then who can this deny, if not a Turk,
The maker still is better than his work?
Sophy. What fruit, what food, what good to men doth flow
But by our God's created and doth grow?   210
Sir Anthony. I grant the sun a vegetative soul
Gives to all fruits of the earth, herbs, plants and trees;
And yet but as a servant swayed by him
Made men like angels and controlleth sin.
Halibeck. Our king of day and our fair queen of nights   215
Walk over us with their perpetual lights,
To see we should not want and to defend us.

Hystory in 1584: see fol. 42v), and reproduce clearly obsolete information. Cf.
Edward Aston's 1611 translation of Boemus' encyclopaedia *Omnium gentium mores*
(1520): 'The Persians beleeve in Heaven, and in *Jupiter*: they have the Sunne also
in great veneration, whom they call *Mitra*, and worship the Moone, *Venus*, the
Fire, Earth, Water, and windes, as gods and goddesses: They have neither Temples,
Sanctuaries, nor Idols, but doe their sacrifices without doores, in some high place, with
great reverence and devotion' (*The Manners, Lawes and Customs of all Nations*, p.
86).

196–8.] Persia was seen as a prime example of a culture fallen from its ancient
glory, partly because many accounts had not caught up with the Safavid reforms of the
sixteenth century—e.g. Boemus/Aston: 'The Persians at this day being overcome by
the Sarrasins, and infected with the madnesse of *Mahomet*, live altogether in darknesse: It
was once a warlike nation, and had for a long space the government of the East: but
now for want of excercise in armes, it fayleth much of his ancient glory' (p. 90). To an
English audience Calimath's resistance to Christian aid and deliverance is meant to
look blindly perverse.

197. *Yon means*] the sun.

207. *if . . . Turk*] a common derogatory tag, though in the context it has a specific
aptness, reflecting the attempt to make Shi'ite Persians side with Christianity against
their Sunni Ottoman rivals.

211. *vegetative soul*] the lowest order of life, 'wherein is the powar and efficacie of
growinge' (T. Elyot, *The Governor*, 1531, III.24, quoted by *OED*). It is distinguished
from the animal and rational souls in the Aristotelian scheme.

Her rain with dews doth all our fruits adorn
Which in his rise are offered to his throne.
He warms, she waters; and to them as due   220
Our knees we give, all other gods eschew.
Sir Anthony. Then all your lives are but to meet a death
That keeps you dying and yet never dead.
And he that speaks in thunder, and whose brow
Is now contract to hear his name denied,   225
Hath vengeance in his hand to strike you down.
Yet with a smile he doth wipe off his frown,
And spares in hope; yet he stores up his doom,
That plagues heaped up fall weightiest when they come.
You then, that scourge my Saviour with your words,   230
My sword hath no assistance for; nor this arm
A growing strength to bear in your defence.
Great emperor, for your favours here's a friend
Should do you manly service in your wars
Did not so just a cause compel me hence.   235
Now back I go upholden with this good:
In my God's cause I ha' shed some pagans' blood.
Sophy. Stay, worthy Englishman, and worthy Christian.
We cannot lose a mould of so much worth.
What is the end thy suit would have of us?   240
Sir Anthony. That you by embassy make league with
                                                    Christendom
And all the neighbour princes bordering here,
And crave their general aid against the Turk,
Whose grants no doubt of. So shall your grace
Enlarge your empire living, and being gone   245
Be called the champion for the holiest one.
These arms shall do you credit, and if I
Miscarry, then 'tis happy so to die.
Sophy. Thy counsel we accept and do applaud it.
Advise us then, ye friends of Persia,   250
Who's fittest in our power to undertake
A business of so great import as this.
Calimath. Who better than the counsellor, my lord,
Being both a Christian and a soldier,
Whom if men envied could not but commend?   255

---

225. *contract*] furrowed in anger.
228. *in hope*] i.e. of repentance and conversion.
239. *mould*] form worthy of imitation, model.
244. *Whose . . . of*] i.e. the princes' offers of support can be relied upon.
255. *if*] even if.

Sophy. And him we'll now prefer as you advise,
　　And grace him forth such an ambassador
　　As never went from Persian emperor.
Halibeck. Yet were it requisite, my noble lord,
　　Some man of worth were joined along with him;   260
　　'Twould give more countenance to his designs.
Calimath. [*Aside*] Good; that's the way to choke him.
Halibeck. So shall your business soonest take effect,
　　The cause be heard, he had in chief respect.
Sophy. Thy counsel we accept, and order thee   265
　　As the fitt'st friend to bear him company.
　　Late Sherley knight, now Lord Ambassador,
　　Chief in commission with Duke Halibeck
　　To make a league 'twixt us and Christendom
　　For furtherance of sharp war against the Turk,   270
　　I'll send thee forth as rich as ever went
　　The proudest Trojan to a Grecian's tent.
　　Call thy best eloquence into thy tongue
　　That may prevail with princes. If thou speed,
　　The Christians' be the honour while Turks bleed.   275
Sir Anthony. My utterance is too short for fitting thanks.
Sophy. And to approve we'll not forget thee absent,
　　Call near the brother of the ambassador.   *Exit* Attendant.

                    Enter ROBERT.

Thy place of general given thee in our wars
From thee we thus take off and here bestow.   280
Halibeck. [*To Calimath*] Heart, how these honours makes me
　　　　　　　　　　　　　　　　　　hate these Christians.
Calimath. Poison finds time to burst, and so shall ours.
Sophy. Though young, I have seen thee valiant; still deserve

256.SP] *om. Q.* we'll] *Bu.*; will *Q.*   257–8.] *one line in Q.*   274. That] *Q;* that't
Bu. 278.SD] *not in Q.*

---

261. *countenance*] credibility.
267–8.] One of Abbas' testimonials delivered to foreign rulers confirms Sherley's
authority: 'An honoured subject of ours goes with him as Ambassador to the sovereigns.
We desire that you shall treat with the said Sir Anthony and consider him as our
supreme commissioner' (CSP *Venice,* 1592–1603, IX.445). This document may have
been fabricated by Sherley; but Abbas like other eastern monarchs is known to have
employed as envoys 'men of little prestige or those who were no longer useful at home'
(Davies, p. 115), and there may be some truth in Sherley's story that Husain 'Ali Beg
was 'in disgrace...for some ill part that he had plaied' (*Relation,* p. 126). If so, his
penance was to keep an eye on the volatile Englishman.
274. *That*] Bullen's emendation 'That't' is attractive.
280. *here*] i.e. on Robert. Presumably some form of insignia is transferred.

And still be honoured. Then this charge forget not,
That in thy battles thou preserve no foe   285
Unto our nation, or for love or wealth.
So prove victorious, while within our eye
Thyself art gracious, stairs to seat thee high.
Robert. If to spend blood may make me honourable
I will be thrifty, yet a prodigal.   290
Halibeck. [*To Calimath*] Enough.
Your plots shall be to try his steps at home,
Let me alone to sink his hopes abroad.
So let us part. At parting only this:
Unto my dearest mistress give this jewel.   295
Say that to leave her here I go from hence
Like one that's banished and for no offence.
Calimath. I'll find fit time to tell your griefs to her.
Sir Anthony. That in my business I will faithful be
I leave my brother as a pledge for me.   300
Sophy. [*To Robert*] You straight shall be dispatched to levy
                                                          forces.

[*To Sir Anthony*] You as befits be furnished on your way.
But first in full cups we'll every other greet
That at next meeting we may prosperous meet.   *Exeunt.*

SCENE iii

Enter the Sophy's NIECE *and* DALIBRA *her maid with a* Boy.

Niece. Dalibra.
Dalibra. Madam?
Niece. Give me thy bosom: what dost thou think of the two
    English brothers?
Dalibra. I think, madam, if they be as pleasant in taste as they   5
    are fair to the eye, they are a dish worth eating.
Niece. A cannibal, Dalibra? Wouldst eat men?
Dalibra. Why not, madam? Fine men cannot choose but be
    fine meat.

0.1. *and . . . Boy*] *and her maide* Q.

286. *or . . . wealth*] either out of compassion or for gain. Cf. i.105–7.
288. *stairs*] i.e. I'll provide the means. Cf. iii.83, and v.50ff, where the image
becomes a visible piece of stagecraft.
3–25.] Probably modelled on the dialogue between Portia and Nerissa in the equivalent scene in *The Merchant of Venice*, a play that is exploited elsewhere in *Travels.*

Niece. Ay, but they are a filling meat.   10
Dalibra. Why, so are most of your sweetmeats; but if a woman
    have a true appetite to them they'll venture that.
Niece. I'd not be free of that company of venturers.
Dalibra. What! Though their voyages be somewhat dangerous,
    they are but short: they'll finish one of their voyages in   15
    forty weeks, and within a month after hoist sail and to't
    again for another.
Niece. You sail clean from the compass, Dalibra! I only
    questioned you about the Christians' habits and behaviours.
Dalibra. That's like their conditions, very civil and comely.   20
Niece. Ay, but they are strangers, Dalibra.
Dalibra. Strangers? I see no strangeness in them. They speak
    as well or, rather, better than our own countrymen;
    and I make no question can do as well if it came once to
    execution.   25
Niece. Their valour shown in the late overthrow of the Turks
    seals that for current.
Dalibra. And yet there are some about the Sophy your uncle
    that look with a sullen brow upon them.
Niece. I hold them the more worthy for that, for envy and   30
    malice are always stabbing at the bosom of worth, when
    folly and cowardice walk up and down in regardless
    security; and here comes one of them.

Enter CALIMATH.

Calimath. Health to your ladyship!
Niece. In wine or beer, my lord?   35
Calimath. In a full bosom of love, madam.
Niece. I pledge no love healths, my lord. But from whence is't?
    If I like the party, my maid shall take it for me.

---

12. venture] venter *Q*.

12. *venture*] try.
13. *free of*] a member of (punning on 'available to'). In 1607 the newly-formed
Virginia Company was seeking investment from would-be adventurers in its joint-
stock enterprise.
20. *like . . . conditions*] in keeping with their social rank.
22. *speak*] i.e. court, chat up. Dalibra is mainly interested in their erotic skills, as *do*
in 24 indicates.
27. *seals . . . current*] gives substance to your view.
32. *regardless*] complacent.
37–60.] The alternation of verse and prose through much of this exchange brings
out the contrast between the Niece's quick assurance and Calimath's pompous formality. The pattern is cleverly varied in 51–2 where his swelling pentameter is deflated
by her poised, mocking alexandrine.

Calimath. From my great brother, warlike Halibeck,
    That makes your love the mark of all his hopes.   40
Niece. I'm sorry for him; 'has missed his mark then. But how
    did the two English brothers bear themselves in the battle?
Calimath. Marched with the rest of meaner action,
    Like stars amongst a regiment of planets
    Shined with the rest—though much below the rest.   45
Niece. That's very strange! It came to us by letters
    The English brothers took more prisoners
    Than any of our commanders in the camp.
Calimath. Indeed they took some straggling runagates,
    Poor heartless snakes that scarce had strength to crawl.   50
    But had you seen the valiant prince my brother—
Niece. Do anything worth note, I should commend him for't!
    Now is the elder of the English Sherleys
    Employed in embassage to Christendom.
Calimath. Only for guide unto my warlike brother,   55
    But neither privy to the business
    Nor party joined in his commission.
Niece. Then fame's a liar.
Calimath. Madam, my brother doth commend himself—
Niece. He could do little and he could not commend himself.   60
    But who comes here?

                Enter ROBERT SHERLEY.

Dalibra. The younger brother of the Sherleys, madam.
Niece. Now by my hopes a goodly personage,
    Composed of such a rich perfection
    As valour seems his servant.—Aught with us?   65
Robert. As servants to their lords, subjects to kings,
    Love mixed with duty worthless Sherley brings
    To your high excellence.
Niece.   From whence and whom?

---

45. rest—though] rest tho Q.   48. of our] *this ed.;* fowre Q.   52–4.] *prose in*
Q.   53. Now] *this ed.;* nor Q.   59. himself—] himselfe. Q.

43–5.] an evidently garbled and perhaps truncated speech, in which Calimath's
grudging admission of the brothers' courage is soured by aspersions on their
competence.
   48. *of our*] Q's 'fowre' is probably a case of type missetting leading to unintended
elision.
   49. *runagates*] fugitives, deserters.
   58. *fame's a liar*] proverbial, but used ironically here. Fame is always in opposition
to false report in this play.
   60. *and*] if.

Robert. Worthy employment having called my brother,
    Your worthless servant, to the Christian states,   70
    Me has he made his trembling messenger
    To bring his dear commends unto your grace.
Niece. Which with no common favour we receive.
    Our hand for his tried service and your own;

              ROBERT *kisses her hand.*

    Our love in fair requital shall be shown.   75
Calimath. Death to a Christian!
Niece.   Nearer yet, more nearer.
Robert. I cannot.
Niece   Why?
Robert.   Your beauty shines too clear.
    Let cloud-born eagles tower about your seat,
    Suffice it me I prosper by the heat.
Niece. The glorious sun of Persia shall infuse   80
    His strength of heat into thy generous veins
    And make thee like himself. In the meantime
    Look high. Find feet, we'll set thee steps to climb.
Robert. I am high enough; the Sherleys' humble aim
    Is not high majesty but honoured fame.   85
Niece. And that you both have won, and with the loss
    Of your best bloods do your high deeds engross
    In time's large volume, where to England's fame
    Ranked with best warriors stands brave Sherley's name.
    Methinks your country should grow great with pride   90
    To see such branches spring out of her sides;
    Your agèd father should grow young again
    To hear his sons live in the friendly pen
    Of kind antiquity. All Persia sings

74.1.] *kisse her hand* Q (*next to* 72–3).

---

76. *Death . . . Christian*] presumably an aside, but perhaps meant to be overheard
by the Niece as a warning not to encourage Robert, who has backed away after
saluting her.

81. *generous*] noble, high-born.

88. *large volume*] The enrolment of the Sherleys in an English pantheon of worthies
had its tentative beginnings in Hakluyt (see note to Epistle, 12); but the full-blooded
comparison with past national heroes awaited the efforts of chroniclers like Purchas
and Drayton. The nineteenth Song of the latter's *Polyolbion* (1622) concludes by
hailing Anthony Sherley as a worthy successor to navigators like Drake, Raleigh and
Cavendish: 'Then *Sherley*, (since whose name such high renowne hath won)/That
Voyage undertooke, as they before had done' (Part II, p. 9).

93–4. *friendly . . . antiquity*] annals of epic achievement. The pen is *friendly* because it
rescues past deeds from oblivion.

The English brothers are co-mates for kings.   95
Robert. You overprize us, madam; and report,
   Striving to right us, doth our worths much wrong.
   'Las! We are men but meanly qualified
   To the rich worthies of our English soil;
   And should they hear what prodigal report   100
   Gives out of us, they would condemn us for't.
   And though these parts would swear us innocent
   Our countrymen would count us insolent,
   For 'tis the nature of our English coast
   Whate'er we do for honour not to boast.   105
Niece. You do your country credit.
Robert.   Honoured princess,
   The mighty Sophy your renownèd uncle
   Expects my service.   *Exit.*
Niece. [*To herself*]   Fare thee well, good Sherley.
   Were thy religion . . . —Wherefore stays your honour?
Calimath. My brother—
Niece.   Is employed. Pray be gone;   110
   Our thoughts are private and would talk alone.
Calimath. [*Aside*] Slighted! 'Tis well; what I intend I'll keep.
   Revenge may slumber but shall never sleep.   *Exit.*
Niece. But he is a Christian, and his state too mean
   To keep even wing with us. Then die the thoughts   115
   Of idle hope, be thy self complete.
   Great in descent, be in thy thoughts as great.
Dalibra. What, dreaming, madam?
Niece. Yes, and my dream was of the wandering knight,
   Aeneas.   120
Dalibra. O, the true Trojan.
Niece. Yet he played false play with the kind-hearted queen of
   Carthage.
Dalibra. And what did you dream of them?

---

  99. *To*] compared to; or perhaps: in the sight of.
  100–01.] Lines which seem to glance at (and aim to salvage) the precarious
reputation of the brothers at this time. Both Anthony and Thomas could indeed be
seen as prodigals (the latter albeit returned to the fold), and the play, like Nixon's
pamphlet, is designed to celebrate their deeds and courage but also to argue that their
activities are not merely self-aggrandising or a threat to national interests.
  102. *parts*] regions.
  112. *keep*] keep secret.
  121. *true Trojan*] A semi-proverbial phrase, reflecting the high estimation of the
Trojans as legendary founders of Rome and London. But Dalibra inflects it in its
colloquial sense of a roisterer or dissolute, and this seems to prompt the Niece's next
thought.

Niece. A very profitable dream, which tells me that as strangers   125
   are amorous, so in the end they prove dangerous, and like
   the industrious bee, having sucked the juice of
   foreign gardens, they make wing to their own homes and
   there make merry with the fraught of their adventures.
Dalibra. Troubled with the fear of suspicion, madam?   130

                    Re-enter CALIMATH.

Niece. 'Tis a disease very incident to our sex. But who comes
   here? My old malady!
Calimath. Madam, the Sophy your renownèd uncle
   Expects your company.
Niece.   It may be so.
Calimath. Presently, madam.
Niece.   And that may be too.   135
Calimath. What to my message?
Niece.   Why, you may be gone.
Calimath. This is no answer.
Niece.   Why, then look for none.
Calimath. I hope for better.
Niece.   This is all you get.
   I cannot come, excuse me by your wit.
Calimath. Cannot, nor will not.

                  Enter ROBERT SHERLEY.

Robert.   Honourable princess,   140
   The mighty Sophy craves your company.
Niece. Instantly, Sherley.—My huge honoured lord,
   If your all-lauded brother Halibeck
   Would aught of love with us, give it our maid.
   She knows our mind, and you may sooner haste.   145
   When emperors call we cannot fly too fast.
                              Exeunt NIECE *and* ROBERT.
Calimath. Then, madam—
Dalibra. Nay, good my lord, if you would aught with me
   deliver't to my boy. I must observe my lady.   *Exit.*
Boy. If you would anything with me tell it to the post.   150
   I must go play again at shittlecock.   *Exit.*

___

130.1. *Re-enter*] *Enter* Q.

___

125–6. *strangers are amorous*] perhaps a proverbial saying.
135. *Presently*] immediately.
142. *huge*] illustrious—but used ironically here.
151. *shittlecock*] common variant of 'shuttlecock', a game in which a shuttlecock is

Calimath. Life, a disgrace! Deluded to my teeth!
    Lives my great brother in so mean respect?
    By Mortus Ali and our Persian gods
    The Sophy shall have note on't; if he pause   155
    To take revenge, no more, I'll put the cause
    To steel's arbitrement. Revenge and Death
    Like slaves attend the sword of Calimath.   *Exit.*

SCENE iv

Enter Chorus.

Chorus. Time, that upon his restless wings conveys
    Hours, days and years, we must entreat you think
    By this hath borne our worthy traveller
    Toward Christendom as far as Russia.
    In his affairs with him's gone Halibeck   5
    Who seems with friendly steps to tread with him,
    But in his heart lurks envy like a snake
    Who hurts them sleeping whom he fears awake.
    Our story then so large, we cannot give
    All things in acts; we should entreat them live   10
    By apprehension in your judging eyes
    Only for taste. Before their embassy
    Had time of hearing with the emperor,
    Great Hali traitorously suggests against him
    Of his low birth, base manners and defects;   15
    Which being fastened in their credulous ears,
    How he was welcome by this show appears.   *Exit.*

---

158. slaves] *conj.Dyce (MS notes in V&A copy)*; slander *Q. Exit.*] *not in Q.* 17.
Exit.] *not in Q.*

---

hit backwards and forwards between two players, or in the air by one player as many
times as possible without dropping it (*OED*). It was fashionable at this date: in *The
Historie of the two Maides of More-clacke* (c.1606) a character declares that to 'play
at shuttle-cock, me thinkes the game[']s now' (F3).
    152. *Deluded*] bamboozled, cheated.
    157. *steel's arbitrement*] the test of the sword. Calimath speaks the language of
duelling but seems to be plotting a squalid revenge.
    0.1. *Chorus*] perhaps now representing Time, with wings and carrying an hourglass.
    10. *acts*] enactments.
    12. *Only . . . taste*] to get the flavour of what happened.
    14–15.] Nixon glosses over Anthony's difficulties in Russia, for which the dra-
matists are probably reliant on William Parry's account of how Husain 'Ali Beg sought
to show 'Sir *Anthony*' to be but a man of meane parentage' (p. 34).

Enter in state the Emperor of Russia, *with three or
four lords to him,* SIR ANTHONY *and* HALIBECK.
SIR ANTHONY *offering to kiss his hand is disgraced
and* HALIBECK *accepted, the Emperor disposing their
affairs to the Council. Exeunt* Emperor *and attendants.*

Only SIR ANTHONY *at the going out of the rest speaks.*

Sir Anthony. Stay and resolve, you counsellors of state,
 What cause, neglects or what offence of ours
 Makes this disgrace wear such a public habit?   20
Halibeck. Sherley, thyself, that art a fugitive,
 A Christian spy, a pirate and a thief.
Sir Anthony. O Halibeck,
 Whom my great master made co-mate with me—
Halibeck. As candles lighted to burn out themselves,   25
 He gave thee grace as parent to disgrace.
 His wisdom there held thee unfit for life
 Yet sent thee hither near thy Christian shore
 That falling there thy shame might be the more.
Sir Anthony. O treason, when thou bear'st the highest wing 30
 Thy tongue seems oily with a venomous sting.
 I stand not, lords, to purge his evidence
 Nor to accuse his slander. These blushless papers

17.5. Emperor *and attendants. not in* Q.   24. master] Mai. Q.   28. shore] *this ed;*
floore Q.

17.1–3. *Enter . . . disgraced*] The Emperor presumably takes the throne used in the
opening scene, and his snub to Anthony is in direct contrast to the Sophy's gesture at
i.32.2–3.
 17.5. *Exeunt . . . attendants*] At least two of the 'three or four' lords need to remain
on stage to take Anthony into custody.
 21–2. *a . . . thief*] The first charge repeats that made at i.159 (see note); the second
is *malapropos* in an Orthodox Christian context, and according to Parry the actual
insinuation was that 'Sherley was come but as a Spie through the Countrey for
purposes tending to his owne good, and not of *Persia* and *Christendome*, as he
pretended. Whereupon they tooke all the kings Letters from him, and opened them, to
know the purport thereof' (p. 34). In 1596 Anthony Sherley had been a privateer in
the Cape Verde islands and West Indies; and before the party left Russia he was to be
accused of selling, in order to defray his debts, gifts from the Shah intended for
European monarchs.
 26. *grace . . . disgrace*] honours and responsibilities that would reveal your lack of
worth.
 28. *shore*] Q's floore is awkward, and its only applicable sense of 'region' is barely
supported by *OED* (8). The emendation is graphically plausible; and cf. iii.104.
 33. *blushless papers*] Sherley carried letters of credence from the Shah, some of
which survive in State Papers (for example, see note to ii.267–8). A document
purporting to be such is reproduced in the 1600 *True Report* of his journey to Persia.
This first brief account of the Persian mission was hastily compiled from letters by
members of the expedition, and immediately suppressed upon publication.

Which his imperial master made to me
Or quit me or condemn me. If I look red   35
'Tis my heart's dye with anger, not with dread.
First Lord. Your letters we'll advise on; in the meantime
We take you to our charge as prisoner.
If fair we find your cause and without rust
Such shall your sentence be, upright and just.   40
Sir Anthony. Howe'er come death, 'tis innocence delight;
Though the world spot her yet her face is white.
                              Exit with first Lord.
Second Lord. Thus by your information have we done
Our justice on that stranger gentleman.
Your princely self we do entreat to feast   45
Till leisure can conclude your business.
Halibeck. Which in our master's name we thank you for.
[*Aside*] Now droops the Christian's honour ne'er to rise,
And in his fall envy hath washed her eyes.   *Exeunt.*

SCENE V

Enter Chorus.

Chorus. Sir Anthony Sherley was thus imprisoned,
And Cushan Halibeck in royal sort
Had entertainment with the Russian.
During which time his council with advice
Had read his letter by the Persian sent,   5
Suspected (by the commendation given
Of his approvèd worth in war and peace,
And his authority assigned to them)
That all suggestions from the other's tongue
Were envy's bolts that spares not whom to wrong.   10
Yet, to make strong their censure, they straight sent

42.1. *with ... Lord*] *not in* Q.

34. *made to me*] wrote on my behalf. The theatre company could have discovered
from a report in Hakluyt that such letters were 'written in golden letters upon red
paper ... being long & narow, about ye length of a foote, and not past three inches
broad. The private signet of the Sophie was a round printed marke about the bignes of
a roial' (III.149).
35. *Or quit*] either vindicate.
49. *envy ... eyes*] i.e. envy is satisfied whilst disguising itself as sympathy. Cf.
Nashe, *Pierce Penilesse*: 'Envie is a Crocodile that weepes when he kils' (*Works*, ed.
McKerrow I.184).
11. *make ... censure*] confirm their assessment. 'Whereupon the Lord Chaunceller
sent for the merchants, enquyring of them what sir *Anthony* was, and whether they

For the English agent and for English merchants,
Where after question of his life and birth
They found him sprung from honourable stock,
And that his country hopes in time to come   15
To see him great, though envièd of some.
They so resolved their master. How he left the court
To please your eyes we in this show report.

A show.

Thus graced by the Muscovian emperor
Envy grew still more rank in Hali's heart.   20
Yet, both dispatched on their designs in hand,
Time now makes short their way, and they at Rome
In state are brought before his Holiness.
Where what succeeded for the former grudge
Give you us leave to show, take leave to judge.   *Exit.*   25

Enter THE POPE *and his* Cardinals.

Pope. With greatest pomp, magnificence and state,
To the adoration of all dazzled eyes,
We do intend the ambassadors once come

---

25. *Exit.*] *not in* Q, *which prints at end of line:* A Shew.

---

durst give hym any credite. To whome they replyed, that hee was nobly descended,
and alied even to the best men of *England*' (Parry, p. 33).

16. *though...some*] Another dig at the Sherleys' detractors. In 1602 Anthony had
written to Cecil complaining that 'the worst sort of the world have taken advantage to
lay upon me all sorts of defamations' (quoted in *The Sherley Brothers*, p. 37). His
fortunes appeared to revive in 1605 when he was sent to Morocco on an embassy of
which James I was one of the sponsors; however, this failed in its aim of producing a
new alliance against the Turks, and by the end of 1606 he was in Spain, engaged in a
variety of schemes. His plans and movements were being closely watched by the
English government in 1607.

18.1.] The *show* interacts with the spoken chorus to economise on dramatic narrative, but it also capitalises on an opportunity for spectacle, probably accompanied
by music.

19–25.] These lines cover the transition to the next episode: a possible staging has
the Emperor and his retinue leave by one door, the ambassadors by another, with the
latter re-appearing on the opposite side and the Pope entering at the door by which
they have just left. Q has a second *A shew* after 25, but this looks more like an
authorial indication of the elaborate processional entry to follow, rather than the
stage-keeper's direction for a summarising dumb show.

24. *succeeded for*] followed, made up for.

25.1.] The command at 30 suggests that the Cardinals appear in the gallery above
the stage, while the Pope makes his entry on the main stage and mounts the dais to the
throne which perhaps is given new trappings appropriate to the occupant. The
Cardinals' descent and entry through the tiring-house doors becomes a procession
which frames the introduction of the ambassadors.

Shall have a hearing, feasting and their welcome.
Descend, O brotherhood of cardinals,   30
And all the holy orders that attend us,
And let your diligence approve your care
To bring them to our presence in Peter's chair.
All. Your Holiness shall have your will obeyed.
Pope. If to the advancement of God's Church and saints   35
    The tenor of their embassage appears,
    They shall have all our furtherance, prayers and tears.
Sir Anthony. Peace to the father of our Mother Church,
    The stair of men's salvations and the key
    That binds or looseth our transgressions.   40
Pope. The virtue of your embassy? Go on.
Sir Anthony. These papers be the precepts taught my tongue,
    The force of whose inscription runneth thus:
    That Christian princes would lend level strength
    To curb the insulting pride of paganism;   45
    And you, the mouth of heaven, advertise them
    To join their bodies to an able arm,
    That, as above's stern vengeance for heaven's foes,
    So men, heaven's friends, should seek their overthrows.
Pope. Ascend, my son; the furtherance of this right   50
    Commands our conscience, is our soul's delight.
Sir Anthony. [*To Halibeck*] Down for thy pride and for the
                                      wrong thou didst me!
    This place admits not thy unhallowed feet,
    And heart being treasonous, fondly climb unto it.
Halibeck. Even step by step, whereas this business tends,   55
    My place admits me and my feet ascends.
Sir Anthony. But Phaethon for climbing had a fall,

---

54. treasonous] *this ed;* treasons *Q.*

---

32. *approve your care*] demonstrate your concern.

41. *virtue*] purpose.

46. *the ... heaven*] strikingly unironic, given the Protestant context. Such titles are usually testimony to Papal presumption, as in Lodowick Lloid's *The Tragicocomedie of Serpents* (1607): 'The Pope ... saith, *Heaven is his*, and he hath the keys of Heaven delivered to him onely' (p. 90).
    advertise them] inform them (of their duty).

50. *Ascend*] The dais on which the throne stood was probably at least four steps high: see Gurr, p. 193.

54.] *treasonous*] Full emendation brings out the sense that is only ambiguously present in 'treason's' (the simplest adjustment to *Q treasons*). The sense is that Halibeck's worldly treachery denies him the Pope's political favour just as his paganism disqualifies him from his blessing.

57. *Phaethon*] son of Phoebus the sun-god, who was permitted to ride his father's

And so shalt thou damnation prove withal.

He strikes HALIBECK.

Pope. Refrain therefore! And whate'er you are,
    If you were kings as but king's ministers   60
    Thinking by privilege of your affairs
    Your outrage hath a freedom, you are deceived.
    For, as unchecked the winds command the seas,
    The best shall shake, our mightiness displeased.
Sir Anthony. Pardon, dread Father, that my heat of blood   65
    Took from me the remembrance of the place
    Wherein all knees should stoop, no hand offend;
    And this repentance for remission plead:
    Rashness doth make the obedient be deceived.
    Nor was't so much my wrongs in Russia,   70
    Wherein his slander made me prisoner,
    Remember me to take revenge on him,
    As that his pagan feet should dare to climb
    Where none but Christian's knees should after mine,
    Much less admit him have the upper way   75
    From men whose souls fear them whom we obey.
Pope. Christian, thy name; that in this register
    To honour thee we may remember it.
Sir Anthony. Sherley, a Christian and a gentleman,
    A pilgrim soldier and an Englishman.   80
Pope. For all these styles we love and honour thee,
    And in thy affairs will so effectually
    Deal for thee in our name to Christian princes,
    They shall so honour thee that thou shalt back
    With power so strong whose sight makes Turkey shake.   85
Sir Anthony. Heaven shall gain souls thereby, religion glory.
Pope. First to Saint Angelo thus hand in hand,
    Then counsel, to make Christian Turkish land.   *Exeunt.*

58.1.] *this ed.; not in* Q.   74. after] *this ed.; and then* Q.

chariot for a day but by failing to control it wrought havoc on earth, and was
destroyed by Jove's thunderbolt. The story was familiar from Ovid's *Metamorphoses*,
II.1–328.
    60. *as but*] instead of being merely.
    62. *outrage*] boldness, presumption.
    80. *pilgrim soldier*] crusader.
    81. *styles*] titles.
    87. *Saint Angelo*] The fortress of Castel Sant'Angelo which stands guard over the
Vatican. But the writer appears to assume that it is a place of worship.

SCENE vi

Enter Chorus.

Chorus. Our traveller here's feasted, banquets done,
    And he with letters is dispatched from Rome
    Unto the States of Venice. Suppose him there
    Where we will leave him, and entreat your thoughts
    To think their eyes transported and they see   5
    Sir Thomas Sherley's following misery.
    From England by desire to see his brother,
    With some few ships, well manned and well provided,
    Suppose him now at sea, where with cross winds
    (Unequal to his merits and his hopes)   10
    He long remained. At last in Italy
    In the great Duke of Florence court he is arrived,
    Feasted and honoured. From thence, being furnished
    With all things fitting for a prosperous voyage,
    He is come unto the straits of Gibraltar;   15
    Then to Leghorn, then to the Duke of Tuscan
    Where divers merchants did corrupt his men
    Against his course, and made them mutinous;
    Which to appease they put to sea again,
    And being in sight of the isle of Sicily   20
    Two of his ships forsook him, and he with one
    Is come to Kea in the Turks' dominion.

A Chamber shot off.

    This latter warning me from speech doth break;
    Suppose him landed here, himself to speak.   *Exit.*

22. Kea] *Ieo* Q.

    7–9. *by . . . sea*] In fact all of Thomas' maritime expeditions were purely privateering ventures.

    9–13. *Suppose . . . honoured*] Nixon records that Thomas 'having long time kept the Seas unprosperously . . . at length landed in *Italie*, and was for a time highly respected in the Duke of *Florence* his Court' (B2).

    16.] Thomas was given a licence by the Grand Duke of Tuscany to attack Turkish shipping, and put out from Livorno (Leghorn) in late 1602. A disastrous attack on a merchant ship in the straits of Gibraltar, in which he lost a hundred men, forced Thomas to return to Livorno, 'where he stayed eight dayes, as well to refresh his hurt men, and to furnish himselfe of fresh water and victuals . . . as also to receive directions from the Duke of *Tuscan*, during which time divers Marchants corrupted his men and made them mutinous, alleaging that the course he tooke was indirect, and dangerous, his plots shallow and unlikely to succeed, & that he faild of warrant and authoritie for his proceedings' (Nixon, B3v).

    22. *Kea*] an island in the Cyclades; Nixon gives it as 'Geo' (Q: *Ieo*) and explains that Sherley landed here but made his raid on a neighbouring island.

Enter SIR THOMAS SHERLEY *with* sailors *and followers.*

Sir Thomas. Welcome ashore, ashore, welcome ashore!   25
　　Forget the past adventures, think that the seas
　　Played with us but as great men do a' land;
　　Hurled us now up, then down; had room to toss,
　　And fed their pleasures though to others' loss.
　　Believe that all misfortunes are like thirst   30
　　That makes your drink taste sweeter when it comes.
　　For me, as you are, so am I a little pile
　　Of earth, slimed earth, and have no greater style
　　Than you have, but a man. And if your blood
　　Have the same heat as mine, we'll never back   35
　　Unto our mother country but our stream
　　Shall lose his vital way or be a theme
　　Unto our sanguine brothers how to raise
　　Paeans of triumphs in our virtue's praise.
　　Or else, even here, this be our fatal lot,   40
　　We'll die unknown, so buried and forgot.
Captain. While we have life, even 'gainst this rocky town
　　We'll find us graves in stones or beat it down.
Sailor. You are our general, and with you we'll stand.
　　Who fear not sea-storms shrink not being a' land.   45
Sir Thomas. I thank you all. Be but your actions thus,
　　Men shall not fright us, nor this lofty town
　　Built upon stony hills to outface the clouds
　　Be able to amaze us, but the men
　　That keep those walls shall perish though not then.   50
　　Then, master gunner, instead of other parley
　　Go let a piece of ordnance summon them.
Gunner. I go.   *Exit.*
Sir Thomas. The rest make good this ground, while that myself
　　At their walls' side will question them to yield.   55

53.SP] *Say.* Q.

　　33. *style*] title.
　　36–7. *but . . . way*] i.e. unless we return home by cowardly flight (or in triumph).
　　49. *amaze*] terrify. The play's turning of a raid on a defenceless village into an heroic siege seems almost to invite the quixotic burlesque in Beaumont's *Knight* (III.210ff). Nixon explains that the raid was a hastily conceived device to occupy his mutinous crew; and his account suggests despite itself that the words he puts into the mouth of the Livorno merchants (see note to 16 above) are a fair assessment of Thomas' leadership.
　　50. *though . . . then*] See note to 100.
　　52. *piece of ordnance*] mounted gun or cannon.

Mercy we'll offer, which if they deny,
In the same hour they do resist, they die.

A chamber shot off.

This tongue proclaims to them we are hither come
With soldiers' hands that bring destruction
To them and their fenced town, if they hold out.   60
Our self will take their answer. If't be proud
The spoil is yours, the earth's for them a shroud.
Arm then, as I do.
Captain.   'Tis for hope of wealth.
Sailor. And pagans' glories to enrich us with.
Sir Thomas. At my return we'll fight to purchase gold,   65
Or tak't with ease, which hope makes cowards bold.   *Exit.*
Captain. But who's too venturous, generals should know,
Instead of gold may meet his overthrow.
For tell me, sailors and my fellow mates,
What gain may be expected from this town   70
That we should venture for? Nay, what from him
We term our general of worth or rule
More than we him enabled in ourselves?
Sailor. Why speaks the captain thus?
Captain. That mischiefs should be shunned ere they're begun,   75
And we ourselves 'void danger ere undone.
For but bethink yourselves: in all our voyage
What prosperous hour hath given encouragement
To make our hopes look cheerful? What have we had
But sickness, sea-storms and contrarious winds?   80
And what can we expect here being landed,
Should but the hardy enemy come and descend,
But wretched slavery and at last our end?

65.SP] *Bu.; Antho. Q.*   66. *Exit.*] *not in Q.*   75. they're] *Bu.;* they *Q.*

58. *tongue*] cannon-shot; cf. i.21.
64. *glories*] valuables, religious booty.
65. *purchase*] gain.
73. *we . . . ourselves*] we have enabled him to achieve through our efforts.
75. *mischiefs*] used primarily in its neutral sense (*OED* 1) of 'troubles', but suggesting also the wilfulness which marked all of Thomas Sherley's exploits. For a devastating comment on one of these, see John Chamberlain's letter to Dudley Carleton on 27 June 1602 (*Letters*, ed. N. E. McClure, 1939, I.151).
77–80. *in . . . winds?*] In keeping with the epic inflation of Thomas' rallying calls, the Captain's speech recalls the great hardships recorded in oceanic narratives like those of Cavendish's final voyage in 1591–3: see Philip Edwards, *Last Voyages*, 1988, pp. 77–9.

Sailor. But how can we prevent it, being here
    And to perform this voyage bound with him?   85
Captain. Why, leave him here and take ourselves to sea
    And every man be captain of himself;
    Where what pillage we can make our prey
    'Twill be our own, and we to none obey.
Servant. Degenerous man,   90
    So big of bone and yet so base of mind
    To counsel against him so good to thee!
    What though our fortune with ungentle hand
    Hath crossed his enterprise and actions,
    Canst then to him whose bounty gave thee means,   95
    Preferment, grace, beyond thy merit's worth,
    Poison thyself and make thy tongue a sting
    Against his life that gives thy fortunes wing?
Captain. What's done is past; times were, fortune's to come,
    And to repay sometimes our speech is dumb.   100
    Then speak, my hearts—if that my motion please,
    Hoist sails, my masters, and again to seas.
Sailors. A captain, a captain!

Enter Gunner.

Gunner. Stay! Whither fly you, feeble mates, in streams
    When I am come to have you bring relief   105
    Unto our general that's oppressed by th' Turks?
All. To sea, to sea!
Gunner. To sea? For what?
    And leave our general in distress a' land?
    The Turks, that at my summons gave their oaths   110
    To hold an hour's parley, break their word,
    Come valiantly upon him; soldier-like
    He hath resisted till his fastened hilt
    Was bladeless in his hand. Nothing now rests
    But present rescue or a present death.   115

---

92. to thee] *Bu.;* then: *Q.* 100. our speech] *this ed.;* to speake *Q;* too, speech
Bu. 103.1.] *not in Q.* 104. Stay!] *Bu.;* Say *Q.*

100.] *Q*'s *speake* is probably the compositor's anticipation of the same word in the
next line; a similar error is apparently made at 50 (*then/Then*); I offer only a
makeshift solution.

104. Stay] Bullen's emendation greatly strengthens the Gunner's entry and urgent
appeal.

113. *fastened*] i.e. to his wrist.

115. *present*] immediate.

Captain. Death unto him that seeks it; we will fly
    For certain safeguard. Wise security
    Seeks shelter ere the storm can trouble.
    To sea, my mates, then! [*To Gunner.*] In you must with us.
    Denial serves not, nor resistance neither;   120
    They are best in health can set them to the weather.
    And so to sea!
All.   To sea! To sea!   *Exeunt all but* Servant.
Servant.   Base villains! Fates,
    Unpartial Fates to spin their lives this length
    Who leave their master and should be his strength.

          Enter SIR THOMAS SHERLEY.

Sir Thomas. Friends, soldiers, sailors!   125
    A rescue, or I am taken prisoner!
Servant. Bootless you call, sir; their unconstant faith
    Is fled from you.
Sir Thomas.   Ha!

          A noise within.

Servant. Hark, they weigh anchor, get your ships to sea
    And leave you to men's tyranny a' land.   130
    They in one knot are knit, and only I
    Stay here, as you, howe'er to live or die.
Sir Thomas. I thank thee; less I cannot give thee.
    Fate, do thy worst. My courage takes no flight
    But here keeps court though my cross destinies fight.   135

          Enter four Turks.

First Turk. Follow, follow, follow!
Second Turk. A Christian, a Christian!
Sir Thomas. Though weaponless I am left, with these I'll fight.
Servant. In what I may I'll show my best of might.

116.SP] *Bu.; Seru. Q.*   122.SD] *not in Q.* villains! Fates,] villaines Fates, *Q.*

    119–28.1 *In . . . within*] One door in the tiring-house leads to the battle (whence the Gunner has come), another back to the beach, where the sounds of embarkation are simulated.
    135.1–137. *Turks . . . Christian*] Sherley's encounter was with the Greek inhabitants of Kea (as Nixon's account fitfully acknowledges): once again the play simplifies the moral structure of events.

Here they fight; SIR THOMAS *being weaponless defends
himself with stones; at last, being oppressed with
multitudes, his servant flies and he is taken.*

First Turk. So, bear him prisoner to Constantinople   140
    To be examined of the emperor.
Sir Thomas. Even where you will, if to my overthrow;
    My mind is high, lie my head ne'er so low.   *Exeunt.*

Enter Servant *again.*

Servant. I will not leave you, master, since I have 'scaped
    From their surprisal, but with my best endeavour   145
    Will strive to see what shall become of you.
    If worse than I could wish, I'll sorrow for't;
    If in my means to help I'll comfort it.   *Exit.*

SCENE vii

Alarum. Enter ROBERT *and other* Persians *with victories.*

Robert. My thanks to heaven that overlooked this day,
    And thus hath aided with an host divine
    The feeble remnants of us thy heralds
    That shall proclaim thy name throughout the world
    And wear this badge of courage on our breasts   5

---

143. *Exeunt*] not in Q.

139.1–3.] The descriptive stage direction is clear evidence that the printer's copy
for Q was the authors' draft or a copy thereof, not the theatre prompt-book.
    0.1. ROBERT... *Persians*] The SD may be a pointer to Robert's costume: both he
and Anthony adopted Persian attire, and Robert was later to cause a considerable stir
by wearing a turban and exotic robes on his European embassies. See S. Chew, *The
Crescent and the Rose* (1937), p. 306. Here Robert probably combines Persian cloak
and headgear (see ii.26 note) with a doublet or vest bearing the Christian cross.
    0.1. *victories*] captives. The word could also mean 'spoils', or more specifically
symbols of military triumph like the heads at i.48. Nixon records that Robert cut off
the heads of his captives and had them 'carried in triumph about the Market place',
but in the play Christian clemency is overridden by obligation, not by the influence of
exotic custom.
    1. *overlooked*] looked over, protected us.
    5. *badge of courage*] the red cross on a white coat, which was standard issue
for English soldiers on Continental campaigns until early in Elizabeth I's reign. By
the early seventeenth century its associations would have been largely nostalgic:
mercenaries like the Sherleys may have been disposed to exploit its crusading associations, but its use here could simply reflect the costume conventions of a patriotic
drama.

Joined with a motto calling on thy name.
This shall redouble valour when it faints;
This says our blood can be no better shed
Than in that blood's behalf that dyed this red.
Let's now recount our victory today: 10
What prisoners have we taken?
Persian. Between thirty and forty of their chief commanders.
Robert. Between thirty and forty of their chief commanders!
We are now here the Persian substitute
And cannot use our Christian clemency   15
To spare a life. Off with all their heads!
Speak, do ye renounce your prophet Mahomet?
Bow to the deity that we adore
Or die in the refusal.
2 or 3 Turks.   For Mahomet we die.
Persian. Join Mortus Ali then with Mahomet,   20
That slew your prophets Omar and Uthman
And on a snowy camel went to heaven,
And yet you shall find grace in Persia.
Turks. For Mahomet, none but Mahomet.
Robert.   To death with
       them,
The rest shall follow.   *Exeunt Turks under guard.*

Enter soldiers with a Christian *in Turk's habit as a prisoner.*

       Off with his head too: 25
We'll have no ransom but conversion.

21. Omar and Uthman] *Hamer* and *Vsman Q.* 25. *Exeunt...guard*] *not in Q.*
soldiers with] *not in Q.*

---

21. *prophets...Uthman*] two of the three caliphs who succeeded the Prophet Muhammad. They are venerated by Sunni Muslims (including the Turks) but rejected by Shi'ites in favour of 'Ali (see second note to i.87). 'Ali succeeded to the caliphate after protracted factional strife but was not certainly implicated in the deaths of his predecessors.

22. *on...heaven*] Probably taken from Geffrey Ducket's account of his visit to Persia in 1574: 'When Mortus Ali died, there came a holy prophet, who gave them warning that shortly there would come a white Camell ... which ... caried the sword & body of Mortus Ali unto the sea side, and the camell going a good way into the sea, was ... taken up into heaven' (Hakluyt III.160). The story is seen as part of the tangle of 'feigned dreames, apparitions, visions, and revelations' that Christian Europe liked to ascribe to Islam (quoted from *The Policy of the Turkish Empire*, 1597, fol. 14); there was indeed a well-developed cult of 'Ali, giving rise to many fabulous stories.

24. *none...Mahomet*] Sunnis in fact accept 'Ali as well as the so-called false caliphs; the Turks' insistence here reflects an erroneous European belief that Shi'ites placed 'Ali on an equal footing with the Prophet.

25. a *Christian*] presumably not the servant of scene vi, since at 49 he can offer no further information.

Christian. I have somewhat to deliver ere I die.
Robert. Be thou a convertite, we'll hear thee; not else.
Christian. Then I must be silent. I'll choose to die
 Before the faith I do profess deny.   30
Robert. Off with his head then.
Christian.   Stay, I am not as I seem.
Robert. Thou seem'st a Turk.
Christian.   Yet am a Christian.
Robert. The more thy crime.
 'Gainst Christians thou hast been a foe today;
 How comes it else thou art our prisoner?   35
Christian. If I be blameful found then let me die.
 First peruse this. (*Shows his arm.*)
Robert. [*Reading*] 'I am prisoner in Constantinople; use your
 best release. Thomas Sherley'.—O heavens!
 Although the news be bitter in itself,
 I cannot but applaud this happy knowledge.   40
 [*Embracing him*] Ten thousand heads now shall not buy
          this head;
 Thou art my best friend's equal for this deed.
 O that the fortune of ten doubtful days
 Were to begin their pale encountering close,   45
 So that my brother stood in armour here
 To join with me. But can ye help
 My understanding with any further notice?
Christian. Not any; letters had I none, but short
 Commends whilst his hand writ down this brief tenor,   50
 So strait is his converse with Christians.
 For him and you this have I undertook:
 First I was forced your most unwilling foe,
 So to become your willing prisoner.
Robert. I thank ye, and I shall remember ye.—
 How many of their commanders are yet living?   55
Persian. Thirty, my lord.
Robert.   Still let them live:
 Those thirty lives shall buy my brother's life
 And I shall think them happily bestowed.
 I'll send an embassy to offer it.   60

60.1.] *not in* Q.

---

45. *pale*] fearful.
close] encounter, military clash.
50. *tenor*] gist.
51. *strait*] limited.

He beckons to an Attendant.

[*To him*] But pray ye be sparing in your speech,
For if by any half-intelligence
He be known my brother, he's sure to die.
                                    Exit Attendant.
So heaven hath aided me thrice 'gainst these Turks
That they would hate the man that loveth me,   65
And to my name they add Sherley the Great;
Though my humility, I vow by heaven,
Doth not affect that overdignity.
But if they do refuse this proffered gift
Sherley shall wish to be no other great   70
Than to be great in their great overthrow.
If that he die within their captive thrall,
Ten thousand Turks shall mourn his funeral.   *Exeunt.*

SCENE viii

Enter THE GREAT TURK, Pashas *and* Attendants.

Great Turk. Thus like the sun in his meridian pride,
        Attended by a regiment of stars,
        Stand we triumphant 'mongst our petty kings.
        Upon the highest promont of either globe
        That heaves his forehead nearest to the clouds   5
        Fix we our foot; and with our eagle's wings
        Canopy o'er three quarters of the world.
        And yet we write *Non ultra*! The proud Sophy,

63.SD] *not in* Q.   72. captive] *this ed.;* Captiues Q.

    64. *thrice*] This scene conflates two campaigns against the Turks (as recorded by Nixon) which, together with the earlier victory in scene ii, would explain Robert's *thrice*.
    4. *either globe*] an image perhaps derived from the Dutch double-hemisphere world maps in which two adjacent globes showing the Old and New Worlds respectively are surrounded by borders illustrating ethnic types and natural wonders. They aptly serve the imperial theme.
    6. *eagle's wings*] appropriating the symbol of Habsburg power: 'The Eagle with two necks in the Imperial arms, and in the arms of the King of Spain, signifies the East and West Empire, and the extension of their power from the East to the West' (John Collet in W. Thoms (ed.), *Anecdotes and Traditions*, 1839, p. 120). But Pliny reports that the walls of ancient Babylon (frequently confused with Baghdad: see 19) 'do resemble an Eagle spreading her wings' (*The Historie of the World*, tr. P. Holland, 1601, p. 136).
    8. Non ultra] This should be *Plus ultra*, echoing the motto of the Emperor Charles V, or *Non sufficit* [*orbis*], the vaunt of Spain in Dekker's *Whore of Babylon*, Cv. See

The Persian beggar that by starts invades us,
Our potent army, like so many wolves   10
Let loose into a flock of senseless sheep,
Shall bait and worry home into their folds,
Whilst Fate and conquest our high state upholds.

Pasha. Yet, mighty and magnificent, your powers
In this late conflict against Persia   15
Have met much loss.

Great Turk.   Base and degenerate coward,
Are not we Hamath, the sole god of earth,
King of all kings, provost of Paradise,
Sultan and Emperor of Babylon,
Of Catheria, Egypt, Antioch;   20
Lord of the precious stones of India;
A champion and defender of the gods;
Prince and conductor from the withered tree
To the green bosom of Achaia mount;
The joy and comfort of great Mahomet,   25
And last protector of the sepulchre

Intro., pp. 10–11. In *The Generall Historie of the Turkes* (1603), Richard Knolles
notes that 'in them is to be noted an ardent and infinit desire of soveraigntie,
wherewith they have long since promised unto themselves the monarchie of the whole
world, a quicke motive unto their so haughtie designes' (A5).

9. *by starts*] sporadically.

17. *Hamath*] apparently a slip; Hamath was a town in Syria. It was however
associated with Turkish military zeal and endurance: Cartwright describes it as a ruin,
'but because it cost many mens lives to winne it; the great Turke will not have it
repaired' (p. 6).

17–27. *the . . . king*] A model for this vaunt was printed in the second half of 1606:
in *Letters from the great Turke . . . unto . . . the Pope*, the Sultan advertises himself as
'Champion of Babilon, God on the earth, Barron of Turkie, Lord of the countrie of
Judea, even unto the earthly Paradise . . . and the future conqueror of Christendome'
(A2v).

20. *Catheria*] probably 'Cathaia', which R. Stafforde names as one of the 'chiefe
Provinces of *Tartarie*' (*A Geographicall . . . description*, 1607, p. 51).

21.] Throughout the sixteenth century the Ottomans had effectively controlled the
overland trade routes to the east.

23.] *withered tree*] 'a little from Ebron [Hebron on the West Bank] there is an Oake
tree . . . commonly called the dry tree, and they say it hath beene from the beginning of
the world, and was aforetime greene & bare leaves, unto the time that our Lord
dyed . . . And some Prophesies say, that a Lord or Prince of the West side of the world
shall win . . . the Holy Land . . . and he shall worship God under that Tree, and the tree
shall waxe greene and beare fruit and leaves, through which miracle many Sarasins
and Jewes shall be turned to the Christian Faith' (Mandeville, sig.E). The Great Turk's
hubris invites the crusading spirit.

24. *Achaia*] now a province on the northwest coast of the Peloponnese, but at that
time often applied generally to southern mainland Greece (the whole country was then
part of the Ottoman empire). 'In this Province is also *Pernassus*, and *Hellicon*,
consecrated to the *Muses*' (Stafforde, p. 24—see note 20).

Of Jewry's god and crucifièd king.
And dares the Persian compare with us?

Enter Messenger.

What and from whom?
Messenger.   The Christian general,
  Sherley the Great, sends you this mild salute   30
  In this his late yet bleeding overthrow,
  Where men like grass stooped to the stroke of death.
  Twenty most choice and valorous commanders
  He has given life to; and in fair exchange
  Tenders them for the life and liberty   35
  Of an imprisoned English gentleman.
Great Turk. Twenty for one! What is the Christian's name?
Messenger. I know not that.
Great Turk.   How shall we know to free him?
Messenger. His stature and proportion
  Is given me by prescription so directly   40
  As from a thousand I can point him out.
Great Turk. Conduct him in, and bring the prisoner forth.
                    Exeunt Attendant *and* Messenger.
  He is sure some prince or else a man of worth,
  That in exchange of him the general
  Proffers so largely.

    Re-enter Attendant *and* Messenger, *followed by*
    a Jailer *with* SIR THOMAS SHERLEY *in bands.*

                    Now is this the man?   45
Messenger. The same, great emperor.
Great Turk.   Then, Christian,
  For by no other title can we call thee,
  Acquaint us with thy parentage and name;
  For from the Christian general Sherley the Great
  We have means that labour thy delivery.   50
Sir Thomas. Great emperor, I am a man whose birth
  And mean attempts were never registered
  Amongst the English worthies. If great Sherley
  Hath aught proposed for my delivery

28.1.] *after* whom? *in* 29 *Q.*   32. stooped . . . stroke] *conj.Bu.;* stept to the streete
Q.   42.1] *not in Q.*   45. *Re-enter* . . . Jailer] *Enter Q.*

  26. *last*] latest; with the implication of 'final and permanent'. The Ottomans took
Jerusalem in 1516.
  45. bands] shackles.

'Twas in a general zeal to Christendom,　　　　　　　55
　　Not any private notice of my worth.
Great Turk. Dissemble not; for, subtle Englishman,
　　We rather judge, nay, absolutely know,
　　Thou either art allied to him by birth,
　　Or some great prince; which till thou dost confess　　60
　　Thy torments shall be more, thy freedom less.
　　As for our captains, let them live or die,
　　The Christian shall in slavish irons lie.
　　Begone with that, and back with him to prison;
　　Double his irons and take back half his diet.　　65
　　Strengthen our powers, and bravely to the field.
　　Our breasts with iron, our spirits with fire are steeled.
　　　　　　　　　Exeunt THE GREAT TURK, Pashas,
　　　　　　　　　　　Attendants *and* Messenger.
Jailer. Come, sir, had not you better confess and be
　　hanged than be starved to death and hanged after?
Sir Thomas. Sir, I'm armed with patience. Tyrants' hate　　70
　　Is bounded within limits: they may will,
　　But there's a God that can prevent their ill.
　　That power I ground on. Here's my greatest cross,
　　A brother's love turns to a brother's loss.
　　My journey? Towards heaven; fate sent me hither,　　75
　　You, like kind guides, send me the next way thither.
Jailer. I will send you the nearest way. But, because
　　you shall not be hungry, I'll diet you with puddle
　　water and bran—you will be the lighter to take your
　　journey.　　　　　　　　　　　　*Exeunt.*　　80

SCENE ix

Enter SIR ANTHONY SHERLEY, *a* Gentleman, *and his*
　　　Servants *who give him letters.*

Sir Anthony. That into England, that to Persia.—
　　And now, dear friend, what tidings at St Mark?

67.1. THE . . . Messenger.] *not in* Q.　75. journey?] Iourney Q; Iourney's Bu.　0.2.
who] *not in* Q.

---

76. *kind guides*] Addressed to those present: one or more of the Attendants remain
until the Jailer leaves with his prisoner.

2. *St Mark*] Piazza San Marco in Venice, 'that famous concourse and meeting of so
many distinct and sundry nations' (*Coryat's Crudities* (1611), repr. 1905, I.318), and
where newsbooks and corantos were sold. In a scene which is clearly exploiting *The
Merchant of Venice*, Anthony's question echoes Shylock's 'What news on the Rialto?'
but places the emphasis on foreign and political, rather than commercial news.

Gentleman. Like to men's minds, distract and variable.
　　You have heard your brother's bloody overthrow
　　Given to the Turks?
Sir Anthony.　　　　　It came to me last night.　　　　5
　　What news from England?
Gentleman.　　　　　Nothing of import.
　　The young'st and greatest grows up here at hand.
Sir Anthony. Aught that concerneth me?
Gentleman.　　　　　About the jewel:
　　It fills the town with admiration,
　　That which great princes for the worth deny,　　10
　　You, but a lord ambassador, should buy.
Sir Anthony. 'Twas for the Sophy, and I wonder much
　　He sends not in the cash.
Gentleman.　　　　　The Jew expects it.

　　　　　　Enter ZARIPH *the Jew.*

Sir Anthony. And here he comes.—Good morrow, honest
　　　　　　　　　　　　　　　　　　Zariph.
Zariph. The Hebrew God and sanctifièd King　　15
　　Bless them that cast kind greeting at the Jew.
Sir Anthony. I owe thee money, Zariph.
Zariph.　　　　　That's the cause
　　Of your kind speech. A Christian spaniel claws
　　And fawns for gain. Jest on, deride the Jew;　　20
　　You may, vexed Zariph will not jest with you.
　　[*Aside*] Now, by my soul, 'twould my spirits much refresh
　　To taste a banquet all of Christians' flesh.
Sir Anthony. I must entreat thee of forbearance, Zariph.
Zariph. No, not an hour.　　　　　　　　25
　　You had my jewel, I must have your gold.
Gentleman. Let me entreat thee, Zariph, for my sake
　　That have stood friend to all thy brethren.

13.1.] *after* 14 *in* Q.　22. spirits] sprits Q.

　7. *young'st*] most recent.
　12. *'Twas . . . Sophy*] The germ of this incident seems to lie in Anthony's dealings
with a Persian merchant who arrived in Venice in 1603 to deal on behalf of the Shah.
His attempts to intimidate the merchant and make money out of his transactions led
to Anthony's arrest and imprisonment; but the Venetian authorities had additional
reasons for wanting to restrain him. Anthony went to Venice in 1601 after the
final rift with Husain 'Ali Beg in Rome, but his planned anti-Turk alliance was seen
as hostile to Venetian commercial interests. See Davies, pp. 139–58, and note to
xii.60–1.

Zariph. You have indeed; for, but this other fast,
    You sold my brother Zachary like a horse,   30
    His wife and children at a common outcry.
Gentleman. That was the law.
Zariph.   And I desire no more;
    And that I shall have. Though the Jew be poor
    He shall have law for money.
Sir Anthony.   Nay, but, Zariph,
    I am, like thee, a stranger in the city.   35
    Strangers to strangers should be pitiful.
Zariph. If we be curst we learnt of Christians
    Who, like to swine, crush one another's bones.
Sir Anthony. Is it a sin in them? 'Tis sin in you.
Zariph. But they are Christians. Zariph is a Jew,   40
    A crucifying hangman trained in sin,
    One that would hang his brother for his skin.
Sir Anthony. But till to morrow.
Zariph.   Well, you shall not say
    But that a Jew will bear with you a day.
    Yet take't not for a kindness, but disgrace,   45
    To show that Christians are than Turks more base;
    They'll not forbear a minute. There's my hand:
    Tomorrow night shall serve to clear your band.
Sir Anthony. I thank thee, and invite thee to a banquet.
Zariph. No banquets; yet I thank you with my heart—   50
    [*Aside*] And vow to play the Jew; why, 'tis my part.   *Exit.*

Enter Servant.

Servant. Sir, here's an Englishman desires access to you.
Sir Anthony. An Englishman? What's his name?

---

37. learnt] learn't *Q*.   38. crush] crash *Q*.   51.SD] *not in Q*.

---

29. *this other fast*] during the recent fast-day. The Jewish calendar recognises four of these apart from Yom Kippur.
    31. *outcry*] auction.
    37. *curst*] malignant, cantankerous.
    41.] Bitter mockery of the long-standing Christian doctrine that Jews are deicides.
    45. *disgrace*] Like Halibeck at iv.26, Zariph predicts that favours granted to Anthony will ultimately bring about his ruin. Though the play does not endorse either character, both Jew and Persian indicate the misguided opportunism and self-righteousness with which the real-life Sherley pursued his mission.
    46. *Turks*] the usual derogatory reflex (cf. ii.207); Zariph is not identifying with these other enemies of Christendom.
    48. *band*] bond.
    49. *banquet*] possibly a full meal, but the word could mean the equivalent of 'dessert'—a course of sweetmeats, fruit and wine (*OED* 3).

Servant. He calls himself Kemp.
Sir Anthony. Kemp! Bid him come in.   *Exit* Servant.   55

                Enter WILL KEMP *and a* Boy.

Welcome, honest Will. And how doth all thy fellows in
  England?
Kemp. Why, like good fellows, when they have no money
  live upon credit.
Sir Anthony. And what good new plays have you?   60
Kemp. Many idle toys, but the old play that Adam and Eve
  acted in bare action under the fig tree draws most of the
  gentlemen.
Sir Anthony. Jesting Will.
Kemp. In good earnest it doth, sir.   65
Sir Anthony. I partly credit thee. But what play of note have
  you?
Kemp. Many of name, some of note, especially one: the name
  was called *England's Joy*. Marry, he was no poet that
  wrote it! He drew more coneys in a pursenet than ever   70
  were taken at any draught about London.

          Enter Servant *with* Harlequin *and his* wife.

55.SD] *not in* Q.   55.1.] *Enter Kempe. Q, next to* 54.   71.1. *with . . .* wife] *not in*
Q.

———————————————————

  56. *Welcome*] Anthony Sherley and Kemp actually met in Rome in 1601, at the
time of the events dramatised in scene v. The two men may have been related. A
contemporary diary reports Kemp as having much to say about Sherley on his return
to England, and as he certainly knew Day and probably his fellow-dramatists as well,
direct observation played its part in the creation of both characters (see S. Chew, *The
Crescent and the Rose*, pp. 275–6, and D. Wiles, *Shakespeare's Clown*, pp. 36–7).
  61–3. *the . . . gentlemen*] i.e. brothels are hot competition for the playhouses.
Kemp's joke is probably that *the old play* does not call to mind the traditional drama
on biblical subjects so much as current exploitation of the oldest profession.
  69. England's Joy] a hoax perpetrated in 1602 by one Richard Venner, who put out
a broadsheet advertising a play to be acted at the Swan on 6 November. John
Chamberlain gives a vivid account of how, having drawn an audience to the theatre
and 'gotten most part of the mony into his hands, he wold have shewed them a fayre
payre of heeles', but 'he was pursued and taken' (*Letters*, ed. N. E. McClure, 1939,
I.172).
  70. *coneys*] rabbits; used figuratively for a dupe or gull.
  pursenet] bag-shaped net with a draw-string, used to catch rabbits.
  71. *draught*] privy. Kemp presumably refers to opportunities for cutpurses and
pickpockets, or perhaps to sexual soliciting.
  71.1. *Harlequin*] The character could be wearing the patchwork costume associated
with Arlecchino, the most famous of the *Zanni* or clown types; but more likely the
term is used loosely to mean an Italian strolling player, since at 101 he proposes to
take the part of Pantalone (see note). The whole episode reveals a rather shaky
understanding of *commedia dell'arte* on the part of the writer.

Servant. Sir, here's an Italian harlequin come to offer a play to
    your lordship.
Sir Anthony. We willingly accept it. Hark, Kemp:
    Because I like thy jesture and thy mirth
    Let me request thee play a part with them.   75
Kemp. I am somewhat hard of study, and like your honour;
    but if they will invent any extemporal merriment, I'll put
    out the small sack of wit I ha' left in venture with them.
Sir Anthony. They shall not deny't. Signior Harlequin, he is   80
    content. [*To Kemp*] I pray thee question him—(*Whispers.*)
Kemp. Now, signior, how many are you in company?
Harlequin. None but my wife and myself, sir.
Kemp. Your wife! Why, hark you, will your wife do tricks in
    public?
Harlequin. My wife can play—   85
Kemp. The honest woman, I make no question; but how if we
    cast a whore's part or a courtesan?
Harlequin. O, my wife is excellent at that! She's practised it
    ever since I married her. 'Tis her only practice.   90
Kemp. But, by your leave, and she were my wife, I had rather
    keep her out of practice a great deal.
Sir Anthony. Yet, since 'tis the custom of the country,
    Prithee make one; conclude upon the project.
    We neither look for scholarship nor art   95
    But harmless mirth, for that's thy usual part.
Kemp. You shall find me no turncoat.

                         Exit SIR ANTHONY.
    But the project: come, and then to casting of the parts.
Harlequin. Marry, sir, first we will have an old Pantaloon.

---

82. *Whispers*] *Whisper. Q.* 98. *Exit* . . . ANTHONY] *Exit. Q* (*next to* 97).

---

75. *jesture*] a common spelling of 'gesture' meaning deportment or acting style,
though a pun is possible in view of Kemp's reputation as a clown. In the dedication to
An Almond for a Parrat Kemp is referred to as '*Jestmonger and* Vice-gerent generall to
the Ghost of Dicke Tarlton' (Nashe, *Works*, ed. McKerrow, III.337).

84–5. *tricks in public*] The female roles in *commedia dell'arte* were taken by
women; cf. the comment in Nashe's *Pierce Penilesse* (1592), which underlines the
relevance of this scene to the play's dramatisation of cultural difference: 'Our players
are not as the players beyond sea, a sort of squirting baudie Comedians, that have
whores and common Curtizens to playe womens partes . . . our Sceane is more statelye
furnisht . . . our representations honourable, and full of gallant resolution, not con-
sisting, like theirs, of a Pantaloun, a Whore, and a Zanie, but of Emperours, Kings,
and Princes' (*Works*, ed. McKerrow, I.215).

89. *practised*] performed.

94. *make one*] i.e. agree on a plot that includes her.

99. *Pantaloon*] Pantalone, the stock figure of the *senex* or old man, typically
dressed in red with a long black cloak and black slippers. He is usually a comic figure

Kemp. Some jealous coxcomb.   100
Harlequin. Right, and that part will I play.
Kemp. The jealous coxcomb?
Harlequin. I ha' played that part ever since—
Kemp. Your wife played the courtesan.
Harlequin. True, and a great while afore. Then I must have a   105
    peasant to my man, and he must keep my wife.
Kemp. Your man, and a peasant, keep your wife? I have known a
    gentleman keep a peasant's wife, but 'tis not usual for a
    peasant to keep his master's wife.
Harlequin. O, 'tis common in our country.   110
Kemp. And I'll maintain the custom of the country. (*He offers
    to kiss his wife.*)
Harlequin. What do you mean, sir?
Kemp. Why, to rehearse my part on your wife's lips. We are
    fellows, and amongst friends and fellows, you know, all   115
    things are common.
Harlequin. But she shall be no common thing, if I can keep her
    several. Then, sir, we must have an Amorado that must
    make me cornuto.
Kemp. O for love sake, let me play that part.   120
Harlequin. No, ye must play my man's part, and keep my wife.
Kemp. Right; and who so fit to make a man a cuckold as he
    that keeps his wife?
Harlequin. You shall not play that part.
Kemp. What say you to my boy?   125
Harlequin. Ay, he may play it and you will.
Kemp. But he cannot make you jealous enough.

---

112. *He offers*] *Offer Q.*

jealously guarding a young wife (which is how Harlequin and Kemp envisage him),
but he is also identified with the *Magnifico* or Venetian grandee, which at 130 they
invoke as a distinct type.
    100. *coxcomb*] fool.
    106. *to . . . man*] as my servant. The rustic peasant with strong regional accent was
one of the minor types of the *commedia dell'arte*.
    keep] attend, wait on—but inviting Kemp's innuendo in the next speech. Harlequin
acts as straight man to Kemp's bawdy clown, and the scene could be played either as
co-operative comedy or as Kemp's outwitting of his foreign rival. The resemblances
between the *commedia* plot and the typical material of the English jig can be seen in
Singing Simpkin, described in 1595 as 'Kemp's new jig' (see C. R. Baskervill, *The
Elizabethan Jig*, 1929, pp. 444–9).
    118. *several*] separate, to myself.
    Amorado] the *innamorato* or young lover.
    119. *cornuto*] a cuckold.
    126. *and . . . will*] if you like.

Harlequin. Tush, I warrant you, I can be jealous for nothing.

Kemp. You should not be a true Italian else.

Harlequin. Then we must have a Magnifico that must take up   130
the matter betwixt me and my wife.

Kemp. Anything of yours, but I'll take up nothing of your
wife's.

Harlequin. I wish not you should. But come, now am I your
master.   135

Kemp. Right, and I your servant.

Harlequin. Lead the way then.

Kemp. No, I ha' more manners than so. In our country 'tis the
custom of the master to go in before his wife, and the man
to follow the master.   140

Harlequin. In—

Kemp. To his mistress.

Harlequin. Ye are in the right—

Kemp. Way to Cuckold's-haven: Saint Luke be your speed.

Exeunt.

SCENE X

Enter ZARIPH.

Zariph. A hundred thousand ducats—sweet remembrance!
I'll read it again; a hundred thousand ducats!
Sweeter still: who owes it? A Christian,
Canaan's brood. Honey to my joyful soul.
If this sum fail, my bond unsatisfied,   5

0.1.] *Q adds: a Iewe.*   1.SP] *Iew. Q (passim).*

130–2. *take up . . . take up*] arbitrate . . . lift (her skirts).

144. *Cuckold's-haven*] a spot on the south side of the Thames between Greenwich
and Charlton marked by a pole with a pair of horns on top. It commemorated a
legend in which King John cuckolded a local miller and in recompense gave him all the
land he could see down-river from his house, on condition that once a year on St
Luke's Day he walked his estate with a pair of horns on his head. St Luke was the
patron of cuckolds. The pole is portrayed in *Eastward Ho!*, IV.i. Kemp's phrase is one
of several variants on the proverb 'to send to Cuckold's Haven' (C886).

0.1.] Zariph probably enters as table and chairs are set for the banquet: the
following dialogue assumes its imminence, and the furniture must be in place for the
entry at 62.1–2.

1. *ducats*] Thomas Coryat explains that in Venice 'this word duckat doth not
signifie any one certaine coyne', but on his figures Zariph's bond was the equivalent
of about £25,000, at that time a 'most stupendious summe of money' (*Crudities*,
repr.1905, I.423, 421).

He's in the Jew's mercy; mercy! Ha, ha!
The lice of Egypt shall devour them all
Ere I show mercy to a Christian.
Unhallowed brats, seed of the bond-woman,
Swine devourers, uncircumcisèd slaves   10
That scorn our Hebrew sanctimonious writ,
Despise our laws, profane our synagogues,
Old Moses' ceremonies, to whom was left
The marble Decalogue twice registered
By high Jehovah's self. Lawless wretches!   15
One I shall gripe, break he but his minute.
Heaven grant he may want money to defray.
O how I'll then embrace my happiness.
Sweet gold, sweet jewel! But the sweetest part
Of a Jew's feast is a Christian's heart.   20

                Enter HALIBECK.

Who's there?—A friend, a friend: good news, good news?
Halibeck. Zariph, the best! The Christian is thine own,
    I'll sell him to thee at an easy rate.
    It shall but cost thy pains, joined with a heart
    Relentless as a flint, that with more strokes   25
    Reverberates his anger with more fire.
    I know it's thine, I'm sure 'tis my desire!
Zariph. It is, it is. Sweeten my longing hopes:
    For charity, give me the happy means.
Halibeck. He should discharge thy bond tonight?   30
Zariph. He should, but I hope he cannot.
Halibeck. He cannot. The money he expected from the Sophy
    Myself have intercepted by the way.
    'Tis (to him unknown) given to my hands,
    And ere this shall aid him—
Zariph.   He shall die with Core,   35

20.1.] *after* 21 *in* Q.

   9. *bond-woman*] Virgin Mary (see *OED* sb[1] 1.c).
   11. *sanctimonious*] holy.
   14. *Decalogue . . . registered*] The Ten Commandments, of which Moses smashed the stone tablets on seeing the idolatry of his people, and returned to the top of Mount Sinai for replacements (Exodus 31–4).
   16. *break . . . minute*] if he fails to meet the deadline.
   17. *want*] lack.
   26. *Reverberates*] Beats up, intensifies (not in *OED* in quite this sense).
   35. *Core*] Proserpina, abducted by Pluto to be his consort in the underworld (Ovid, *Metamorphoses*, V.385ff).

As poor and loathsome as was leprous Job;
Sink down with Dathan to hell's black abyss.
A Christian's torture is a Jew's bliss.
For further execution, say, say.
Halibeck. Sit at his banquet with a smiling cheek;   40
Let him run out his prodigal expense
To the full length. The beggar has a hand
As free to spread his coin as the swollen clouds
Throw down their wat'ry pillage, which from the sea
The misty pirates fetch. Then seize on him,   45
Defer not, this night; vengeance in height of mirth
Galls deepest, like a fall from heaven to earth.
Zariph. O that thou wert one of the promised seed
To sleep with blessed Abraham when thou diest
For this good news. Here shall be cannibals   50
That shall be ready to tear him piecemeal
And devour him raw; throw him in the womb
Of unpitied misery, the prison.
There let him starve and rot, his dungeon cry
To Zariph's ears shall be sweet harmony.   55
Halibeck. It is enough; determine, follow it.
Myself will presently back to Persia,
And by the way I will invent such tales
As shall remove the Sophy's further love.
Ere any stranger shall with me walk even,   60
I'll hate him, were his virtues writ in heaven. (*Music*)
The music says the banquet is at hand.

           Enter SIR ANTHONY *with some Venetians, and
                  others with a banquet.*

Sir Anthony. Let us abridge the office of our breath
To give to each of you a several welcome.
I do beseech ye take it all at once:
Ye are all welcome. Now, I pray ye, sit.   65

62.1. *with*] *not in* Q.   66. Ye are] Yee'are Q.

---

37. *Dathan*] who joined a rebellion against the authority of Moses in the wilderness,
and was swallowed up by an earthquake (Numbers 16).
    41–2. *Let...length*] Anthony Sherley's extravagant lifestyle at other people's
expense was a recurrent feature of his travels.
    45. *misty pirates*] i.e. the clouds.
    46. *in...mirth*] i.e. when the victim is most carefree.
    57. *presently*] without delay.
    60. *with...even*] be on an equal footing with me.
    63. *office*] duty.
    64. *several*] individual.

Zariph. We'll not strive for first.
Halibeck.   'Tis more used than fit.
Zariph. O this sweet music is heaven's rhetoric!
   The art was first revealed to Tubal Cain,
   Good Hebrew. 'Tis now forgot, 'tis grown stale;   70
   Newfangled ages makes old virtues fail.
Sir Anthony. So much the Hebrew writ doth testify,
   Yet are there different to that opinion:
   The Grecians do allow Pythagoras,
   The Thracians give it to their Orpheus   75
   As first inventors of the harmony.
Zariph. All errors; Tubal, Tubal, Hebrew Tubal.

Enter Prologue.

Sir Anthony. But howsoever, we'll hold no dispute;
   Our attention is tied to some other sports.
Prologue. Our act is short, your liking is our gains;   80
   So we offend not, we are paid our pains.
Zariph. No more of this, we'll have a Jew's jig.

Enter Sergeants *and take hold on* SIR ANTHONY.

   To your business, delay not.   *Exit* Prologue.
Sir Anthony. What means this violence?
Zariph.   We'll not stand
   Upon interr'gatories; away with him.   85
Sir Anthony. Jew—
Zariph.   Christian. Away with him.
Sir Anthony.   Hear me—
Zariph. In prison; I'll listen to laugh at thee.
Sir Anthony. Be merciful—
Zariph.   Merciful? Ha, ha!
Sir Anthony. No, not to me, I scorn to ask it of thee.
   But to thine own black soul be merciful.   90

77.1.] *after* 79 *in* Q.   83.SD] *not in* Q.   82–5.] *prose in* Q.   85. interr'gatories]
Intergatories Q.

---

   67. *first*] prime position at table. Having first declined the invitation at ix.50,
Zariph elects to keep a low profile until his moment of triumph.
   used than fit] common than appropriate.
   69.] Tubal Cain was by tradition 'the forger of every cutting instrument of brass
and iron'; both parts of the name (cf. Arabic *qayin*) derive from words for 'smith'.
   77.1.] Presumably either Harlequin or Kemp's boy.
   82. *jig*] trick, joke. But Zariph plays sardonically on the sense of a theatrical end-
piece: 'the Jyg at the end of an Enterlude, wherein some pretie knaverie is acted'
(Cotgrave, 'Farce').

Inhuman dog, that in midst of courtesy
Dost yoke me in a serpent's arm, true seed
Of that kiss-killing Judas, can thy black soul
Have hope of pity, being pitiless?
Zariph. Pray for thyself, I am saved already.   95
Sir Anthony. Halibeck, does not your eye discover
A treacherous heart in this?
Halibeck.   Ha, ha!
Sir Anthony.   Dost laugh at me?
Citizen. Sir, be comforted. Venice shall not see
Your fortunes long oppressed for a greater
Matter than this.
Sir Anthony.   I am not moved, sir.   100
It hath not emptied the least pipe of blood
That are within my cheeks. Only this is all
That wraps my senses in astonishment:
In all my travels I ne'er saw hell till now.
'Tis here true portrayed, set in open view   105
In an envious knave and a bloody Jew.
                              Exeunt Sergeants *with him,*
                              followed by Venetian citizens.
Zariph. There rot and starve, starve and rot. O my delight!
I shall dream of this happiness tonight.   *Exit.*
Halibeck. To Persia now; while Sherley here sinks low,
There Halibeck above his height shall grow.   *Exit.* 110

SCENE xi

Enter THE SOPHY, CALIMATH *and* Attendants.

Sophy. No more! By Mortus Ali, we are moved.
Dares that proud Sherley, whom our powerful heat
Drew from the earth, refined and made up great;
Dares he presume to contradict our will
And save a man whom we command him kill?   5
He would not, nay he durst not; he brews his death,

96–100.] *prose in* Q.   104. travels] trauailes Q.   106.1.] *Exeunt with him* Q.

91. *in . . . courtesy*] i.e. whilst Anthony is his host.
92. *arm*] embrace, grip.
2–3. *our . . . great*] alchemical imagery, describing the process of sublimation whereby gross matter is vaporised to remove impurities. (Cf. Jonson, *Alchemist,* I.i.64–9.)
6. *brews*] causes, brings about.

Rides in a cloud of our offended breath.
Calimath. He knows it.
Sophy.   And he fears it.
Calimath.   All yourself,
   I speak not to disparage Sherley's worth
   Nor to divorce him from your gracious favour,   10
   But to maintain the custom of our wars
   Which most contemptuously he has broke down
   In giving life to thirty prisoners,
   And talking with the Turk by messengers.
Sophy. Send to the Turk, and save our prisoners' lives!   15
Calimath. With proffer to return them ransomless.
Sophy. By Mortus Ali and our Persian gods,
   For every man he saved I'll have a joint,
   And for conversing with the Turk, his head—
Calimath. Besides, your gracious niece—
Sophy.   Ha? What of her?   20
   Dares the proud Christian think upon our niece?
Calimath. And look and love her.
Sophy.   How!
Calimath.   And she on him.
Sophy. To save the body we must lose a limb:
   Sherley shall off.
Calimath.   And time.
Sophy.   One call our niece.
                              Exit Attendant.

   Alter our customs, steal our subjects' bosoms,   25
   And like a cunning adder twine himself
   About our niece's heart! She once his own,
   He's lord of us and of the Persian crown.

        Enter NIECE, DALIBRA *and* Attendants.

Niece. What craves the mighty Sophy?
Sophy.   Loose your train.
                Exeunt DALIBRA *and* Attendants.
   And to the purpose. When and what commends   30
   Came to your hands from our new general,
   Sherley the Great?
Niece.   That he is great in name

---

8. All] *Q; Calm conj.Bu.* 24.1.] *not in Q.* 29.1.] *not in Q.*

8. *All yourself*] possibly the dramatists' notion of a pagan honorific, but more likely the text is corrupt.
30. *commends*] remembrances, compliments.

Springs not from aught in us, but his own fame.
But for what reason doth your greatness make
This privy search in my concealèd thoughts
Touching the English general?   35
Sophy.   Thy bosom
Harbours a traitor: dost thou not love young Sherley?
Niece. I do not hate him; should I answer so,
Against my tongue my conscience would say 'no'.
Sophy. Why, then you love him?
Niece.   Should I not say 'Ay',   40
My honoured thoughts would give my tongue the lie.
Calimath. She has confessed.
Niece.   That I love him: true.
Calimath. And English Sherley—
Niece.   If he had his due
You should all love him; he has spent a sea
Of English blood to honour Persia.   45
Sophy. And through that bloody sea his treacherous head
Shall make a purple voyage to the shade
Where treason lives apparelled in red flames.
Niece. For me? Because your niece does honour him?
Sophy. For thee, because my niece doth dote on him,   50
Forgetful of thy fortunes and high birth,
More bestial in thine appetite than beasts.
The princely lioness disdains to mate
But with a lion; time and experience shows
That eagles scorn to build or bill with crows.   55
Niece. What means all this?
Sophy.   That with thy love to Sherley
Thou buyest our hate.
Niece.   By'r Lady, a hard bargain,
But merchant venturers cannot always win.
You forced my thought to love him, and like a tutor
First taught my tongue to call him honourable.   60
Your breath commanded knees to bow to him,
Tongue to adore, and duty to attend him.

---

41. honoured] *Q*; honest *conj.Bu.*

---

55. *bill*] kiss.
57. *By'r Lady*] a Christian oath (despite iii.109–15). Thomas Herbert, however, in his warm obituary of Robert Sherley, reminded his readers that 'Lady *Terezia*, his faithfull Wife … was ever Christian' (*A Relation*, 1634, p. 125).
58.] Cf. iii.13. The Niece's irony acknowledges that she now sees herself as love's agent rather than its victim, and this fortifies her against the challenge that follows.

And is affection turned *apostata*?
But I have found your humour; you grow jealous
Lest I should rob you of your minion.   65
In faith, you need not.
Sophy.   Our enkindled rage
Is grown too strong to be blown out with jests.
Thou lovest—
Niece.   The very ground he goes upon.
But why? Because it bears my body's want?
By Jove and by a virgin's modest thought,   70
Which like a laurel garland decks my brows,
I love not Sherley; never harboured thought
That told me he was lovely, at least equal
To maintain wing with us.
Sophy.   Come, you dissemble.
Niece. I loved him to please you; to humour you   75
Gave him kind language; if I praised his worth
'Twas not my tongue but yours. If 'twere a lie
It came from these, they authored it, not I.
Yet I'll recant it too—call him uncivil,
Ill-favoured, treacherous, disobedient;   80
And, to appease the tempest of your wrath,
Swear him a coward worse than Calimath.
Lord. I'll not endure!
Calimath.   Unequalled excellence,
She doth disgrace us all to honour him.
Niece. You all disgrace yourselves to envy him   85
Whose worth has been an honour to you all.

Enter ROBERT SHERLEY.

Robert. Conquest and peace attend you.
Sophy.   A strong guard.

ROBERT *is surrounded.*

87.1.] *not in Q.*

   63. apostata] faithless, inconstant.
   64. *your humour*] what's discomposing you.
   69. *want*] need, desire.
   71.] Daphne fleeing Apollo was turned into a laurel, 'a never-withering tree, to shew what immortall honour a virgin obtaines by preserving her chastity' (Sandys, *Ovid*, p. 36).
   73–4. *at . . . wing*] or even that he was on an equal footing.
   77–8. *yours . . . these*] The Niece is careful to distinguish between the Sophy's judicious praise of Robert and insincere hero-worship by members of the court.

Robert. What means the Sophy? here are none—
Sophy.   But traitors.
    Ignoble Sherley, treacherous Christian,
    How durst thou 'gainst the custom of our kingdom   90
    Reserve those prisoners' lives?
Robert.   Dread majesty,
    Not proud contempt but Christian charity,
    The pilot of mine actions.
Sophy.   But we know
    You come not empty of excuse, proud Sherley.
    Have we breathed life into thy sickly fortunes,   95
    And, like the low and mean-bred Saraber,
    Having allowed thee seat-room at our foot,
    Dar'st thou presume to climb up to our crown?
    Presumptuous, know our breath can shake thee down.
Robert. Look through my bosom: if you find one thought   100
    Basely conditioned or ambitious—
Sophy. Th' art all ambition, and hast drawn the love
    Out of our subjects' breasts, who, to defeat
    Us of our due, title thee Sherley the Great.
Robert. Great was their error that informed you so.   105
    My thoughts are like my fortunes, mean and low.
    If the high favours you have thrown on me
    By my dear industry I have increased,
    Adds honour to your own. For saving of my prisoners
    Let but a brother's love plead my excuse.   110
Sophy. Ambitious like your own are his
    Proceedings; 'tis brought to us by letter
    How much he has abused himself and us
    In his employments.
Robert.   Dearest excellence,
    Let not his want of duty fall on me,   115
    Nor mine return to him.
Calimath.   Yet, for his love
    You do confess you save these prisoners?

---

96. *Saraber*] Probably a garbled version of 'Saracen', generally at this time seen as marauding desert Arabs who had overrun Persia in the distant past.

109. *Adds*] i.e. this adds.

113–14. *How . . . employments*] The Shah's dissatisfaction with Anthony, and consequent misuse of Robert, are not recorded in any of the printed accounts, but were known to Cecil and his agents who intercepted letters written by both brothers. In September 1606 Robert wrote desperately to Anthony of the Shah's complaint 'that it is seven yeares since he sentt you into cristendum, he knowes not wheare [you] are, nor what you have dun in his service, nor the reason you retorne not unto him . . . I . . . am in hazzarde to loose my selfe' (quoted in *The Sherley Brothers*, pp. 58–9).

Robert. True, for a brother's love, but not for his.
    I have an elder brother, so every way complete
    With virtuous qualities that even his foes   120
    Cannot but speak him well. Desire of fame,
    That in all ages has been Sherleys' aim,
    Drew him from home; mischances, that like hail
    Fall on bold minds, did him so hard assail
    That by the Turk he was surprised and taken.   125
    By many strokes the tallest oaks are shaken.
    To ransom him, not to infringe your right,
    I freed these prisoners, manly ta'en in fight.
Calimath. And was not that ambition?
Robert.   If to save
    A worthy brother from a worthless grave   130
    Be held ambitious, I have in a sin
    Waded so deep that I must perish in.
Niece. Perish may twenty cowards first.
Sophy. Away with her to prison!   *Exit* NIECE *under guard.*
                          Suppose, as you infer,
    To ransom him you saved your prisoners' lives,   135
    For whose sake do you love our niece?
Robert.   Yon fire
    That lightens all the world knows my desire
    Durst never look so high.
Sophy.   Come! You, that durst
    Break our land's custom for a brother's sake,
    Durst for your own sake dote upon our niece.   140
    But see what credit your ambition bears:
    Go, mount those prisoners' heads on thirty spears.
Robert. First be my blood their ransom, ere the Turk
    Should have that proud advantage to report
    A Christian and a true-born English soldier   145
    Promised, and had not power to perform.
Sophy. Then learn to promise nothing but your own.
Robert. Nor did I, mighty prince. With my own hands
    I took those captive Turks; with my dear blood
    I bought them of proud danger. This being known,   150
    In giving them I gave nought but my own.
Calimath. Come, y'are too peremptory.
Robert.   I am indeed:

---

134. *Exit* NIECE] *next to* 133 *in* Q.   *under guard*] *not in* Q.

126.] proverbial: 'Many little strokes fell great oaks' (S941).

Before mine honour let my man's heart bleed.
Were it mine equal did me half this wrong,
He should find sharper vengeance than my tongue.   155
Calimath. You can produce no probable excuse.
Robert. Your ears will hear no reason, Calimath.
  Thou hast a brother, Persian. So have I:
A prisoner brother. To redeem his life,
That all this while lies on the edge of death,   160
I saved these prisoners. Wert to do again,
Again I'd venture. Have ye shapes of men
And want their spirits? We in all are three
Sons of one father, branches of one tree.
Should a rough hand but violently tear   165
One scion from a tree, the rest must bear
Share in the hurt. The smallest wound that drains
Blood from our breasts empties our father's veins.
Sophy. Hast thou another brother?
Robert.   We in all are three;
  The young'st and meanest spirit speaks in me.   170
Yet, ere the Turk should think I had not power
To back my word, O be this instant hour
My latest minute; with your warlike sword
Strike off my head. Life's cheaper than my word.
Sophy. Be master of thy wish. But first we here take off   175
Thy offices and titles, and bestow them
Upon this worthy gentleman—

    ROBERT *is stripped of his insignia and Calimath invested*
               with them.

                  —charging thee
By that first mover whom thou call'st thy god,
The blest Messiah, and the sacrament
Which Christians hold so ceremonious,
Thy father's blessing and thy brother's love   180
And the long progress which thy soul must go,
Whether thou ever levelled'st at our crown
Or an unlawful contract with our niece?
Robert. Never; for had I harboured such intent   185
Nothing could make me basely to repent.

---

166. scion] *Bu;* siens *Q.*   177.SD] *not in Q.*

---

166. *scion*] twig.
173. *latest*] last.

But I had never. Any life nor death
Can make a Christian falsify his breath.
Sophy. Withdraw the Christian.   *Exit* ROBERT *under guard.*
                              And produce our niece,
    And—

> *Enter an officer with a counterfeit head like Sherley's.*

              —officer, 'tis well.   190

> *Enter* NIECE. *She approaches the officer holding the head.*

Will you speak yet? Yet can ambition read
Your hateful practice?
Niece. [*Seizes the head.*]   Had young Sherley's head—
Sophy. A traitor's head whose proud ambitious tongue
    Did at his death basely confess his wrong.
    Do you as much, and take our princely pardon.   195
    Speak, did you love that Christian or no?
Niece. I never loved him living, but being dead
    Thus I'll embrace, thus kiss his lovely head.
    Alas, good Sherley, did thy warlike hand
    For this defend the Sophy, guard his land?   200
    Didst thou for this forsake thy country, friends
    And weeping father? That's a kind amends!
Calimath. Speak: did you love him?
Niece.   No; for if I had,
    I should have grown impatient, wild and mad;
    Washed off this blood with tears, and—
Sophy.   Take her hence.   205
    She dies but she acknowledge her offence.
Niece. Stay; since I must, I will. I did offend
    'Cause undeserved I wrought brave Sherley's end.
    I did offend, for careless I stood by
    And let true valour amongst cowards die.   210
Calimath. Cowards!
Niece.   Ay, cowards! His worth recorded stands
    Upon yon file of stars. He has the hands
    Of all the holy angels to approve

189.SD] *not in* Q.   190.1. *She...head*] *not in* Q.

---

187. *Any...death*] No chance of life or prospect of death.
190. *with...Sherley's*] The Q stage direction informs readers but not audiences,
and the head is handled and accepted as real by the Niece at 198.
206. *but*] unless.
212. *file*] catalogue, roll.

What blood he's spent in quest of Christian love.
I speak not like a strumpet that, being filled
With spirit of lust, her own abuse to gild   215
Slanders her friend. Till now I never loved him,
And now by yonder sun I dote on him.
I never heard him vow, protest or speak
Word that might his approved allegiance break.   220
O you have done a deed blacker than night,
A murder that would murders foul affright!
Your very foes will say, when this is known,
In cutting off his head you have scarred your own.
Were I his brother, countryman, or slave   225
I'd kill his murderer, or dig my grave
Under the Sophy's feet. O you have won
The ire of heaven and hate of Christendom.

Sophy. If he be innocent.
Niece.   By heaven he is.
Sophy. Then we confess our spleen has done amiss.   230
Niece. Redeem it then, and in his winding sheet
    Let his dissevered head and body meet.
    Return them me, let me the credit have
    And lay his mangled body in a grave.
Sophy. Take it with our best love and furtherance.   235
    And having joined his body to the head
    His winding sheet be thy chaste marriage bed.

                  Enter ROBERT SHERLEY.

Niece. Then lives young Sherley?
Sophy.   Yea, and still shall stand
    Loved of the Sophy, honoured in his land.
    All styles and offices we late took off   240
    We back restore. And now to Calimath.
    Thus far on your report we have proceeded,
    And had we found them either culpable
    Their heads had paid for 't; but being clear
    We here restore them to their former state,   245
    Renew them with our love, thee with our hate.
Robert. For this dear favour, as for all the rest,
    Low-minded Sherley counts him highly blessed.

                  Enter Messenger.

---

233. *the ... have*] be entrusted with them.

Sophy. Your sweating news?
Messenger.   To the great general.
　　To your demand thus sends the haughty Turk: 250
　　That were your thirty prisoners petty kings
　　He would not free the English gentleman.
Sophy. Would not? Lead on, we'll talk with him in steel.
　　What he denies to hear we'll force him feel.
　　Will not return them? Then will we head our spears   255
　　With viceroys' skulls, and o'er his craven ears
　　Batter his castles like a shower of hail.
　　On to the field! Heaven and our right prevail.
　　　　　　　　　　　Exeunt all except CALIMATH.
Calimath. Hell on our wrongs! Give him his niece in marriage!
　　First like an ass load me with ornaments   260
　　To see how I'd become his golden traps,
　　And the same minute snatch them off again!
　　O, I am vexed! Damnation and black hell
　　Author my actions; in my passions dwell
　　Commotive thoughts; envy and hate   265
　　Strive in my breast like twins inseparate.
　　My spleen's in travail, and till they be born
　　My swollen heart labours and my breast is torn.
　　To ease which torment, and to free my breath,
　　I'll be delivered: my kind midwife's death.   *Exit.* 270

　　　　　　　　SCENE xii

　　　Enter Jailer with a paper in his hand.

Jailer. According to this my warrant here, I must this morning
　　fetch my prisoner to airing. He had need be hung out lest
　　his flesh should mould, for I am sure his clothes are musty

---

258.1.] *Exeunt. Manet Cally. Q.*

　　256. *viceroys'*] Pashas of the Ottoman empire.
　　261. *traps*] trappings. But Calimath's awareness of how the Sophy has tested him at
175–7 prompts a half-realised pun.
　　265. *commotive*] tumultuous.
　　267. *spleen*] thought to be the source of passionate anger.
　　270. *death*] i.e. Robert's; but this self-destructive torment seems to yearn for a more
personal oblivion.
　　2. *airing . . . hung out*] The Jailer's meaning is clear if the stocks are thrust out
from the discovery space at the start of the scene. If they are not produced until later
(e.g. at 27), his words sound like gallows humour.

already. We Turks are to these Christians for all the world
like usurers to young heirs—make picking meat of their   5
carcases even to the very bones, and then leave them to the
hangman, for they'll none of them; and not like Englishmen
to their oxen, the nearer fat the nearer fed upon. Well,
hither he must come; and yet I think scarcely too, unless he
be carried, for I am sure—let me see—these five   10
or six months at least he has had nothing but the hard
boards for his bed, dry bread for his food and miserable
water for his drink. And we Turks think that it is too good
for these Christians too; for why should we do any better
to them, since they do little better one to another? But   15
where are you here? Ha!

He opens a door. Enter SIR THOMAS.

Sir Thomas. What would thy tongue with me, unless to have
    Thy tyrannies, writ here, fright thine own soul?
    Or art thou come to add unto my bones,
    Having no sense of suffering in my flesh?
    Speak out thy worst; our spirit's not afraid   20
    At what can come, though in our looks dismayed.
Jailer. All this, sir, is to be left to the discretion of
    the higher powers; I ha' nothing to do with it. Only,
    sir, I have a warrant here to make two knots to tie   25
    your ankles in, all the teeth in your head cannot tell
    how to undo 'em; and here they are ready, sir.

He leads him towards the stocks.

Sir Thomas. How, slave?
Jailer. Nay, come, resist not, but remember we have cold
    irons, a good cudgel and a strong arm. Put in your   30
    bearers.

16.1. *He . . . door*] *not in* Q.   27.1.] *not in* Q.

5. *make . . . of*] feed daintily on.
8. *nearer*] more.
14–15. *why . . . another?*] A familiar comment on the divisions within Christendom,
as in the Epistle to *The Turkes Secretorie* (1607): 'Why then are we afraid of any
forrain Turks? Seeing we . . . are Turkes unto our selves . . . and turne our swords
against our own sides' (A4r–v). But the comparison in 4–5 has already initiated a
more specific allusion to the urban jungle of Jacobean city comedy.
18. *writ here*] i.e. in his emaciated body.
19–20. *add . . . flesh*] turn your attention to my bones now that I've lost all bodily
sensation.
31. *bearers*] legs.

Sir Thomas. Blind Fortune, when thou lookest askance on men
    Thou art without conscience in thy plaguing them.
Jailer. Come, come; your legs are shrunk as you had been
    at your lechery lately—we shall ha' them slip their   35
    collars anon. So, you may say your prayers now. You
    shall ha' more company presently.

        Exit Jailer leaving SIR THOMAS *in the stocks.*

Sir Thomas. What folly were't in me to sigh at this
    Or chide my fortune being common, that she brings
    Full hands to fools and knaves, grief even to kings.   40
    Or what avails it me to rail at them
    That fled from me, whose faiths I built upon?—
    Since 'tis as ripe in trust to find some slaves
    As honest men to die and have due graves;—
    Or that my flesh is shrunk and my blood paled,   45
    Since I have this to make my courage bold.
    Men have but done a part of what death should.
    Or why should my captivity afflict me?
    Good minds know this: imprisonment's no shame
    Unless the cause be foul which blots the name.   50
    Then all the griefs in my remembrance be
    Is that my father's eyes should weep for me
    And my misfortune. For mine own mishaps
    Are to my mind as are heaven's thunderclaps
    Who clears the air of foul infection;   55
    And in my thoughts do only publish this:
    Affliction's due to man as life and sin is.

      Enter THE GREAT TURK *with a* Pasha *followed by* Jailer
              and Attendants.

Great Turk. Speak: where is this captive English Christian?
Pasha. Here, as appointed by our emperor.

---

35. ha' them] ha' 'hem Q.   38. were't] wert Q.   43. ripe Q; rife *conj.Dyce (MS
notes).*   57.1. *followed by*] *not in* Q.

34–5. *legs . . . lechery*] Quasi-proverbial: cf. Falstaff's description of Justice Shallow
in *2Henry IV*: 'When a was naked, he was for all the world like a forked radish . . . a
was the very genius of famine, yet lecherous as a monkey' (Arden ed., III.ii.304–8).
    43. *'tis . . . slaves*] it's a safe assumption that some will prove untrustworthy. Dyce's
conjecture ('rife' for *ripe*) makes easier sense but removes Thomas' emphasis on
personal judgement ripened by adversity.
    57.2. *Attendants*] Some of these form the Great Turk's retinue, others are the
jailer's assistants and carry on the rack (perhaps removing the stocks when Thomas is
freed).

Great Turk. Say, Christian: yet resolve us thy descent   60
  And promise of the ransom that's assigned thee,
  Or tortures shall enforce it from thy tongue.
  With the sun's light this day we have thee graced
  Which till this hour we have exempt from thee;
  Which grace of ours unless thou do confess,   65
  Thy tortures shall be more, thy freedom less.
Sir Thomas. That I enjoy yon benefit of heaven,
  The life and solace of each living creature,
  Here to refresh mine eyes, I do confess;
  By you kept from me, by yon bounty given me.   70
  And this some comfort to my misery:
  That sun shines on my father looks on me.
  But to resolve your grace to pay a ransom
  And know not how to make my promise good,
  I had rather you should take, I yield, my blood.   75
Great Turk. Why, think'st thou, Christian, our belief's so slight,
  Great Sherley for thy ransom would send back
  Thirty of chiefest note in our respect,
  And thou of obscure parentage and birth?
  Thou hast waked our anger. Put him on the rack,   80
  Where four and twenty hours he shall remain.
  Upon your lives I charge it quickly done,
  Ourself will see the execution.
Sir Thomas. 'Tis but the farthest way about to death
  To give men ling'ring tortures, when a small prick   85
  Is man's conclusion. But howsoe'er, my lord,
  I ha' patience to accept what you afford,
  The dungeon; this, now that. If back again
  Unto your loathsome prison after rack,
  True constancy's my forefront, and my back.   90
Great Turk. We'll try your patience, Christian. Hoist him up.
Sir Thomas. [*Screams.*] O! O!

---

62. Or] *Bu;* Our *Q.*

60–1. *thy...ransom*] Robert's initiative to rescue Thomas is the dramatists' invention, but the Turkish interest in his affiliations had an actual parallel in Anthony's trial by a government commission in Venice (see note to ix.12), where he was questioned closely about his connections with Thomas (who had attacked Venetian shipping in the Mediterranean). The playwrights could not, however, have learned of this from Nixon, who is silent about Anthony's Venetian ordeal.

91. *Hoist him up*] The command suggests that the rack is not one which stretches the victim in a prone position (which would be less visible to spectators in the yard) but a structure on which he is lifted by means of ropes attached to his wrists.

Great Turk. Now where's your haughty courage durst
                                        withstand us,
  And Roman spirit that forswore to yield?
Sir Thomas. Here, emperor, here, even in these outstretched
                                      veins 95
  Lives my amazeless vitals, here's an undaunted heart
  That never yields by Turkish tyranny.
  I am the same through all that made me man,
  Scorn pagan's threats to die a Christian.
Great Turk. Wrench him again.   100
Sir Thomas. O! O!
Great Turk. Yet wilt thou tell thy blood and parentage
  And yield unto the ransom we have assigned thee?
Sir Thomas. No, emperor, no.
  Even in this hell of pain I answer 'never'.   105
  I once denied thee, and my tongue's no liar.
Great Turk. We stand amazèd at thy constancy.
  Yet answer us: wilt thou forsake thy faith,
  Become as we are, and to Mahomet
  Our holy prophet, and his Alcoran   110
  Give thy devotion?—and by our kings we swear
  We will accept thee in the place of kings.
Sir Thomas. First shall the sun melt from his restless seat
  Ere that our name shall turn *apostata*;
  Thy kingdoms be unpeopled, and thy nations   115
  Become as free for beasts as now for men;
  Thyself (as sometimes were thy ancestors)
  Fed in a cage and dragged at conqueror's heels.
Great Turk. Presumptuous Christian!
Sir Thomas. And thy bad life meet such a hateful death 120
  Even fowls shall loathe thy body, men thy breath.
Great Turk. Thy strength of faith hath bred a wonder in us.
  One take him down and bear him back to prison;
  We yet resolve not how to deal with him.
Sir Thomas. Even where you will; to torture back again. 125
  Our comfort's this: hell stores for you like pain.
                         Exit SIR THOMAS *under guard.*

126.1.] *Exit Tho.* Q.

---

96. *amazeless*] imperturbable, intrepid. Not in *OED*.
110. *Alcoran*] Qur'an or Koran, the holy book of Islam.
114. *turn* apostata] be that of one who denies the true faith.
117–18. *Thyself . . . cage*] An allusion to Timur's humiliation of the Ottoman Emperor Bajazeth I in 1399, made famous by Part I of Marlowe's *Tamburlaine*.

Enter Messenger.

Great Turk. The hasty news?
Messenger. The English agent craves access to you.
Great Turk. Admit him.

Enter Agent.

Agent. From my dread master, England's royal king,   130
    By these his letters, fair commends to you.
Great Turk. We greet him with like love. [*Reads.*] His letters
                                           crave
    A prisoner that's called Sherley, we should have.
Agent. An English knight, whom his misfortunes cast
    Upon your Turkish shore.
Great Turk. We have as yet had notice of no such.   135
Agent. By name perhaps, dread emperor. Yet in this place
    By your commandment he lives prisoner,
    And brother to that Sherley called 'the Great'—
Great Turk. Ha!
Agent. Which in the Persian wars is general.   140
Great Turk. Had I known that, by Mahomet he had died.
Agent. His miseries have spoke unto our king,
    Joined with his worth; and he hath sent for him.
Great Turk. We'll not deny your master his request.   145
    Yet how to know we do not send him back
    His subject, but a present given from us,
    Whom we esteem of an unvalued worth,
    One bring him forth.

Enter one with SIR THOMAS.

                Receive him, English agent.
    To thee,   150
    As to thy master's hand, we thus present him.
    Bid him accept him as our thoughts did hold;
    A gem could not be bought from us with gold.
    His pass shall be for Florence, then for England,

---

149. *Enter* . . . THOMAS] *after* agent *in* Q.

151.] Presumably Thomas is handed over with considerable ceremony to drive
home the distinction made in 146–7.
154.] Thomas was released through James I's intercession in December 1605,
returning to England via Corfu and a number of Italian cities, including Florence
where he reaffirmed his allegiance to the Grand Duke of Tuscany (see note to vi.16).
He would have had no interest in going to Persia.

Lest he in Persia should embrace his brother   155
And prove a plague to us as great as the other.   *Exeunt.*

SCENE xiii

Enter MASTER ROBERT SHERLEY *and a* Hermit *with him.*

Robert. Grave father, for the reverence of your age,
          And justice of the cause for which you come—
          Being to advance the glory of our God
          Wherein no soul should have neglectful thoughts—
          I have lain by particular affairs   5
          To give a hearing to your business.
Hermit. Go on, my son; to Him being dutiful
          Virtue will make thy name more honourable.
          Myself from far have on these agèd feet,
          Whose knees do buckle and have scarce their strength   10
          To bear me further than a grave's in length,
          With easy paces but a swift desire
          Enquired thee out; that hearing thee a Christian
          So gracious with this Persian emperor,
          A mind so noble in thy actions,   15
          A body fortunate in his designs,
          Thou might'st as well bestow thy pains and blood
          To advance religion as for heathen's good.
Robert. Heaven knows,
          Knew I the means, I were His willing servant.   20
Hermit. If, like thy tongue, thy intention have a care,
          Climb up to heaven by this ascending stair.
          Entreat thy emperor thou may'st raise a church
          To sacrifice thy prayers unto that name
          To whom all names should kneel. When if his priests,   25
          Himself, his council, any heathen breath
          Should contradict the high authority
          Of thy devoted zeal, spare not to say
          Their god's His servant whom thy thoughts obey.
          And win, as by persuasion kings are won,   30
          Or else confute them by religion.
Robert. Alas, sir, my ungrown experience
          To argue a difference of that height

---

22. *this . . . stair*] the stepped dais on which the throne stands.
32. *ungrown*] immature, limited.

Betwixt their god and ours is so far unfit,
I rather shall abuse than honour it.
Hermit. Why, why, my son? Dost thou forget to know　　　35
　　Our God's the spring whence eloquence doth flow,
　　And can infuse into thee, wert thou dumb,
　　Words thunderlike, a contradictless tongue?
　　That when thou speak'st for the honour of that name　　40
　　Made earth to hang betwixt yon heavenly frame
　　Borne on no axletree, angels do sit
　　About thine ears and breathe into thy wit.
　　And if thou shouldest in such a quarrel die
　　Martyrs look on thee with a joyful eye.　　45
Robert. Ye have given unto my life another soul!
　　And never, reverend father, could you have come
　　In time that's fitter wherein I may prove
　　My duty to the Highest, to Christian's love.
　　This present day I have an infant born　　50
　　Who, though descended from the emperor's niece,
　　A pagan, I'll baptise in Christian faith;
　　Confute their ignorance, heaven assisting me,
　　That mine own soul this comfort may partake:
　　Sherley in Persia did the first Christian make.　　55
　　Then raise a temple for our further good,
　　Or in the fair adventure spend my blood.
Hermit. In all necessities I'll further thee,
　　And if by my advice thou diest I'll die with thee.
Robert. And so to die your life were new begun.　　60
　　Old age to die with him 'a made God's son.

　　　　Enter THE SOPHY, HALIBECK *and* CALIMATH *with*
　　　　　　　Attendants.

Sophy. Hali, go on; and of your great affairs
　　Deliver us every several circumstance.
Halibeck. From thence I left, dread sovereign, thus ensues.

---

45. look] *this ed.;* lookes *Q.*　61.1. *with* Attendants] *not in Q.*

---

41. *Made*] who made.
45.] The appeal to the intercession of saints is another distinctively Catholic note in the play. See Intro, p. 10.
55.] There were in fact several Christian communities in Persia in the sixteenth century.
57. *adventure*] enterprise.
61.] An obscure, possibly corrupt line. Robert may be thinking of his own death as timely (as in old age) if it comes in such a cause.
64. *thence...left*] where I left off.

That Sherley whom you joined with me in embassy,   65
Having our footing once on Christian ground,
Became so proud, so wild, so prodigal
All eyes contemn him; only some few
That gave his rising looks, but for the due
Your grace bestowed on him in princes' courts.   70
His fellowship was fools, his actions sports
For wise men's tables. I often did advise him
That such behaviours no way did befit
The glory of his place, nor would you suffer it
When his return gave place for punishment.   75
When first in Russia, he abused your greatness,
For which the just State did imprison him;
Yet for the honour of the cause in hand
Ere long he was released. We come to Rome,
Where I but striving to ascend as chief,   80
Being in person there your sacred self,
His hand first struck me, while his tongue did chime
'No pagans must ascend where Christians climb'.
Sophy. Durst he say so?
Halibeck.   He did, my lord.
Yet passed we thence to Venice, where, as before,   85
He kept his flood of riot and abuse,
For which he's there kept prisoner; and the State
Returned me back, nothing determined of.
Calimath. Now may my sovereign evidently see
Their subtle glosings have this inward kind: 90
They'll wound your heart though seem to please your mind.
Sophy. By day! if this be true, no Christian lives
Within the compass where our word may kill.
[*To Robert*] Speak!
How canst thou answer this appeal of theirs?   95
Robert. O let the emperor but desist a while
From the remembrance of a tale he heard;

---

68. *contemn*] despise.
69. *That . . . looks*] countenanced his presumption.
but for] simply because of.
72. *tables*] dinner conversation.
85. *Yet . . . Venice*] Husain 'Ali Beg actually set off for Persia after breaking with Sherley in Rome, but died on the journey home.
87. *kept prisoner*] Anthony was released in 1603, shortly after the accession of James I, who gave him a licence to remain overseas, thus legalising his original departure from England (Davies, p. 162). He remained in Venice until the end of 1604, when he was expelled for pursuing his scheme of a Perso-Christian alliance.
90. *glosings*] flatteries, deceptions.

Or else but think great men may face a lie
Till truth appear and give their cheek a dye.
These letters in your eyes first speak for me,   100
　　　He presents letters to THE SOPHY.
Whilst in their ears a story I'll unfold
Shall make their heads shake and their hearts cold.
The first from Russia, where this envious man
Accused my brother as a fugitive,
A thief, a pirate, and a Christian spy;   105
For which he was imprisoned, till evidently
The State had knowledge of his innocence.
Then him released, sent that intelligence.
At Rome I not deny my brother struck him
For pride, so just the Father of that seat   110
In his behalf doth in his letter speak.
Now let your eyes but look what Venice writes:
That this man by suggestions wrought the State
Against my brother's labours; withheld the treasure
Your princely self sent to discharge the Jew   115
For the rich jewel that my brother bought.
And all the benefit to Christendom
And to your honour is by him undone.
Sophy. Treasons unheard of! Such shall the revenge be.
His silence and his looks approves his guilt.   120
Great Sherley, at thy censure there he stands;
To doom him death may equal his offence.
Unto thy brother's life he stretched his sin;
Be his alike, we freely give thee him.
Robert. Then here's my justice for so vile a crime.   125
Since that it reached unto my brother's life
And blemish of his honour and his worth,
And hindered that ordained for Christian glory,
He shall confess unto your sacred self
All treasons in those letters mentionèd   130
To be his plots and actions 'gainst my brother.
And tell the world, to shut up scandal's tongue,
All that thou didst from roots of envy sprung
And no desert of his. They satisfied

100.1.] *not in* Q.

117–18. *benefit . . . honour*] i.e. to both sides from the proposed alliance against the Turks.

134–6. *They . . . him*] The trial of Halibeck is pure invention (see note to 85), but in Nixon's version Robert is less actively magnanimous, merely recommending that

For all conspiracy, all envy's sin,   135
We thus will love thee, learn but to love him.
Sophy. Thou art too merciful.
Calimath. In this as merciful as honourable.
Halibeck. Thy clemency doth make me see myself
To have been a villain to that gentleman   140
Deserves so well of all men, best of me.
Great emperor, not a letter that is there,
If every character were doubled twice,
But the attempts are mine against his life.
Death I have deserved; then much I owe to thee   145
That might have ta'en my life, and set me free.
Sophy. Stay there, sir.
Sherley has pardoned the offence to him,
Not the transgressions thou hast done to us.
We sent thee forth as our ambassador,   150
To deal for us as we ourself were there,
Which dignity of ours thy tongue profaned;
For which we do adjudge thee lose thy tongue.
We made thy hand, like ours, to strike or spare,
Which power and grace of ours thou didst abuse;   155
For which thou shalt go handless to thy grave.
And that thy head, that made the rest offend,
Shall off.
All.   Mercy, dread emperor.
Sophy. Who talks of mercy tastes our wrath with him.
And you that are akin to him in blood,   160
Whose eyes being brother's should taste grief alike,
We charge you see the execution.
Calimath. Dread emperor—
Sophy.   Speak not, we are resolved.
Halibeck. And I to die.
Ambition still lies lowest, seeking to fly.   165
                              Exit under guard.

165.1. *under guard*] *not in* Q.

the Persian should be put out of his misery after losing his hands and tongue (13). The
dramatists are pursuing the theme of clemency begun in scene i. But see Intro., p. 16,
and next note.
   147–58.] Cartwright comments approvingly on Persian justice, 'which kind of
severity were very needfull for some parts of Christendome, I will not say for *England*
though we have faulted therein' (p. 67).
   165.] A version of the proverb 'Ambition is the last affection a noble mind can put
off' (A234).

Sophy. [*To Robert*] His honours and possessions now are
                                                    thine.
    If yet unsatisfied thy griefs remain
    Ask yet; to please thyself it shall be granted.
Robert. I fear to be too bold.
Sophy.   Ask and obtain.
Robert. My child may be baptised in Christian faith   170
    And know the same God that the father hath.
Sophy. Baptize thy child, ourself will aid in it;
    Ourself will answer for't, a godfather.
    In our own arms we'll bear it to the place
    Where it shall receive the complete ceremony.   175
    Speak, what else thou wouldst have granted thee.
Robert. You are too lavish of your high favours.
    I would entreat I might erect a church
    Wherein all Christians that do hither come
    May peaceably hear their own religion.   180
Sophy. 'Tis granted, erect a stately temple.
    It shall take name from thee, Great Sherley's Church.
    Finish thy suit, whate'er it be.
Robert. You are too prodigal, I too presuming.
    Yet sith yourself doth thus authorise me,   185
    I will not hide my heart. Your further leave:
    I would by your permission raise a house
    Where Christian children from their cradles
    Should know no other education,
    Manners, language nor religion   190
    Than what by Christians is delivered them.
Sophy. We'll ask no council to confirm that grant,
    'Tis obtained. Speak all.
Robert. Your favour, love and good estimation,
    And my suit is ended.   195

172–3. *ourself...godfather*] Nixon records two children of the marriage 'both Christened in that Countrey...the King himselfe beeing a witnesse to one of them in Baptisme' (K4v). John Cartwright was scornful: 'that hee should have a child in *Persia*, and that the King (a professed enemie to the Name of our blessed Saviour) should bee the God-father; this certainly is more fitte for a Stage, for the common people to wonder at, then for any mans private studies' (pp. 70–1).

178–91.] Based on Nixon: 'Robert Sherley hath already erected there a church, called after his own name, in which he hath divine service...duely read...Hee hath also obtained of the King a number of young infants of that country to be brought up in a house appointed for that purpose, that altogether estranged, & kept from hearing or speaking their owne Language, may in time learne our English Speech, and come at length to Christian knowledge.' But the playwrights tactfully avoid having Robert voice his hope (as Nixon puts it) that the Sophy 'may in time bee brought to become a Christian' (K4v).

Sophy. In the best embrace of our endearèd love
    We do enclose thee. Sherley shall approve
    Our favours are no cowards, to give back;
    They shall abide till death. Thou shalt not lack
    Our love's plenitude, our dearest nephew.   200
    Now for the temple, where our royal hand
    Shall make thy child first Christian in our land.   *Exeunt.*

A show of the Christening.

EPILOGUE

Enter Chorus *as* Fame.

Fame. Thus far hath Fame with her proclaiming trump
    Sounded the travels of our English brothers.
    Unhappy they (and hapless in our scenes)
    That in the period of so many years
    Their destinies' mutable commandress   5
    Hath never suffered their regreeting eyes
    To kiss each other at an interview.
    But would your apprehensions help poor art,
    Into three parts dividing this our stage,
    They all at once shall take their leaves of you.   10
    Think this England, this Spain, this Persia.
    Your favours then, to your observant eyes
    We'll show their fortunes' present qualities.

Enter three several ways the three brothers: ROBERT *with*
the state of Persia as before; SIR ANTHONY *with the*
King of Spain *and others, where he receives the Order*
of Saint Iago, and other offices; SIR THOMAS *in England,*

0.1.] *Enter fame. Q.* 5. Their] *this ed; That Q.*

---

202. Exeunt] I have retained *Q*'s clearing of the stage which doubtless preceded the
formal dumb show, but technically this leaves it stranded between the final scene and
the Epilogue (not designated as such in *Q*, but Fame's speech clearly balances the
Prologue). The Chorus presumably enters and begins to speak during a second,
processional *exeunt.*
    5. *Their*] *Q*'s *That* was probably caught by the compositor from the preceding line.
commandress] Dame Fortune.
    13.1. *three . . . ways*] The central discovery space might have been used for one of
the 'entries', drawing the curtain to reveal (perhaps) a mime of Thomas' homecoming,
flanked by the exotic contexts of the two brothers still abroad.
    13.3–4. *where . . . offices*] Cf. Nixon, I4v–K: 'He stayed not long in Spaine, before
the King installed him one of the Knights of the Honourable Order of S. Iago, and

with his father and others. Fame *gives to each a*
prospective glass: they seem to see one another
and offer to embrace, at which Fame *parts them, and*
so exeunt all except Fame.

To those that need further description
We help their understandings with a tongue.   15
Sir Anthony Sherley we have left in Spain,
Knight of Saint Iago, one of the council
Of his highness' wars against the infidels,
Captain of th' Armado, with other honours.
The eldest in England is, to few unknown   20
His worth, his merit, and his offices.
The last in Persia, as you have seen.
This is the utmost of intelligence.
If we should prosecute beyond our knowledge,
Some that fill up this round circumference,   25
And happily better know their states than we,
Might justly call the authors travellers,
And give the actors too the soldier's spite.
Then here we leave them; now the rest to you:

13.8. *and . . . Fame*] *and so: Exeunt. Manet Fame. Q.*

---

created him Captaine of his Galleyes for the warres against the Turkes.' This was
announced only in March 1607 (*The Sherley Brothers*, p. 65), so Nixon's information
was up to date.

13.6. *prospective glass*] traditionally a magical device for seeing distant or future
events; at this date also a magnifying glass, which the instrument used on stage
probably resembled. See illustration on p. 19. (The telescope was not invented until
the year after the play was written.) In Barnabe Barnes' *The Divils Charter* (1607)
Pope Alexander performs similar feats with a 'Magicall glasse' (F4v), and Hariot
intrigued the Indians in Virginia with 'strange sights' in 'a perspective glass' (Hakluyt
VIII.378).

20–1.] Readers of the play, and perhaps its later audiences, might have known that
in September 1607 Thomas was imprisoned in the Tower for interfering with the
Levant trade (Davies, pp. 181–5). He was released in the following year.

22. *as . . . seen*] In fact the play gives a rosy picture of Robert's fortunes in the
period after Anthony's departure from Persia. He was effectively held hostage for his
brother's successful discharging of the embassy, and when the latter failed Robert fell
into disfavour. (See xi.113–14 note.) His situation improved only late in 1607 when
the Shah decided to send him to Europe on an embassy of his own.

25. *this . . . circumference*] referring to the Curtain theatre where the play was first
performed (see title-page note). The Red Bull was probably square (Bentley VI.216).

26. *happily*] haply, perhaps. But the word also conveys an awareness that some in
the audience (those who move in diplomatic and court circles) might have privileged
access to information about the Sherleys that is not in the printed accounts.

27.] because 'a traveller may lie with authority' (T476).

28. *the . . . spite*] Soldiers' tales were regarded as highly unreliable.

Since they have safely passed so many perils   30
(For what through danger passes is the best),
Since they in all places have found favourites,
We make no doubt of you: 'twere too hard doom
To let them want your liking here at home.   *Exit.*

FINIS

31.] A variant of the proverb 'The more danger the more honour' (D35).

THE SEA VOYAGE
A comedy

The Persons represented in the Play.

ALBERT, *a French pirate, in love with Aminta.*
TIBALT DUPONT, *a merry gentleman, friend to Albert.*
Master of the Ship, *an honest merry man.* 5
LAMURE, *an usuring merchant.*
FRANVILLE, *a vainglorious gallant.*
MORILLAT, *a shallow-brained gentleman.*
Boatswain, *an honest man.* 10
SEBASTIAN, *a noble gentleman of Portugal, husband to Rosellia.*
NICUSA, *nephew to* Sebastian. *(Both cast upon a desert island.)*
RAYMOND, *brother to* Aminta.
Surgeon.
Sailors. 15

Women.

AMINTA, *mistress to* Albert, *a noble French virgin.*
ROSELLIA, *governess of the Amazonian Portugals.*
CLARINDA, *daughter to* Rosellia, *in love with Albert.*

2–28.] *F2; not in F.*

---

5. TIBALT] The name is synonymous with a combative nature from Shakespeare's use of it in *Romeo and Juliet*, though Tibalt's role here is more reminiscent of Mercutio. Fletcher may have been guided in naming him by the description in Warner's *Syrinx* of the character of Chebron on whom Tibalt is modelled: 'a lustie taule fellow, of a cholericke complexion and an invincible courage...bending his browes and laying hand on his weapon' (B4v).

17. AMINTA] Fletcher may be the first writer to treat this as a feminine name, which became a literary favourite later in the century, though 'Minta' was apparently in ordinary usage for girls by 1598 (see W. Goddard, *A Mastif Whelp*, H3); Tasso gives it to the eponymous shepherd-hero of his *Aminta* (1573).

18. ROSELLIA] Variously spelled in F and F2; 'Rosella' occurs several times, and the chosen form might be modernised to 'Roselia'.

19–22.] Fletcher is repetitive with female names, using three of these four in other plays between 1620 and 1623. Hippolita was queen of the Amazons in some versions of the legend, and a character of that name, described as 'guerrière, & ... orgueilleuse

HIPPOLITA ⎫ *three ladies, members of the Female*   20
CROCALE   ⎬ *Commonwealth.*
JULETTA   ⎭

The Scene: first at sea, then
in the desert islands.

The Principal Actors were   25

Joseph Taylor.   John Lowin.
William Eglestone.   John Underwood.
Nicholas Tooley.

---

entre les armes' (p. 472) appears in the *Histoire . . . de Lysandre & de Caliste* (Paris 1620), a romance by Audiguier (also featuring a character named Clarinda) on which Fletcher was to base his 1623 play *The Lover's Progress*, and which may have suggested the situation in our play in which 'une nouvelle Amazonne' (p. 574) threatens to usurp the hero's love for the heroine.

21. CROCALE] Borrowed from Ovid's account of the goddess of chastity's train: '*Diana* bathes her selfe . . . attended by six Nymphs whose names sute well with that service. *Crocale* signifieth pibble stones in the fountaine which serve as a strainer to clarifie the water' (Sandys, *Ovid*, p. 99).

25.] Bentley speculates that F2 gives 'only five names instead of the usual eight' because the play has an unusually small number of adult roles and no less than six for boy actors (III.413).

26–8.] All prominent members of the King's Men. Taylor was the most recent recruit but had made a name for himself with other companies: he inherited several of Richard Burbage's roles, including Hamlet, and presumably played Albert here. Lowin was remembered for several major comic parts with the company, such as Falstaff and Volpone (Nungezer, p. 241), and probably took the part of Tibalt. Nicholas Tooley, in his late forties in 1622, perhaps played Sebastian.

ACT I

A tempest, thunder and lightning.

Enter Master *and two* Sailors.

Master. Lay her aloof! The sea grows dangerous.
    How it spits against the clouds, how it capers,
    And how the fiery element frights it back!
    There be devils dancing in the air: I think
    I saw a dolphin hang i'th'horns of the moon   5
    Shot from a wave. Heyday, heyday,
    How she kicks and yerks!
    Down with the main mast, lay her at hull,
    Furl up all her linens and let her ride it out.
First Sailor. She'll never brook it, master!   10
    She's so deep laden that she'll bulge.
Master.   Hang her!
    Can she not buffet with a storm a little?
    How it tosses her! She reels like a drunkard.
Second Sailor. [*Above*] We have discovered the land, sir!
    Pray let's make in—she's so drunk else,   15
    She may chance to cast up all her lading.
First Sailor. Stand in, stand in! We are all lost else, lost
    And perished.
Master.   Steer her a-starboard there.
Second Sailor. Bear in with all the sail we can! See, master,
    See, what a clap of thunder there is, what   20

ACT I SCENE i] *Actus Primus—Scoena Prima F.* 8. the] *F2;* 'e *F.*

---

    1. *Lay . . . aloof*] keep (or turn) the ship's head into the wind. (Cf. nautical 'luff'.)
    2–3.] Recalling the descriptions of the storm in *The Tempest* by Miranda (I.ii.3–5) and Ariel (I.ii.197ff), but Shakespeare's opening scene dramatises the shipwreck itself in more rigorously functional language.
    5. *dolphin*] this, or more usually the porpoise with which it was often confused, was said to play before a storm (P483).
    7. *yerks*] pitches, shudders.
    8. *lay . . . hull*] drift with the sails furled.
    11. *bulge*] spring a leak in the bilge or bottom of the hull.
    16. *cast*] vomit.
    17. *Stand in*] Make for the shore.

A face of heaven, how dreadfully it looks!
Master. Thou rascal, thou fearful rogue! Thou hast been
                                            praying,
    I see't in thy face. Thou hast been mumbling
    When we are split, you slave. Is this a time
    To discourage our friends with your cold orisons?   25
    Call up the boatswain. How it storms!—Holla!

              Enter Boatswain.

Boatswain. What shall we do, master? Cast over all
    Her lading? She will not swim an hour else.
Master. The storm is loud; we cannot hear one another.
    What's the coast?
Boatswain.   We know not yet. Shall we make in?   30

      Enter ALBERT, FRANVILLE, LAMURE,
          TIBALT DUPONT *and* MORILLAT.

Albert. What comfort, sailors?
    I never saw since I have known the sea,
    Which has been these twenty years, so rude a tempest.
    In what state are we?
Master.   Dangerous enough, captain.
    We have sprung five leaks, and no little ones.   35
    Still rage!—Besides, her ribs are open,
    Her rudder almost spent. Prepare yourselves
    And have good courages: death comes but once,

26.1.] *not in* F.

24. *split*] being wrecked.
25.] implying that prayer saps morale as well as being a neglect of vital duties.
Sailors were more often rebuked for blaspheming at times of stress, and the master's
cynical impiety replaces the usual profanities (cf. opening scene of *The Tempest*). As
nautical scenes go, this one is fairly decorous, perhaps because Fletcher was mindful of
the tastes of a more genteel audience.
29. *The . . . loud*] The staging of this scene at Blackfriars (and perhaps at the Globe)
would draw upon the company's experience in presenting, *inter alia*, its equivalent in
The Tempest. Blackfriars provided the necessary technology: thunder run, wind
machine, a revolving drum filled with pebbles to simulate the sound of the sea, and
squibs to provide the lightning. The tiring-house galleries would have been used for
lookouts (e.g. at 14) and in conjunction with the main stage for the handling of ropes
and lowering of sails.
    we . . . another] Several maritime accounts (and plays) refer to the master and
boatswain being equipped with whistles, and this was probably reflected in Jacobean
staging of such scenes. Cf. Heywood, *Fortune by Land and Sea*, IV (*Works*, 1874,
VI.417).
36. *Still rage!*] either a comment on the continuing storm, or a command issued to
the general tumult.

And let him come in all his frights.
Albert.   Is't not possible
To make in to th' land? 'Tis here before us.   40
Morillat. Here hard by, sir.
Master.   Death is nearer, gentlemen.
Yet do not cry; let's die like men.

Enter AMINTA.

Tibalt. Shall's hoist the boat out and go all at one cast?
The more the merrier.
Master.   You are too hasty, monsieur.
Do ye long to be i'th' fishmarket before your time?   45
Hold her up there.
Aminta.   O miserable Fortune,
Nothing but horror sounding in mine ears,
No minute to promise to my frighted soul.
Tibalt. Peace, woman!
We ha' storms enough already—no more howling.   50
Aminta. Gentle master—
Master.   Clap this woman under hatches.
Albert. Prithee speak mildly to her.
Aminta.   Can no help?
Master. None that I know.
Aminta.   No promise from your goodness?
Master. Am I a god? For Heaven's sake, stow this woman.
Tibalt. Go, take your gilt prayer book and to your business.   55
Wink and die, there an old haddock stays for ye.
Aminta. Must I die here in all the frights, the terrors,
The thousand several shapes death triumphs in?
No friend to counsel me?
Albert.   Have peace, sweet mistress.
Aminta. No kindred's tears upon me? O my country!   60
No gentle hand to close mine eyes?
Albert.   Be comforted.
Heaven has the same power still, and the same mercy.
Aminta. O, that wave will devour me!
Master.   Carry her down, captain,
Or, by these hands, I'll give no more direction,
Let the ship sink or swim. We have ne'er better luck   65

---

46. *her*] the sail: the master has assented to the general plea to make for land. The
basic situation recalls the episode in Ariosto's *Orlando Furioso* (19.35–42) where
Marfisa is wrecked on the Amazons' shoreline, but there the master's reluctance to
make for land derives from his knowledge of its inhabitants.
56. *Wink*] sleep.

When we ha' such stowage as these trinkets with us,
These sweet sin-breeders. How can heaven smile on us
When such a burden of iniquity
Lies tumbling like a potion in our ship's belly?
                    Exeunt Master, Boatswain and Sailors.
Tibalt. Away with her, and if she have a prayer   70
That's fit for such an hour, let her say't quickly
And seriously.
               Exeunt TIBALT, FRANVILLE, LAMURE *and* MORILLAT.
Albert.   Come, I see it clear, lady.
Come in and take some comfort. I'll stay with ye.
Aminta. Where should I stay? To what end should I hope?
Am I not circled round with misery?   75
Confusions in their full heights dwell about me.
O monsieur Albert, how am I bound to curse ye,
If curses could redeem me! How to hate ye!
You forced me from my quiet, from my friends—
Even from their arms that were as dear to me   80
As daylight is, or comfort to the wretched.
You forced my friends from their peaceful rest;
Some your relentless sword gave their last groans.
Would I had there been numbered!
And to Fortune's never-satisfied afflictions   85
Ye turned my brother, and those few friends I'd left
Like desperate creatures to their own fears
And the world's stubborn pities. O merciless!
Albert. Sweet mistress—
Aminta. And whether they are wandered to avoid ye,   90
Or whether dead and no kind earth to cover 'em—
Was this a lover's part? But heaven has found ye,
And in his loud voice, his voice of thunder,
And in the mutiny of his deep wonders
He tells ye now ye weep too late.
Albert.   Let these tears   95

69.1.] *Exit F.*   72.SD] *Exit. F.*   93. loud] *F;* loudest *F2.*

66. *trinkets*] useless adornments. The misogyny of the following lines is driven by the superstition that women on board bring bad luck to a voyage.
69.] i.e. is churning up our insides. This vivid image of the ship as ailing organism refers to the queasy effects of medicine but also exploits the licentious associations of 'tumble'.
72.] *F*'s *Exit* is designed to leave Albert and Aminta alone on stage, since Tibalt (who must leave at this point) is the only character whose re-entry is not marked later in the scene.
86. *turned*] turned out, abandoned.

Tell how I honour ye. Ye know, dear lady,
Since ye were mine how truly I have loved ye,
How sanctimoniously observed your honour;
Not one lascivious word, not one touch, lady—
No, not a hope that might not render me   100
The unpolluted servant of your chastity.
For you I put to sea to seek your brother—
Your captain, yet your slave—that his redemption,
If he be living where the sun has circuit,
May expiate your rigour and my rashness.   105
Aminta. The storm grows greater! What shall we do?
Albert.
                                          Let's in,
And ask heaven's mercy. My strong mind yet presages
Through all these dangers we shall see a day yet
Shall crown your pious hopes and my fair wishes.
                              Exeunt ALBERT *and* AMINTA.

              Enter Master, Sailors, Gentlemen, Boatswain
                          and Surgeon.

Master. It must all overboard.
Boatswain.   It clears to seaward!   110
Master. Fling o'er the lading there, and let's lighten her.
All the meat and the cakes—we are all gone else—
That we may find her leaks and hold her up.
Yet save some little biscuit for the lady
Till we come to the land.
Lamure.   Must my goods over too?   115
Why, honest master, here lies all my money,
The money I ha' racked by usury

109.1.] *Exit F.* 110–11. seaward!/*Master.* Fling] Sea-ward mast./Fling *F.* 112.
cakes] *F*; casks *conj.Mason;* cates *conj.H.Weber* (ed. *Works of B&F,* 1812).

---

98. *sanctimoniously*] religiously, piously.
102.] On the conflicting purposes of the voyage, see Intro., pp. 20–1.
107. *strong*] resolute.
109.2–3.] *F2* omits the Surgeon, who does not speak in this scene; but *F* clearly
intends to assemble the full cast of characters to be marooned. The *Gentlemen* are the
four who left the stage at 72.
112. *cakes*] Various emendations are on offer (see collation); but cakes in the old
sense of hard-baked loaves were staple fare on board ship: in one of the early accounts
of privation in Virginia, voyage provisions are used to alleviate hunger but 'extended
not above ... two Cakes a day' (Purchas XIX.53).
117–19. *racked ... banished*] A Jacobean audience would be reminded of the
recent exiling of Sir Giles Mompesson for gross extortion, celebrated in a 1621

To buy new lands and lordships in new countries
'Cause I was banished from mine own. I ha' been
This twenty years a-raising it.
Tibalt.   Out with it.   120
The devils are got together by the ears
Who shall have it, and here
They quarrel in the clouds.
Lamure.   I am undone, sir.
Tibalt. And be undone! 'Tis better than we perish.
Lamure. O save one chest of plate!   125
Tibalt. Away with it lustily, sailors.
It was some pawn that he has got unjustly.
Down with it low enough, and let crabs breed in't.

              Enter ALBERT.

Master. Over with the trunks too.
Albert. Take mine and spare not.
Master.   We must over with all.   130
Franville. Will ye throw away my lordship that I sold,
Put it into clothes and necessaries
To go to sea with?
Tibalt. Over with it. I love to see a lordship sink!
Sir, you left no wood upon't to buoy it up;   135
You might ha' saved it else.
Franville.   I am undone
Forever!
Albert.   Why, we are all undone: would you
Be only happy?
Lamure.   Sir, you may lose too.
Tibalt. Thou liest, I ha' nothing but my skin
And my clothes, my sword here, and myself;   140
Two crowns in my pocket; two pair of cards
And three false dice. I can swim like a fish,

---

135. buoy] *F2;* bovy *F.*

broadside which declared: 'For greedie gaine hee thrust the weake to wall.../He
outlawde therefore was and banisht quite' (STC 18003.9). Lamure's name might even
be a sly allusion to this indictment. But Fletcher would have found a relevant French
connection in reports of Louis XIII's campaign in 1621 against the Huguenot strong-
hold of La Rochelle (a major privateering base): Edward Herbert, as ambassador to
France, reported a proposal that the rebels should be 'banished into other Countreys',
and made a protest to the French government against such a policy (*The Life of
Herbert of Cherbury*, ed. J. M. Shuttleworth, 1976, pp. 104, 118).
     127. *pawn*] security against a debt.
     141. *pair*] packs.

Rascal, nothing to hinder me.
Boatswain. In with her of all hands!
Master. Come, gentlemen, come captain—ye must help all.   145
    My life now for the land! 'Tis high and rocky,
    And full of perils.
Albert.   However, let's attempt it.
Master. Then cheer lustily, my hearts!   *Exeunt.*

ACT I SCENE ii

Enter SEBASTIAN *and* NICUSA.

Sebastian. Yes, 'tis a ship! I see it now, a tall ship.
    She has wrought lustily for her deliverance.
    Heaven's mercy, what a wretched day has here been!
Nicusa. To still and quiet minds that knew no misery
    It may seem wretched, but with us 'tis ordinary.   5
    Heaven has no storm in store, nor earth no terror
    That can seem new to us.
Sebastian.   'Tis true, Nicusa,
    If fortune were determined to be wanton
    And would wipe out the stories of men's miseries.
    Yet we two living, we could cross her purpose,   10
    For 'tis impossible she should cure us,
    We are so excellent in our afflictions.
    It would be more than glory to her blindness,
    And style her power beyond her pride, to quit us.
Nicusa. Do they live still?
Sebastian.   Yes, and make to harbour.   15
Nicusa. Most miserable men, I grieve their fortunes.
Sebastian. How happy had they been had the sea covered 'em!
    They leap from one calamity to another.
    Had they been drowned, they had ended all their sorrows.

---

1. *1 . . . ship*] Sebastian's best vantage-point for the sighting is the gallery in the tiring-house, and at 62 he speaks of descending to the main stage. The scene is short enough to be played 'above' in its entirety.
    tall] stout.
6–8.] The abrupt transition suggests a cut: Sebastian appears to be replying not to Nicusa's last remark but to something like the view that the uncertainty of fortune leaves them the hope of a change for the better. Nicusa's fatalism in this scene is less confirmed than his uncle's.
12. *excellent*] surpassing.
14. *quit*] redeem.
18. *leap*] i.e. from the ship into the boat (or the sea): see note to 59.

What shouts of joy they make!
Nicusa.   Alas, poor wretches,   20
   Had they but once experience of this island,
   They'd turn their tunes to wailings.
Sebastian.   Nay, to curses,
   That ever they set foot on such calamities.
   Here's nothing but rocks and barrenness,
   Hunger and cold to eat. Here's no vineyards   25
   To cheer the heart of man, no crystal rivers
   After his labour to refresh his body
   If he be feeble. Nothing to restore him
   But heavenly hopes. Nature that made those remedies
   Dares not come here, nor look on our distresses,   30
   For fear she turn wild like the place and barren.
Nicusa. O uncle, yet a little memory of what we were
   'Twill be a little comfort in our calamities.
   When we were seated in our blessed homes
   How happy in our kindreds, in our families,   35
   In all our fortunes!
Sebastian. Curse on those French pirates that displanted us!
   That flung us from that happiness we found there,
   Constrainèd us to sea, to save our lives,
   Honours and our riches,   40
   With all we had, our kinsmen and our jewels,
   In hope to find some place free from such robbers.
   Where a mighty storm severed our barks,
   That where I know not went my wife, my daughter
   And my noble ladies that went with her,   45
   Virgins and loving souls, to 'scape those pirates.
Nicusa. They are living yet; such goodness cannot perish.
Sebastian. But never to me, cousin; never to me again.
   What bears their flag-staves?
Nicusa.   The arms of France sure.

---

39. Constrainèd] Constrain'd *F*.   44. That ... wife] *this ed;* That, where my wife *F*.

24–31.] The type of the desert isle could be found even in the fruitful Canaries:
Robert Harcourt commented that on the outlying island of Allegranza in 1608 'we
found no inhabitants, nor fresh-water, neither fruitfull tree, plant, herbe, grasse, nor
any thing growing that was good, onely an abundance of unwholsome Sea-foule ... &
a few ... wilde Goats, which the craggy rocks defended from our hands, and hungry
mouths' (*A Relation of a Voyage to Guiana*, 1613, pp. 2–3).
   44. *That*] so that. *F*'s line is defective (see collation), and the repetition of *where*
from 43 may imply the omission of a line or more preceding this one. Various
emendations have been proposed, none of them persuasive.
   49. *arms of France*] indicating that the ship is on a privateering mission and not

Nay, do not start, we cannot be more miserable.   50
  Death is a cordial now, come when it will.
Sebastian. They get to shore apace. They'll fly as fast
  When once they find the place. What's that which swims
                              there?
Nicusa. A strong young man, sir, with a handsome woman
  Hanging about his neck.
Sebastian.   That shows some honour.   55
  May thy brave charity, whate'er thou art,
  Be spoken in a place that may renown thee
  And not die here.
Nicusa.   The boat it seems turned over,
  So forcèd to their shifts; yet all are landed.
  They're pirates, on my life.
Sebastian.   They will not rob us,   60
  For none will take our misery for riches.
  Come cousin, let's descend and try their pities.
  If we get off, a little hope walks with us;
  If not, we shall but load this wretched island
  With the same shadows still that must grow shorter.   65
                                        Exeunt.

ACT I   SCENE iii

Enter ALBERT, AMINTA, TIBALT, MORILLAT, LAMURE,
  Master, FRANVILLE, Surgeon *and* Sailors.

Tibalt. Wet-come ashore, my mates! We are safe arrived yet.
Master. Thanks to heaven's goodness, no man lost.
  The ship rides fair too, and her leaks in good plight.
Albert. The weather's turned more courteous. How does
  My dear? Alas, how weak she is, and wet!   5
Aminta. I am glad yet I 'scaped with life, which certain,
  Noble captain, next to heaven's goodness
  I must thank you for; and which is more
  Acknowledge your dear tenderness, your firm love

---

simply engaged in lawless piracy. During periods of war or poor relations with Spain,
French and English vessels were licensed by their home governments to prey on Iberian
shipping.
  51. *cordial*] relieving medicine.
  59. *forcèd . . . shifts*] i.e. overloaded by too many desperate men.
  65. *that . . . shorter*] presumably as they shrink with age.
  3. *rides fair*] is buoyant.

To your unworthy mistress, and recant too   10
(Indeed I must) those harsh opinions,
Those cruel unkind thoughts I heaped upon ye.
Further than that, I must forget your injuries;
So far I am tied and fettered to your service.
Believe me, I will learn to love.
Albert.   I thank ye, madam;   15
And it shall be my practice to serve.
What cheer, companions?
Tibalt. No great cheer, sir. A piece of soused biscuit
And half a hard egg, for the sea has taken order.
Being young and strong we shall not surfeit, captain!   20
For mine own part, I'll dance till I'm dry.
Come surgeon, out with your glister-pipe
And strike a galliard.
Albert.   What a brave day again,
And what fair weather after so foul a storm!
Lamure. Ay; an't pleased the master, he might ha' seen   25
This weather and ha' saved our goods.
Albert.   Never think on 'em,
We have our lives and healths.
Lamure.   I must think on 'em,
And think 'twas most maliciously done
To undo me.
Franville.   And me too—I lost all. I ha'n't
Another shirt to put upon me, nor clothes   30
But these poor rags. I had fifteen fair suits!
The worst was cut upon taffety.
Tibalt. I am glad you ha' lost: give me thy hand.

---

16. serve] F; deserve you *conj.Dyce.*

13. *your injuries*] the harm that you've done me.
18. *soused*] soaked. The word usually means pickled or steeped in alcohol.
19. *taken order*] ordained it so, asserted itself (by taking the rest of the food). OED does not support the sardonic idea of the sea ordering a meal.
20. *surfeit*] be gorging ourselves.
22. *glister-pipe*] tube for inserting enemas (clysters) or suppositories. Tibalt humorously presses it into service as a musical recorder.
23. *galliard*] lively dance in triple time.
brave] fine.
31. *Suits*] 'an ensemble of harmonizing or matching garments: doublet, hose, coat, jerkin, mandilion [short coat with hanging sleeves], or cloak' (Linthicum, p. 212).
32. *taffety*] silk. Similar pretensions earned a contemptuous reference to 'our Tuftaffety humorists' amongst the gentlemen settlers in Virginia, in *A Map of Virginia* (Oxford 1612), p. 13.

    Is thy skin whole? Art thou not purled with scabs?
No ancient monuments of madam Venus?   35
Thou hast a suit then will pose the cunning'st tailor,
That will never turn fashion, nor forsake thee
Till thy executors, the worms, uncase thee.
They take off glorious suits, Franville; thou art happy
Thou art delivered of 'em. Here are no brokers,   40
No alchemists to turn 'em into metal,
Nor leathered captains with ladies to adore 'em.
Wilt thou see a dogfish rise in one of thy brave doublets
And tumble like a tub to make thee merry?
Or an old haddock rise with thy hatched sword   45
Thou paid'st a hundred crowns for?
A mermaid in a mantle of your worship's?
Or a dolphin in your double ruff?
Franville.   Ye are merry;
    But if I take it thus, if I be foisted
And jeered out of my goods—
Lamure.   Nor I, I vow thee.   50
    Nor master nor mate, I see your cunning.
Albert. O be not angry, gentlemen.
Morillat.   Yes sir,
    We have reason, and some friends I can make.
Master. What I did, gentlemen, was for the general safety.
    If ye aim at me, I am not so tame.   55
Tibalt. Pray take my counsel, gallants.
    Fight not till the surgeon be well;

---

34. *purled*] embroidered, adorned—likening round scabs to the loops of purl stitch.

35. *ancient . . . Venus*] old syphilitic scars.

36. *pose*] perplex.

40–1. *brokers . . . metal*] pawnbrokers to relieve you of your finery when you get into debt. The vulnerability of high-living gallants to city opportunists is a recurrent theme in the period, and Albert suggests ironically that Franville will feel encumbered by his clothes if he has no opportunity to lose them.

42. *leathered captains*] gallants sporting the military look; cf. *Antipodes* III.161–3 and notes. The fashion must have been a recurrent one.

43. *dogfish . . . doublet*] a witty variation on the proverbial 'as proud as a dog in a doublet' (D452).

44. *tumble . . . tub*] waddle around. At this date *tub* was already applied to a clumsy ship, and *dogfish* was a common term of contempt.

45. *hatched sword*] one whose handle and scabbard are inlaid with jewels.

48. *double ruff*] the 'French fall' ruff which hung down in two or more pleats rather than sticking out at right angles.

49. *foisted*] cheated.

53. *some . . . make*] presumably a threat to encourage mutiny among the crew.

He's damnable sea-sick, and may spoil all.
Besides, he has lost his fiddlestick, and the best
Box of boar's grease. Why do you make such faces   60
And hand your swords?
Albert.   Who would ye fight with,
                                         gentlemen?
Who has done ye wrong? For shame, be better tempered.
No sooner come to give thanks for our safeties
But we must raise new civil broils amongst us?
Inflame those angry powers to shower new vengeance on
                                                    us?   65
What can we expect for these unmanly murmurs,
These strong temptations of their holy pities
But plagues in another kind, a fuller, so dreadful
That the singing storms are slumbers to it?
Tibalt. Be men, and rule your minds.   70
If you will needs fight, gentlemen,
And think to raise new riches by your valours,
Have at ye! I have little else to do now
I have said my prayers. You say you have lost,
And make your loss your quarrel,   75
And grumble at my captain here, and the master,
Two worthy persons—indeed, too worthy for such
                                                    rascals.
Thou galloon-gallant, and [*To Lamure*] Mammon, you
That build on golden mountains, thou money maggots!
Come, all draw your swords: ye say ye are miserable.   80
Albert. Nay hold, good Tibalt.
Tibalt.   Captain, let me correct 'em.—
I'll make ye ten times worse!—I will not leave 'em,
For look ye, fighting is as nourishing to me
As eating. I was born quarrelling.
Master.   Pray sir—
Tibalt. I will not leave 'em skins to cover 'em!   85
Do ye grumble when ye are well, ye rogues?
Master. Noble Dupont—
Tibalt.   Ye have clothes now, and ye prate!
Aminta. Pray gentlemen, for my sake be at peace.

---

59. *fiddlestick*] The word suitably describes the *glister-pipe* (22), but OED records
it as a nonce-substitute, here meaning something like 'his whatsit'. Tibalt means that
his companions need purging; in modern idiom, they are full of shit.

78. *galloon*-] frilly. Galoon was a tape or braid used for binding or trimming
(Linthicum); cf. Cotgrave: 'Gallonne... *edged, laced, or tyed with galloone lace*'.

Let it become me to make all friends.
Franville.   You
Have stopped our angers, lady.
Albert.   This shows noble.
Tibalt. 'Tis well, 'tis very well. There's half a biscuit,   90
Break't amongst ye all, and thank my bounty.
This is clothes and plate too! Come, no more quarrelling.

Enter SEBASTIAN *and* NICUSA.

Aminta. But ha! What things are these? Are they
Human creatures?
Tibalt.   I have heard of sea-calves.
Albert. They are no shadows sure, they have legs and arms.   95
Tibalt. They hang but lightly on, though.
Aminta.   How they look!
Are they men's faces?
Tibalt.   They have horse-tails growing to 'em,
Goodly long manes.
Aminta.   Alas, what sunk eyes they have!
How they are crept in, as if they had been frighted!
Sure they are wretched men.   100
Tibalt.   Where are their wardrobes?
Look ye, Franville: here are a couple of courtiers!
Aminta. They kneel. Alas, poor souls.
Albert.   What are ye? Speak:
Are ye alive, or wand'ring shadows
That find no peace on earth till ye reveal   105
Some hidden secret?
Sebastian.   We are men as you are;
Only our miseries make us seem monsters.

---

89. Let ... friends] *given to Lamure in F.*

---

89. *Let ... friends*] Attributed to Lamure in F, which suggests that a speech of his
has been cut.

95. *sea-calves*] seals.

96. *shadows*] ghosts.

97–108. *How ... hearts*] In Warner, Arbaces and his companion are 'altogether
unweaponed and naked, saving that their pined bodies were in some parts disorderly
covered with a fewe unhandsome rags: their lokes seemed wilde, their countenance
full of heavinesse, their colour swarth, their heare & beardes long, lothsome, and
unkembde ... being men in shape, they seemed monsters in show: but such monsters
as were rather to be pitied than to be feared' (Bv).

104–6. *Are ... secret?*] Testifying to the enduring popularity of the ghost in *Hamlet*, a
play of which distant echoes have already been heard in the opening scene (lines 58,
67).

If ever pity dwelt in noble hearts—
Albert. We understand 'em too: pray mark 'em, gentlemen.
Sebastian.   Or that heaven is pleased with human charity;   110
          If ever ye have heard the name of friendship,
          Or suffered in yourselves the least afflictions;
          Have gentle fathers that have bred ye tenderly
          And mothers that have wept for your misfortunes,
          Have mercy on our miseries.
Albert.   Stand up, wretches.   115
          Speak boldly, and have release.
Nicusa   If ye be Christians,
          And by that blessed name bound to relieve us,
          Convey us from this island.
Albert.   Speak, what are ye?
Sebastian. As you are, gentle born. To tell ye more
          Were but to number up our own calamities   120
          And turn your eyes wild with perpetual weepings.
          These many years, in this most wretched island
          We two have lived, the scorn and game of fortune.
          Bless yourselves from it, noble gentlemen!
          The greatest plagues that human nature suffers   125
          Are seated here: wildness and wants innumerable.
Albert. How came ye hither?
Nicusa.   In a ship, as you do;
          And—as you might have been, had not heaven
          Preserved ye for some more noble use—
          Wrecked desperately; our men and all consumed   130
          But we two, that still live and spin out
          The thin and ragged threads of our misfortunes.
Albert. Is there no meat above?
Sebastian.   Nor meat nor quiet;
          No summer here to promise anything,

109.] Cf. *The Tempest*, II.ii.65–7: 'This is some monster of the isle ... Where the
devil should he learn our language?' Both Shakespeare and Fletcher, working in a
romance idiom, none the less give exotic encounters a topical grounding. A French
pirate captain is presumably a good linguist, and contemporary accounts supply
models for Fletcher's Portuguese outcasts: Richard Jobson in *The Golden Trade*
(1623), an account of exploration up the Gambia river in 1620–1, tells of the 'vagrant
Portingall ... another sort of people we finde dwelling, or rather lurking ... only some
certaine way up the River ... these are, as they call themselves, *Portingales* ... It doth
manifestly appeare, that they are such, as have beene banished, or fled away, from
forth either of *Portingall*, or the Iles belonging unto that governement ... [They]
become in a manner naturalized ... still reserving carefully, the use of the *Portingall*
tongue, and with a kinde of an affectionate zeale, the name of Christians' (pp. 28–30).
    133. *above*] further inland.

Nor autumn to make full the reaper's hands.   135
The earth, obdurate to the tears of heaven,
Lets nothing shoot but poisoned weeds.
No rivers, nor no pleasant groves; no beasts.
All that were made for man's use fly this desert;
No airy fowl dares make his flight over it,   140
It is so ominous.
Serpents and ugly things, the shames of nature,
Roots of malignant tastes, foul standing waters.
Sometimes we find a fulsome sea-root
And that's a delicate! A rat sometimes,   145
And that we hunt like princes in their pleasure.
And when we take a toad, we make a banquet.

Aminta. For heaven's sake, let's aboard.

Albert. D'ee know no farther?

Nicusa.   Yes, we have sometimes seen
The shadow of a place inhabited,
And heard the noise of hunters, and have   150
Attempted to find it. So far as a river,
Deep, slow, and dangerous, fenced with high rocks
We have gone; but, not able to achieve
That hazard, return to our old miseries.
If this sad story may deserve your pities—   155

Albert. Ye shall aboard with us. We will relieve your miseries.

Sebastian. Nor will we be unthankful for this benefit.
No, gentlemen, we'll pay for our deliverance.
Look, ye that plough the seas for wealth and pleasures,   160
That outrun day and night with your ambitions,
Look on those heaps. They seem hard, ragged quarries:
Remove 'em and view 'em fully.

Master.   O heaven,

144–5. sea-root/And that's] *F;* sea-root and/That is *Dyce.*

---

136. *obdurate . . . heaven*] Warner's picture of desolation avoids Fletcher's awkward sentimentality: the island 'seemed abhorred of the gods, and wee founde it utterlye abandoned of men, beasts, fowles, fruites, and every other thing necessarye for mans behoofe' (C4).

140–3.] A cut may have weakened the syntax of this rather slack passage. The first line clumsily modifies the idea of flight in 139, and lazily anticipates II.ii.9–10, where the image is much more at home.

144. *fulsome*] stinking.

154–5. *achieve . . . hazard*] pass beyond that obstacle.

162–3. *Look . . . fully*] Sebastian reveals the treasure by drawing the curtain across the discovery space, and invites them to carry it out on to the main stage.

They are gold and jewels!
Sebastian.   Be not too hasty,
    Here lies another heap.
Morillat.   And here another.   165
    All perfect gold!
Albert.   Stand further off. You must
    Not be your own carvers.
Lamure.   We have shares, and deep ones.
Franville. Yes, sir, we'll maintain it. Ho, fellow sailors!

                    Enter Sailors.

Lamure. [*Draws his sword.*] Stand all to your freedoms. I'll
                                        have all this.
Franville. And I this.
Tibalt.   You shall be hanged first!   170
Lamure. My losses shall be made good.
Franville.   So shall mine,
    Or with my sword I'll do it! All that will share
    With us, assist us.
Tibalt.   Captain, let's set in.
Albert. This money will undo us, undo us all!
Sebastian. This gold was the overthrow of my happiness.   175
    I had command too, when I landed here,
    And led young, high and noble spirits under me.
    This cursèd gold enticing 'em, they set
    Upon their captain, on me that owned this wealth,
    And this poor gentleman;   180
    Gave us no few wounds, forced us from our own.
    And then their civil swords—who should be owners
    And who lords over all—turned against their own lives.
    First in their rage consumed the ship,
    That poor part of the ship that 'scaped the first wreck;   185
    Next their lives by heaps. O be you wise and careful!

168.1.] *not in F.*

---

167. *be ... carvers*] take what you please. Proverbial (C110).

shares] Booty was a familiar motive in early voyaging (see note to 202), but such opportunism sounded particularly shallow at a time when the Virginia Company could say that at Jamestown 'the Colony beginneth now to have the face and fashion of an orderly State ... each man having the shares of Land due to him set out, to hold and enjoy to him and his Heires' (*A Declaration of the State of the Colony and Affaires in Virginia*, 1620, pp. 4–5). Investors in the company were very likely to be found in the Blackfriars audience. Fletcher intensifies the satire at III.112.

178–86. *This ... heaps*] A summary of the harrowing account of the Assyrian party's self-destruction in Warner, Ch.V.

Lamure. We'll ha' more: sirrah, come, show it.
Franville. Or ten times worse afflictions than thou speak'st of.
Albert. Nay, and ye will be dogs. (*Beats 'em out.*)
Tibalt.　　　　　　　　　　　　　Let me come, captain:
　This golden age must have an iron ending.　　　　190
　Have at the bunch.

　　　　He beats 'em off. Exeunt fighting all except
　　　　　AMINTA, SEBASTIAN *and* NICUSA.

Aminta.　　　　　O Albert! O gentleman, O friends. *Exit.*
Sebastian. Come, noble nephew: if we stay here we die.
　Here rides their ship, yet all are gone to th' spoil.
　Let's make a quick use.
Nicusa.　　　　　　　Away dear uncle.
Sebastian. This gold was our overthrow.　　　　195
Nicusa. It may now be our happiness.　　　*Exeunt.*

　　　　Re-enter TIBALT *and the rest,* AMINTA *above.*

Tibalt. You shall have gold—yes, I'll cram it int'ee.
　You shall be your own carvers; yes, I'll carve ye.
Morillat. I am sore! I pray, hear reason—
Tibalt.　　　　　　　　　　I'll hear none.
　Covetous base minds have no reason.　　　　200
　I am hurt myself, but whilst I have a leg left
　I will so haunt your gilded souls. How d'ye, captain?
　Ye bleed apace—curse on the causers on't!
　Ye do not faint?
Albert.　　　　No, no; I am not so happy.
Tibalt. [*To the others*] D'ye howl? Nay, ye deserve it.　205
　Base, greedy rogues!—Come, shall we make an end of
　　　　　　　　　　　　　　　　　　'em?
Albert. They are our countrymen, for heaven's sake spare 'em.
　Alas, they are hurt enough, and they relent now.

---

191. *Exeunt ...* NICUSA] *Exit. F.　196.SD*] *Exit. F (in 195).　196.1. Re-enter*] *Enter*
F. AMINTA *above*] *next to 208–9 in* F.

196.1.] F does not specify an entry for Aminta at this point (see collation), but she
anxiously pursues the combatants at 191, and can use her vantage-point in the gallery
to observe them until her attention is caught by the departing ship.
　202. *gilded*] money-loving; specious. In *The Proceedings of the English Colonie in
Virginia* (Oxford, 1612), 'the worst mischiefe was, our gilded refiners with their
golden promises, made all men their slaves in hope of recompence, there was no talke,
no hope, no worke, but dig gold, wash gold, refine gold, load gold' (p. 21).

Aminta. O captain! captain!

Albert.   Whose voice is that?

Tibalt.   The lady's.

Aminta. Look, captain, look! Ye are undone, poor captain—   210
    We are all undone, all, all! We are all miserable.
    Mad, wilful men, ye are undone—your ship, your ship!

Albert. What of her?

Aminta.   She's under sail and floating.
    See where she flies—see, to your shames, you wretches,
    Those poor starved things that showed you gold.   *Exit.* 215

>   LAMURE *and* FRANVILLE *go up with* Sailors *to see the ship.*

First Sailor. They have cut the cables and got her out.
    The tide too has befriended 'em.

Master. Where are the sailors that kept her?

Boatswain.   Here, here in
    The mutiny, to take up money; and left
    No creature. Left the boat ashore too! This gold,   220
    This damned enticing gold!

Second Sailor.   How the wind drives her,
    As if it vied to force her from our furies!

Lamure. Come back, good old men!

Franville.   Good honest men, come back.

Tibalt. The wind's against ye: speak louder.

Lamure. Ye shall have all your gold again.—They see us!   225

Tibalt. Hold up your hands, and kneel, and howl, ye
                                        blockheads,
    They'll have compassion on ye—yes, yes,
    'Tis very likely! Ye have deserved it.
    D'ye look like dogs now?
    Are your mighty courages abated?   230

Albert. I bleed apace, Tibalt.

Tibalt.   Retire, sir,
    And make the best use of our miseries.
    They but begin now.

215.SD] *not in* F.   215.1. *with* Sailors] *not in* F.   233. *below*] *not in* F.

---

220. *boat*] i.e. the ship's boat or shallop used to ferry people and goods from anchorage to shore. The sailors clearly break a prime rule in leaving the boat where it can be found and taken.

221–2. *How...furies!*] Fletcher is less explicit than Warner in mitigating the heartlessness of the absconders: 'the two *Meades*...moved with compassion towards the ungratefull people, indeavoured in all they possible might to returne backe againe into their succour: but all in vaine, doe what they might, contrarie windes resisted their mercifull meaning' (sig.D).

Enter AMINTA *below.*

Aminta.   Are ye alive still?
Albert. Yes, sweet.
Tibalt.   Help him off, lady, and wrap him
  Warm in your arms. Here's something that's comfortable.   235
  Off with him handsomely. I'll come to ye straight—
                          Exeunt ALBERT *and* AMINTA.
  But vex these rascals a little.
Franville.   O, I
  Am hungry, and hurt, and I am weary.
Tibalt. Here's a pestle of a portigue, sir;
  'Tis excellent meat with sour sauce.
  And here's two chains—suppose 'em sausages.   240
  Then there wants mustard; but the fearful surgeon
  Will supply ye presently.
Lamure. O for that surgeon! I shall die else.
Tibalt. Faith, there he lies in the same pickle too.   245
Surgeon. My salves and all my instruments are lost,
  And I am hurt, and starved. Good sir, seek for
  Some herbs.
Tibalt.   Here's herb graceless: will that serve?
  Gentlemen, will ye go to supper?
All.   Where's the meat?
Tibalt. [*Mimics*] Where's the meat? What a veal voice is there!   250
Franville. Would we had it, sir, or anything else.
Tibalt. I would now cut your throat, you dog,
  But that I would not do you such a courtesy
  To take you from the benefit of starving.
  O, what a comfort will your worship have   255
  Some three days hence! Ye things beneath pity,
  Famine shall be your harbinger.

257. Famine] *F2; om. F.*

---

239. *pestle . . . portigue*] hunk of gold. *OED* treats *pestle* as a diminutive (i.e. a morsel); but cf. Cotgrave: 'jambe de pourceau. *A pestle of porke; a gammon*'. A *portigue* was a Portuguese coin worth between three and five sovereigns.

242. *mustard*] used as an emetic; but Mason, defending *fearful* in the same line, commented that the 'mustard that Tibalt alludes to, is . . . produced by fear' (pp. 315–16). *OED* gives no examples of this slang usage, but the scatology of 59–60 (and later III.i.39) lends support.

248. *herb graceless*] Perhaps Tibalt produces a dagger, which is the opposite of rue (pity), 'sour herb-of-grace' (*Richard II*, III.iv.106).

250. *veal*] pathetic, spineless—from the idea of 'bloodless', though *OED* does not support this figurative usage before the nineteenth century.

You must not look for down beds here
Nor hangings—though I could wish ye strong ones!
Yet here be many lightsome cool star chambers   260
Open to every sweet air, I'll assure ye,
Ready provided for ye, and so I'll leave ye.
Your first course is served, expect the second.   *Exit.*
Franville. A vengeance on these jewels.
Lamure.   O, this cursèd gold!
                                                    Exeunt.

---

259. ones] *F2;* on's *F.*

258.] A familiar admonition, particularly to gentlemen colonists in the harsh
conditions of Virginia: Thomas Hariot, in his *Briefe and True Report* on the 1585
settlement, noted that for those who 'were of a nice bringing up ... there were not to
be found any English cities, nor such faire houses, nor at their owne wish any of
their old accustomed dainty food, nor any soft beds of downe or feathers' so that
'the countrey was to them miserable, and their reports thereof according' (Hakluyt
VIII.351–2). This passage was closely paraphrased by Captain John Smith in his
description of recalcitrant elements in the colony twenty-five years later (*A Map of
Virginia*, 1612, p. 38), and this may have helped to give it the force of a literary trope.
    259. *hangings*] bed-hangings.
    strong ones!] i.e. halters.
    260. *star chambers*] Commentators have been inclined to see an allusion to Star
Chamber, the instrument of royal jurisdiction which became a symbol of authoritarian
rule under the early Stuarts, but Fletcher does not romanticise the escape from tyranny
into the wilderness. The allusion serves merely to emphasise Franville's removal from
courtly comforts and perhaps to remind him that he is in no position to pull rank on
Tibalt.

ACT II

SCENE i

Enter ALBERT *and* AMINTA.

Albert. Alas, dear soul, ye faint.
Aminta.   You speak the language
  Which I should use to you. Heaven knows, my weakness
  Is not for what I suffer in myself
  But to imagine what you endure, and to what fate
  Your cruel stars reserve ye.
Albert.   Do not add   5
  To my afflictions by your tender pities.
  Sure we have changed sexes: you bear calamity
  With a fortitude would become a man;
  I like a weak girl suffer.
Aminta.   O, but your wounds
  How fearfully they gape! And every one   10
  To me is a sepulchre. If I loved truly—
  Wise men affirm that true love can do wonders—
  This bathed in my warm tears would soon be cured
  And leave no orifice behind. Pray give me leave
  To play the surgeon and bind 'em up;   15
  The raw air rankles 'em.
Albert.   Sweet, we want means.
Aminta. Love can supply all wants.

                She binds his wounds with her hair.

Albert.   What have ye done, sweet?
  O sacrilege to beauty! There's no hair
  Of these pure locks by which the greatest king
  Would not be gladly bound, and love his fetters.   20
Aminta. O Albert, I offer
  This sacrifice of service to the altar
  Of your staid temperance, and still adore it.
  When with a violent hand you made me yours

ACT II SCENE i] *Actus Secundus F.*   17.SD] *not in F.*

17. SD] A common motif in the European romance tradition; on the Jacobean stage
Aminta perhaps used a sharp stone or a property rock to mime cutting her hair.

I cursed the doer; but now I consider   25
How long I was in your power, and with what honour
You entertained me! It being seldom seen
That youth and heat of blood could e'er prescribe
Laws to itself. Your goodness is the Lethe
In which I drown your injuries, and now   30
Live truly to serve ye. How do you, sir?
Receive you the least ease from my service?
If you do I am largely recompensed.
Albert. You good angels
That are engaged, when man's ability fails,   35
To reward goodness, look upon this lady.
Though hunger gripes my croaking entrails,
Yet when I kiss these rubies, methinks
I'm at a banquet, a refreshing banquet.
Speak, my blessed one: art not hungry?   40
Aminta. Indeed I could eat to bear you company.
Albert. Blush, unkind Nature,
If thou hast power or being to hear
Thyself, and by such innocence accused,
Must print a thousand kinds of shames upon   45
Thy various face. Canst thou supply a drunkard,
And with a prodigal hand reach choice of wines
Till he cast up thy blessings?—Or a glutton,
That robs the elements to soothe his palate
And only eats to beget appetite,   50
Not to be satisfied? And suffer here
A virgin, which the saints would make their guest,
To pine for hunger?

Horns within.

Ha! If my sense
Deceive me not, these notes take being from
The breath of men. Confirm me, my Aminta.   55
Again: this way the gentle wind conveys it to us.
Hear you nothing?
Aminta.   Yes, it seems free hunters' music.

---

29. *Lethe*] oblivion. In classical myth Lethe was the river of forgetfulness in Hades.
30. *your injuries*] the memory of your kidnapping me.
38. *rubies*] lips.
46. *various*] changeable.
47. *reach*] dish out.
48. *cast*] vomit.
57. *free . . . music*] the sound of horns accompanying the chase.

Albert. Still 'tis louder; and I remember the Portugals
    Informed us they had often heard such sounds,
    But ne'er could touch the shore from whence it came.   60
    Follow me, my Aminta. My good genius,
    Show me the way! [*Horns sound again.*] Still, still we are
                           directed.
    When we gain the top of this near rising hill
    We shall know further.   *Exeunt and enter above.*
                  Courteous Zephyrus
    On his dewy wings carries perfumes to cheer us.   65
    The air clears too, and now we may discern
    Another island, and questionless
    The seat of fortunate men. O that we could
    Arrive there!
Aminta.   No, Albert, 'tis not to be hoped.
    This envious torrent's cruelly interposed.
    We have no vessel that may transport us,   70
    Nor hath nature given us wings to fly.
Albert. Better try all hazards,
    Than perish here remediless. I feel
    New vigour in me, and a spirit that dares   75
    More than a man to serve my fair Aminta.
    These arms shall be my oars, with which I'll swim;
    And my zeal to save thy innocent self like wings
    Shall bear me up above the brackish waves.
Aminta. Will ye then leave me? Till now I ne'er was wretched.   80
Albert. My best Aminta, I swear by goodness 'tis
    Nor hope nor fear of myself that invites me
    To this extreme. 'Tis to supply thy wants, and believe me,
    Though pleasure met me in most ravishing forms,
    And happiness courted me to entertain her,   85
    I would nor eat nor sleep till I returned

---

80. Till . . . wretched] *given to Albert in F.*

---

61. *good genius*] guardian angel.

64. SD] The gallery was reached by a staircase behind the tiring-house façade.
While the actors are offstage, dramatic momentum would be maintained by the
elaborate winding of the horns, perhaps supplemented by musical effects which
continue through and provide an evocative backing to the rest of Albert's speech.
Blackfriars reputedly had the best orchestra in London, and many plays made extensive
use of music.

79. *brackish*] salty. *Another island* (67) implies a swim across open sea; but earlier
(I.iii.152) the barrier is a river which, if it were tidal, would be *brackish* in the proper
sense—fresh water contaminated by salt.

And crowned thee with my fortunes.
Aminta.   O, but your absence!
Albert. Suppose it but a dream; and as you may
    Endeavour to take rest. And when that sleep
    Deceives your hunger with imagined food,   90
    Think you have sent me for discovery
    Of some most fortunate continent, yet unknown,
    Which you are to be queen of.
    And now, ye powers that e'er heard lovers' prayers
    Or cherished pure affection, look on him   95
    That is your votary; and make it known
    Against all stops you can defend your own.   *Exeunt.*

ACT II   SCENE ii

Enter HIPPOLITA, CROCALE *and* JULETTA,
armed with bows and quivers.

Hippolita. How did we lose Clarinda?
Crocale.   When we
    Believed the stag was spent, and would take soil,
    The sight of the black lake which we supposed
    He chose for his last refuge frighted him more
    Than we that did pursue him.
Juletta.   That's usual,   5

_____

0.2.] *Dyce.*

92. *fortunate*] fertile, full of natural wealth—like the Americas.
96. *votary*] devotee.
0.1–2.] As Albert's first glimpse of them (81–3) implies, the women com-
bine bucolic grace with Amazonian power-dressing. The latter may have recalled
the description of Zelmane in Sidney's *New Arcadia*, richly dressed in 'a doublet of
sky-colour satin covered with plates of gold . . . on her thigh she ware a sword,
which . . . witnessed her to be an Amazon or one following that profession' (ed. V.
Skretkowicz, 1987, pp. 68–9). But it is also just possible that the three who appear
now did so in 1622 as 'Masculine-women' in a more topical sense, alluding to a recent
cross-dressing controversy in London by sporting broad-brimmed hats and French
doublets, and humorously confronting the polemicist's belief that the like of these
London transvestites 'are not found . . . in any Sea-mans travell' (*Hic Mulier*, 1620,
A3v). The use of boy-actors would play up the idea of ambivalent sex-roles, though
the actual gender of the characters is not meant to be in doubt.
2. *take soil*] take refuge in water.
3–5. *The . . . him*] A Renaissance audience would be reminded of the classical
Avernus (explicitly evoked in 9–10), but a closer analogue is the description of the
lake inhabited by the monster Grendel in *Beowulf*, 1367–72: 'A deer/Hunted through
the woods by packs of hounds,/ . . . prefers to die/On these shores, refuses to save its
life/In that water' (tr. B. Raffel, 1963). Such a reference would have been available
only to a tiny circle of scholars in 1622.

For death itself is not so terrible
To any beast of chase.
Hippolita.   Since we lived here,
We ne'er could force one to it.
Crocale.   'Tis so dreadful,
Birds that with their pinions cleave the air
Dare not fly over it. When the stag turned head   10
And we even tired with labour, Clarinda,
As if she were made of air and fire and had
No part of earth in her, eagerly pursued him.
Nor need we fear her safety: this place yields
Not fauns nor satyrs, or more lustful men.   15
Here we live secure,
And have among ourselves a commonwealth
Which in ourselves begun, with us must end.
Juletta. Ay, there's the misery.
Crocale.   But being alone,
Allow me freedom but to speak my thoughts.   20
The strictness of our governess that forbids us
On pain of death the sight and use of men
Is more than tyranny! For herself, she's past
Those youthful heats, and feels not the want
Of that which young maids long for; and her daughter   25
The fair Clarinda, though in few years
Improved in height and large proportion,
Came here so young
That scarce rememb'ring that she had a father
She never dreams of man. And should she see one,   30

9–10. *Birds . . . it*] Traditional lore about lake Avernus near Naples, familiar from
Virgil's *Aeneid*, VI.238–43, and repeated even in up-to-date guides like Peter Heylyn's
Microcosmos (Oxford 1621): '*lacus Avernus*, the stincke of which killeth birds as they
flie over it' (p. 92).

9. *pinions*] wings.

12–13. *made . . . her*] like Shakespeare's Cleopatra (*A&C*, V.ii.284–5), who was
perhaps for the Blackfriars audience an acceptable type of militant femininity.

15. *fauns . . . satyrs*] originally Roman rural deities; in pastoral, lustful goat-men
'with long tailes, and hornes on their heads, their bodies all hairy' (Sandys, *Ovid*, p.
154). The discoverers inevitably found them in exotic locations: André Thevet reports
that in the vicinity of the Moluccas 'ther are foure Ilands desert inhabited (as they say)
onely with *Satyres*' (*New found worlde*, 1568, fol. 90), and Torquemeda tells of an
Atlantic landfall on '*the Iland of Satyres*' where 'appeared certaine wilde men, of a
fierce & cruell resemblance, all covered with haire somewhat reddish, resembling in
each other part men, but onely that they had long tailes full of brissled haires like unto
horses'; a captured woman is subjected by them to 'all sort of fleshly abomination and
filthy lust' (p. 25).

17. *a commonwealth*] The Amazon ideal of a state run by women was a popular
debating point in the period.

In my opinion, 'a would appear
A strange beast to her.
Juletta.   'Tis not so with us!
Hippolita. For my part, I confess it. I was not made
    For this single life, nor do I love hunting so
    But that I had rather be the chase myself!   35
Crocale. By Venus—out upon me, I should have sworn
    By Diana!—I am of thy mind too, wench.
    And though I have ta'en an oath, not alone
    To detest but never to think of man,
    Every hour something tells me I am forsworn.   40
    For I confess, imagination helps me sometimes,
    And that's all is left for us to feed on;
    We might starve else! For if I have any pleasure
    In this life but when I sleep, I am a pagan.
    Then, from the courtier to the country clown,   45
    I have strange visions.
Juletta.   Visions, Crocale?
Crocale. Yes, and fine visions, too.
    And visions I hope in dreams are harmless
    And not forbid by our canons. The last night
    (Troth, 'tis a foolish one, but I must tell it)   50
    As I lay in my cabin, betwixt sleeping and waking—
Hippolita. Upon your back?
Crocale.   How should a young maid lie, fool,
    When she would be entranced?
Hippolita.   We are instructed.
    Forward, I prithee.
Crocale.   Methought a sweet young man
    In years some twenty, with a downy chin   55
    Promising a future beard, and yet no red one,
    Stole slyly to my cabin, all unbraced,
    Took me in his arms and kissed me twenty times,
    Yet still I slept.
Juletta.   Fie, thy lips run over, Crocale!

---

27. *Improved*] grown.

34–5. *nor . . . myself!*] In Shakespeare's *Dream* and *Two Noble Kinsmen*, Hippolyta is a keen hunter but has been tamed by marriage.

37. *Diana*] goddess of chastity. See note on Characters, 21.

53. *entranced*] transported—with an obvious sexual pun.

56. *and . . . one*] i.e. but not your typical man. A red beard was associated with lechery (which would hardly deter Crocale) but also functioned, via the medieval stage presentation of Judas with a red beard, as a dramatic symbol of deception and betrayal.

57. *unbraced*] with his doublet unfastened.

But to the rest.

Crocale.   Lord, what a man is this,   60
Thought I, to do this to a maid! Yet then,
For my life, I could not wake. The youth,
A little daunted, with a trembling hand
Heaved up the clothes—

Hippolita.   Yet still you slept.

Crocale.   I'faith I did.
And when methoughts he was warm by my side,   65
Thinking to catch him, I stretched out both mine arms.
And when I felt him not, I shrieked out
And waked for anger.

Hippolita.   'Twas a pretty dream.

Enter ALBERT, *staggering and collapsing.*

Crocale. Ay, if it had been a true one.

Juletta.   But stay,
What's here cast o'th' shore?

Hippolita.   'Tis a man!   70
Shall I shoot him?

Crocale.   No, no! 'Tis a handsome beast,
Would we had more o' the breed. Stand close, wenches,
And let's hear if he can speak.

Albert.   Do I yet live?
Sure it is air I breathe: what place is this?
Sure something more than human keeps residence here,   75
For I have passed the Stygian gulf and touch
Upon the blessed shore! 'Tis so: this is
The Elysian shade; these, happy spirits that here
Enjoy all pleasures.

Hippolita.   He makes towards us.

Juletta. Stand, or I'll shoot.

Crocale.   Hold! He makes no resistance.   80

Albert. Be not offended, goddesses, that I fall
Thus prostrate at your feet. Or if not such,

68.1. *staggering and collapsing*] not in F.

76–8. *Stygian . . . shade*] The Styx is the river surrounding the classical underworld
which the dead must cross to reach the Elysian fields.

81. *goddesses*] The Amazons were thought of as tall and stately, and Purchas
records a Mexican legend in which they are 'accounted of the people for Goddesses,
and whiter then other women' (XVIII.59–60).

But nymphs of Dian's train that range these groves
Which you forbid to men, vouchsafe to know
I am a man, a wicked, sinful man; and yet not sold   85
So far to impudence as to presume
To press upon your privacies, or provoke
Your heavenly angers. 'Tis not for myself
I beg thus poorly, for I am already
Wounded, wounded to death, and faint. My last breath   90
Is for a virgin comes as near yourselves
In all perfection, as what's mortal may
Resemble things divine. O pity her,
And let your charity free her from that desert—
If heavenly charity can reach to hell,   95
For sure that place comes near it. And where'er
My ghost shall find abode, eternally
I shall pour blessings on ye. [*He faints.*]
Hippolita.   By my life
I cannot hurt him.
Crocale.   Though I lose my head
For it, nor I. I must pity him, and will.   100

Enter CLARINDA.

Juletta. But stay—Clarinda.
Clarinda. What new game have ye found here, ha?
What beast is this lies wallowing in his gore?
Crocale. Keep off.
Clarinda.   Wherefore, I pray? I ne'er turned
From a fell lioness robbed of her whelps,   105
And shall I fear dead carrion?
Juletta.   O, but—
Clarinda. But? What is't?
Hippolita.   It is infectious.
Clarinda.   Has it not
A name?
Crocale.   Yes, but such a name from which,
As from the devil, your mother commands us fly.
Clarinda. Is it a man?
Crocale.   It is.
Clarinda.   What a brave shape   110

83–7. *groves . . . privacies*] alluding to the story of Actaeon who spied on Diana
and her nymphs bathing, and was punished by being turned into a stag and torn apart
by his own hounds (Ovid, *Metamorphoses*, III.174ff).
    105. *fell*] savage.

It has in death! How excellent would it
Appear had it life. Why should it be
Infectious? I have heard my mother say
I had a father, and was not he a man?
Crocale. Questionless, madam.
Clarinda.   Your fathers too were men?   115
Juletta. Without doubt, lady.
Clarinda.   And without such
It is impossible we could have been.
Hippolita. A sin against nature to deny it.
Clarinda.   Nor
Can you or I have any hope to be
A mother without the help of men.
Crocale.   Impossible!   120
Clarinda. Which of you then most barbarous, that knew
You from a man had being and owe to it
The name of parent, durst presume to kill
The likeness of that thing by which you are?
Whose arrows made these wounds? Speak or, by Dian,   125
Without distinction I'll let fly at ye all.
Juletta. Not mine.
Hippolita.   Nor mine.
Crocale.   'Tis strange to see her moved thus.
Restrain your fury, madam. Had we killed him
We had but performed your mother's command.
Clarinda. But if she command unjust and cruel things   130
We are not to obey it.
Crocale.   We are innocent.
Some storm did cast him shipwrecked on the shore—
As you see, wounded. Nor durst we be surgeons
To such your mother doth appoint for death.
Clarinda. Weak excuse! Where's pity?   135
Where's soft compassion? Cruel and ungrateful!
Did providence offer to your charity
But one poor subject to express it on,
And in't to show our wants too, and could you
So carelessly neglect it?
Hippolita.   For aught I know   140
He's living yet; and you may tempt your mother

---

126. *distinction*] discriminating one from another.
139. *our wants*] just what we've been missing.
141. *tempt*] i.e. to be less rigorous.

By giving him succour.
Clarinda.   Ha! Come near, I charge ye.
So, bend his body. Softly! Rub his temples—
Nay, that shall be my office. How the red
Steals into his pale lips! Run and fetch   145
The simples with which my mother healed my arm
When last I was wounded by the boar.
Crocale.   Do!
  [_Aside to Hippolita_] But remember her to come after ye
That she may behold her daughter's charity.
                                    Exit HIPPOLITA.

Clarinda. Now he breathes! The air passing through   150
The Arabian groves yields not so sweet an odour—
Prithee taste it; taste it, good Crocale.
Yet I envy thee so great a blessing. 'Tis
Not sin to touch these rubies, is it?
Juletta.   Not,
  I think.
Clarinda.   Or thus to live chameleon-like?   155
  I could resign my essence to live ever thus.

              Re-enter HIPPOLITA _with simples._

O welcome! Raise him up gently. Some soft hand
Bound up these wounds. A woman's hair! What fury
For which my ignorance does not know a name
Is crept into my bosom? But I forget   160
My pious work. Now if this juice hath power
Let it appear. [ALBERT _stirs._] His eyelids ope: prodigious!
Two suns break from these orbs.
Albert.   Ha, where am I?
  What new vision's this? To what goddess do I owe
This second life? Sure thou art more than mortal,   165

156.1.] _Enter Hipolita F (next to_ 160).

146. _simples_] herbal remedies.
150–1. _The . . . odour_] Arabia Felix was renowned for the aroma of its spices,
which provided a favourite metaphor for the sweetness of a woman's breath. Clarinda
appropriates it in feminist fashion.
153. _Yet . . . thee_] Having invited Crocale to kiss Albert, she perhaps prevents her
with these words: this might motivate Crocale's slightly sour comment at 179–80.
154. _rubies_] lips. Clarinda may not have seen a man but she knows the idiom of
love poetry. Cf. II.i.38–9.
155. _chameleon-like_] i.e. on air.
156. _resign my essence_] surrender my being. Clarinda's paradoxical statement
registers the crumbling of her feminist sense of self.

And any sacrifice of thanks or duty
In poor and wretched man to pay, comes short
Of your immortal bounty. But to show
I am not unthankful, thus in humility
I kiss the happy ground you have made sacred   170
By bearing of your weight.
Clarinda.   No goddess, friend,
But made of that same brittle mould as you are.
One too acquainted with calamities
And from that apt to pity. Charity ever
Finds in the act, reward, and needs no trumpet   175
In the receiver. O forbear this duty—[*Raises him.*]
I have a hand to meet with yours, and lips
To bid yours welcome.
Crocale.   I see that by instinct,
Though a young maid hath never seen a man,
Touches have titillations and inform her.   180

Enter ROSELLIA.

But here's our governess.
Now I expect a storm!
Rosellia.   Child of my flesh,
And not of my fair unspotted mind,
Unhand this monster!
Clarinda.   Monster, mother?
Rosellia.   Yes!
And every word he speaks, a siren's note   185
To drown the careless hearer. Have I not taught thee
The falsehood and the perjuries of men?
On whom but for a woman to show pity
Is to be cruel to herself. The sovereignty
Proud and imperious men usurp upon us   190
We confer on ourselves, and love those fetters
We fasten to our freedoms. Have we, Clarinda,
Since thy father's wrack, sought liberty
To lose it uncompelled? Did fortune guide—
Or rather destiny—our bark, to which   195
We could appoint no port, to this blest place,

---

167. *In*] that is within the capacity of.
185. *siren's note*] a nice feminist inversion of the Siren myth.
188. *but*] merely.
193. *wrack*] overthrow, ruin. *F*'s spelling (modernised to 'wreck' at I.iii.130) here preserves the wider meaning of the word: Rosellia doesn't yet know that Sebastian was a castaway after the storm separated their ships.

Inhabited heretofore by warlike women
That kept men in subjection? Did we then,
By their example, after we had lost
All we could love in man, here plant ourselves   200
With execrable oaths never to look
On man but as a monster? And wilt thou
Be the first precedent to infringe those vows
We made to heaven?

Clarinda.   Hear me, and hear me with justice.
And as ye are delighted in the name   205
Of mother, hear a daughter that would be
Like you. Should all women use this obstinate
Abstinence you would force upon us, in
A few years the whole world would be peopled
Only with beasts.

Hippolita.   We must and will have men!   210

Crocale. Ay, or we'll shake off all obedience.

Rosellia.   Are
Ye mad? Can no persuasion alter ye?
Suppose you had my suffrage to your suit:
Can this shipwrecked wretch supply them all?

Albert. Hear me, great lady.   215
I have fellows in my misery, not far hence,
Divided only by this hellish river.
There live a company of wretched men
Such as your charity may make your slaves.
Imagine all the miseries mankind   220
May suffer under, and they groan beneath 'em.

Clarinda. But are they like to you?

Juletta.   Speak they your language?

Crocale. Are they able, lusty men?

Albert.   They were, good ladies.
And in their May of youth, of gentle blood
And such as may deserve ye. Now cold and hunger   225
Hath lessened their perfection; but restored
To what they were, I doubt not they'll appear

---

203. precedent] president *F*.   214. them] *F*; ye *Dyce*.

---

197. *warlike women*] The Amazons, variously located by classical authorities in
Africa and Asia Minor, and discovered in America by Renaissance travellers.
200. *plant*] a common term in the period for the act of establishing a colony.
201. *execrable*] cursing.
213. *suffrage*] assent (literally 'vote').
214. *them all*] i.e. the needs of you all.

Worthy your favours.

Juletta.   This is a blessing
We durst not hope for.

Clarinda.   Dear mother, be not obdurate.

Rosellia. Hear then my resolution, and labour not   230
To add to what I'll grant, for 'twill be fruitless.
You shall appear as good angels to these wretched men.
In a small boat we'll pass o'er to 'em,
And bring 'em comfort. If you like their persons
And they approve of yours—for we'll force nothing,   235
And since we want ceremonies, each one
Shall choose a husband, and enjoy his company
A month, but that expired you shall no more
Come near 'em. If you prove fruitful
The males ye shall return to them, the females   240
We will reserve ourselves. This is the utmost
Ye shall e'er obtain. As ye think fit,
Ye may dismiss this stranger, and prepare
Tomorrow for the journey.   *Exit.*

Clarinda.   Come, sir, will ye walk?
We will show ye our pleasant bowers, and something ye   245
Shall find to cheer your heart.

Albert.   Excellent lady,
Though 'twill appear a wonder one near starved
Should refuse rest and meat, I must not take
Your noble offer. I left in yonder desert
A virgin almost pined.

Clarinda.   She's not your wife?   250

Albert. No, lady, but my sister. [*Aside*] 'Tis now dangerous
To speak truth.—To her I deeply vowed
Not to taste food or rest, if fortune brought it me,
Till I blessed her with my return. Now if
You please to afford me an easy passage   255
To her, and some meat for her recovery,

---

236. *want*] lack.

240–1. *The . . . ourselves*] This practice was a prominent part of the Amazon legend, and ascribed by travel writers to warrior groups like the 'legion of women' which is said to form part of the Emperor of Monomotapa's defence force: 'These women have places appointed them to dwell in by themselves, and at certayne times have the company of men, that they may have children, which if they be boyes, they send unto their fathers, if daughters, they keepe them' (Linschoten, *Voyages*, 1598, p. 212).

251. *dangerous*] Albert may be rationalising his unwillingness to disappoint Clarinda, but his reaction also registers the sexual volatility of the women.

I shall live your slave, and thankfully she shall
Ever acknowledge her life at your service.
Clarinda. You plead so well, I can deny ye nothing.
I myself will see you furnished,   260
And with the next sun visit and relieve thee.
Albert. Ye are all goodness!   *Exeunt.*

ACT III

Enter severally LAMURE, FRANVILLE *and* MORILLAT.

Lamure. O, what a tempest have I in my stomach!
    How my empty guts cry out! My wounds ache;
    Would they would bleed again, that I might get
    Something to quench my thirst.
Franville. O Lamure, the happiness my dogs had   5
    When I kept house at home! They had a storehouse,
    A storehouse of most blessed bones and crusts.
    Happy crusts! O, how sharp hunger pinches me!
Morillat. O my importunate belly! I have nothing
    To satisfy thee. (*Exit* Franville.) I have sought as far   10
    As my weak legs would carry me, yet can
    Find nothing—neither meat nor water,
    Nor anything that's nourishing. My belly's
    Grown together like an empty satchel.

Re-enter FRANVILLE.

Lamure. How now, what news?
Morillat.   Hast any meat yet?   15
Franville. Not a bit that I can see. Here be
    Goodly quarries, but they be cruel hard
    To gnaw. I ha' got some mud, we'll eat it with spoons,
    Very good thick mud—but it stinks damnably.
    There's old rotten trunks of trees too, but not a leaf   20
    Nor blossom in all the island.
Lamure.   How it looks!
Morillat. It stinks too.
Lamure.   It may be poison.
Franville.   Let it
    Be anything, so I can get it down. Why man,
    Poison's a princely dish.
Morillat.   Hast thou no biscuit?
    No crumbs left in thy pocket? Here's my doublet: 25

ACT III] *Actus Tertius. F.*   14.1. *Re-enter*] *Enter F.*

17. *quarries*] rocks, but punning on the sense of game meat.

Give me but three small crumbs.
Franville.   Not for three kingdoms,
  If I were master of 'em. O Lamure,
  But one poor joint of mutton we ha' scorned, man!
Lamure. Thou speakest of paradise.
Franville.   Or but the snuffs
  Of those healths we have lewdly at midnight   30
  Flung away.
Morillat.   Ah, but to lick the glasses!

Enter Surgeon.

Franville. Here comes the surgeon.—What hast thou
                                          discovered?
  Smile, smile and comfort us.
Surgeon.   I am expiring;
  Smile they that can. I can find nothing, gentlemen.
  Here's nothing can be meat without a miracle.   35
  O that I had my boxes and my lints now,
  My stupes, my tents and those sweet helps of nature,
  What dainty dishes could I make of 'em!
Morillat. Hast ne'er an old suppository?
Surgeon. O would I had, sir.   40
Lamure. Or but the paper where such a cordial,
  Potion or pills hath been entombed.
Franville. Or the blessed bladder where a cooling glister—
Morillat. Hast thou no cerecloths left? Nor any old poulties?
Franville. We care not to what it hath been ministered.   45
Surgeon. Sure, I have none of these dainties, gentlemen.
Franville. Where's the great wen
  Thou cutt'st from Hugh the sailor's shoulder?
  That would serve now for a most princely banquet.
Surgeon. Ay, if we had it, gentlemen.   50

---

29. *snuffs*] dregs.
30. *healths*] toasts.
31. *Flung away*] knocked back.
36. *boxes*] of drugs and ointments (one of the original senses of the word).
lints] soft dressings.
37. *stupes . . . tents*] pieces or rolls of medicated material used to probe and cleanse wounds.
43. *bladder*] skin or leather container. This line has no end-punctuation in F, suggesting either that Franville is interrupted or that a cut was made, possibly to truncate a particularly disgusting suggestion.
44. *cerecloths*] waxed bandages used to treat bruises and muscular pain.
poulties] poultices.
47. *wen*] lump, tumour.

I flung it overboard, slave that I was.
Lamure. A most unprovident villain!
Surgeon.   If I
  Had anything that were but supple now,
  I could make salads of your shoes, gentlemen,
  And rare ones—anything unctuous.
Morillat. Ay, and then we might fry the soles i'th'sun.   55
  The soles would make a second dish.
Lamure. Or souse 'em in the salt water,
  An inner sole well soused—

Enter AMINTA.

Franville.   Here comes the woman.
  It may be she has meat, and may relieve us.   60
  Let's withdraw and mark and then be ready;
  She'll hide her store else and so cozen us.

They conceal themselves.

Aminta. How weary and how hungry am I!
  How feeble and how faint is all my body!
  Mine eyes, like spent lamps glowing out, grow heavy,   65
  My sight forsaking me; and all my spirits
  As if they heard my passing bell go for me
  Pull in their powers and give me up to destiny.
  O for a little water! a little, little meat,
  A little to relieve me ere I perish.   70
  I had whole floods of tears awhile that nourished me,
  But they are all consumed for thee, dear Albert.
  For thee they are spent, for thou art dead;
  Merciless fate hath swallowed thee. O, I
  Grow heavy; sleep is a salve for misery.   75
  Heaven look on me, and either take my life
  Or make me once more happy. [*She sleeps.*]
Lamure. [*Advancing*]   She's fast asleep
  Already. Why should she have this blessing
  And we wake still, wake to our wants?
Morillat. This thing hath been our overthrow, and all   80
  These biting mischiefs that fall on us are come

62.1.] *not in F.*   77. She's F2; Hee's F.

---

55. *unctuous*] oily, like an ointment.
59. *soused*] pickled.

Through her means.
Franville.   True. We were bound, ye all know,
For happy places and most fertile islands
Where we had constant promises of all things.
She turned the captain's mind, and must   85
Have him go in search, I know not of who
Nor to what end—of such a fool her brother,
And such a coxcomb her kinsman, and we
Must put in everywhere! She has put us in now,
I'faith.
Lamure.   Why should we consume thus, and starve?   90
Have nothing to relieve us, and she live there
That bred all our miseries, unroasted
Or unsod?
Morillat.   I have read in stories—
Lamure. Of such restoring meats: we have examples,
Thousand examples and allowed for excellent.   95
Women that have eat their children, men their slaves;
Nay, their brothers. But these are nothing:
Husbands devoured their wives (they are their chattels),
And of a schoolmaster that in a time of famine
Powdered up all his scholars.
Morillat.   She's young and tidy;   100
In my conscience she'll eat delicately,
Just like young pork a little lean.
Your opinion, surgeon.
Surgeon.   I think she may
Be made good meat. But look, we shall want salt.

83.] *happy . . . islands*] Phrasing which reveals the literary and mythical roots of the colonist's dream. Torquemeda (p. 90) declares that amongst the ancients 'the commonest opinion was, that the Elisian fields were those, which we now call the fortunate Ilands'—i.e. the Canary Isles, renowned 'for their fertility, and rare immunities' (P. Heylyn, *Microcosmos*, 1621, p. 398). The Atlantic islands had mostly proved very productive.

84. *constant promises*] The propaganda designed to attract funds and colonists to Virginia was insistent, from Hariot's 1588 catalogue of 'Merchantable commodities' (Hakluyt VIII.353ff) to the latest advertisement in 1620: 'We rest in great assurance, that this Countrey, as it is seated neere the midst of the world, betweene the extreamities of heate and cold . . . is capable . . . of the richest commodities of most parts of the earth' (*A Declaration of . . . Virginia*, pp. 2–3). The writer is careful to point out, for the benefit of gentlemen, that this means not just abundant raw materials but also products like wines and silks.

89. *put in*] i.e. to port.

90. *consume*] waste away.

93. *unsod*] unboiled.

100. *Powdered up*] salted and preserved.

tidy] firm.

Franville. Tush, she needs no powdering.

Surgeon.   I grant ye;   105
　　But to suck out the humourous parts, by all means
　　Let's kill her in a chase, she'll eat the sweeter.

Lamure. Let's kill her any way, and kill her quickly
　　That we might be at our meat.

Surgeon.   How if the captain—

Morillat. Talk not of him. He's dead, and the rest famished.   110
　　Wake her, surgeon, and cut her throat,
　　And then divide her, every man his share.

Franville. She wakes herself.

Aminta.   Holy and good things keep me!
　　What cruel dreams have I had.—Who are these?
　　O they are my friends! For heaven's sake, gentlemen,   115
　　Give me some food to save my life. If ye have aught to
　　　　　　　　　　　　　　　　　　　　　　　　spare,
　　A little to relieve me. I may bless ye,
　　For, weak and wretched, ready to perish
　　Even now I die.

Morillat.   You'll save a labour then.
　　You bred these miseries, and you shall pay for't.   120
　　We have no meat, nor where to have we know not;
　　Nor how to pull ourselves from these afflictions.
　　We are starved too, famished, all our hopes deluded.
　　Yet ere we die thus, we'll have one dainty meal.

Aminta. Shall I be with ye, gentlemen?   125

Lamure. Yes, marry shall ye! In our bellies, lady.
　　We love you well—

Aminta.   What said you, sir?

Lamure.   Marry,
　　We'll eat your ladyship.

Franville. You that have buried us in this base island,
　　We'll bury ye in a more noble monument.   130

Surgeon. Will ye say your prayers, that I may perform, lady?
　　We are wondrous sharp set. Come, gentlemen,

---

106. *humourous parts*] morbid fluids. Humours theory—the doctrine that physical
health depends on the proper balance of four essential elements in the body—is here
invoked to support the widespread belief that hunted or baited flesh makes better
eating. Game meats were thought to be otherwise hard to digest.

111–12. *cut . . . share*] Fletcher creates black comedy with this parody of Sebastian's
reductive logic in *The Tempest*, II.i.285–9.

132. *sharp set*] ravenous; the innuendo of 'sexually aroused' is more apparent when
the phrase is repeated at 152.

Who are for the hinder parts?
Morillat.   I.
Franville.   I.
Lamure.   And I.
Surgeon. Be patient,
    They will not fall to every man's share.   135
Aminta. O hear me! Hear me, ye barbarous men.
Morillat. Be short and pithy.
    Our stomachs cannot stay a long discourse.
Surgeon. And be not fearful, for I'll kill ye daintily.
Aminta. Are ye not Christians?   140
Lamure. Why, do not Christians eat women?
Aminta. Eat one another? 'Tis most impious!
Surgeon. Come, come—
Aminta.   O, help, help, help!
Tibalt. [*Off stage*]   The lady's voice!

    Enter TIBALT, Master *and Sailors.*

    Stand off, slaves! What do you intend, villains?
    I have strength enough left me, if you abuse this soul, to—   145
Master. They would have ravished her, upon my life.
    Speak, how was it, lady?
Aminta. Forgive 'em, 'twas their hungers.
Tibalt.   Ha, their hungers!
Master. They would have eaten her.
Tibalt.   O damned villains!
    Speak, is it true?
Surgeon.   I confess an appetite.   150
Tibalt. An appetite? I'll fit ye for an appetite!
    Are ye so sharp set that her flesh must serve you?
    Murder's a main good service with your worships.
    Since ye would be such devils, why did you not
    Begin with one another handsomely,   155
    And spare the woman to beget more food on?
Aminta. Good sir—
Tibalt.   You shall grow mummy, rascals;

---

    133. *hinder parts*] hindquarters.
    141. *do . . . women?*] The gallants seem to have been listening to the renegades who deserted the Jamestown colony in 1609–10 and once back in England 'roared out the tragicall historie of the man eating of his dead wife in *Virginia*' (*A true declaration of Virginia*, 1610, p. 38). In putting the record straight, the Virginia Company goes to some lengths (pp. 38–9) to make clear that this notorious case had nothing to do with famine.
    153. *service*] (1) course (of a meal); (2) armed (military) action.
    157. *mummy*] dead meat. Since dried flesh was also used for various medicinal purposes, Tibalt echoes the repulsive recipes of 37–50.

    I'll make you fall to your brawns and your buttocks
    And worry one another like keen bandogs.
Aminta. Good sir, be merciful.   160
Tibalt. You shall know what 'tis to be damned cannibals.

                        Enter ALBERT.

Aminta. O my best friend!
Albert.   Alas, poor heart—here,
    Here's some meat and sovereign drink to ease you.
    Sit down, gentle sweet.
Aminta.   I am blessed to see you.
Tibalt. Sir, not within forty foot of this food!   165
    If you do, dogs—
All.   O captain, captain, captain!
Albert. Ye shall have meat, all of you.
Tibalt.   Captain,
    Hear me first. Hark, 'tis so inhuman!
    I would not ha' the air corrupted with it. [*Whispers.*]
Albert. O barbarous men!—Sit down, Dupont! Good master,   170
    And honest sailors!
Tibalt.   But stand you off and wait
    Upon our charity. I'll wait on you else!
    And touch nothing but what's flung t'ye as if you
    Were dogs. If you do, I'll cut your fingers, friends;
    I'll spoil your carving.
Aminta. [*Giving food*]   There, wretches, there.   175
Tibalt. Eat your meat handsomely now, and give heaven
                                                  thanks.
Albert. There's more bread.
Tibalt.   See, they snarl like dogs.
    Eat quietly, you rascals, eat quietly.
Albert. There is drink too.
Tibalt.   Come, come, I'll fill you each
    Your cups. Ye shall not surfeit!
Aminta.   And what   180

---

165. Sir, not] *F;* Stir not *F2.*

---

    158. *brawns*] arms or calves.
    159. *bandogs*] fierce chained dogs, usually mastiffs.
    165. *Sir*] F2's *Stir not* is attractive, but the implied SD in *F* provides a more specific
focus, as Tibalt warns off the first man to try his luck.
    170–1. *Sit . . . sailors!*] Albert is trying to prevent a general assault on the would-be
cannibals.
    172. *wait on*] attend to, deal with.

Have you discovered?
Albert.   Sweet, a paradise.
A paradise inhabited with angels—
Such as you are! Their pities make 'em angels.
They gave me these viands, and supplied me
With these precious drinks.   185
Aminta. Shall not we see 'em?
Albert.   Yes, they will see you
Out of their charities. Having heard our story
They will come and comfort us, come presently.
We shall no more know wants nor miseries.
Aminta. Are they all women?
Albert.   All, and all in love with us.   190
Aminta. How!
Albert. Do not mistake: in love with our misfortunes;
They will cherish and relieve our men.
Tibalt. [*To the gallants*] Do you shrug now,
And pull up your noses? You smell comfort!   195
See, they stretch out their legs like dottrels,
Each like a new Saint Denis.
Albert.   Dear mistress,
When you would name me, and the women hear,
Call me your brother, you I'll call my sister,
And pray, observe this all—   200
Why do you change colour, sweet?
Aminta. Eating too much meat.
Albert.   Sauced with jealousy.
Fie, fie, dear saint: i'faith, ye are to blame.
Are ye not here? Here, fixed in my heart? [*Horns sound.*]
All. Hark, hark!   205

---

202. Sauced] *F2;* Sawce *F.*

---

188. *presently*] without delay.
196. *stretch . . . dottrels*] The dotterel is a species of plover, which because it was easily caught became synonymous with a dupe or simpleton. Thomas Fuller describes it as 'so *ridiculously Mimical*, that . . . As the *Fowler* stretcheth forth his *Arms* and *Legs*, going towards the *Bird*, so the *Bird* extendeth his *Legs* and *Wings* approaching the *Fowler*, till surprised in the Net' (*Worthies*, 1642, II.149).
197. *Saint Denis*] The patron saint of France, martyred in AD 250. After being decapitated he picked up his head and walked five miles to his place of burial. Tibalt may be drawing an irreverent analogy with the gallant who is all leg and no brain; but probably this is an allusion to the story of St Denis in the wilderness, told in Richard Johnson's *The Most Famous History of the Seaven Champions of Christendome* (1596): 'he indured such a pennurie and scarcitie of victualles: that hee was forced . . . to feede upon the hearbes of the fields, & the fruits of trees, till the haires of his head were like to Egles feathers, and the nayles of his fingers to birds clawes' (p. 34).

Enter ROSELLIA, CLARINDA, CROCALE, HIPPOLITA
and JULETTA.

Albert. They are come. Stand ready, and look nobly,
   And with all humble reverence receive 'em.
   Our lives depend upon their gentle pities,
   And death waits on their anger. [*Takes Aminta aside.*]
Morillat.   Sure they are fairies.
Tibalt. Be they devils, devils of flesh and blood,   210
   After so long a lent and tedious voyage
   To me they are angels.
Franville.   O for some eringoes!
Lamure. Potatoes, or cantharides.
Tibalt.   Peace, you rogues
   That buy abilities of your 'pothecaries!
   Had I but took the diet of green cheese   215
   And onions for a month, I could do wonders.
Rosellia. Are these the jewels you run mad for?
   What can you see in one of these
   To whom you would vouchsafe a gentle touch?
   Can nothing persuade you to love yourselves   220
   And place your happiness in cold and chaste
   Embraces of each other?
Juletta.   This is from
   The purpose.
Hippolita.   We had your grant to have them
   As they were.
Clarinda. [*Aside*] 'Tis a beauteous creature,
   And to myself I do appear deformed
   When I consider her. And yet she is   225
   The stranger's sister: why then should I fear?
   She cannot prove my rival.
Rosellia.   When you repent

---

211. *lent*] slow, drawn-out (from Italian *lento*); F's *Lent* reinforces the idea of a
spell of enforced abstinence. The sex-starved sailor is a common figure: cf. *Pericles*,
IV.vi.42 (Arden ed.), 'Faith, she would serve after a long voyage at sea.'
   212–13. *eringoes . . . cantharides*] all considered aphrodisiacs in the period: unlike
Tibalt, his companions clearly do not feel up to the sexual challenge of the women.
Eringo is the shrub known as sea-holly, though the word usually described its candied
root (cf.V.ii.44), and cantharides were dried beetles used for cosmetic and medicinal
purposes.
   213. *Potatoes*] These came to Europe from the Americas; it appears to be the sweet
potato from 'hotte regions' that was thought to 'strengthen the bodie' and 'procure
bodily lust' (Gerard's *Herball*, 1597, pp. 780–1).
   214. *abilities*] bodily strength; here, sexual capacity.
   215. *but took*] eaten nothing but.

That you refused my counsel, may it add
To your afflictions that you were forewarned,   230
Yet leaped into the gulf of your misfortunes.
But have your wishes.
Master.   Now she makes to us.
Aminta. I am instructed. But take heed, Albert,
You prove not false.
Albert.   Ye are your own assurance,
And so acquainted with your own perfections   235
That weak doubts cannot reach you. Therefore fear not.
Rosellia. That you are poor and miserable men
My eyes inform me; that without our succours
Hope cannot flatter you to dream of safety.
The present plight you are in can resolve you   240
That to be merciful is to draw near
The heavenly essence. Whether you will be
Thankful I do not question, nor demand
What country bred you; what names, what manners.
To us it is sufficient we relieve   245
Such as have shapes of men; and I command you,
As we are not ambitious to know
Further of you, that on pain of death
You presume not to enquire what we are
Or whence derived.
Albert.   In all things we obey you,   250
And thankfully we ever shall confess
Ourselves your creatures.
Rosellia.   You speak as becomes you.
First then, and willingly, deliver up
Those weapons we could force from you.
Albert. We lay 'em down most gladly at your feet.   255
Tibalt. I have had many a combat with a tall wench,
But never was disarmed before.
Rosellia.   And now hear comfort.
Your wants shall be supplied, and though it be
A debt women may challenge to be sued to,
Especially from such they may command,   260

---

230. forewarned] *Sympson* (ed. *Works of B&F*, 1750); forward *F.*

240. *resolve you*] i.e. save you by convincing us.
256. *tall*] lusty, spirited.
258–9. *though . . . to*] although women are entitled to choose from among their suitors.

We give up to you that power, and therefore
Freely each make his choice.
Franville.   Then here I fix.
Morillat. Nay, she is mine—I eyed her first.
Lamure.   This mine.
Tibalt. Stay, good rascals. You are too forward, sir gallant.
You are not giving order to a tailor   265
For the fashion of a new suit.
Nor are you in your warehouse, master merchant.
Stand back and give your betters leave, your betters,
And grumble not. If ye do, as I love meat
I will so swinge the salt itch out on you.   270
Captain, master, and the rest of us
That are brothers and good fellows, we have been
Too late by the ears, and yet smart for our follies.
To end therefore all future emulation:
If you please to trust to my election, you   275
Shall say I am not partial to myself.
I doubt not give content to all.
All.   Agreed, agreed!
Tibalt. Then but observe how learnèd and discreetly
I will proceed, and as a skilful doctor
In all the quirks belonging to the game   280
Read over your complexions. [*To Albert*] For you,
                                        captain,
Being first in place and therefore first to be served,
I give my judgement thus: for your aspect
Y'are much inclined to melancholy, and that tells me
The sullen Saturn had predominance   285
At your nativity, a malignant planet;

---

282. Being] *F2*; Beinst *F*.

262–3. *Then . . . first*] The woman in dispute is perhaps Crocale, whose silence in
the preceding dialogue seems to indicate that she is busy fraternising with the gallants
(cf. Tibalt's comment at 298).
270. *swinge*] thrash.
salt] lustful.
273. *by the ears*] at each other's throats.
279–81. *as . . . complexions*] Judicial astrology was still a recognised tool of
medical diagnosis, and indeed gave academic authority to the physician, but it was
frequently under attack, as in J. Melton's *Astrologaster* (1620) and by implication in
the irreverent language of 280.
280. *quirks*] tricky arguments.
283. *aspect*] facial expression; but perhaps also alluding to the idea that planetary
position or *aspect* determines temperament.

And if not qualified by a sweet conjunction
Of a soft and ruddy wench born under Venus
It may prove fatal. Therefore to your arms
I give this rose-cheeked virgin.

Clarinda.   To my wish!   290
Till now I never was happy.

Aminta.   Nor I accursed.

Tibalt. Master, you are old
Yet love the game, that I perceive too;
And if not well spurred up you may prove rusty.
Therefore, to help ye, here's a Bradamanta,   295
Or I am cozened in my calculation.

Crocale. A poor old man allotted to my share!

Tibalt. Thou wouldst have two—nay, I think twenty!
But fear not, wench. Though he be old he's tough;
Look on's making, he'll not fail I warrant thee.   300

Rosellia. A merry fellow; [*Aside*] and were not man a creature
I detest, I could endure his company.

Tibalt. Here's a fair herd of does before me;
And now for a barren one.
For though I like the sport, I do not love   305
To father children. Like the Grand Signior
Thus I walk in my seraglio
And view 'em as I pass; then draw I forth
My handkercher, and having made my choice
I thus bestow it.

Rosellia.   On me!

Tibalt.   On you; now   310
My choice is made. To it, you hungry rascals.

Albert. Excellent!

Aminta.   As I love goodness

---

287. *conjunction*] Saturn and Venus were thought never to be astronomically proximate, and symbolised the incompatibility of age and youth (Cf. Falstaff and Doll in *2Henry IV*, II.iv.265–6); but Tibalt sees them instead as a complementary alignment.

295. *Bradamanta*] Bradamante is the warrior maiden of Ariosto's *Orlando Furioso*, available to English readers in Harington's translation (1591).

296.] Unless I've misjudged what's needed.

300. *on's making*] at his frame.

306. *Grand Signior*] the Ottoman Sultan, whose seraglio was a subject of prurient fascination to Europeans: 'his Virgins . . . are indeede the choisest beauties of the Empire. . . . When it is his pleasure to have one, they stand ranckt in a gallery; and she prepareth for his bed to whom he giveth his handkercher' (Sandys, *Relation*, p. 74).

311. *To . . . rascals*] The three unengaged men are left to share Hippolita and Juletta, unless Tibalt means also to apportion to them the now abandoned Aminta.

It makes me smile i'th' height of all my fears.
Clarinda. What a strong contention you may behold
    Between my mother's mirth and anger.   315
Tibalt. Nay, no coyness. Be mistress of your word:
    I must and will enjoy you.
Rosellia.   Be advised, fool.
    Alas, I am old; how canst thou hope content
    From one that's fifty?
Tibalt.   Never talk on't; I
    Have known good ones at threescore and upwards.   320
    Besides, the weather's hot, and men that have
    Experience fear fevers. A temperate
    Diet is the only physic. Your juleps,
    Nor gujacum, prunellos, camphire pills
    Nor gourd-water come not near your old woman.   325
    Youthful stomachs are still craving, though there be
    Nothing left to stop their mouths with. And believe me,
    I am no frequent giver of those bounties.
    Laugh on, laugh on, good gentlemen, do. I shall
    Make holiday and sleep when you dig in   330
    The mines till your hearts ache.
Rosellia.   A mad fellow.
    Well, sir, I'll give you hearing, and as I like
    Your wooing and discourse. But I must tell ye, sir,
    That rich widows look for great sums in present,
    Or assurances of ample jointers.
Tibalt.   That   335
    To me is easy, for instantly I'll do it.
    Hear me, comrades.
Albert.   What sayst thou, Tibalt?
Tibalt. Why, that to woo a wench with empty hands

---

335. jointers] *F; jointures Dyce.*

---

323. *juleps*] sweetened medicinal drinks.
324. *gujacum*] A medicinal brew was made from the powdered wood of the West Indian guaiacum tree, esteemed in the sixteenth century principally as a cure for syphilis.

prunellos] possibly dried plums (*OED*), but more likely the common herb prunel or 'self-heal', described by R. Dodoens as 'temperate betwixt heat and cold...The decoction of Prunell made with wine or water, doth joyne together and make whole and sound all wounds both inward and outward' (*A New Herbal*, 1619, p. 93).

camphire] camphor oil, a bitter aromatic tree extract used medicinally and as an antaphrodisiac. It is described by Linschoten (*Voyages*) as 'one of the principallest wares in India' (p. 126), whence it was imported from China and the spice islands.
325. *gourd-water*] distilled liquor of some kind, a medicinal.
335. *jointers*] jointures, financial settlements.

Is no good heraldry; therefore let's to the gold
And share it equally. 'Twill speak for us   340
More than a thousand compliments or cringes,
Ditties stol'n from Patrick, or discourse
From Ovid. Besides, 'twill beget us respect,
And if ever fortune 'friend us with a bark
Largely supply us with all provision.   345
Albert. Well advised, defer it not.
Tibalt.   Are ye all
Contented?
Men.   We are.
Tibalt.   Let's away then.
Straight we'll return, and you shall see our riches.
                                        Exeunt men.
Rosellia. Since I knew what wonder and amazement was
I ne'er was so transported.
Clarinda. [*To Aminta*]   Why weep ye, gentle maid?   350
There is no danger here to such as you.
Banish fear, for with us I dare promise
You shall meet all courteous entertainment.
Crocale. We esteem ourselves most happy in you.
Hippolita. And bless fortune that brought you hither.   355
Clarinda. Hark in your ear: I love you as a friend
Already; ere long you shall call me by
A nearer name. I wish your brother well—
I know you apprehend me.
Aminta. [*Aside*]   Ay, to my grief I do.—
Alas, good ladies, there is nothing left me   360
But thanks to pay ye with.
Clarinda.   That's more than yet
You stand engagèd for.

        Enter ALBERT, TIBALT *and the rest with treasure.*

Rosellia.   So soon returned!

        The men bestow jewels on the women.

347. SP *Men*] *All.* F.   348.1.] *Exit.* F.   349. knew] F2; know F.   362.1.] *this ed.;
not in* F.

_____

  339. *Is...heraldry*] isn't exactly classy.
  341. *cringes*] obsequious bows.
  342. *Ditties...Patrick*] Petrarchan verses, the staples of love poetry.
  342–3. *discourse...Ovid*] perhaps from Marlowe's translation of the *Amores*, or
from the *Ars Amatoria*, but the ever-popular *Metamorphoses* could also supply a
winning tale.
  344. *'friend...bark*] favour us with a ship.

Albert. Here, see the idol of the lapidary.

Tibalt. These pearls for which the slavish negro dives
   To the bottom of the sea.   365

Lamure. To get which the industrious merchant touches
   At either pole.

Franville.   The never-failing purchase
   Of lordships and of honours.

Morillat.   The world's mistress
   That can give everything to the possessors.

Master. For which the sailors scorn tempestuous winds   370
   And spit defiance in the sea.

Tibalt.   Speak, lady:
   Look we not lovely now?

Rosellia.   Yes, yes! O my stars
   Be now for ever blessed that have brought
   To my revenge these robbers! Take your arrows
   And nail these monsters to the earth.

The women draw their bows.

Albert.   What mean ye, lady?   375
   In what have we offended?

Rosellia.   O my daughter,
   And you, companions with me in all fortunes,
   Look on these caskets and these jewels.
   These were our own when first we put to sea
   With good Sebastian; and these the pirates   380
   That not alone deprived him of this treasure
   But also took his life.

Crocale.   Part of my present
   I well remember was mine own.

Hippolita.   And these
   Were mine!

Juletta.   Sure I have worn this jewel.

Rosellia.   Wherefore
   Do ye stay then and not perform my command?   385

375.SD] *this ed.; not in F.*   383. well] F; will F2.

---

363. *lapidary*] cutter and polisher of precious stones, a jeweller.

364–71. *These . . . sea*] a version of the traditional encomion to Lady Money: cf.
Jonson, *Staple of News*, I.vi.62ff (Revels ed., citing various parallels).

364–7. *These . . . pole*] Pearl-trading was a global business, as the pages of Hakluyt
reveal; in Caribbean and South American waters African slaves replaced the native
pearl fishers as they were exterminated.

Albert. O heaven, what cruel fate pursues us!
Tibalt.   I
    Am well enough served, that must be off'ring jointures,
    Jewels and precious stones more than I brought with me.
Rosellia. Why shoot ye not?
Clarinda.   Hear me, dear mother.
    And when the greatest cruelty is justice   390
    Do not show mercy. Death to these starved wretches
    Is a reward, not punishment. Let 'em live
    To undergo the full weight of your displeasure.
    And that they may have sense to feel the torments
    They have deserved, allow 'em some small pittance   395
    To linger out their tortures.
Rosellia.   'Tis well counselled.
    And we'll follow it.
Men.   Hear us speak—
Rosellia.   Peace, dogs.
    Bind 'em fast. When fury hath given way to reason
    I will determine of their sufferings,
    Which shall be horrid. Vengeance though slow-paced   400
    At length o'ertakes the guilty, and the wrath
    Of the incensèd powers will fall most sure
    On wicked men when they are most secure.   *Exeunt.*

---

397. And ... it] *given to All. in F (with* Heare us speake). SP *Men*] *All. F.*

ACT IV

SCENE i

Enter RAYMOND, SEBASTIAN, NICUSA *and* Sailors.

First Sailor. Here's nothing, sir, but poverty and hunger;
   No promise of inhabitance, neither tract
   Of beast nor foot of man. We have searched all
   This rocky desert, yet cannot discover
   Any assurance here is or hath been such men.   5
Second Sailor. Not a relic of anything they wore,
   Nor mark left by 'em either to find relief
   Or to warn others from the like misfortune.
   Believe it, these fellows are both false,
   And to get a little succour in their misery   10
   Have framed this cunning tale.
Raymond. The ship I know is French and owned by pirates,
   If not by Albert my arch-enemy.
   You told me too there was a woman with 'em,
   A young and handsome woman.
Sebastian.   There was so, sir.   15
Raymond. And such and such young gallants.
Nicusa.   We told ye true,
                                     sir,
   That they had no means to quit this island.
Raymond. And that amidst their mutiny, to save your lives
   You got their ship.
Sebastian.   All is most certain, sir.
Raymond. Where are they then? Where are these men   20
   Or woman? We are landed where your faiths
   Did assure us we could not miss their sights.
   For this news we took ye to our mercy;
   Relieved ye when the furious sea and famine
   Strove which should first devour ye; clothed   25
   And cherished ye; used ye as those ye say
   Ye are, fair gentlemen. Now keep your words

ACT IV SCENE i] *Actus quartus. Scoena prima.* F.

---

2. *tract*] print, trace.
21. *faiths*] sworn testimony.

And show us this company your own free pities spoke
                                                     of—
    These men ye left in misery, the woman.
    Men of those noble breedings you pretend to   30
    Should scorn to lie, or get their food with falsehood.
    Come, direct us.
Sebastian.   Alas, sir, they are gone,
    But by what means or providence we know not.
Second Sailor. Was not the captain
    A fellow of a fiery yet brave nature,   35
    A middle stature and of brown complexion?
Nicusa. He was, sir.
Raymond.   'Twas Albert,
    And my poor wretched sister.
First Sailor.   'Twas he, certain.
    I ha' been at sea with him, many times at sea.
Raymond. Come, show us these men.   40
    Show us presently, and do not dally with us.
Sebastian. We left 'em here—what should we say, sir?—here
    In this place.
Second Sailor.   The earth cannot swallow 'em. They have
    No wings, they cannot fly, sure.
Raymond.   You told us too
    Of heaps of treasure and of sums concealed   45
    That set their hearts a-fire. We see no such thing,
    No such sign. What can ye say to purge ye?
    What have ye done with these men?
Nicusa.   We, sir?
Raymond.   You, sir.
    For certain I believe ye saw such people.
Sebastian. By all that's good, by all that's pure and honest,   50
    By all that's holy—
Raymond.   I dare not credit ye.
    Ye have so abused my hope that now I hate ye.
First Sailor. Let's put 'em in their ragged clothes again,
                                                     captain,
    For certain they are knaves. Let's e'en deliver 'em
    To their old fruitful farm. Here let 'em walk the island.   55
Sebastian. If ye do so we shall curse your mercies.

---

    30. *pretend to*] claim to have.
    41. *presently*] immediately.
    55. *farm*] in its proper sense of land leased for cultivation, as it was on a large scale
in the colonies; but used ironically here.

Nicusa. Rather put us to sea again.
Raymond.   Not so.
　Yet this I'll do, because ye say ye are Christians—
　Though I hardly credit it. Bring in the boat,
　And all aboard again but these two wretches.   60
　Yet leave 'em four days' meat. If in that time—
　For I will search all nooks of this strange island—
　I can discover any tract of these men
　Alive or dead, I'll bear ye off and honour ye.
　If not, ye have found your graves. So farewell.   65
                          Exeunt RAYMOND *and* Sailors.
Nicusa. That goodness dwells above, and knows us innocent,
　Comfort our lives and at his pleasure quit us.
Sebastian. Come, cousin, come. Old time will end our story;
　But no time, if we end well, ends our glory.   *Exeunt.*

ACT IV   SCENE ii

Enter ROSELLIA, CLARINDA, CROCALE, HIPPOLITA
and JULETTA.

Rosellia. Use 'em with all the austerity that may be;
　They are our slaves. Turn all those pities,
　Those tender reluctations that should become your sex
　To stern anger. And when ye look upon 'em
　Look with those eyes that wept those bitter sorrows,   5
　Those cruelties ye suffered by their rapines.
　Some five days hence that blessèd hour comes,
　Most happy to me, that knit this hand to my
　Dear husband's, and both our hearts in mutual bands.
　That hour, ladies—   10
Clarinda. What of that hour?
Rosellia.   Why, on that hour, daughter,
　And in the height of all our celebrations,
　Our dear remembrances of that dear man
　And those that suffered with him, our fair kinsmen,
　Their lives shall fall a sacrifice to vengeance—   15
　Their lives that ruined his. 'Tis a full justice.
　I will look glorious in their bloods,

65.1.] *Exit. F.*

3. *reluctations*] aversion (to violence).

And the most noble spirit of Sebastian,
That perished by the pride of these French pirates,
Shall smile in heaven and bless the hand that killed him.   20
Look strictly all unto your prisoners;
For he that makes a 'scape beyond my vengeance,
Or entertains a hope by your fair usage—
Take heed, I say—she that deceives my trust,
Again take heed: her life! And that's but light   25
Neither: her life in all the tortures my spirit
Can put on.
All.   We shall be careful.
Rosellia.   Do so.   *Exit.*
Clarinda. You are angry, mother, and ye are old too,
Forgetting what men are. But we shall temper ye.
How fare your prisoners, ladies? In what forms   30
Do they appear in their afflictions?
Juletta. Mine fare but poorly, for so I am commanded;
'Tis none of their fault.
Clarinda.   Of what sort are they?
Juletta. They say they are gentlemen, but they show
Mongrels.   35
Clarinda.   How do they suffer?
Juletta.   Faith, like boys.
They are fearful in all fortunes. When I smile
They kneel, and beg to have that face continued;
And like poor slaves adore the ground I go on.
When I frown, they hang their most dejected heads
Like fearful sheephounds. Show 'em a crust of bread   40
They'll saint me presently, and skip like apes
For a sup of wine. I'll whip 'em like hackneys,
Saddle 'em, ride 'em, do what I will with 'em.
Clarinda. Tush, these are poor things. Have they names like
Christians?
Juletta. Very fair names: Franville, Lamure, and Morillat;   45
And brag of great kindreds too. They offer
Very handsomely, but that I am a fool
And dare not venture. They are sound too, i' my
conscience,
Or very near upon't.
Clarinda.   Fie, away fool!

---

35. *Mongrels*] poorly bred.
41. *saint me presently*] bless me instantly.
42. *hackneys*] common horses.
48. *sound*] undiseased.

Juletta. They tell me, if they might be brought before you   50
    They would reveal things of strange consequence.
Clarinda. Their base poor fears.
Juletta.   Ay, that makes me hate 'em too.
    For if they were but manly to their sufferance
    Sure I should strain a point or two.
Clarinda. An hour hence I'll take a view of 'em   55
    And hear their business. Are your men thus too?
Crocale. Mine? No, gentle madam, mine were not cast
    In such base moulds. Afflictions, tortures
    Are names and natures of delight to my men.
    All sorts of cruelties they meet like pleasures.   60
    I have but two: the one they call Dupont,
    Tibalt Dupont; the other the shipmaster.
Clarinda. Have they not lives and fears?
Crocale.   Lives they have, madam;
    But those lives never linked to such companions
    As fears or doubts.
Clarinda.   Use 'em nobly,   65
    And where you find fit subjects for your pities
    Let it become ye to be courteous.
    My mother will not always be thus rigorous.
Hippolita. Mine are sailors, madam, but they sleep soundly
    And seldom trouble me, unless it be when   70
    They dream sometimes of fights and tempests.
    Then they roar and whistle for cans of wine
    And down they fling me; and in that rage—
    For they are violent fellows—they play such wreaks!
    If they have meat, they thank me; if none,   75
    They heartily desire to be hanged quickly.
    And this is all they care.
Clarinda.   Look to 'em diligently,
    And where your pities tells ye they may deserve,
    Give comfort.
All.   We will.
         Exeunt CROCALE, HIPPOLITA *and* JULETTA.

---

79. *Exeunt . . .* JULETTA] *Exit. F.*

   53. *to . . . sufferance*] in coping with their ordeal.
   59. *names . . . delight*] A modern equivalent would be 'meat and drink'; the phrase
derives from the proverb 'Names and natures do often agree' (N32).
   73. *down . . . me*] i.e. the drink down their throats (rather than Hippolita to the
ground).
   74. *play . . . wreaks*] cause such havoc. Cf. Cotgrave, 'Jouer ses jeux . . . *to play
reakes, or keep a terrible coile.*'

Enter AMINTA.

Clarinda.   Come hither, be not frighted.
   Think not ye steal this liberty, for we give it.   80
   Your tender innocence assures me, virgin,
   Ye had no share in those wrongs these men did us.
   I find ye are not hardened in such mischiefs.
   Your brother was misled sure, foully misled.
Aminta. How much I fear these pities!
Clarinda.   Certain he was,   85
   So much I pity him; and for your sake
   Whose eyes plead for him. Nay, for his own sake.
Aminta.   Ha!
Clarinda. For I see about him—women have subtle eyes
   And look narrowly, or I am much abused—
   Many fair promises; nay, beyond those,   90
   Too, many shadowed virtues.
Aminta.   I think he
   Is good.
Clarinda.   I assure myself he will be.
   And out of that assurance take this comfort,
   For I perceive your fear hath much dejected ye:
   I love your brother.
Aminta.   Madam—   95
Clarinda. Nay, do not take it for a dreamt-of favour
   That comforts in the sleep, and awake vanishes.
   Indeed I love him.
Aminta.   Do ye indeed?
Clarinda. You doubt still because ye fear his safety.
   Indeed he is the sweetest man I e'er saw—   100
   I think the best! Ye may hear without blushes
   And give me thanks, if ye please, for my courtesy.
Aminta. Madam, I ever must. [*Aside*] Yet witness, heaven,
   They are hard pulled from me.—Believe me, madam,
   So many imperfections I could find   105
   (Forgive me grace for lying), and such wants
   ('Tis to an honest use), such poverties
   Both in his main proportion and his mind too.
   There are a hundred handsomer (I lie lewdly!).

---

  89. *narrowly*] attentively.
  91. *shadowed*] underlying.
  106. *wants*] deficiencies.
  108. *main proportion*] general build.

    Your noble usage, madam, hath so bound me to ye   110
    That I must tell ye—
Clarinda.   Come, tell me your worst.
Aminta. He is no husband for ye. I think ye mean
    In that fair way.
Clarinda.   Ye have hit it.
Aminta. [*Aside*]   I am sure
    Ye have hit my heart!—You will find him dangerous,
                        madam,
    As fickle as the flying air, proud, jealous,   115
    Soon glutted in your sweets, and soon forgetful.
    I could say more, and tell ye I have a brother—
    Another brother, that so far excels this
    Both in the ornaments of man and making.
Clarinda. If you were not his sister I should doubt   120
    Ye mainly; doubt ye for his love, ye deal
    So cunningly. Do not abuse me: I
    Have trusted ye with more than life, with my
    First love. Be careful of me.
Aminta.   In what use, madam?
Clarinda. In this, lady. Speak to him for me, you   125
    Have power upon him. Tell him I love him,
    Tell him I dote on him: it will become
    Your tongue.
Aminta. [*Aside*] Become my grave! O fortune,
    O cursèd fortune.
Clarinda.   Tell him his liberty
    And all those with him; all our wealth and jewels,   130
    Good sister—for I'll call ye so.
Aminta.   I shall, lady
    [*Aside*]—Even die, I hope.
Clarinda.   Here's meat and wine, pray
                         take it;
    And there he lies. Give him what liberty
    You please, but still concealed. What pleasure you
    Shall please, sister; he shall ne'er want again.   135

112–13. *ye . . . way*] i.e. that's what you're after.

118. *Another brother*] Aminta finds her way blocked, since Albert has already misused the lover's conventional recourse to an imaginary sibling as a way of resolving romantic tangles. Contrast Viola's valid and effective use of it in *Twelfth Night*, II.iv.107ff.

121. *ye . . . love*] your loyalty to him.

129. *Tell*] Promise.

134. *still concealed*] always discreetly—remembering Rosellia's threat at 23–7.

Nay, see an' you'll take it. Why do you study thus?
Aminta. To avoid mischiefs if they should happen.
Clarinda.   Go,
    And be happy for me.   *Exit.*
Aminta.   O blind fortune.
    Yet happy thus far, I shall live to see him.
    In what strange desolation lives he here now?   140
    Sure this curtain will reveal.

                ALBERT *is discovered.*

Albert.   Who's that? Ha!
    Some gentle hand, I hope, to bring me comfort.
    Or if it be my death 'tis sweetly shadowed.
Aminta. Have ye forgot me, sir?
Albert.   My Aminta?
Aminta.   She, sir,
    That walks here up and down an empty shadow;   145
    One that for some few hours but wanders here,
    Carrying her own sad coffin,
    Seeking some desert place to lodge her griefs in.
Albert. Sweet sorrow, welcome! Welcome, noble grief.
    How got you this fair liberty to see me?   150
    For sorrows in your shape are strangers to me.
Aminta. I come to counsel ye.
Albert.   Ye are still more welcome,
    For good friends in afflictions give good counsels.
    Pray then, proceed.
Aminta.   Pray eat first, ye show faint.
    Here's wine to refresh ye too.
Albert.   I thank ye, dear.   155
Aminta. Drink again.
Albert.   Here's to our loves. How, turn and weep?
    Pray pledge it. This happiness we have yet left:
    Our hearts are free.—Not pledge it? Why,
    And though beneath the axe this health were holy.

---

136. an'] an F.   138.SD] *not in* F.   141.SD] *this ed.; Enter Albert* F.

---

136. *see . . . it*] don't be bashful about taking a look.
study] hesitate.
141. *curtain*] either across the discovery space in the tiring-house façade, or in front
of a booth—possibly one thrust out from the discovery space at the start of the scene.
143. *shadowed*] foretold.
154. *show*] look, seem.
159. *And though*] Even if (it were pledged).
health] toast.

Why do ye weep thus?
Aminta.   I come to woo ye.   160
Albert. To woo me, sweet? I am wooed and won already.
    You know I am yours. This pretty way becomes ye.
    But you would deceive my sorrows—that's your intent.
Aminta. I would I could; I should not weep, but smile.
    Do ye like your meat and wine?
Albert.   Like it?
Aminta.   Do you like   165
    Your liberty?
Albert.   All these I well may like.
Aminta. Then pray like her that sent 'em. Do ye like wealth
    And most unequalled beauty?
Albert.   Peace. Indeed,
    You'll make me angry.
Aminta.   Would I were dead that ask it;
    Then ye might freely like and I forgive ye.   170
Albert. What like, and who? Add not more misery
    To a man that's fruitful in afflictions.
    Who is't you would have me like? Who sent these comforts?
Aminta. I must tell.
Albert.   Be bold.
Aminta.   But be you temperate.
    If you be bold I die. The young fair virgin—   175
    Sorrow hath made me old!—O hearken,
    And wisely hark: the governess's daughter,
    That star that strikes this island full of wonder,
    That blooming sweetness—
Albert.   What of her?
Aminta.   She sent it,
    And with it—it must be out—she dotes on ye   180
    And must enjoy ye, else no joy must find ye.
Albert. And have you the patience to deliver this?
Aminta. A sister may say much, and modestly.
Albert. A sister?
Aminta.   Yes, that name undid ye;
    Undid us both. Had ye named wife, she had feared ye,   185
    And feared the sin she followed. She had shunned ye,
    Her virgin modesty had not touched at ye.

---

186. shunned ye,] shun'd, yea *F.*

---

163. *would . . . sorrows*] are trying to cheer me up by teasing me.
172. *fruitful in*] already laden with.

But thinking you were free hath kindled a fire
I fear will hardly be extinguished.
Albert.   Indeed
I played the fool.
Aminta.   O my best sir, take heed,   190
Take heed of lies. Truth, though it trouble some minds,
Some wicked minds, that are both dark and dangerous,
Yet it preserves itself, comes off pure, innocent,
And like the sun, though never so eclipsed,
Must break in glory. O sir, lie no more.   195
Albert. Ye have read me a fair lecture, and put a spell
Upon my tongue for feigning. But how will
You counsel now?
Aminta.   Ye must study to forget me.
Albert. How!
Aminta.   Be patient.
Be wise and patient, it concerns ye highly.   200
Can ye lay by our loves? But why should I doubt it?
Ye are a man, and men may shift affections;
'Tis held no sin. To come to the point,
Ye must lose me—many and mighty reasons.
Albert. Hear me, Aminta.   205
Have you a man that loves you too? That feeds ye,
That sends ye liberty? Has this great governess
A noble son too, young and apt to catch ye?
Am I, because I am in bonds and miserable,
My health decayed, my youth and strength half blasted,   210
My fortune like my waning self, for this despised?
Am I for this forsaken? A new love chosen?
And my affections, like my fortunes, wanderers?
Take heed of lying, you that chid me for it,
And showed how deep a sin it was and dangerous,   215
Take heed yourself. You swore you loved me dearly,
No few nor little oaths you swore, Aminta,
Those sealed with no small faith, I then assured myself.
O seek no new ways to cozen truth.
Aminta. I do not. By love itself, I love thee,   220
And ever must; nor can all deaths dissolve it.

---

195. *Must break*] proverbial (T591).
196–7. *put . . . feigning*] i.e. cured me of telling lies.
207–8. *Has . . . too*] A gesture towards the plot symmetry that was to characterise the Dryden/Davenant *Tempest* (1667).

Albert. Why do you urge me thus then?
Aminta.   For your safety,
    To preserve your life.
Albert.   My life I do confess
    Is hers, she gives it.
    And let her take it back, I yield it.
    My love's entirely thine, none shall touch at it,   225
    None, my Aminta, none.
Aminta.   Ye have made me happy.
    And now I know ye are mine, fortune I scorn thee.
    Go to your rest and I'll sit by ye.
    Whilst I have time I'll be your mate, and comfort ye,
    For only I am trusted. You shall want nothing,   230
    Not a liberty that I can steal ye.
Albert. [*Embracing her*] May we not celebrate our loves,
                                   Aminta?
    And where our wishes cannot meet—
Aminta.   You are wanton.
    But with cold kisses I'll allay that fever;
    Look for no more, and that in private too.   235
    Believe me, I shall blush else. But let's consider,
    We are both lost else.
Albert.   Let's in, and prevent fate.   *Exeunt.*

ACT IV   SCENE iii

Enter CROCALE *and* JULETTA *with* TIBALT *and* Master.

Tibalt. You do well to air us, ladies; we shall be musty else.
    What are your wise wills now?
Crocale.   You are very crank still.
Tibalt. As crank as a holy friar fed with hailstones!
    But do ye bring us out to bait like bulls?
Master. Or are you weary of the charge ye are at?   5
    Turn us abroad again—let's jog, ladies.
    We are gross and coarse, unfit for your sweet pleasures.
Tibalt. Knock off our shoes, and turn 's to grass.

---

237. *prevent*] outwit, forestall. Albert may still be pressing her to make love, but more likely he agrees on the need to go in and make contingency plans.

2. *crank*] lively, boisterous. Crocale is encouraging him to put his energy into sexual play.

3. *as ... hailstones!*] an enigmatic simile, and not recorded as proverbial. Perhaps *hailstones* was Protestant slang for the devotional ritual of repeating Hail Marys.

Crocale. You are determined
    Still to be stubborn then. It well becomes ye!   10
Tibalt. An humour, lady, that contents a prisoner.
    A sullen fit sometimes serves for a second course.
Juletta. Ye may as well be kind and gain our favours;
    Gain meat and drink and lodging to rest your bones.
Tibalt. My bones have bore me thus long   15
    And had their share of pains and recreations.
    If they fail now they are no fair companions.
Crocale. Are ye thus harsh to all our sex?
Master.   We cannot
    Be merry without a fiddler. Pray strike up
    Your tabors, ladies.
Crocale.   The fools despise us.   20
Juletta. We know ye are very hungry now.
Tibalt. Yes, 'tis very wholesome, ladies,
    For we that have gross bodies must be careful.
    Have ye no piercing air to stir our stomachs?
    We are beholding to ye for our ordinary.   25
Juletta. Why, slaves, 'tis in our power to hang ye.
Master. Very likely.
    'Tis in our powers then to be hanged and scorn ye.
    Hanging's as sweet to us as dreaming to you.
Crocale. Come, be more courteous.
Juletta.   Do, and then ye shall   30
    Be pleased and have all necessaries.
Tibalt.   Give me
    Some ratsbane then.
Crocale.   And why ratsbane, monsieur?
Tibalt. We live like vermin here and eat up your cheese,
    Your mouldy cheese that none but rats would bite at;
    Therefore 'tis just that ratsbane should reward us.   35
    We are unprofitable, and our ploughs are broken.

---

8. *Knock . . . shoes*] like retired horses.

20. *tabors*] small drums.

24. *stir . . . stomachs*] (1) give us an appetite; (2) arouse us sexually. Tibalt slights
the women's erotic appeal.

25. *ordinary*] daily fare.

29. *sweet*] erotically satisfying; an allusion to the belief that hanging invariably
produces orgasm: Gerard in his *Herball* (1597) explains that the mandrake grows
under a gallows 'where the matter . . . hath fallen from the dead bodie' (p. 281). The
reference to *dreaming* recalls Crocale's salacious musings at II.ii.49ff.

32. *ratsbane*] rat-poison.

33–6.] For tactical reasons Tibalt no longer argues that his sexual performance is
unimpaired by meagre diet (cf. III.215–16).

There is no hope of harvest this year, ladies.
Juletta. Ye shall have all content.
Master. Ay, and we'll serve your uses!
    I had rather serve hogs, there's more delight in't.   40
    Your greedy appetites are never satisfied;
    Just like hungry camels, sleeping or waking
    You chew the cud still.
Crocale.   By this hand, we'll starve ye.
Master. 'Tis a noble courtesy. I had as lief
    Ye should famish me as founder me—
    To be jaded to death is only fit for a hackney.   45
    Here be certain tarts of tar about me,
    And parcels of potargo in my jerkin;
    As long as these last—
Juletta.   Which will not last ever.
Tibalt. Then we'll eat one another like good fellows.
    A shoulder of his for a haunch of mine!   50
Juletta. 'Tis excellent.
Tibalt.   'Twill be as we'll dress it, ladies.
Crocale. Why, sure ye are not men.
Master.   Ye had best come search us.
    A seaman is seldom without a salt eel.
Tibalt. I am bad enough,   55
    And in my nature a notorious wencher;
    And yet ye make me blush at your immodesty.
    Tell me, good master, didst ever see such things?
Master. I could like 'em though they were lewdly given,
    If they could say no; but fie on 'em, they gape   60
    Like oysters.
Tibalt.   Well, ye may hang or starve us.
    But your commanding impudence shall never fear us.
    Had ye by blushing signs, soft cunnings, crept

---

39. *we'll . . . uses*] in return we'll have to sleep with you.

45. *founder me*] make me lame.

46. *jaded*] worn out—with a pun on 'jade', an inferior horse (cf. the modern 'hack').

48. *potargo*] variant form of 'botargo', a relish made with the roe of the mullet or tunny. Presumably a sardonic reference to marine detritus on his clothes.

52. *dress*] prepare, cook.

54. *salt eel*] rope's end used for flogging (*OED*)—which, apart from carrying the obvious innuendo, also alludes to the sado-masochistic tastes that Crocale described with relish at IV.ii.58–60. Tibalt's next speech is apparently motivated by Crocale accepting the master's invitation.

60–1. *gape . . . oysters*] proverbial (O114).

62. *fear*] frighten.

Into us and showed us your necessities,
We had met your purposes, supplied your wants.   65
We are no saints, ladies.
I love a good wench as I love my life,
And with my life I will maintain my love.
But such a sordid impudence I'll spit at.
Let's to our dens again. Come, noble master.   70
You know our minds, ladies. This is the faith
In which we'll die.   *Exeunt* TIBALT *and* Master.
Crocale.   I do admire 'em.
Juletta.   They
     Are noble fellows, and they shall not want
     For this.

               Enter CLARINDA.

Crocale.   But see, Clarinda comes. Farewell,
     I'll to my charge.   *Exit.*   75
Clarinda.   Bring out those prisoners now
     And let me see 'em, and hear their business.
Juletta. I will, madam.   *Exit.*
Clarinda. I hope she hath prevailed upon her brother.
     She has a sweet tongue, and can describe
     The happiness my love is ready to fling on him.   80
     And sure he must be glad, and certain, wonder
     And bless the hour that brought him to this island.
     I long to hear the full joy that he labours with.

     Re-enter JULETTA *with* MORILLAT, FRANVILLE *and* LAMURE

Morillat. Bless thy divine beauty.
Franville. Mirror of sweetness.   85
Lamure. Ever-springing brightness. [*All three kneel.*]
Clarinda. Nay, stand up gentlemen, and leave your flatteries.
Morillat. She calls us gentlemen! Sure we shall have some meat
                                                       now.
Clarinda. I am a mortal creature. Worship heaven
     And give these attributes to their divinities.   90
     Methinks ye look but thin.
Morillat.   O we are starved,
     Immortal beauty.
Lamure.   We are all poor starved knaves.

75.SD] *not in* F.   83.1. *Re-enter . . . with*] *Enter Juletta* F.

Franville. Neither liberty nor meat, lady.

Morillat.   We
    Were handsome men, and gentlemen, and sweet men,
    And were once gracious in the eyes of beauties.   95
    But now we look like rogues, like poor starved rogues.

Clarinda. What would ye do if ye were to die now?

Franville. Alas, were we prepared! If you will hang us
    Let's have a good meal or two to die with
    To put 's in heart.

Morillat.   Or if you'll drown us   100
    Let's be drunk first, that we may die merrily
    And bless the founders.

Clarinda.   Ye shall not die so hastily.
    What dare ye do to deserve my favour?

Lamure. Put us to any service.

Franville.   Any bondage,
    Let's but live.

Morillat.   We'll 'get a world of children;   105
    For we know ye are heinously provided that way.
    And ye shall beat us when we offend ye, beat us
    Abundantly, and take our meat from us.

Clarinda. [*To the women*] These are weak, abject things, that
                                        show ye poor ones!—
    What's the great service ye so oft have threatened   110
    If ye might see me and win my favour?

Juletta. [*Prompting*] That business of discovery.

Morillat.   O,
    I'll tell ye, lady.

Lamure.   And so will I!

Franville.   And I!
    Pray let me speak first.

Morillat.   Good, no confusion.
    We are before a lady that knows manners;   115
    And, by the next meat I shall eat, 'tis certain
    This little gentlewoman that was taken with us—

Clarinda. Your captain's sister, she you mean.

Morillat.   Ay, ay,
    She's the business that we would open to ye.

---

98. were we] *conj.Dyce;* we were *F.*   106. provided] *F;* unprovided *F2.*

102. *bless the founders*] Proverbial (Dent F619.11).
106. *heinously*] very poorly, appallingly.
109. *that . . . ones!*] i.e. for fancying them.

You are cozened in her.
Lamure.   How, what is't you would open?   120
Franville. She is no sister.
Morillat.   Good sirs, how quick you are.
     She is no sister, madam.
Franville.   She is his—
Morillat. Peace I say.
Clarinda.   What is she?
Morillat.   Faith, sweet lady,
     She is, as a man would say, his—
Clarinda.   What?
Lamure.   His mistress.
Morillat. Or as some new translators read, his—   125
Clarinda. O me!
Morillat. And why should he delude you thus, unless
     He meant some villainy? These ten weeks he
     Has had her at sea for his own proper appetite.
Lamure. His cabin-mate, I'll assure ye.
Clarinda.   No sister, say ye?   130
Morillat. No more than I am brother to your beauty.
     I know not why he should juggle thus.
Clarinda. Do not lie to me!
Morillat.   If ye find me lie,
     Lady, hang me empty.
Clarinda.   How am I fooled!
     Away with 'em, Juletta, and feed 'em—   135
     But hark ye, with such food as they have given me.
     New misery!
Franville.   Nor meat nor thanks for all this?   *Exit.*
Clarinda. Make 'em more wretched.
     O I could burst! Curse and kill now,
     Kill anything I meet. Juletta, follow me,   140

---

127. should he] *this ed.;* he should F.

120–21. *How . . . sister*] The two sentences are bracketed in *F* to indicate that they are spoken together, as both characters try to pre-empt Morillat; but each forms part of a serviceable verse line.

124–5. *mistress . . . translators*] The meaning of *mistress* in the 1620s is unstable, often having its old sense of one who possesses the heart of the lover rather than being possessed sexually by him, but beginning to acquire the latter connotation. The line is obviously completed by a monosyllable such as 'whore'.

129. *proper*] exclusive.

132. *juggle*] deceive.

137. *Exit.*] Franville tries to storm off, and is presumably hauled back by Juletta, or by Clarinda as physical accompaniment to her final outburst. Cf. his impetuous exit at III.i.10.

And call the rest along.

Juletta.   We follow, madam.   *Exeunt.*

ACT IV   SCENE iv

Enter ALBERT *and* AMINTA.

Aminta. I must be gone now, else she may suspect me.
   How shall I answer her?
Albert.   Tell her directly.
Aminta. That were too sudden, too improvident.
   Fires of this nature must be put out cunningly;
   They'll waste all come near 'em else. Farewell   5
   Once more.
Albert.   Farewell, and keep my love entire.
   Nay, kiss me once again; methinks we should
   Not part.
Aminta.   O be wise, sir.
Albert.   Nay, one kiss more.
Aminta. Indeed you're wanton. We may be taken too.

Enter CLARINDA, JULETTA, CROCALE *and* HIPPOLITA.

Clarinda. Out thou base woman. By heaven, I'll shoot 'em
                                           both.   10
Crocale. Nay, stay, brave lady, hold! A sudden death
   Cuts off a nobler vengeance.
Clarinda.   Am I made bawd
   To your lascivious meetings? Are ye grown
   So wise in sin? Shut up that villain! And sirrah,
   Now expect my utmost anger. Let him there starve.   15
Albert. I mock at your mischiefs.   *Exit* CROCALE *with* ALBERT.
Clarinda.   Tie that false witch
   Unto that tree. There let the savage beasts
   Gnaw off her sweetness, and snakes embrace her beauties.
   Tie her, and watch that none relieve her.   *Exit.*
Hippolita.   We
   Could wish ye better fortune, lady, but dare   20

16.SD] *Exit.* F.   19.SD] *not in* F.

16–17. *Tie...tree*] At the Globe she would probably be tied to one of the stage
pillars (as, according to William Kemp, were pickpockets in the audience 'when at a
play they are taken pilfring': *Kemp's Nine Daies Wonder* (1600), repr.1923, p. 4).
Blackfriars may have used some sort of property tree.

   Not help ye.
Aminta.   Be your own friends, I thank ye.
                Exeunt HIPPOLITA *and* JULETTA.
   Now only my last audit, and my greatest,
   O heaven, be kind unto me,
   And if it be thy will, preserve.

              Enter RAYMOND.

Raymond.   Who is this?
   Sure 'tis a woman! I have trod this place   25
   And found much footing; now I know 'tis peopled.
   Ha, let me see: 'tis her face? O heaven!
   Turn this way, maid.
Aminta.   O Raymond! O brother!
Raymond. Her tongue too! 'Tis my sister. What rude hand—
   Nay, kiss me first. O joy! [*He begins to untie her.*]

    Enter JULETTA, CROCALE *and* CLARINDA.

Aminta.   Fly, fly, dear brother!   30
   You are lost else.
Juletta.   A man, a man! A new man!
Raymond. What are these? [*Draws his sword.*]
Crocale.   An enemy, an enemy!
Clarinda. Dispatch him. Take him off, shoot him straight.
Raymond. I dare not use my sword, ladies, against
   Such comely foes.
Aminta.   O brother, brother!   35
Clarinda. Away with 'em, and in dark prisons bind 'em.
   One word replied, ye die both. Now, brave mother,
   Follow thy noble anger, and I'll help thee.   *Exeunt.*

21.1] *not in* F.

---

22. *audit*] court of appeal.
38. *Follow*] act upon. Clarinda has forgotten her earlier desire (IV.ii.28–9) to
restrain her mother's vengefulness.

ACT V

SCENE i

Enter ROSELLIA, CLARINDA, CROCALE, JULETTA
and HIPPOLITA.

Rosellia. I am deaf to all your entreaties. She that moves me
    For pity or compassion to these pirates
    Digs up her father's or her brother's tomb
    And spurns about their ashes. Couldst thou
    Remember what a father thou hast once,   5
    'Twould steel thy heart against all foolish pity.
    By his memory, and the remembrance of
    His dear embraces, I am taught
    That in a noble cause revenge is noble;
    And they shall fall the sacrifices to appease   10
    His wandering ghost and my incensèd fury.
Clarinda. The new-come prisoner too?
Rosellia.   Him too.
    Yet that we may learn
    Whether they are the same, or near allied
    To those that forced me to this cruel course,   15
    Better their poor allowance, and permit 'em
    To meet together and confer
    Within the distance of your ear. Perhaps
    They may discover something that may kill
    Despair in me, and be a means to save 'em
    From certain ruin.
Crocale.   That shall be my charge.   20
Rosellia. Yet to prevent
    All hope of rescue—for this new-come captain
    Hath both a ship and men not far off from us,
    Though ignorant to find the only port

ACT V SCENE i] *Actus quintus, Scoena prima F.* 6. all] *F2; not in F.* 24. far off
from] *F;* far from *F2.*

---

3. *brother's*] used loosely of the men lost with Sebastian; Crocale later talks of their
'long-lost husbands' (V.ii.117) though this could be typical wishful thinking on her
part.
   4. *spurns about*] tramples on.

That can yield entrance to our happy island—   25
Guard the place strongly, and ere the next sun
Ends his diurnal progress I will be
Happy in my revenge, or set 'em free.   *Exeunt.*

ACT V   SCENE ii

Enter CROCALE, JULETTA *and* HIPPOLITA.
A Table furnished.

Crocale. So serve it plentifully, and lose not time
To enquire the cause. There is a main design
That hangs upon this bounty. See the table
Furnished with wine too, that discovers secrets
Which tortures cannot open.   5
Open the doors too of the several prisons
And give all free entrance into this room.
Undiscovered I can here mark all.
                    Exeunt JULETTA *and* HIPPOLITA.

Enter TIBALT *and* Master.

Here's captain careless and the tough shipmaster.
The slaves are nosed like vultures: how wild they look!   10
Tibalt. Ha, the mystery of this some good hobgoblin
Rise and reveal.
Master.   I am amazed at it,

8.1.] *not in* F.

19. *discover*] reveal.
26. *happy island*] See note to III.83.
0.1.] An awkward re-entry of characters who have just left the stage. The new scene carries out Rosellia's order at V.i.16, and in performance the action would be continuous; but it seems likely that a scene has been omitted from F, perhaps one showing Sebastian and Nicusa and reminding us that they are the key to the tragi-comic balance registered in V.i's final line. If so, the omission probably reflects an original theatrical cut to sustain the momentum and flow of the action in the closing stages.
5–6. *open./Open*] The half-line and repeated word suggest another cut, but it is covered by a pause while flagons and cups are fetched.
6. *several*] various, separate. The other women open the stage doors, presumably using them to leave the stage, while Crocale conceals herself behind the curtain in front of the discovery space (or behind a stage pillar in the public theatre).
9. *captain careless*] recalling the proverbial alcoholic sentiment of 'Hang care' (C85), which Beaumont & Fletcher give to the misogynist Captain Jacomo in *The Captain* (c.1612), IV.ii.92.
10–46.] A good example of Fletcher's use of vigorous accentual verse; attempts to restore the original lineation must remain provisional.

Nor can I sound the intent.
Tibalt.   Is not this bread,
  Substantial bread, not painted?
Master.   But take heed,
  You may be poisoned.
Tibalt.   I am sure I am famished.   15
  And famine, as the wise man says, gripes the guts
  As much as any mineral. This may be treacle
  Sent to preserve me after a long fast;
  Or be it viper's spittle I'll run the hazard.
Master. We are past all fear; I'll take part with ye.
Tibalt.   Do.   20
  And now i'faith, how d'e feel yourself? I find
  Great ease in't. What's here? Wine, and it be thy will!
  Strong lusty wine. [*Drinks deep.*] Well, fools may talk
  Of mithridate, cordials and elixirs,
  But from my youth this was my only physic.   25
  Here's a colour!
  What lady's cheek, though cerused over, comes near it?
  It sparkles too, hangs out diamonds. O
  My sweetheart, how I will hug thee again and again!
  They are poor drunkards, and not worth thy favours,   30
  That number thy moist kisses in these crystals.
Master. But monsieur, here are suckets and sweet dishes.
Tibalt. Tush, boys' meat; I am past it. Here's strong food
  Fit for men—nectar, old lad! Mistress of merry hearts,
  Once more I am bold with you.
Master.   Take heed, man. Too much   35
  Will breed distemper.
Tibalt.   Hast thou lived at sea
  The most part of thy life, where to be sober
  While we have wine aboard is capital treason?

---

16. *famine*] F2; *om.* F.

---

13. *sound*] fathom.
14. *not painted*] i.e. to deceive us. Cf. the painted waxworks used to torment the
Duchess in another Blackfriars play, Webster's *Duchess of Malfi* (1614).
17. *mineral*] poison (OED 2c).
treacle] medicinal preparation.
19. *Or be it*] but even if it's.
24. *mithridate*] cure-alls. Loosely applied to medicines, the word derived from the
legend of King Mithridate who guarded against being poisoned by regularly taking
antidotes.
27. *cerused*] painted, made up. (Ceruse was a lead-based cosmetic.)
28. *hangs out*] effervesces.
32. *suckets*] sweets.
36–8. *Hast . . . treason?*] A rosy view of ship life for the working sailor, who could

And dost thou preach sobriety?

Master.   Prithee forbear.
    We may offend in it: we know not for whom   40
    It was provided.

Tibalt.   I am sure for me;
    Therefore, foutra! When I am full, let 'em hang me,
    I care not.

Master. [*Aside*] This has been his temper ever.—
    See, provoking dishes: candied eringoes
    And potatoes.

Tibalt.   I'll not touch 'em. I will drink,   45
    But not a bit on a march. I'll be an eunuch
    Rather.

    Enter ALBERT, AMINTA, RAYMOND, LAMURE, MORILLAT
            and FRANVILLE *severally.*

Master.   Who are these?
Tibalt.   Marry, who you will.
    [*Drinks.*] I keep my text here.

Albert.   Raymond!
Raymond.   Albert!

Tibalt. Away, I'll be drunk alone. Keep off, rogues, or
    I'll belch ye into air. Not a drop here!   50

Aminta. Dear brother, put not in your eyes such anger.
    Those looks poisoned with fury shot at him
    Reflect on me. O brother, look milder, or
    The crystal of his temperance will turn
    'Em on yourself.

Albert. [*To Raymond*] Sir, I have sought ye long   55
    To find your pardon. You have ploughed the ocean
    To wreak your vengeance on me for the rape
    Of this fair virgin. Now our fortune guides us

---

expect only a daily ration of beer that not long into the voyage was usually flat and
sour.

    42. *foutra!*] fuck it. A common expletive derived from French 'Foutre. *To leacher'*
(Cotgrave).

    44–5. *provoking . . . potatoes*] See note to III.212–13.

    46. *bit*] bite to eat.

    47. *Who are these?*] The master has never seen Raymond before, and the gallants
are the worse for their humiliating confinement.

    48. *text*] Trinculo in *The Tempest* similarly makes his bottle his book (II.ii.141).

    54–5. *The . . . yourself*] The *crystal* of Albert's benevolence is seen here not as a
transparent medium but as a reflective and repelling surface. Cf. William Bourne's
reference to 'very perfect and good looking glasses, either of steele or Christall' in
Inventions or Devises (1578), p. 93.

To meet on such hard terms that we need rather
A mutual pity of our present state   60
Than to expostulate of breaches past
Which cannot be made up. And though it be
Far from your power to force me to confess
That I have done ye wrong, or, such submission
Failing to make my peace, to vent your anger,   65
You being yourself 'slaved, as I, to others;
Yet for your sister's sake, her blessed sake,
In part of recompense of what she has suffered
For my rash folly—the contagion
Of my black actions catching hold upon   70
Her purer innocence—I crave your mercy;
And wish however several motives kept us
From being friends while we had hope to live,
Let death which we expect, and cannot fly from,
End all contention.   75
Tibalt.   Drink upon't,
  'Tis a good motion. Ratify it in wine,
  And 'tis authentical.
Raymond.   When I consider
  The ground of our long difference, and look on
  Our not to be avoided miseries,
  It doth beget in me—I know not how—   80
  A soft religious tenderness; which tells me,
  Though we have many faults to answer for
  Upon our own account, our fathers' crimes
  Are in us punished. O Albert, the course
  They took to leave us rich was not honest,   85
  Nor can that friendship last which virtue joins not,
  When first they forced the industrious Portugals
  From their plantations in the happy islands.
Crocale. [*Aside*] This is that I watch for.
Raymond. And did omit no tyranny which men   90
  Inured to spoil and mischief could inflict
  On the grieved sufferers. When by lawless rapine
  They reaped the harvest which their labours sowed,
  And not content to force 'em from their dwelling
  But laid for 'em at sea, to ravish from 'em   95
  The last remainder of their wealth—then, then,

---

72. *several motives*] various causes.
95. *laid*] lay in wait.

After a long pursuit, each doubting other
As guilty of the Portugals' escape,
They did begin to quarrel like ill men
(Forgive me, piety, that I call 'em so).   100
No longer love or correspondence holds
Than it is cemented with prey or profit.
Then did they turn those swords they oft had bloodied
With innocent gore upon their wretched selves,
And paid the forfeit of their cruelty   105
Shown to Sebastian and his colony
By being fatal enemies to each other.
Thence grew Aminta's rape, and my desire
To be revenged. And now observe the issue:
As they for spoil ever forgot compassion   110
To women, who should be exempted from
The extremities of a lawful war,
We now, young able men, are fall'n into
The hands of women that, against the soft
Tenderness familiar to their sex,   115
Will show no mercy.

       CROCALE *reveals herself. Enter* HIPPOLITA *and* JULETTA.

Crocale.   None, unless you show us
Our long-lost husbands.
We are those Portugals you talked of.
Raymond.   Stay—
I met upon the sea in a tall ship
Two Portugals famished almost to death.   120
Tibalt. Our ship, by this wine! And those the rogues
That stole her; left us to famish in
The barren islands.
Raymond.   Some such tale they told me;
And something of a woman, which I find
To be my sister.
Crocale.   Where are these men?
Raymond.   I left 'em,   125

116.SD] *this ed.; Enter Crocale. F (next to 115).*

    97. *doubting*] suspecting.
    99. *ill*] evil.
    116.SD] *F* provides only the direction '*Enter Crocale*', but her ensuing speech demands that she be flanked by her companions, who could enter either above in the gallery or at the doors on either side of the discovery space where Crocale has probably been concealed (see note to 6 above).

Supposing that they had deluded me
With forged tales, in the island where they said
They had lived many years the wretched owners
Of a huge mass of treasure.
Albert.   The same men;
And that the fatal muck we quarrelled for.   130
Crocale. They were Portugals, you say.
Raymond.   So they professed.
Crocale. They may prove such men as may save your lives,
And so much I am taken with fair hope
That I will hazard life to be resolved on't.
How came you hither?
Raymond.   My ship lies by the river's mouth   135
That can convey ye to these wretched men
Which you desire to see.
Crocale.   Back to your prisons
And pray for the success. If they be those
Which I desire to find, you are safe. If not,
Prepare to die tomorrow, for the world   140
Cannot redeem ye.
Albert.   However, we are armed
For either fortune.   *Exeunt all but* TIBALT *and* CROCALE.
Tibalt.   What must become of me now,
That I am not dismissed?
Crocale.   O sir, I purpose
To have your company.
Tibalt.   Take heed, wicked woman!
I am apt to mischief now.
Crocale.   You cannot be   145
So unkind to her that gives you liberty.
Tibalt. No, I shall be too kind, that's the devil on't!
I have had store of good wine; and when I am drunk
Joan is a lady to me, and I shall
Lay about me like a lord. I feel strange motions—   150
Avoid me, temptation!
Crocale.   Come sir, I'll help ye in.   *Exeunt.*

---

126. Supposing that they] *conj.Dyce;* Supposing they *F.*   142.SD] *Exit. F*

149. *Joan*] Every common wench.

ACT V SCENE iii

Enter SEBASTIAN *and* NICUSA *above.*

Nicusa. What may that be that moves upon the lake?
Sebastian. Still it draws nearer, and now I plainly can
    Discern it. 'Tis the French ship.
Nicusa.   In it
    A woman, who seems to invite us to her.
Sebastian. Still she calls with signs of love to hasten   5
    To her. So lovely hope doth still appear!
    I feel nor age nor weakness.
Nicusa.   Though it bring death
    To us 'tis comfort, and deserves a meeting.
    Or else fortune, tired with what we have suffered
    And in it overcome, as it may be,   10
    Now sets a period to our misery.   *Exeunt.*

ACT V SCENE iv

Enter severally RAYMOND, ALBERT *and* AMINTA. *Horrid music.*
An altar prepared.

Raymond. What dreadful sounds are these?
Aminta.   Infernal music,
    Fit for a bloody feast.
Albert.   It seems prepared
    To kill our courages ere they divorce
    Our souls and bodies.
Raymond.   But they that fearless fall
    Deprive them of their triumph.

Enter ROSELLIA, CLARINDA, JULETTA *and* HIPPOLITA *with*
LAMURE, FRANVILLE *and* MORILLAT.

0.1. *above*] not in F.   0.2. *An . . . prepared*] *before SD in 5 F.*

11. *period*] limit, end.
0.1. Horrid music] Presumably a harsh combination of woodwind and trumpets,
setting the scene for barbaric acts. Fletcher uses similar effects in other plays, e.g. the
travesty of holy ritual in *The Queen of Corinth*, II.i.50, danced 'to a horrid Musick'
(*Works*, ed. Bowers, 1992, VIII.29).

Aminta.   See the furies   5
    In their full trim of cruelty.
Rosellia.   'Tis the last
    Duty that I can pay to my dead lord.
    Set out the altar. I myself will be
    The priest, and boldly do those horrid rites
    You shake to think on. Lead these captains nearer,   10
    For they shall have the honour to fall first
    To my Sebastian's ashes.

    ALBERT *and* RAYMOND *are led to the altar.*

                        And now, wretches,
    As I am taught already that you are
    (And lately by your free confession)
    French pirates, and the sons of those I hate   15
    Even equal with the devil, hear with horror
    What 'tis invites me to this cruel course
    And what you are to suffer. No Amazons we,
    But women of Portugal, that must have from you
    Sebastian and Nicusa. We are they   20
    That groaned beneath your fathers' wrongs; we are
    Those wretched women
    Their injuries pursued and overtook.
    And from the sad remembrance of our losses
    We are taught to be cruel—when we were forced   25
    From that sweet air we breathed in by their rapine,

---

5. with . . . MORILLAT] &c. F.   12.SD] not in F.

    5.SD] This is the most logical point of entry for the gallants, who have been under
the charge of Hippolita and Juletta and who must be present for the denouement.
    6. *trim*] array. On the Jacobean stage the women characters are likely to have worn
robes of some kind, and possibly masks, and Rosellia carries a sacrificial knife or
sword.
    9. *priest . . . rites*] Rosellia's prospective act is an apotheosis of Amazonian cruelty,
but it also recalls in its ritual formality the practices of human sacrifice in the
Americas, particularly the graphic accounts of 'horrid rites' in Aztecan Mexico
available to English readers in Joseph Acosta's *Naturall and Morall Historie of the
Indies* (1604) and in Purchas' potted version of that book in the 1617 *Pilgrimage*. It is
possible that the theatre selectively used accounts like the following to design such
exotic and grotesque scenes: 'Six of the Priests were appointed to this execution; foure
to hold the hands and feet of him that should be sacrificed, the fift to hold his head,
the sixt to open the stomacke, and pull out his heart. . . . The sixt, which killed the
Sacrifice, was as a high Priest, or Bishop [who] carried a great knife in his hand of a
large and sharpe flint' (*Purchas His Pilgrimage*, pp. 987–8). The Mexican victims
were led up a staircase down which they were thrown after being killed: this was a
famous image in Renaissance Europe (see p. 29), and could have been recalled by the
use of a stage dais.

And sought a place of being. As the seas
And winds conspired with their ill purposes
To load us with afflictions, in a storm
That fell upon us, the two ships that brought us   30
To seek new fortunes in an unknown world
Were severed. The one bore all the able men,
Our treasure and our jewels. In the other
We women were embarked, and fell upon
After long tossing in the troubled main   35
This pleasant island. But in few months
The men that did conduct us hither died;
We long before had given our husbands lost.
Rememb'ring what we had suffered by the French
We took a solemn oath never to admit   40
The cursed society of men. Necessity
Taught us those arts not usual to our sex;
And the fertile earth yielding abundance to us
We did resolve, thus shaped like Amazons,
To end our lives. But when you arrived here   45
And brought as presents to us our own jewels—
Those which were borne in the other ship—
How can ye hope to 'scape our vengeance?
Aminta. It boots not then to swear our innocence?
Albert. Or that we never forced it from the owners?   50
Raymond. Or that there are a remnant of that wreck,
    And not far off?
Rosellia.   All you affirm, I know
    Is but to win time. Therefore prepare your throats,
    The world shall not redeem ye.

            She takes up a knife from the altar.

                            And that your cries
May find no entrance to our ears, to move   55
Pity in any, bid loud music sound
Their fatal knells. If ye have prayers use 'em
Quickly to any power will own ye.

        Enter CROCALE *with* SEBASTIAN, NICUSA *and* TIBALT.

                            But ha!
Who are these? What spectacles of misfortune?

54.SD] *not in* F.   58.1. *with*] *not in* F.

35. *main*] high sea.

Why are their looks so full of joy and wonder?   60
Crocale. O lay by
These instruments of death, and welcome to
Your arms what you durst never hope to embrace!
This is Sebastian, this Nicusa, madam,
Preserved by miracle. Look up, dear sir,   65
And know your own Rosellia. Be not lost
In wonder and amazement. Or if nature
Can by instinct instruct you what it is
To be blessed with the name of father,
Freely enjoy it in this fair virgin.   70
Sebastian. Though my miseries
And many years of wants I have endured
May well deprave me of the memory
Of all joys past, yet looking on this building,
This ruined building of a heavenly form   75
In my Rosellia, I must remember
I am Sebastian.
Rosellia.   O my joys!
Sebastian. [*Embracing Clarinda*] And here
I see a perfect model of thyself
As thou wert when thy choice first made thee mine.
These cheeks and front, though wrinkled now with time   80
Which art cannot restore, had equal pureness
Of natural white and red, and as much ravishing,
Which by fair order and succession
I see descend on her. And may thy virtues
Wind into her form, and make her a perfect dower,   85
No part of thy sweet goodness wanting to her.
I will not now, Rosellia, ask thy fortunes,
Nor trouble thee with hearing mine.
Those shall hereafter serve to make glad hours
In their relation, all past wrongs forgot.
I am glad to see you, gentlemen; but most
That it is in my power to save your lives.

---

80. front] *Mason;* fronts *F.*

---

73. *deprave*] OED calls this an 'erroneous' substitution for 'deprive', but its own examples suggest that it is a specially intensified form of the latter. Sebastian means that past griefs may have corrupted his capacity for positive recollection; Fletcher is attempting the note struck at the end of *The Winter's Tale*, where joyful reconciliation is tempered by a sense of what is irrecoverably lost.

80. *front*] brow.

85. *dower*] i.e. wife (lit., marriage portion or dowry).

You saved ours when we were near starved at sea,
And I despair not, for if she be mine
Rosellia can deny Sebastian nothing.   95
Rosellia.   She does give up
Herself, her power and joys and all to you,
To be discharged of 'em as too burdensome.
Welcome in any shape!
Sebastian. [*To Raymond*] Sir, in your looks
I read your suit of my Clarinda: she is yours.   100
[*To Aminta*] And lady, if it be in me to confirm
Your hopes in this brave gentleman,
Presume I am your servant.
Albert.   We thank you, sir.
Aminta. O happy hour!
Albert.   O my dear Aminta,
Now all our fears are ended.
Tibalt. [*Embracing Crocale*]   Here I fix.   105
She's mettle, steel to the back, and will cut
My leaden dagger if not used with discretion.
Crocale. You are still no changeling!
Sebastian.   Nay,
All look cheerfully, for none shall be
Denied their lawful wishes. When awhile   110
We have here refreshed ourselves, we'll return
To our several homes; and well that voyage ends
That makes of deadly enemies, faithful friends.   *Exeunt.*

FINIS

106–7. *cut . . . dagger*] wear me out (*leaden* = limp, ineffectual).
108. *You . . . changeling*] you're incorrigible!

THE ANTIPODES

To
The Right Honourable
William, Earl of Hertford, &c.

My lord,
    The long experience I have had of your Honour's favourable 5
intentions towards me hath compelled me to this presumption.
But I hope your goodness will be pleased to pardon what your
benignity was the cause of, viz., the error of my dedication.
Had your candour not encouraged me in this, I had been
innocent; yet, I beseech you, think not I intend 10
it any other than your recreation at your retirement from
your weighty employments, and to be the declaration of your
gracious encouragements towards me, and the testimony of my
gratitude. If the public view of the world entertain 15
it with no less welcome than that private one of the stage
already has given it, I shall be glad the world owes you the
thanks. If it meet with too severe construction, I hope your
protection. What hazards soever it shall justle with, my desires

---

15–16. entertain it with] Q (corr.); entertain with Q (uncorr.).

The title-page of Q informs us that the play was 'Acted in the yeare 1638, by the
Queenes Majesties Servants, at *Salisbury* Court in Fleet-street'. The last London
theatre to be built before the Restoration, Salisbury Court was an indoor or 'private'
theatre on the other side of the city wall from Blackfriars and drawing a similar
audience. The Queen's Men acted there from 1637 until the closing of the theatres.
    The title-page also bears the epigraph 'Hic totus volo rideat Libellus', from Martial,
Epigrams, XI.15, 3: 'I will this Book should laugh throughout and jest' (tr. R.
Fletcher, 1656). Brome used the same tag as epigraph to several other plays.

    3.] *William Seymour* (1588–1660), created Marquis of Hertford in 1640, and
admitted to the Privy Council in the same year. During the 1630s his was one of
several noble families that found themselves at odds with Charles I's government.
    9. *candour*] kindliness.
    11. *retirement*] spare time.
    18. *construction*] interpretation.

are it may pleasure your lordship in the perusal, which is the   20
only ambition he is conscious of who is,
                    My lord,
                        Your Honour's humbly devoted
                            Richard Brome

Courteous Reader,
                    You shall find in this book more than was
presented upon the stage, and left out of the presentation for
superfluous length (as some of the players pretended). I thought
good all should be inserted according to the allowed original,   5
and as it was at first intended for the Cockpit stage, in the right
of my most deserving friend Mr. William Beeston, unto whom
it properly appertained. And so I leave it to thy perusal as it
was generally applauded, and well acted, at Salisbury Court.
                        Farewell,   10
                            Richard Brome.

To Censuring Critics On The Approved Comedy, *The Antipodes*

Jonson's alive! The world admiring stands,
And to declare his welcome there, shake hands.
Apollo's pensioners may wipe their eyes
And stifle their abortive elegies;
Taylor his goose quill may abjure again,   5
And to make paper dear, scribbling refrain;

1–11. Courteous ... Brome.] *after* Epilogue *in* Q.   11. Richard] Ri. Q.
1–15.] *after* The Prologue *in* Q.

5. *allowed original*] the text submitted to and licensed for performance by the Master of the Revels.
6. *as ... stage*] In the 1630s Brome was under contract to the Salisbury Court company, but when plague closed the theatres in May 1636 he was denied his regular salary, and he turned for help to his friend William Beeston, who commissioned him to write a play for his company of boy actors at the Cockpit theatre in Drury Lane. The ensuing legal tussle is discussed by Ann Haaker in *Renaissance Drama* I (1968), 283–306.
3. *Apollo's pensioners*] Jonson's literary circle, the Sons of Ben, which after his death continued to meet in the Apollo room of the Devil and St Dunstan tavern near Temple Bar. See HS XI.294–300.
4. *abortive elegies*] *Jonsonius Virbius*, a collection of commemorative poems by Jonson's friends and disciples, was published in 1638.
5. *Taylor*] John Taylor, Thames waterman turned writer, and notoriously prolific. He published his collected works in 1630 but continued to produce pamphlets and hack verse, some of it commemorating his own colourful travels through Britain and on the Continent.
6.] i.e. and stop driving up the price of paper by using so much.

For sure there's cause of neither. Jonson's ghost
Is not a tenant i'the Elysian coast,
But vexed with too much scorn at your dispraise,
Silently stole unto a grove of bays.   10
Therefore bewail your errors, and entreat
He will return unto the former seat,
Whence he was often pleased to feed your ear
With the choice dainties of his theatre.
But I much fear he'll not be easily won   15
To leave his bower, where grief and he alone
Do spend their time, to see how vainly we
Accept old toys for a new comedy.
Therefore repair to him, and praise each line
Of his *Volpone, Sejanus, Catiline.*   20
But stay, and let me tell you where he is:
He sojourns in his Brome's *Antipodes.*

C.G.

To The Author On His Comedy,
The Antipodes

Steered by the hand of Fate o'er swelling seas,
Methought I landed on th'antipodes,
Where I was straight a stranger; for 'tis thus:
Their feet do tread against the tread of us.
My scull mistook; thy book, being in my hand,   5
Hurried my soul to th'antipodean strand,

---

15. Robert Chamberlain] R.C. *some copies of Q.*

9. *vexed . . . dispraise*] Jonson's *The New Inn* had been a flop in 1629, in stark contrast to Brome's triumphs in the same year with *The Lovesick Maid* and *The Northern Lass.* Jonson's response was the *Ode to Himself,* in which he poured scorn on the audience's taste and judgement for, *inter alia,* not distinguishing his work from 'Broomes sweeping' (HS VI.492). Although the rift between the playwrights was soon mended, Jonson had little success with his final plays, and it was his protégé Brome, together with Shirley and Massinger, who commanded the London stage in the 1630s.

18. *old toys*] There were many revivals of Elizabethan plays in the 1630s, mostly in the popular theatres like the Red Bull, but also in more exclusive venues like the Cockpit: see the latter's repertory list for 1639 in Bentley, I.331. The old-fashioned 'journeying' play also had an influence on contemporary writing for the stage, e.g. on John Kirke's *Seven Champions of Christendom* (1638), acted at both the Cockpit and the Red Bull.

23. *C.G.*] Probably Charles Gerbier, minor writer and associate of Brome, and a regular contributor of commendatory verses (Haaker).

5. *scull*] small rowing boat.
mistook] was wrecked.

Where I did feast my fancy and mine eyes
With such variety of rarities,
That I perceive thy muse frequents some shade
Might be a grove for a Pierian maid.   10
Let idiots prate; it boots not what they say.
Th'Antipodes to wit and learning may
Have ample priv'lege, for among that crew
I know there's not a man can judge of you.
                                              Robert Chamberlain.   15

The Persons in the Play (in order of appearance)

Prologue.
BLAZE, *an herald painter.*
JOYLESS, *an old country gentleman.*
HUGHBALL, *a doctor of physic.*
BARBARA, *wife to Blaze.*   5
MARTHA, *wife to Peregrine.*
LETOY, *a fantastic lord.*
QUAILPIPE, *his curate.*
PEREGRINE, *son to Joyless.*
DIANA, *wife to Joyless.*   10
BYPLAY, *a conceited servant to Letoy.*
TRUELOCK, *a close friend to Letoy.*
Followers *of the Lord Letoy's, who are actors in the byplay.*

0.1. (in . . . appearance)] *not in* Q *(which gives them in this order).*

    6.] Probably glancing at Andrea's passage to the underworld in Kyd's much-parodied play *The Spanish Tragedy* (c.1587): 'When I was slain, my soul descended straight/To pass the flowing stream of Acheron' (I.i.18–19).
    10. *Pierian maid*] one of the Muses, who were born in Pieria on the slopes of Mount Olympus.
    15. *Robert Chamberlain*] writer and wit whose play The *Swaggering Damsel* was published in the same year as The *Antipodes.*
    2. BLAZE . . . painter] To *blaze* is to describe in heraldic terms the arms that a herald painter depicts on shields, banners etc. Brome's character derives his role as host and presenter from the word's figurative sense of 'portray', carrying a hint of ostentation and panache.
    7. fantastic] eccentric.
    8. *QUAILPIPE*] suggesting a high-pitched and querulous voice, clearly then as now part of the stereotype of the curate. A quailpipe was a whistle used by fowlers to lure quails by imitating their call.
    11–13. BYPLAY . . . byplay] *OED*'s definition, 'action carried on aside . . . while the main action proceeds' accords better with the character's role than with the function of the 'inner' play; but in neither case does it suggest the fluid relationship between the parts of Brome's action. *OED*'s first example is from 1812.
    11. conceited] quick-witted, inventive.

THE PROLOGUE

Enter Prologue.

Opinion, which our author cannot court
For the dear daintiness of it, has of late
From the old way of plays possessed a sort
Only to run to those that carry state
In scene magnificent and language high,   5
And clothes worth all the rest, except the action.
And such are only good, those leaders cry;
And into that belief draw on a faction
That must despise all sportive, merry wit,
Because some such great play had none in it.   10

But it is known (peace to their memories)
The poets late sublimèd from our age,
Who best could understand and best devise
Works that must ever live upon the stage,
Did well approve and lead this humble way   15
Which we are bound to travel in tonight.
And though it be not traced so well as they
Discovered it by true Phoebean light,
Pardon our just ambition yet that strive

0.1.] *not in* Q.   16. travel] trauaile Q.

---

3. *possessed a sort*] seduced a particular set. Brome alludes to the fashion at the Caroline court for plays on elevated themes like platonic love and ideal friendship; his play *The Love-sick Court* (c.1635) is a sustained burlesque of the mode.
4–6. *those . . . rest*] The sumptuous staging and design of some of the court drama of the 1630s drew criticism from various quarters; a notorious example was Suckling's *Aglaura* (staged a few months before *Antipodes*) which according to a contemporary report 'cost three or four hundred Pounds setting out, eight or ten Suits of new Cloaths he gave the Players; an unheard of Prodigality' (cited by Haaker from Bentley, V.1202).
12. *poets . . . age*] Brome's mentor Jonson had recently died in 1637; the range of his own work suggests that as well as recalling other dramatists who wrote citizen comedy, like Dekker (died 1632), Marston and Chapman (died 1634), he also cherished the memory of Fletcher and Shakespeare.
16. *travel*] Q's *travaile* carries the equally forceful sense of 'labour'. The pun is a very common one; see note to I.i.175.
18. *Phoebean*] In Virgil's *Eclogues* Phoebus Apollo is the patron of poetry and music; the term reinforces the oracular authority claimed in 11–15 for an elder generation of dramatists.

To keep the weakest branch o'th' stage alive.   20

I mean the weakest in their great esteem
That count all slight that's under us, or nigh,
And only those for worthy subjects deem,
Fetched, or reached at (at least) from far or high,
When low and homebred subjects have their use   25
As well as those fetched from on high or far.
And 'tis as hard a labour for the muse
To move the earth as to dislodge a star.
See yet those glorious plays, and let their sight
Your admiration move; these, your delight.   *Exit.*

---

30. *Exit.*] *not in* Q.

20. *weakest . . . stage*] the endangered traditions of English comedy. In the lines that
follow Brome establishes his claim to use exotic ideas and subjects for 'homebred'
purposes.
    22. *under . . . nigh*] conflating two fashionable prejudices: first, against plays that do
not deal with elevated subjects, and second, the supposed English disdain for what lies
near to home. The phrase *under us* also slyly anticipates the action to come.
    30. *admiration*] sense of wonder.

ACT I

SCENE i

Enter BLAZE *and* JOYLESS.

Blaze. To me, and to the city, sir, you are welcome,
    And so are all about you. We have long
    Suffered in want of such fair company.
    But now that time's calamity has given way
    (Thanks to high Providence) to your kinder visits,   5
    We are, like half-pined wretches that have lain
    Long on the planks of sorrow, strictly tied
    To a forced abstinence from the sight of friends,
    The sweetlier filled with joy.
Joyless   Alas, I bring
    Sorrow too much with me to fill one house   10
    In the sad number of my family.
Blaze. Be comforted, good sir. My house, which now
    You may be pleased to call your own, is large
    Enough to hold you all. And for your sorrows,
    You came to lose 'em, and I hope the means   15
    Is readily at hand. The doctor's coming
    Who, as by letters I advertised you,
    Is the most promising man to cure your son
    The kingdom yields. It will astonish you
    To hear the marvels he hath done in cures   20
    Of such distracted ones as is your son,
    And not so much by bodily physic (no,
    He sends few recipes to th'apothecaries)
    As medicine of the mind, which he infuses
    So skilfully, yet by familiar ways,   25

1.SP] *not in* Q.

3. *Suffered . . . want*] felt the absence. This is also the actors' welcome to their
returning public (see next note and Bentley II.664), foreshadowing the Joyless family's
role of audience to Letoy's play.
4. *time's calamity*] The plague had closed London's theatres from 12 May 1636 to
2 October 1637, except for a single week during the winter.
6. *half-pined*] half-starved, like sailors on an arduous ocean voyage.
23. *recipes*] medical prescriptions.

That it begets both wonder and delight
In his observers, while the stupid patient
Finds health at unawares.

Joyless.   You speak well of him.
Yet I may fear my son's long-grown disease
Is such he hath not met with.

Blaze.   Then I'll tell you, sir.   30
He cured a country gentleman that fell mad
For spending of his land before he sold it;
That is, 'twas sold to pay his debts. All went
That way for a dead horse, as one would say;
He had not money left to buy his dinner   35
Upon that wholesale day. This was a cause
Might make a gentleman mad, you'll say; and him
It did, as mad as landless squire could be.
This doctor by his art removed his madness
And mingled so much wit among his brains   40
That, by the overflowing of it merely,
He gets and spends five hundred pound a year now
As merrily as any gentleman
In Derbyshire. I name no man; but this
Was pretty well, you'll say.

Joyless.   My son's disease   45
Grows not that way.

Blaze.   There was a lady mad—
I name no lady—but stark mad she was
As any in the country, city, or almost
In court could be.

Joyless.   How fell she mad?

Blaze.   With study,
Tedious and painful study. And for what   50
Now, can you think?

Joyless.   For painting, or new fashions?

---

26. *both . . . delight*] Cf. Prologue, 30; but Brome is now claiming by analogy to offer both in his own play.

27. *stupid*] stunned.

33–4. *All . . . horse*] proverbial (H699); this expression of wasted effort survives in the phrase 'to flog a dead horse'.

36. *wholesale*] sell-out.

44. *Derbyshire*] Then, as now, a prosperous county.

48–9. *almost . . . court*] Another dig at court excesses.

51. *painting*] putting on make-up. Cosmetics were an elaborate art in the period, and a frequent target of satirists.

I cannot think for the philosopher's stone.
Blaze. No, 'twas to find a way to love her husband,
　　　Because she did not, and her friends rebuked her.
　　　Joyless. Was that so hard to find, if she desired it?　　55
Blaze. She was seven years in search of it, and could not,
　　　Though she consumed his whole estate by it.
Joyless. 'Twas he was mad then.
Blaze.　　　　　　　　　　　No, he was not born
　　　With wit enough to lose! But mad was she
　　　Until this doctor took her into cure.　　　　　　　60
　　　And now she lies as lovingly on a flockbed
　　　With her own knight as she had done on down
　　　With many others; but I name no parties.
　　　Yet this was well, you'll say.
Joyless.　　　　　　　　　　Would all were well!
Blaze. Then, sir, of officers and men of place,　　　　65
　　　Whose senses were so numbed they understood not
　　　Bribes from due fees, and fell on praemunires,
　　　He has cured divers that can now distinguish
　　　And know both when and how to take of both,
　　　And grow most safely rich by't. T'other day　　　70
　　　He set the brains of an attorney right
　　　That were quite topsy-turvy overturned
　　　In a pitch o'er the bar, so that (poor man)
　　　For many moons he knew not whether he
　　　Went on his heels or's head, till he was brought　　75
　　　To this rare doctor; now he walketh again
　　　As upright in his calling as the boldest
　　　Amongst 'em. This was well, you'll say.
Joyless.　　　　　　　　　　　　'Tis much.
Blaze. And then for horn-mad citizens, my neighbours,

---

52. *philosopher's stone*] the elusive formula sought by alchemists to enable the transformation of base metals into gold and silver. Single-minded effort coupled with moral purity were essential to its discovery; Joyless detects the former but not the latter in female habits and pursuits.

61. *flockbed*] mattress stuffed with coarse wool and cotton tufts; a poor quality bed.

65. *men of place*] public officials.

66. *understood not*] had forgotten how to distinguish.

67. *fell ... praemunires*] got mixed up in shady practices. Technically, praemunire is the offence of taking a case to a court outside crown jurisdiction, but the term was often used more loosely of legal irregularities.

73. *In ... bar*] by being disbarred.

79. *horn-mad*] insanely jealous (fearing the cuckold's horns).

He cures them by the dozens, and we live   80
As gently with our wives as rams with ewes.
Joyless. We do, you say—were you one of his patients?
Blaze. [*Aside*] 'Slid, he has almost catched me.—No, sir, no.
I name no parties, I, but wish you merry.
I strain to make you so, and could tell forty   85
Notable cures of his to pass the time
Until he comes.
Joyless   But, pray, has he the art
To cure a husband's jealousy?
Blaze. Mine, sir, he did—[*Aside*] 'Sfoot, I am catched again.
Joyless. But still you name no party. Pray, how long,   90
Good Master Blaze, has this so famous doctor,
Whom you so well set out, been a professor?
Blaze. Never in public; nor endures the name
Of doctor—though I call him so—but lives
With an odd lord in town, that looks like no lord.   95
My doctor goes more like a lord than he.

Enter Doctor HUGHBALL.

O, welcome sir. I sent mine own wife for you.
Ha' you brought her home again?
Doctor.   She's in your house
With gentlewomen who seem to lodge here.
Blaze. Yes, sir, this gentleman's wife and his son's wife.   100
They all ail something, but his son, 'tis thought,
Is falling into madness, and is brought
Up by his careful father to the town here
To be your patient. Speak with him about it.
Doctor. [*To Joyless*] How do you find him, sir? Does his
                                             disease   105
Take him by fits, or is it constantly
And at all times the same?
Joyless.   For the most part

---

82. *We*] *emph. this ed.;* We *Q.*   96.1.] *Ex.Doctor. Q.*   98.] *Act* I.*Scen.*2. *Blaze,
Doctor, Ioylesse. Q* (*after* againe?)

---

83. *'Slid*] common oath (by God's eyelid).
89. *'Sfoot*] by God's foot.
92. *a professor*] practising.
98.] Q and subsequent editors begin a new scene here. This edition abandons
Brome's Jonsonian practice of marking the entry of a new character with a scene
break: see Note on the Text.
103. *careful*] worried.

It is only inclining still to worse
As he grows more in days. By all the best
Conjectures we have met with in the country,   110
'Tis found a most deep melancholy.
Doctor. Of what years is he?
Joyless.   Of five and twenty, sir.
Doctor. Was it born with him? Is it natural
Or accidental? Have you or his mother
Been so at any time affected?
Joyless.   Never.   115
Not she unto her grave, nor I till then,
Knew what a sadness meant; though since I have,
In my son's sad condition, and some crosses
In my late marriage, which at further time
I may acquaint you with.
Blaze. [*Aside*]   The old man's jealous   120
Of his young wife! I find him by the question
He put me to ere while.
Doctor.   Is your son married?
Joyless. Divers years since; for we had hope a wife
Might have restrained his travelling thoughts, and so
Have been a means to cure him, but it failed us.   125
Doctor. What has he in his younger years been most
Addicted to? What study, or what practice?
Joyless. You have now, sir, found the question which, I think,
Will lead you to the ground of his distemper.
Doctor. That's the next way to the cure. Come quickly,
                                        quickly.   130
Joyless. In tender years he always loved to read
Reports of travels and of voyages.
And when young boys like him would tire themselves
With sports and pastimes, and restore their spirits
Again by meat and sleep, he would whole days   135
And nights (sometimes by stealth) be on such books
As might convey his fancy round the world.

113–5. *Was...affected*] 'That other inward inbred cause of Melancholy is our temperature ... which wee receive from our parents ... looke what disease the father had when he begot him, such his sonne will have after him' (Burton, I.2.i.6). Burton distinguishes this natural cause from those that are 'outward and adventitious', like bad diet.

118. *crosses*] snags, problems.

127. *study*] Excessive bookishness was a proverbial cause of melancholy.
practice] kind of activity.

130. *next*] quickest.

Doctor. Very good; on.

Joyless.   When he grew up towards twenty,
His mind was all on fire to be abroad.
Nothing but travel still was all his aim;   140
There was no voyage or foreign expedition
Be said to be in hand, but he made suit
To be made one in it. His mother and
Myself opposed him still in all and, strongly
Against his will, still held him in and won   145
Him into marriage, hoping that would call
In his extravagant thoughts. But all prevailed not,
Nor stayed him—though at home—from travelling
So far beyond himself that now, too late,
I wish he had gone abroad to meet his fate.   150

Doctor. Well, sir, upon good terms I'll undertake
Your son. Let's see him.

Joyless.   Yet there's more: his wife, sir.

Doctor. I'll undertake her, too. Is she mad, too?

Blaze. They'll ha' mad children then!

Doctor.   Hold you your peace.

Joyless. Alas, the danger is they will have none.   155
He takes no joy in her, and she no comfort
In him; for though they have been three years wed,
They are yet ignorant of the marriage bed.

Doctor. I shall find her the madder of the two, then.

Joyless. Indeed, she's full of passion, which she utters   160
By the effects, as diversely as several
Objects reflect upon her wand'ring fancy:
Sometimes in extreme weepings, and anon
In vehement laughter; now in sullen silence,
And presently in loudest exclamations.   165

Doctor. Come, let me see 'em, sir; I'll undertake
Her, too. Ha' you any more? How does your wife?

Joyless. Some other time for her.

Doctor.   I'll undertake
Her, too. And you yourself, sir, by your favour

---

147. *extravagant*] roving, wandering.

161–2.] unpredictably, depending on what happens to strike her.

166. *undertake*] At the second repetition the word's bawdy implication begins to obtrude, especially as Martha's symptoms are clearly those of melancholy caused by female celibacy (see Burton, I.3.ii.4, a passage Brome appears to be following here).

And some few yellow spots which I perceive   170
About your temples, may require some counsel.

Enter BARBARA.

Blaze. [*Aside*] So, he has found him.
Joyless.   But my son, my son, sir!
Blaze. Now, Bab, what news?
Barbara.   There's news too much within
          For any homebred, Christian understanding.
Joyless. How does my son?
Barbara.   He is in travail, sir.   175
Joyless. His fit's upon him?
Barbara.   Yes. Pray, Doctor Hughball,
          Play the man-midwife and deliver him
          Of his huge tympany of news—of monsters,
          Pygmies and giants, apes and elephants,
          Griffins and crocodiles, men upon women,   180
          And women upon men, the strangest doings—
          As far beyond all Christendom as 'tis to't.
Doctor. How, how?
Barbara.   Beyond the moon and stars, I think,
          Or Mount in Cornwall either.
Blaze. How prettily like a fool she talks!   185
          And she were not mine own wife, I could be
          So taken with her.
Doctor.   'Tis most wondrous strange.

171.1.] *Act* 1.Scene 3. *Enter Barbara. Q.*

170. *some ... spots*] Hughball mischievously interprets age-spots as symptoms of jealousy—appropriate to the conventional figure of the old man with a young wife.

175. *in travail*] on another of his journeys. The word was pronounced 'travel', and here puns on 'in labour', setting up the childbirth image in 177.

178. *huge ... news*] collection of inflated tales. A *tympany* was literally a morbid swelling or tumour.

news] The items of popular lore that follow were an enduring kind of news (as they still are in some tabloid journalism), and testify to a world-view shaped by sixteenth-century cosmographies and Pliny's *Naturall History*, as well as by Peregrine's immediate source, Mandeville's *Voyages and Travailes*.

180. *Griffins*] Mythical beasts with 'the body before as an Eagle, and behinde as a Lyon ... but ... greater then eight Lyons, and stronger then an hundred Eagles' (Mandeville, R2v).

180–1. *men ... doings*] 'in another Ile are folks that are both men and women, and have members of both, for to engender with, & when they will, they use one at one time, & another at another time' (Mandeville, O3).

182.] As alien to Christian practice as these regions are distant from us.

184. *Mount*] St Michael's Mount near Penzance.

Barbara. He talks much of the kingdom of Cathaya,
     Of one Great Khan and goodman Prester John
     (Whate'er they be), and says that Khan's a clown   190
     Unto the John he speaks of; and that John
     Dwells up almost at Paradise. But sure his mind
     Is in a wilderness, for there he says
     Are geese that have two heads apiece, and hens
     That bear more wool upon their backs than sheep—   195
Doctor. O, Mandeville. Let's to him. Lead the way, sir.
Barbara. And men with heads like hounds!
Doctor.   Enough, enough.
Barbara. You'll find enough within, I warrant ye.
                    Exeunt DOCTOR, BLAZE *and* JOYLESS.

                    Enter MARTHA.

     And here comes the poor mad gentleman's wife,
     Almost as mad as he. She haunts me all   200
     About the house to impart something to me.
     Poor heart, I guess her grief, and pity her.
     To keep a maidenhead three years after marriage
     Under wedlock and key! Insufferable, monstrous!

198.1–2.] *Ex.3.Ent.Mar. Q (scene division omitted).*   204. key!...monstrous!] key,
insufferable! monstrous, *Q.*

---

188. *Cathaya*] China—though contemporary writers are often unsure whether they
are one and the same. The name evoked for Europeans a vast and distant region.
    189. *Great Khan*] Emperor of China.
    Prester John] The legendary Christian priest-king of Ethiopia, a vaguely defined
region which was often conflated with 'the Indies' by medieval geographers. Scholarly
opinion rejected the African connection, and held that Prester John had been a
powerful Christian prince in north-east Asia whose dominions were overrun by the
Tartars under Genghis Khan in the thirteenth century. See E. Brerewood, *Enquiries
touching the Diversity of Languages* (1614), pp. 74–5, and Torquemeda, p. 114.
    190–1. *Khan's...John*] Haaker points out that Peregrine rejects Mandeville's
assessment (Q2), which echoed most authorities in asserting the superior power of the
Great Khan. One effect of transposing Prester John to Africa was to renew the myth of
his vast empire: in 1636 Mercator's *Atlas* (which Peregrine doubtless pored over)
affirmed that he 'ought to be ranked among the greatest Monarchs of our age, whose
Dominions reach from the one to the other Tropick; from the *Red-Sea* unto the
Æthiopicke Ocean' (II.431).
    191–2. *John...Paradise*] 'Beyond the Iles of the land of *Prester John*' lies a
wilderness which 'lasteth to Paradise *terrestre*, where *Adam* and *Eve* were set...Men
say that Paradise *terrestre* is the highest land of all the world' (Mandeville, T3).
    194–7. *geese...hounds*] All are illustrated by wood-cuts in editions of Mandeville
(in 1625 ed. on sigs.N4v, Ov, O4).
    196. *Mandeville*] Mandeville's *Travels* (see Intro., note 2) was reprinted five times
between 1612 and 1639. As Haaker points out (p. 27), Brome appears to be using the
1625 edition.

It turns into a wolf within the flesh,　　　　　　　　　　205
Not to be fed with chickens and tame pigeons.
I could wish maids be warn'd by't not to marry
Before they have wit to lose their maidenheads
For fear they match with men whose wits are past it.
What a sad look! And what a sigh was there!—　　　210
Sweet Mistress Joyless, how is't with you now?

Martha. When I shall know, I'll tell. Pray tell me first,
How long have you been married?

Barbara. [*Aside*]　　　　　　　　Now she is on it.—
Three years, forsooth.

Martha.　　　　　　　And, truly, so have I;
We shall agree, I see.

Barbara.　　　　　　If you'll be merry.　　　　　215

Martha. No woman merrier, now I have met with one
Of my condition. Three years married, say you? Ha, ha,
　　　　　　　　　　　　　　　　　　　　　　ha!

Barbara. What ails she, trow?

Martha.　　　　　　Three years married! Ha, ha, ha!

Barbara. Is that a laughing matter?

Martha.　　　　　　　'Tis just my story.
And you have had no child; that's still my story. Ha, ha,
　　　　　　　　　　　　　　　　　　　ha! 220

Barbara. Nay, I have had two children.

Martha.　　　　　　　　Are you sure on't,
Or does your husband only tell you so?
Take heed o' that, for husbands are deceitful.

Barbara. But I am o'the surer side. I am sure
I groan'd for mine and bore 'em, when at best　　225
He but believes he got 'em.

Martha.　　　　　　Yet both he
And you may be deceived, for now I'll tell you,
My husband told me, faced me down and stood on't,
We had three sons, and all great travellers—

205–6. *wolf . . . pigeons*] Haaker cites Topsell, *The Historie of Four-Footed Beastes* (1607), p. 746: 'There is a disease called a wolfe, because it consumeth and eateth up the flesh in the bodie next the sore, and must every day be fed with fresh meat, as Lambes, Pigeons, and such other things wherein is bloode, or else it consumeth al the flesh of the body, leaving not so much as the skin to cover the bones.'

218. *trow*] I wonder.

229–30.] Probably alluding to the Sherley brothers, whose exploits were recorded by Purchas and who had recently been recalled by Sir Thomas Herbert in his *Relation of Some Yeares Travaile* (1634). Herbert offers a warm appreciation of Robert Sherley, 'the greatest Traveller in his time' (p. 125), who was still remembered for his exploits against the Turks.

That one had shook The Great Turk by the beard.   230
I never saw 'em, nor am I such a fool
To think that children can be got and born,
Trained up to men, and then sent out to travel,
And the poor mother never know nor feel
Any such matter. There's a dream indeed!   235
Barbara. Now you speak reason, and 'tis nothing but
Your husband's madness that would put that dream
Into you.
Martha.   He may put dreams into me, but
He ne'er put child, nor anything towards it yet
To me to making. (*Weeps.*) Something, sure, belongs   240
To such a work; for I am past a child
Myself to think they are found in parsley beds,
Strawberry banks, or rosemary bushes, though
I must confess 1 have sought and searched such places,
Because I would fain have had one.
Barbara. [*Aside*]   'Las, poor fool!   245
Martha. Pray tell me, for I think nobody hears us,
How came you by your babes? I cannot think
Your husband got them you.
Barbara. [*Aside*]   Fool, did I say?
She is a witch, I think.—Why not my husband?
Pray, can you charge me with another man?   250
Martha. Nor with him neither. Be not angry, pray now;
For were I now to die, I cannot guess
What a man does in child-getting. I remember
A wanton maid once lay with me, and kissed
And clipped and clapped me strangely, and then wished   255
That I had been a man to have got her with child.
What must I then ha' done, or (good now, tell me)
What has your husband done to you?
Barbara. [*Aside*]   Was ever
Such a poor piece of innocence three years married!
Does not your husband use to lie with you?   260
Martha. Yes, he does use to lie with me, but he does not

---

240. (Weeps.)] *weepe.* Q.   262. he] *Baker; she* Q.   278. *Exeunt*] *Ex.* (*after 277 in*
Q).

---

242. *parsley beds*] a common piece of English folk-lore; see OED for examples.
249. *She . . . witch*] because she has apparently divined Barbara's infidelity.
255. *clipped and clapped*] embraced and patted. In this suggestive context the
second word may imply something more firmly administered; 'slap and tickle' is a
recent equivalent.

Lie with me to use me as he should, I fear;
Nor do I know to teach him. Will you tell me?
I'll lie with you and practise, if you please.
Pray take me for a night or two, or take   265
My husband and instruct him but one night.
Our country folks will say you London wives
Do not lie every night with your own husbands.
Barbara. Your country folks should have done well to ha' sent
Some news by you! But I trust none told you there   270
We use to leave our fools to lie with madmen.
Martha. Nay, now again y'are angry.
Barbara.   No, not I,
But rather pity your simplicity.
Come, I'll take charge and care of you—
Martha.   I thank you.
Barbara. And wage my skill against my doctor's art   275
Sooner to ease you of these dangerous fits
Than he shall rectify your husband's wits.
Martha. Indeed, indeed, I thank you.   *Exeunt.*

ACT I   SCENE ii

Enter LETOY *dressed like a servant and carrying a letter,*
with BLAZE.

Letoy. Why, broughtst thou not mine arms and pedigree
Home with thee, Blaze, mine honest herald's painter?
Blaze. I have not yet, my lord, but all's in readiness
According to the herald's full directions.
Letoy. But has he gone to the root; has he derived me   5
Ex origine, ab antiquo? Has he fetched me
Far enough, Blaze?
Blaze.   Full four descents beyond
The conquest, my good lord, and finds that one

ACT I SCENE ii] *Act.1.Scene.5. Q.   0.1–2.] this ed.; Letoy, Blaze. Q.*

267–8. *you . . . husbands*] A familiar satire on city wives; cf. *The Court Begger,* I.i
(*Works* 1873, I.294).
271. *We . . . leave*] We're in the habit of deserting.
6. *fetched me*] traced me back.
7–9. *Full . . . Conqueror*] Henry Peacham explains that 'the ancients of our Nobility
for the greater part, acknowledge themselves to bee descended out of *Normandy,* and
to have come in with the Conquerour, many retaining their ancient *French* names'
(*The Compleat Gentleman,* 1622, p. 142).

Of your French ancestry came in with the Conqueror.
Letoy. Jeffrey Letoy; 'twas he from whom the English   10
Letoys have our descent, and here have took
Such footing that we'll never out while France
Is France, and England England,
And the sea passable to transport a fashion.
My ancestors and I have been beginners   15
Of all new fashions in the court of England
From before *Primo Ricardi Secundi*
Until this day.
Blaze. [*Indicating Letoy's attire*] I cannot think, my lord,
They'll follow you in this though.
Letoy.   Mark the end.
I am without a precedent for my humour.   20
But is it spread, and talked of in the town?
Blaze. It is, my lord, and laughed at by a many.
Letoy. I am more beholding to them than all the rest.
Their laughter makes me merry; others' mirth
And not mine own it is that feeds me, that   25
Battens me as poor men's cost does usurers.
But tell me, Blaze, what say they of me, ha?
Blaze. They say, my lord, you look more like a pedlar
Than like a lord, and live more like an emperor.
Letoy. Why, there they ha' me right! Let others shine   30
Abroad in cloth o' bodkin; my broadcloth
Pleases mine eye as well, my body better.
Besides, I'm sure 'tis paid for—to their envy.
I buy with ready money; and at home here
With as good meat, as much magnificence,   35
As costly pleasures, and as rare delights
Can satisfy my appetite and senses
As they with all their public shows and braveries.

23.SP] *Baker; om. Q.*

17. Primo . . . Secundi] Richard II's reign, beginning in 1377, was thought to mark
an increase in the influence of French fashion in England.
  19. *this*] adopting such humble attire.
  20. *humour*] whim, caprice.
  26. *Battens*] sustains, fattens.
  31. *Abroad*] in public.
  cloth o'bodkin] cloth, usually silk or linen, worked with gold and silver thread and
embroidered with raised patterns (Linthicum).
  broadcloth] woollen cloth of plain weave, two yards wide, which was the staple of
the garment industry until displaced by new fabrics; by the seventeenth century it was
worn mainly by servants (Linthicum).

They run at ring and tilt 'gainst one another;
I and my men can play a match at football,   40
Wrestle a handsome fall, and pitch the bar,
And crack the cudgels, and a pate sometimes,
'Twould do you good to see't.
Blaze.   More than to feel't!
Letoy. They hunt the deer, the hare, the fox, the otter,
Polecats, or harlots, what they please, whilst I   45
And my mad grigs, my men, can run at base,
And breathe ourselves at barley-break and dancing.
Blaze. Yes, my lord, i'th' country, when you are there.
Letoy. And now I am here i'th' city, sir, I hope
I please myself with more choice home delights,
Than most men of my rank.   50
Blaze.   I know, my lord,
Your house in substance is an amphitheatre
Of exercise and pleasure.
Letoy.   Sir, I have
For exercises, fencing, dancing, vaulting,
And for delight, music of all best kinds.
Stage plays and masques are nightly my pastimes,   55
And all within myself: my own men are
My music and my actors. I keep not
A man or boy but is of quality;
The worst can sing or play his part o'th' viols   60
And act his part, too, in a comedy,
For which I lay my bravery on their backs.

40–2.] Burton sees these as the 'common recreations of country folks' (II.2.iv.1), and Peacham agrees: 'For throwing and wrestling, I hold them exercises not so well beseeming Nobilitie, but rather Souldiers in a Campe' (p. 179).

42. *crack ... pate*] Each player at cudgels wielded two staffs, one to defend himself and the other to attack his opponent's head.

44. *They*] the gentry.

45. *Polecats*] Regarded as vermin rather than sport. The word was also slang for a prostitute, and prompts Letoy's last item of prey.

46. *mad grigs*] wild boys, exuberant fellows.

base] Game played by two teams, in which anyone caught outside their base is taken prisoner by the opposing side.

47. *barley-break*] Game in which one couple is placed between two others whom they have to catch.

52. *amphitheatre*] The word was associated with classical arenas and places of contest, but its technical sense of 'double theatre' is used here figuratively to suggest the variety of entertainment on offer.

57. *within myself*] created out of my own resources.

61. *comedy*] play.

62. *bravery*] finery.

And where another lord undoes his followers,
I maintain mine like lords. (*Hoboys*) And there's my
                                        bravery.

*A service as for dinner pass over the stage, borne by
many servitors richly apparelled, doing honour to
Letoy as they pass. Exeunt.*

Now tell me, Blaze, look these like pedlar's men?   65
Blaze. Rather an emperor's, my lord.
Letoy.   I tell thee,
These lads can act the emperors' lives all over,
And Shakespeare's chronicled histories, to boot.
And were that Caesar or that English earl
That loved a play and player so well now living,   70
I would not be outvied in my delights.
Blaze. My lord, 'tis well.
Letoy.   I love the quality
Of playing: ay, I love a play with all
My heart, a good one; and a player that is
A good one, too, withal. As for the poets,   75
No men love them, I think, and therefore
I write all my plays myself, and make no doubt
Some of the court will follow
Me in that, too. Let my fine lords
Talk o' their horse tricks, and their jockeys that   80
Can out-talk them. Let the gallants boast
Their May-games, play-games, and their mistresses;

---

64. *Hoboys.*] *prefaces* 64.1–3 *in* Q.   75. *withal*] *this ed.; with all my heart* Q.

---

63. *undoes*] dismisses.
64. Hoboys] Common English spelling of 'hautboy', the forerunner of the modern oboe.
69. *Caesar . . . earl*] The emperor Nero patronised lavish theatrical spectacles; the Earl of Leicester had been an important sponsor of Elizabethan players, and his troupe established the first permanent theatre in London in 1576.
72. *quality*] profession.
75. *withal*] besides. Q reads *with all my heart*, but the phrase makes the line hypermetrical, and seems to have been caught from 73–4, with the compositor lulled into repetition by the second occurrence of 'withall' in the MS.
78–9. *Some . . . too*] A dig at the courtier-dramatists who produce plays which they 'boast to have made . . . when for ought you know they bought 'em of Universitie Scholars' (Epilogue to *The Court Begger*, *Works 1873*, I.271, cited by Haaker).
82. *May-games*] frolics. Cf. John Fletcher's complaint that his pastoral play *The Faithful Shepherdess* failed because 'the people . . . missing whitsun ales, creame, wassel and morris-dances, began to be angry' (*Works*, ed. Bowers, III.497). But the

I love a play in my plain clothes—ay,
And laugh upon the actors in their brave ones.

Enter QUAILPIPE.

Quailpipe. My lord, your dinner stays prepared.
Letoy.   Well, well,   85
    Be you as ready with your grace as I
    Am for my meat, and all is well.   *Exit Quailpipe.*
        Blaze, we have rambled
    From the main point this while. It seems by his letter
    My doctor's busy at thy house. I know who's there,
    Beside. Give him this ring; tell him it wants   90
    A finger. Farewell, good Blaze.   *Exit* LETOY.
Blaze. Tell him it wants a finger? My small wit
    Already finds what finger it must fit.   *Exit.*

ACT I SCENE iii

Enter Doctor HUGHBALL, PEREGRINE *with a book in his hand,*
JOYLESS *and* DIANA.

Doctor. Sir, I applaud your noble disposition,
    And even adore the spirit of travel in you,
    And purpose to wait on it through the world,
    In which I shall but tread again the steps
    I heretofore have gone.
Peregrine. All the world o'er ha' you been already?   5
Doctor. Over and under, too.
Peregrine.   In the antipodes?
Doctor. Yes, through and through;
    No isle nor angle in that nether world

---

83. —ay,] I, Q.   85.SP *Quailpipe.*] *Re.* Q.   91,93. SDs] *not in* Q.
ACT I SCENE iii] *Act.1.Scene 6.* Q.   0.1. *with*] *not in* Q.

---

slighting reference may also allude to the fact that traditional festivities had an
important political dimension after Charles I reissued the *Book of Sports* in 1633 and
insisted that rural custom be sustained by the nobility and gentry. See Leah Marcus,
The Politics of Mirth, 1986, pp. 3–15.
    play-games] trivial diversions.
    85. SP] Instead of the character's name Q has *Re.*, which editors interpret as
'retainer'; more plausibly it is short for 'reader', the role later ascribed to Quailpipe
(II.ii.70). But it is also possible that the actor rather than the character is nominated
here, and that Quailpipe was played by Timothy Reade, who specialised in clown roles
with the Queen's Men. See II.ii.70 note.

But I have made discovery of. Pray, sir, sit.   10
[*To Joyless*] And, sir, be you attentive. I will warrant
His speedy cure without the help of Galen,
Hippocrates, Avicen, or Dioscorides.
Diana. A rare man! Husband, truly I like his person
As well as his rare skill.
Joyless.   Into your chamber!   15
I do not like your liking of men's persons.
Doctor. Nay, lady, you may stay. Hear and admire,
If you so please, but make no interruptions.
Joyless. [*Aside to Diana*] And let no looser words, or
                                        wand'ring look,
Bewray an intimation of the slight   20
Regard you bear your husband, lest I send you
Upon a further pilgrimage than he
Feigns to convey my son.
Diana.   O jealousy!
Doctor. Do you think, sir, to th' antipodes such a journey?
Peregrine. I think there's none beyond it; and that Mandeville,   25
Whose excellent work this is, was th'only man
That e'er came near it.
Doctor.   Mandeville went far.
Peregrine. Beyond all English legs that I can read of.
Doctor. What think you, sir, of Drake, our famous
                                        countryman?
Peregrine. Drake was a didapper to Mandeville.   30
Candish, and Hawkins, Furbisher, all our voyagers
Went short of Mandeville. [*Turns pages.*] But had he
                                        reached

12–13. *Galen...Dioscorides*] Hippocrates was the father of Greek medical science, and his successors, including Dioscorides in the first century AD and especially Galen in the second, laid the foundations of European practice until early modern times. The Arab physician Avicenna (Ibn-Sina) helped to transmit the classical legacy to the West in the eleventh century.

20. *Bewray*] reveal.

30. *didapper*] dabchick, a small water-fowl—often used as term of ridicule.

31. *Candish*] Thomas Cavendish, who in 1586–8 emulated Drake's circumnavigation of the globe.

Hawkins] Either Sir Richard, who failed to complete a voyage to Japan in 1593 but 'whose mighty mind small things could not suffice', or his father Sir John Hawkins, 'who with his furrowing Keele,/ . . . touch'd the goodly rich *Brazeel*' (Michael Drayton, *Polyolbion* (1622), 19th Song, Pt.2, sig.C).

Furbisher] Martin Frobisher, the first Englishman to search for the North-West passage in the 1570s.

To this place here—yes, here—this wilderness,
And seen the trees of the sun and moon, that speak
And told King Alexander of his death, he then   35
Had left a passage ope for travellers
That now is kept and guarded by wild beasts—
Dragons, and serpents, elephants white and blue,
Unicorns, and lions of many colours,
And monsters more, as numberless as nameless.   40
Doctor. Stay there—
Peregrine.   Read here else. Can you read?
Is it not true?
Doctor.   No truer than I ha' seen't.
Diana. Ha' you been there, sir? Ha' you seen those trees?
Doctor. And talked with 'em, and tasted of their fruit.
Peregrine. Read here again then: it is written here   45
That you may live four or five hundred year.
Diana. Brought you none of that fruit home with you, sir?
Joyless. You would have some of't, would you, to have hope
T'outlive your husband by't?
Diana,   I'd ha't for you,
In hope you might outlive your jealousy.   50
Doctor. Your patience both, I pray. I know the grief
You both do labour with, and how to cure it.
Joyless. Would I had given you half my land, 'twere done.
Diana. Would I had given him half my love, to settle
The t'other half free from encumbrances   55
Upon my husband.
Doctor.   Do not think it strange, sir.
I'll make your eyes witnesses of more
Than I relate, if you'll but travel with me.

33–46.] A close paraphrase of the account in Mandeville of the wilderness beyond the land of Prester John, where are to be found 'the trees of the Sunne, and of the Moone, that speke to King *Alexander*, and told him of his death, and men say, that those that keepe those trees and eat of the fruits of them, live foure or five hundred yeere through vertue of the fruit, and wee would gladly have gone thither, but I thinke that an hundred thousand men of armes could not passe that wildernesse for the plentie of wilde beasts, as Dragons, and Serpents ... Elephants, both white and blue, without number, & Unicornes, and Lyons of many colours' (T2).

36. *a ... travellers*] In fact passage to the East had been effectively closed since the fourteenth century by the spread of Islam. Cf. *Travels*, viii.21 note.

44. *tasted ... fruit*] A boast which recalls the Mandevillian claim 'Of that fruit I have eaten', when describing a type of gourd which 'when it is Ripe men cut it asunder, and they find therein a Beast as it were of flesh, bone and bloud, as it were a litle Lambe' (Rv). The vaunt is found only in the Cotton MS.

53. *'twere done*] i.e. if only that would get the job over with.

You hear me not deny that all is true
That Mandeville delivers of his travels;   60
Yet I myself may be as well believed.
Peregrine. Since you speak reverently of him, say on.
Doctor. Of Europe I'll not speak; 'tis too near home.
Who's not familiar with the Spanish garb,
Th'Italian shrug, French cringe, and German hug?   65
Nor will I trouble you with my observations
Fetched from Arabia, Paphlagonia,
Mesopotamia, Mauritania,
Syria, Thessalia, Persia, India,
All still is too near home. Though I have touched   70
The clouds upon the Pyrenean mountains,
And been on Paphos Isle, where I have kissed
The image of bright Venus, all is still
Too near home to be boasted.
Diana. [*Aside*]   That I like well
In him, too; he will not boast of kissing   75
A woman too near home.
Doctor.   These things in me
Are poor. They sound in a far traveller's ear
Like the reports of those that beggingly

63–70.] British travel in Europe had become very common by the 1630s, and published accounts proliferated. By 1615 George Sandys could say: 'France I forbeare to speake of, and the lesse remote parts of Italy: daily survaide and exactly related' (*Relation*, p. 1); and two years later Joseph Hall declared: 'This age is so full of light, that there is no one country of the habitable world, whose beames are not crossed and interchanged with other . . . Even China itselfe, and Japonia, and those other remotest Isles, & continents . . . have received such discoveries, as would rather satisfie a Reader, then provoke him to amend them' (*Quo Vadis*, 1617, p. 36).

64. *garb*] dandyism. The word meant elegant manners and deportment as well as 'attire'. English familiarity with Europe did not get rid of foreign stereotypes: as late as 1630 an advice manual was disparaging 'the Italian huffe of the shoulder . . . or the French Apishnesse' (G. Botero, *Relations*, p. 51).

65. *cringe*] low bow.

67. *Paphlagonia*] ancient kingdom on the north coast of Asia Minor.

68. *Mauritania*] part of the region of north Africa known as Barbary, and comprising modern Morocco and part of Algeria.

72. *Paphos Isle*] Cyprus, 'sacred of old unto Venus', who first emerged from the waves there, and had her principal shrine at Paphos on the west coast of the island. George Sandys casts doubt on the doctor's touristy claim with the information that 'her Temples . . . were razed to the ground by the procurement of Saint Barnaby' (*Relation*, pp. 218, 221).

78–80. *those . . . Madrid*] The practice of betting on a private journey, putting down a stake to be repaid threefold or more if it is successfully completed. Brome echoes Jonson's satire on such enterprises in his poem *The Famous Voyage* (*Epigram* 133, lines 32–3, HS VIII.85).

Have put out on returns from Edinburgh,
Paris, or Venice, or perhaps Madrid,   80
Whither a milliner may with half a nose
Smell out his way, and is not near so difficult
As for some man in debt, and unprotected,
To walk from Charing Cross to th'old Exchange.
No, I will pitch no nearer than th' Antipodes,   85
That which is farthest distant, foot to foot
Against our region.
Diana.   What, with their heels upwards?
Bless us! How 'scape they breaking o' their necks?
Doctor. They walk upon firm earth, as we do here,
And have the firmament over their heads,   90
As we have here.
Diana.   And yet just under us!
Where is hell then? If they whose feet are towards us,
At the lower part of the world, have heaven too
Beyond their heads, where's hell?
Joyless.   You may find that
Without enquiry. Cease your idle questions.   95
Diana. Sure hell's above ground, then, in jealous husbands!
Peregrine. What people, sir—I pray, proceed—what people
Are they of the Antipodes? Are they not such
As Mandeville writes of, without heads or necks,
Having their eyes placed on their shoulders, and   100
Their mouths amidst their breasts?
Diana.   Ay so, indeed;
Though heels go upwards, and their feet should slip,
They have no necks to break!
Doctor.   Silence, sweet lady;

---

81. *milliner*] vendor of small items of clothing and accessories, who would search out the latest foreign fashions.

84. *old Exchange*] Sir Thomas Gresham's old Royal Exchange, which stood between Cornhill and Threadneedle Street, replaced by the New Exchange in the Strand in 1609. Both were shopping centres and places of business.

87–91. *with ... here*] evidently a favourite debating point as people came to terms with the idea of a globe inhabited in every region. In 1604 Joseph de Acosta testified to English readers from hard experience that 'wee that live now at *Peru*, and inhabite that part of the world which is oposite to *Asia* and their Antipodes finde not our selves to bee hanging in the aire, our heades downward' (*Historie of the ... Indies*, p. 22). But many continued to have difficulty grasping 'why do not the Antipodes, that have their feete opposite to ours, fall into the Heavens' (J. Melton, *Astrologaster*, 1620, p. 29).

98–101. *such ... breasts*] One of the best-known exotic legends of the period, illustrated on Ptolemaic maps as well as in Mandeville (O2v).

Pray give the gentleman leave to understand me.
The people through the whole world of Antipodes,   105
In outward feature, language, and religion,
Resemble those to whom they are supposite.
They under Spain appear like Spaniards;
Under France, Frenchmen; under England, English
To the exterior show; but in their manners,   110
Their carriage, and condition of life,
Extremely contrary. To come close to you:
What part o'th' world's antipodes shall I now
Decipher to you, or would you travel to?
Peregrine. The furthest off.
Doctor.   That is th' antipodes of England.   115
The people there are contrary to us,
As thus: here (heaven be praised) the magistrates
Govern the people; there the people rule
The magistrates.
Diana.   There's precious bribing then!
Joyless. You'll hold your peace.
Doctor.   Nay, lady, 'tis by nature.   120
Here generally men govern the women—
Joyless. I would they could else.
Diana.   You will hold your peace!
Doctor. But there the women overrule the men.
If some men fail here in their power, some women
Slip their holds there. As parents here and masters   125
Command, there they obey the child and servant.
Diana. But pray, sir, is't by nature or by art
That wives o'ersway their husbands there?
Doctor.   By nature.
Diana. Then art's above nature, as they are under us.
Doctor. In brief, sir, all   130
Degrees of people, both in sex and quality,
Deport themselves in life and conversation
Quite contrary to us.
Diana.   Why then, the women
Do get the men with child, and put the poor fools
To grievous pain, I warrant you, in bearing.   135
Joyless. Into your chamber! Get you in, I charge you.
Doctor. By no means, as you tender your son's good.
No, lady, no; that were to make men women,

---

107. *supposite*] directly below.
119. *precious*] costly.
122. *else*] elsewhere.
131. *quality*] rank.

And women men. But there the maids do woo
The bachelors, and 'tis most probable,   140
  The wives lie uppermost.
Diana.   That is a trim,
  Upside down, antipodean trick indeed!
Doctor. And then at christenings and gossips' feasts,
  A woman is not seen: the men do all
  The tittle-tattle duties, while the women   145
  Hunt, hawk, and take their pleasure.
Peregrine. Ha' they good game, I pray, sir?
Doctor.   Excellent;
  But by the contraries to ours, for where
  We hawk at pheasant, partridge, mallard, heron,
  With goshawk, tercel, falcon, lanneret,   150
  Our hawks become their game, our game their hawks.
  And so the like in hunting: there the deer
  Pursue the hounds; and, which you may think strange,
  I ha' seen one sheep worry a dozen foxes
  By moonshine in a morning before day.   155
  They hunt train-scents with oxen, and plough with dogs.
Peregrine. [*Laughing*] Hugh, hugh, hugh!
Diana. Are not their swans all black, and ravens white?
Doctor. Yes, indeed are they, and their parrots teach
  Their mistresses to talk.
Diana.   That's very strange.   160
Doctor. They keep their cats in cages,
  From mice that would devour them else; and birds
  Teach 'em to whistle and cry 'Beware the rats, Puss!'.
  But these are frivolous nothings. I have known
  Great ladies ride great horses, run at tilt,   165
  At ring, races, and hunting matches, while

150.] Tercel is the male of any peregrine falcon or goshawk; lanneret is the male of the lanner, another species of falcon.

156. *train-scents*] something 'trained' or dragged along the ground to provide a scent for hounds to follow (*OED*).

158. *Are ... black*] Juvenal compared a chaste wife to a black swan, establishing the latter as a standard contradiction in terms (*Satires* VI.165). Ian Donaldson points out, however, that such a bird was first sighted in Australia just before the play was written (*The World Upside-Down*, 1970, pp. 83–4).

159–60. *their ... talk*] like Lady Pol in Jonson's *Volpone*.

165–6.] Burton agrees that these are the 'disports of greater men, and good in themselves, though many Gentlemen by that meanes, gallop quite out of their fortunes' (II.2.iv.1). The joke is directed at gentry wives like Lady Frugal in Massinger's *City Madam* (1632) who come to town and dissipate their husbands' estates.

165. *tilt*] jousting.

166. *At ring*] sport in which a rider endeavours to carry off on the point of his lance a metal ring suspended from a post (Haaker).

Their lords at home have painted; pawned their plate
And jewels to feast their honourable servants.
And there the merchants' wives do deal abroad
Beyond seas, while their husbands cuckold them   170
At home.
Diana.   Then there are cuckolds, too, it seems,
As well as here.
Joyless.   Then you conclude here are!
Diana. By hearsay, sir. I am not wise enough
To speak it on my knowledge yet.
Joyless.   Not yet!
Doctor. Patience, good sir.
Peregrine.   Hugh, hugh, hugh!   175
Doctor. What, do you laugh that there is cuckold-making
In the Antipodes? I tell you, sir,
It is not so abhorred here as 'tis held
In reputation there: all your old men
Do marry girls, and old women, boys,   180
As generation were to be maintained
Only by cuckold-making.
Joyless.   Monstrous!
Doctor.   Pray, your patience.
There's no such honest men there in their world
As are their lawyers. They give away
Their practice, and t'enable 'em to do so,   185
Being all handicrafts or labouring men,
They work (poor hearts, full hard) in the vacations
To give their law for nothing in the term times.
No fees are taken, which makes their divines,
Being generally covetous, the greatest wranglers   190
In lawsuits of a kingdom. You have not there
A gentleman in debt, though citizens
Haunt them with cap in hand to take their wares
On credit.
Diana.   What fine sport would that be here now!
Doctor. All wit and mirth and good society   195
Is there among the hirelings, clowns, and tradesmen;

---

167. *painted*] put on make-up.
181. *As*] so that.
186. *handicrafts*] skilled artisans.
193. *take*] make them accept.
196. *clowns*] country folk.

And all their poets are puritans.

Diana.   Ha' they poets?

Doctor. And players, too. But they are all the sob'rest,
Precisest people picked out of a nation.

Diana. I never saw a play.

Doctor.   Lady, you shall.

Joyless.   She shall not!   200

Doctor. She must, if you can hope for any cure.
Be governed, sir; your jealousy will grow
A worse disease than your son's madness else.
You are content I take the course I told you of
To cure the gentleman?

Joyless.   .   I must be, sir.   205

Doctor. Say, Master Peregrine, will you travel now
With me to the Antipodes, or has not
The journey wearied you in the description?

Peregrine. No, I could hear you a whole fortnight, but
Let's lose no time; pray, talk on as we pass.   210

Doctor. First, sir, a health to auspicate our travels,
And we'll away. (*Fills cups from a bowl on the table.*)

Enter BLAZE *with a letter.*

Peregrine.   Gi'me't.—What's he? One sent,
I fear, from my dead mother to make stop
Of our intended voyage.

Doctor.   No, sir; drink.

Blaze. [*Aside to Doctor*] My lord, sir, understands the course   215
                                              y'are in
By your letters, he tells me, and bade me gi' you
This ring, which wants a finger here, he says.

Peregrine. We'll not be stayed?

Doctor.   No, sir, he brings me word

---

212. *Fills . . . table*] *A Bowle on the table.* Q (*next to* 209–10). *Enter . . . letter*]
Act.I.Scene.7. Ent.Bla. Q.

200.] Women went more freely to the theatre in England than in other countries,
which helped to fuel William Prynne's admonition that 'Stage-playes are the immediate
common occasions of much actuall lewdnesse, adultery, and other grosse uncleanesse:
which cause all Christians to abominate them, and to keepe *their wives and children
from them* . . . for feare they should corrupt their chastity and draw them on to publike
lewdnesse' (*Histrio-mastix*, 1633, pp. 433–4).

212.SD] The table could be a fixture in Act I (if not the whole play); the opening
scene probably also involves dispensing of hospitality.

212–13. *One . . . mother*] Peregrine's fantasies extend to paranoid delusion. Cf.
I.i.143–7.

The mariner calls away. The wind and tide
Are fair, and they are ready to weigh anchor,   220
Hoist sails, and only stay for us. Pray drink, sir.
Peregrine. A health then to the willing winds and seas,
  And all that steer towards th' Antipodes.
Joyless. He has not drunk so deep a draught this twelvemonth.
Doctor. 'Tis a deep draught indeed, and now 'tis down,   225
  And carries him down to the Antipodes!
  I mean but in a dream.
Joyless.   Alas, I fear!
  See, he begins to sink.
Doctor.   Trust to my skill.
  Pray take an arm, and see him in his cabin.
  Good lady, save my ring that's fallen there.   230
Diana. In sooth, a marvellous neat and costly one!
Blaze. [*Aside*] So, so, the ring has found a finger.
Doctor. Come, sir, aboard, aboard, aboard, aboard!
                    Exeunt all except BLAZE.
Blaze. To bed, to bed, to bed! I know your voyage,
  And my dear lord's dear plot. I understand   235
  Whose ring hath passed here by your sleight of hand.
                    Exit.

233.1.] *not in* Q.   236.1.] *not in* Q.

225. *draught*] potion.

ACT II

SCENE i

Enter LETOY *and* Doctor HUGHBALL.

Letoy. Tonight, sayest thou, my Hughball?
Doctor.   By all means,
    And if your play takes to my expectation,
    As I not doubt my potion works to yours,
    Your fancy and my cure shall be cried up
    Miraculous. O, y'are the lord of fancy.   5
Letoy. I'm not ambitious of that title, sir.
    No, the Letoys are of antiquity
    Ages before the fancies were begot,
    And shall beget still new to the world's end.
    But are you confident o' your potion, Doctor?   10
    Sleeps the young man?
Doctor.   Yes, and has slept these twelve
                                                      hours,
    After a thousand mile an hour outright
    By sea and land, and shall awake anon
    In the Antipodes.
Letoy.   Well, sir, my actors
    Are all in readiness, and, I think, all perfect   15
    But one, that never will be perfect in a thing
    He studies. Yet he makes such shifts extempore
    (Knowing the purpose what he is to speak to)
    That he moves mirth in me 'bove all the rest.
    For I am none of those poetic furies   20
    That threats the actor's life, in a whole play
    That adds a syllable or takes away.

0.1.] *Letoy, Doctor. Q.* 1.SP *Letoy.*] *not in Q.*

---

4. *fancy*] imagination.
8. *fancies*] trivial entertainments (?).
12. *After*] at the rate of (Baker).
17. *makes . . . extempore*] is so good at improvisation.
20. *poetic furies*] i.e. playwrights, who complained when actors failed to do justice
to the products of their *furor poeticus*, or creative frenzy.

    If he can fribble through, and move delight
    In others, I am pleased.
Doctor. It is that mimic fellow which your lordship   25
    But lately entertained.
Letoy.   The same.
Doctor. He will be wondrous apt in my affair,
    For I must take occasion to interchange
    Discourse with him sometimes amidst their scenes,
    T'inform my patient, my mad young traveller,   30
    In divers matters.
Letoy. Do; put him to't. I use't myself sometimes.
Doctor. I know it is your way.
Letoy.   Well, to the business.
    Hast wrought the jealous gentleman, old Joyless,
    To suffer his wife to see our comedy?   35
Doctor. She brings your ring, my lord, upon her finger,
    And he brings her in's hand. I have instructed her
    To spur his jealousy off o'the legs.
Letoy. And I will help her in't.
Doctor.   The young distracted
    Gentlewoman, too, that's sick of her virginity,   40
    Yet knows not what it is, and Blaze and's wife
    Shall all be your guests tonight, and not alone
    Spectators, but (as we will carry it) actors
    To fill your comic scenes with double mirth.
Letoy. Go fetch 'em then, while I prepare my actors.   45
                    Exit DOCTOR.
    [*Calls.*] Within there, ho!
1. (*within*)   This is my beard and hair.
2. (*within*) My lord appointed it for my part.
3. (*within*)   No,
    This is for you; and this is yours, this grey one.
4. (*within*) Where be the foils and targets for the women?

---

43. actors] Actor *Q* (*final s fractured in Q printing*).

---

   23. *fribble*] extemporise. As used here, the word seems to imply a ready fluency
denied by *OED*'s definition 'falter, stammer out'. The word often has a negative
connotation, but when used of theatrical practice this has more to do with disapproval
of actors who readily improvise off the script: cf. *Hamlet*, III.ii.38–45, and Middleton,
Hengist, King of Kent, V.i.385, on those who 'abuse simple people, with a printed
play . . . they speak but what they list on't and fribble out the rest' (Oxford ed.).
   26. *entertained*] took into service.
   35. *suffer*] allow.
   38. *spur . . . legs*] make him wild with jealousy.
   49. *targets*] shields.

1. (*within*) Here, can't you see?
Letoy.   What a rude coil is there!   50
     But yet it pleases me.
1. (*within*)   You must not wear
     That cloak and hat.
2. (*within*)   Who told you so? I must
     In my first scene, and you must wear that robe.
Letoy. What a noise make those knaves! Come in, one of you.

          Enter QUAILPIPE, three actors, *and* BYPLAY.

Letoy. Are you the first that answers to that name?
Quailpipe. My lord.   55
Letoy.   Why are not you ready yet?
Quailpipe. I am not to put on my shape before
     I have spoke the prologue. And for that, my lord,
     I yet want something.
Letoy. What, I pray, with your grave formality?   60
Quailpipe. I want my beaver shoes and leather cap
     To speak the prologue in, which were appointed
     By your lordship's own direction.
Letoy.   Well, sir, well— [*Fetches them.*]
     There they be for you. I must look to all.
Quailpipe. Certes, my lord, it is a most apt conceit,   65
     The comedy being the world turned upside down,
     That the presenter wear the capital beaver
     Upon his feet, and on his head shoe leather.
Letoy. Trouble not you your head with my conceit,
     But mind your part. Let me not see you act now   70
     In your scholastic way you brought to town wiᵗ ye,
     With seesaw sack-a-down, like a sawyer.
     Nor in a comic scene play *Hercules Furens*,

54.1.] *after 55 in Q (preceded by: Act 2.Scene 2.).*

---

50. *coil*] disturbance.
55. *that name*] i.e. knave.
67. *capital beaver*] headgear (a beaver fur hat).
71–2.] i.e. speaking the lines in a monotonous chant (Haaker cites a nursery rhyme which uses the phrase in question). Thomas Heywood in his *Apology for Actors* (1612), whilst defending university drama as a training in rhetoric, warns the actor against standing 'in his place like a livelesse Image, demurely plodding, & without any smooth & formal motion' (C4).
73–4.] The usual complaint against ranting styles of performance; cf. *Travels*, ii.1–2 note, and Hamlet's disparagement of the actor who will 'tear a passion to tatters, to very rags, to split the ears of the groundlings' (*Hamlet*, III.ii.10–11). *Hercules Furens* is a Senecan drama which Jasper Heywood translated into English in 1561.

Tearing your throat to split the audients' ears.
[To another] And you, sir, you had got a trick of late   75
Of holding out your bum in a set speech,
Your fingers fibulating on your breast
As if your buttons or your band-strings were
Helps to your memory. Let me see you in't
No more, I charge you. No, nor you, sir, in   80
That over-action of the legs I told you of,
Your singles and your doubles. Look you: thus—
Like one o'th' dancing masters o'the Bear-garden.
And when you have spoke, at end of every speech,
Not minding the reply, you turn you round   85
As tumblers do, when betwixt every feat
They gather wind by firking up their breeches.
I'll none of these absurdities in my house,
But words and action married so together
That shall strike harmony in the ears and eyes   90
Of the severest, if judicious, critics.
Quailpipe. My lord, we are corrected.
Letoy.   Go, be ready.
                         Exeunt QUAILPIPE *and the three* actors.
[To Byplay] But you, sir, are incorrigible, and
Take licence to yourself to add unto
Your parts your own free fancy, and sometimes   95
To alter or diminish what the writer
With care and skill composed. And when you are
To speak to your co-actors in the scene,
You hold interlocutions with the audients—
Byplay. That is a way, my lord, has been allowed   100
On elder stages to move mirth and laughter.

92.1.] *not in* Q.   121.SD] *Ex.Byp.* Q.

74. *audients'*] listeners'. The modern form used possessively would violate the metre.
77. *fibulating*] fiddling.
78. *band-strings*] ties used to fasten a ruff or collar.
82. *singles . . . doubles*] dance steps in twos and fours.
83. *Bear-garden*] The Hope theatre on Bankside was built in 1614 on the site of the old Bear-garden as a dual purpose arena—plays and bear baiting—but by the 1630s it catered exclusively to the latter and had reverted to its old name.
87. *firking*] hoisting.
99. *audients*] Retained to agree with 74; in the present instance the old spelling also suggests the actor's extempore engagement with individual members of the audience.

Letoy. Yes, in the days of Tarlton and Kemp,
Before the stage was purged from barbarism,
And brought to the perfection it now shines with.
Then fools and jesters spent their wits, because   105
The poets were wise enough to save their own
For profitabler uses. Let that pass.
Tonight I'll give thee leave to try thy wit
In answering my doctor and his patient
He brings along with him to our Antipodes.   110
Byplay. I heard of him, my lord. Blaze gave me light
Of the mad patient, and that he never saw
A play in's life. It will be possible
For him to think he is in the Antipodes
Indeed when he is on the stage among us,   115
When't has been thought by some that have their wits
That all the players i'th' town were sunk past rising.
Letoy. Leave that, sir, to th'event. See all be ready,
Your music, properties, and—
Byplay.   All, my lord.
Only we want a person for a mute.   120
Letoy. Blaze when he comes shall serve. Go in.   *Exit* BYPLAY.
My guests, I hear, are coming.

        Enter BLAZE, JOYLESS, DIANA, MARTHA *and* BARBARA.

Blaze. My lord, I am become your honour's usher
To these your guests: the worthy Master Joyless,
With his fair wife, and daughter-in-law.
Letoy.   They're welcome,   125
And you in the first place, sweet Mistress Joyless.
You wear my ring, I see; you grace me in it.
Joyless. His ring? What ring? How came she by't?
Blaze. [*Aside*]   'Twill work.
Letoy. I sent it as a pledge of my affection to you,

122.1.] *Act 2.Scene 3. Q (before* SD).

---

102. *Tarlton . . . Kemp*] Richard Tarlton was the most celebrated of Elizabethan
theatrical clowns (see Nungezer, pp. 347–65 for many contemporary tributes); when
he died in 1588, Kemp was his natural successor in public esteem (see *Travels*,
Characters, 19 note).
105–7. *Then . . . uses*] The implication that an older generation of playwrights was
more interested in substance than superficial wit somewhat qualifies Letoy's first
statement, and recalls the artistic priorities declared in the Prologue.
116–17.] A further reference to the plague: see I.i.4 note.

For I before have seen you, and do languish   130
Until I shall enjoy your love.
Joyless. [*Aside*]   He courts her!
Letoy. Next, lady—you—I have a toy for you, too.
Martha. My child shall thank you for it, when I have one.
I take no joy in toys since I was married.
Letoy. Prettily answered.—I make you no stranger,   135
Kind Mistress Blaze.
Barbara.   Time was your honour used
Me strangely, too, as you'll do these, I doubt not.
Letoy. Honest Blaze,
Prithee go in; there is an actor wanting.
Blaze. Is there a part for me? How shall I study't?   140
Letoy. Thou shalt say nothing.
Blaze.   Then if I do not act
Nothing as well as the best of 'em, let me be hissed.   *Exit.*
Joyless. [*Aside to Diana*] I say restore the ring, and back with
                                                       me.
Diana. To whom shall I restore it?
Joyless.   To the lord that sent it.
Diana. Is he a lord? I always thought and heard   145
I'th' country, lords were gallant creatures. He
Looks like a thing not worth it. 'Tis not his;
The doctor gave it me, and I will keep it.
Letoy. I use small verbal courtesy, Master Joyless,
You see; but what I can in deed, I'll do.   150
You know the purpose of your coming, and
I can but give you welcome. If your son
Shall receive ease in't, be the comfort yours,
The credit of't my doctor's. You are sad.
Joyless. My lord, I would entreat we may return;   155
I fear my wife's not well.
Letoy. Return! Pray, slight not so my courtesy.
Diana. Besides, sir, I am well, and have a mind,
A thankful one, to taste my lord's free bounty.
I never saw a play, and would be loath   160
To lose my longing now.
Joyless. [*Aside*]   The air of London
Hath tainted her obedience already,
And should the play but touch the vices of it,

---

135. *I . . . stranger*] I remember you. Earlier it was hinted (I.i.89) that Barbara's
husband has had past reason to be jealous, and this lends a touch of irony to Letoy's
casting of him in a self-effacing role.

She'd learn and practise 'em.—Let me beseech
Your lordship's reacceptance of the un-   165
Merited favour that she wears here, and
Your leave for our departure.
Letoy.   I will not
Be so dishonoured, nor become so ill
A master of my house to let a lady
Leave it against her will, and from her longing.   170
I will be plain wi' ye therefore. If your haste
Must needs post you away, you may depart;
She shall not till the morning, for mine honour.
Joyless. Indeed, 'tis a high point of honour in
A lord to keep a private gentleman's wife   175
From him.
Diana.   I love this plain lord better than
All the brave, gallant ones that e'er I dreamt on.
Letoy. 'Tis time we take our seats. So, if you'll stay,
Come sit with us; if not, you know your way.
Joyless. Here are we fallen through the doctor's fingers   180
Into the lord's hands. Fate, deliver us!   *Exeunt omnes.*

ACT II   SCENE ii

Enter, in sea gowns and caps, Doctor HUGHBALL *and*
PEREGRINE *brought in a chair by two* sailors. *Cloaks and
hats are brought in.*

Doctor. Now the last minute of his sleeping fit
Determines. Raise him on his feet. So, so,
Rest him upon mine arm. Remove that chair.—
Welcome ashore, sir, in th' Antipodes.
Peregrine. Are we arrived so far?
Doctor.   And on firm land.   5

ACT II SCENE ii] *Act.2.Scene 4. Q.*

170. *from*] contrary to.
0.1. sea gowns] Cf. Cotgrave, 'Esclavine . . . *a sea-gowne; or a course, high-collered,
and short-sleeved gowne, reaching down to the mid leg, and used most by sea-men,
and Saylors.*' But a scene in the *Chronicle History of King Leir* (1605; TLN 1991–
2037) shows that it was not only a tough working garment (one sailor has 'a good
sheeps russet sea-gowne') but also one worn by gentlemen passengers; and (*pace OED*
sea 18) was not a nightgown.
0.2. chair] sedan-chair: see IV.227–9 note.
2. *Determines*] is elapsed.

Sailors, you may return now to your ship.   *Exeunt* sailors.
Peregrine. What worlds of lands and seas have I passed over,
   Neglecting to set down my observations!
   A thousand thousand things remarkable
   Have slipped my memory, as if all had been   10
   Mere shadowy phantasms, or fantastic dreams.
Doctor. We'll write as we return, sir; and 'tis true,
   You slept most part o'th' journey hitherward,
   The air was so somniferous. And 'twas well:
   You 'scaped the calenture by't.
Peregrine.   But how long do   15
   You think I slept?
Doctor.   Eight months, and some odd days,
   Which was but as so many hours and minutes
   Of one's own natural country sleep.
Peregrine. Eight months?!
Doctor.   'Twas nothing for so young a brain.
   How think you one of the seven Christian champions,   20
   David by name, slept seven years in a leek bed?
Peregrine. I think I have read it in their famous history.
Doctor. But what chief thing of note now in our travels
   Can you call presently to mind? Speak like a traveller.
Peregrine. I do remember, as we passed the verge   25
   O'th' upper world, coming down, downhill,
   The setting sun, then bidding them good night,
   Came gliding easily down by us and struck
   New day before us, lighting us our way,

8.] The traveller was encouraged to keep a diary, and humanist advice manuals
gave clear guidelines as to what he should note and investigate.

15. *calenture*] 'the Calentura, which is the Spanish name of . . . a very burning and
pestilent ague' experienced by sailors in the tropics ('Drakes West Indian Voyage . . .
1585', in Hakluyt, X.120).

20. *seven . . . champions*] the patron saints of England, Scotland, Wales, Ireland,
Spain, Italy and France (see 'To Censuring Critics', n.18, and also note to *Sea Voyage*,
III.197).

21–2.] Peregrine remembers the incident (the Welsh saint's leek bed is the Doctor's
embellishment) from Richard Johnson's *Most Famous History of the Seaven
Champions of Christendome* (1596), where 'foure spirites, in the similitude . . . of
foure beautifull Damsels . . . wrapped the drousie Champion in a sheete of the finest
Arabian silke, and convayed him into a Cave . . . where they laide him upon a soft bed'
and by singing 'continually▸kept him sleeping for the tearme of seaven yeares' (M4).

25–9. *as . . . way*] Torquemeda notes that 'the farther we goe from the Equinoc-
tiall . . . the day and successively the night should encrease . . . and that when it were
[day] in the one part, it should be night in the other . . . these Landes goe alwayes
downe-hill, or slope-wise, in respect of the course of the Sunne' (p. 253).

But with such heat that till he was got far   30
Before us, we even melted.
Doctor. [*Aside*]   Well-wrought potion!—
Very well observed, sir.
But now we are come into a temperate clime,
Of equal composition of elements
With that of London, and as well agreeable   35
Unto our nature as you have found that air.
Peregrine. I never was at London.
Doctor.   Cry you mercy.
This, sir, is Anti-London. That's the antipodes
To the grand city of our nation:
Just the same people, language, and religion,
But contrary in manners, as I ha' told you.   40
Peregrine. I do remember that relation
As if you had but given it me this morning.
Doctor. Now cast your sea weeds off, and don fresh garments.

*They shift their sea gowns and caps for the cloaks and hats.
Hoboys play.*

Hark, sir, their music.   45

They sit. Enter LETOY, JOYLESS, DIANA, MARTHA, *and* BARBARA
in masks. They sit at the other end of the stage.

Letoy. Here we may sit, and he not see us.
Doctor. Now see one of the natives of this country.
Note his attire, his language, and behaviour.

Enter QUAILPIPE *as Prologue.*

Quailpipe. Our far-fetched title over lands and seas
Offers unto your view th' Antipodes.   50
But what Antipodes now shall you see?

---

38. the antipodes] the'Antipodes *Q.* 44.1. *They . . . hats*] *as Baker; Act 2. Scene
5. Shift. Q (after 46).* 44.2. *Hoboys play*] *Hoboyes. Q (after 46, preceding SD).*
45.1. *They sit*] *not in Q.* 48.1. *as*] *not in Q.*

37.] The initial journey from the provinces to London is forgotten; Peregrine's
amnesia might jeopardise the satiric therapy to come, but 'the Doctor instantly
resolves to humour him' (Baker).
39. *grand*] principal.
44. *fresh garments*] the traditional theatrical sign of the hero's renewal.
49. *title*] The title of a play was sometimes displayed on a sign hung in a con-
spicuous part of the stage, though surviving examples of this are usually of a play
within the play (cf. Kyd's *Spanish Tragedy*, IV.iii.17; Beaumont's *Knight*, Induction;
Wily Beguiled, Prologue).

Even those that foot to foot 'gainst London be,
Because no traveller that knows that state
Shall say we personate or imitate
Them in our actions; for nothing can,   55
Almost, be spoke but some or other man
Takes it unto himself and says the stuff,
If it be vicious or absurd enough,
Was woven upon his back. Far, far be all
That bring such prejudice mixed with their gall.   60
This play shall no satiric timist be
To tax or touch at either him or thee
That art notorious. 'Tis so far below
Things in our orb that do among us flow,
That no degree, from kaiser to the clown,   65
Shall say this vice or folly was mine own.
Letoy. This had been well now, if you had not dreamt
    Too long upon your syllables.   *Exit* QUAILPIPE.
Diana. The Prologue call you this, my lord?
Barbara. 'Tis my lord's reader, and as good a lad   70
    Out of his function as I would desire
    To mix withal in civil conversation.
Letoy. Yes, lady, this was prologue to the play,
    As this is to our sweet ensuing pleasures. (*Kisses her.*)
Joyless. Kissing indeed is prologue to a play   75
    Composed by th' devil, and acted by the Children
    Of his Black Revels; may hell take ye for't.
Martha. Indeed I am weary, and would fain go home.

---

68. *Exit* QUAILPIPE] *Ex.Prol. Q.*   74.SD] *Kiss. Q.*

---

59. *woven . . . back*] modelled on him, meant as personal attack. The assertion that satire attacks types of vice and folly rather than real-life individuals is frequently made in Jonson's work, not always convincingly.

61. *timist*] opportunist.

65. *no . . . clown*] no rank, from king to country bumpkin.

67. *dreamt*] hung, dwelt. Quailpipe clearly delivers the affected performance he was warned against giving at II.i.70.

70. *reader*] one who reads divine service; but the word does not seem to have been commonly used in this sense, and its purpose here may be to supply a pun on 'Reade' (see I.ii.85 note).

71. *Out . . . function*] when he's not doing that job.

76–7. *Children . . . Revels*] Joyless interprets Letoy's analogy in the spirit of William Prynne (see note to I.iii.200), who argued vociferously and at length that 'Stage-Playes are the very workes, and Pompes of Satan' (*Histrio-mastix*, p. 48). The allusion is to the King's Revels Company (also known as the Children of the Revels, probably because it had a high proportion of boy players—Bentley I.283) which acted at Salisbury Court until the 1636 plague.

Barbara. Indeed but you must stay, and see the play.

Martha. The play? What play? It is no children's play,   80
　　Nor no child-getting play, pray, is it?

Barbara. You'll see anon. (*Flourish*) O, now the actors enter.

　　　　Enter two Sergeants, with swords drawn, running before
　　　　　　　　　　a Gentleman.

Gentleman. Why do you not your office, courteous friends?
　　Let me entreat you stay, and take me with you.
　　Lay but your hands on me; I shall not rest   85
　　Until I be arrested. A sore shoulder-ache
　　Pains and torments me till your virtuous hands
　　Do clap or stroke it.

1 Sergeant.   You shall pardon us.

2 Sergeant. And I beseech you pardon our intent,
　　Which was indeed to have arrested you.   90
　　But sooner shall the charter of the city
　　Be forfeited than varlets like ourselves
　　Shall wrong a gentleman's peace. So, fare you well, sir.
　　　　　　　　　　　　　　Exeunt Sergeants.

Gentleman. O, y'are unkind.

Peregrine.   Pray, what are those?

Doctor.   Two
　　　　　　　　　　　　　　　　catchpoles
　　Run from a gentleman, it seems, that would   95
　　Have been arrested.

　　　　Enter Old Lady *and* BYPLAY *like a servingman.*

Lady.   Yonder's your master.
　　Go, take him you in hand, while I fetch breath.

Byplay. O, are you here? My lady and myself
　　Have sought you sweetly—

Letoy. [*Aside*]   You and your lady,
　　You should ha' said, puppy.

Byplay.   For we heard you were   100

82.SD] *after* enter *in* Q.   82.1–2.] Act 2.Scene 6. Q (*before* SD).   93.1.] *Ex.* Q.
96.] Act 2.Scene 7. Q (before SD).

82.1. Sergeants] Normally, in the drama of the period, a byword for hard-hearted
rigour, particularly towards the improvident gentry they must arrest for debt.
　94. *catchpoles*] contemptuous term for sergeants.
　95. *would*] wished to.
　97. *fetch*] catch my.
　99–100. *You . . . said*] presumably because in the Antipodes the order of courtesy is
reversed.

To be arrested. Pray, sir, who has bailed you?
I wonder who, of all your bold acquaintance
That knows my lady, durst bail off her husband.
Gentleman. Indeed, I was not touched.
Byplay.   Have you not made
An end by composition, and disbursed   105
Some of my lady's money for a peace
That shall beget an open war upon you?
Confess it if you have, for 'twill come out.
She'll ha' you up, you know. I speak it for your good.
Gentleman. I know't, and I'll entreat my lady wife   110
To mend thy wages t'other forty shillings
A year for thy true care of me.
Lady.   'Tis well, sir.
But now—if thou hast impudence so much
As face to face to speak unto a lady
That is thy wife and supreme head—tell me   115
At whose suit was it? or upon what action?
Debts I presume you have none, for who dares trust
A lady's husband who is but a squire
And under covert-barne? It is some trespass—
Answer me not till I find out the truth.   120
Gentleman. The truth is—
Lady.   Peace! How dar'st thou speak the truth
Before thy wife? I'll find it out myself.
Diana. In truth, she handles him handsomely.
Joyless.   Do you like it?
Diana. Yes, and such wives are worthy to be liked
For giving good example.
Letoy.   Good! Hold up   125
That humour by all means.
Lady.   I think I ha' found it.
There was a certain mercer sent you silks
And cloth of gold to get his wife with child;
You slighted her, and answered not his hopes,
And now he lays to arrest you. Is't not so?   130
Gentleman. Indeed, my lady wife, 'tis so.
Lady.   For shame!

_____

105. *composition*] coming to an agreement.
119. *covert-barne*] corruption of 'covert-baron'; used of a married woman because she is under the protection and influence of her husband (*OED*).
123–6. *In . . . means*] Here and at 138–46 below the actors in the inner play are probably directed by Letoy to 'freeze': see III.8–9.

Be not ingrateful to that honest man,
To take his wares and scorn to lie with his wife.
Do't, I command you. What did I marry you for?
The portion that you brought me was not so   135
Abundant, though it were five thousand pounds
(Considering, too, the jointure that I made you),
That you should disobey me.
Diana.   It seems the husbands
In the Antipodes bring portions, and
The wives make jointures.
Joyless.   Very well observed!   140
Diana. And wives, when they are old and past childbearing,
Allow their youthful husbands other women.
Letoy. Right. And old men give their young wives like licence.
Diana. That I like well. Why should not our old men
Love their young wives as well?
Joyless.   Would you have it so?   145
Letoy. Peace, Master Joyless, you are too loud. Good still.
Byplay. Do as my lady bids. You got her woman
With child at half these words.
Gentleman.   O, but another's
Wife is another thing. Far be it from
A gentleman's thought to do so, having a wife   150
And handmaid of his own that he loves better.
Byplay. There said you well, but take heed, I advise you,
How you love your own wench or your own wife
Better than other men's.
Diana.   Good Antipodean counsel.
Lady. Go to that woman; if she prove with child,   155
I'll take it as mine own.
Gentleman.   Her husband would
Do so, but from my house I may not stray.
Martha. If it be me your wife commends you to,
You shall not need to stray from your own house.
I'll go home with you.
Barbara.   Precious! What do you mean?   160
Pray keep your seat; you'll put the players out.
Joyless. Here's goodly stuff! She's in the Antipodes, too.

---

135. *portion*] dowry.
137. *jointure . . . you*] sum of money I settled on you.
147. *woman*] servant.
160. *Precious!*] common oath (By God's precious blood).

Peregrine. [*Seeing Letoy and guests*] And what are those?
Doctor.   All Antipodeans.
    Attend, good sir.

        Enter Waiting Woman, great-bellied.

Lady.   You know your charge; obey it.
Woman. What is his charge? Or whom must he obey,   165
    Good madam, with your wild authority?
    You are his wife, 'tis true, and therein may,
    According to our law, rule and control him.
    But you must know withal, I am your servant
    And bound by the same law to govern you   170
    And be a stay to you in declining age,
    To curb and qualify your headstrong will
    Which otherwise would ruin you. Moreover,
    Though y'are his wife, I am a breeding mother
    Of a dear child of his, and therein claim   175
    More honour from him than you ought to challenge.
Lady. In sooth, she speaks but reason.
Gentleman.   Pray, let's home then.
Woman. You have something there to look to, one would
                              think,
    If you had any care. How well you saw
    Your father at school today! And knowing how apt   180
    He is to play the truant.
Gentleman.   But is he not
    Yet gone to school?
Woman.   Stand by, and you shall see.

      Enter three Old Men *with satchels, &c.*

All 3. [*Singing and dancing*] Domine, domine duster.
    Three knaves in a cluster, &c.
Gentleman. O, this is gallant pastime! Nay, come on,   185
    Is this your school? Was that your lesson, ha?
1 *Old Man.* Pray now, good son, indeed, indeed.
Gentleman.   Indeed,

164.SD] *after* obey it. *and preceded by* Act.2.Scene.8. *Q.*   182.1.]   Act.2.Scene.9 *Q*
(*before* SD).

    182.1. &c.] conveniently filled out by Brome's imitator in *News in the Antipodes*:
'the old men . . . are put to Schoole again, with a peece of bread and butter in their
hands . . . they goe every day with satchels at their backs, and bottles in their hands' (p.
3).
    183. *Domine*] schoolmaster. Presumably a popular nursery rhyme.

You shall to school. Away with him, and take
Their wagships with him, the whole cluster of 'em.
2 *Old Man.* You shan't send us now, so you shan't.   190
3 *Old Man.* We be none of your father, so we bean't.
Gentleman. Away with 'em, I say; and tell their schoolmistress
   What truants they are, and bid her pay 'em soundly.
All 3. O, o, o.
Byplay.   Come, come, ye gallows-clappers.
Diana. Alas, will nobody beg pardon for   195
   The poor old boys?
Doctor.   Sir, gentle sir, a word with you.
Byplay. To strangers, sir, I can be gentle.
Letoy.   Good!
   Now mark that fellow; he speaks extempore.
Diana. Extempore call you him? He's a dogged fellow
   To the three poor old things there. Fie upon him!   200
Peregrine. Do men of such fair years here go to school?
Byplay. They would die dunces else.
Peregrine. Have you no young men scholars, sir, I pray,
   When we have beardless doctors?
Doctor. [*Aside*]   He has wiped
   My lips.—You question very wisely, sir.   205
Byplay. So, sir, have we, and many reverend teachers,
   Grave counsellors at law, perfect statesmen,
   That never knew use of razor, which may live
   For want of wit to lose their offices.
   These were great scholars in their youth; but when   210
   Age grows upon men here, their learning wastes,
   And so decays that if they live until
   Threescore, their sons send them to school again.
   They'd die as speechless else as newborn children.

---

189. *Their wagships*] i.e. his fellow mischief-makers.

193. *pay*] thrash.

194. *gallows-clappers*] old scarecrows—likening a swinging body to the clapper of a bell.

196. *Sir . . . you*] The Doctor anticipates Peregrine's first intervention.

203–4. *Have . . . doctors*] Peregrine shifts the meaning of *scholar* from 'student' to 'man of learning', prompted by the paradoxical contrast between the youthful doctor/professor (cf.I.i.91–2) and the aged pupils, and this yields a further gloss on Hughball's pretensions.

204–5. *wiped my lips*] scored a point off me. Cf. 'I gave him a wipe, I spoke something that galled him' (E. Partridge, *Dictionary of the Underworld*).

209. *For . . . wit*] until they are witless enough.

214. *speechless*] 'Sans teeth' in 'second childishness and mere oblivion': the seventh age of man (*As You Like It*, II.vii.165–6). In this case the Antipodes do not invert nature but find a social remedy for it.

Peregrine. 'Tis a wise nation; and the piety   215
    Of the young men most rare and commendable.
    Yet give me, as a stranger, leave to beg
    Their liberty this day; and what they lose by't,
    My father, when he goes to school, shall answer.
Joyless. [*Aside*] I am abus'd on that side, too.
Byplay.   'Tis granted.   220
    Hold up your heads and thank the gentleman,
    Like scholars, with your heels now.
All 3. Gratias, Gratias, Gratias.   *Exeunt skipping.*
Diana. Well done, son Peregrine!—He's in's wits, I hope.
Joyless. If you lose yours the while, where's my advantage?   225
Diana. And trust me, 'twas well done, too, of Extempore
    To let the poor old children loose. And now
    I look well on him, he's a proper man.
Joyless. She'll fall in love with the actor, and undo me.
Diana. Does not his lady love him, sweet my lord?   230
Letoy. Love? Yes, and lie with him as her husband does
    With's maid. It is their law in the Antipodes.
Diana. But we have no such laws with us.
Joyless.   Do you
    Approve of such a law?
Diana.   No, not so much
    In this case, where the man and wife do lie   235
    With their inferior servants. But in the other,
    Where the old citizen would arrest the gallant
    That took his wares and would not lie with's wife,
    There it seems reasonable, very reasonable.
Joyless.   Does it?
Diana. Make't your own case: you are an old man;   240
    I love a gentleman; you give him rich presents
    To get me a child (because you cannot). Must not
    We look to have our bargain?
Joyless.   Give me leave
    Now to be gone, my lord, though I leave her
    Behind me; she is mad and not my wife,   245
    And I may leave her.
Letoy.   Come, you are moved, I see.
    I'll settle all; but first prevail with you

223.SD] *Exit. Q.*

---

225. *the while*] in the meantime.
228. *proper*] good-looking.
248. *comedians*] players. (Cf. I.ii.61.)

To taste my wine and sweetmeats. The comedians
Shall pause the while. This you must not deny me.

Exit LETOY *with* MARTHA, DIANA *and* BARBARA.

Joyless. I must not live here always: that's my comfort.   *Exit.* 250
Peregrine. I thank you, sir, for the poor men's release.
    It was the first request that I have made
    Since I came in these confines.
Byplay.   'Tis our custom
    To deny strangers nothing—yea, to offer
    Of anything we have that may be useful   255
    In courtesy to strangers. Will you therefore
    Be pleased to enter, sir, this habitation,
    And take such viands, beverage, and repose
    As may refresh you after tedious travels?
Doctor. Thou tak'st him right, for I am sure he's hungry.   260
Peregrine. All I have seen since my arrival are
    Wonders, but your humanity excels.
Byplay. Virtue in the Antipodes only dwells.   *Exeunt.*

249.1.] *Exit. Q.*   263.SD] *not in Q.*

---

249. *Shall pause*] An interval after each Act, in which music played while the lights
were trimmed, was standard practice in the indoor theatres.

ACT III

Enter LETOY, JOYLESS, DIANA, MARTHA *and* BARBARA

Letoy. Yet, Master Joyless, are you pleased? You see
    Here's nothing but fair play, and all above board.
Joyless. But it is late, and these long intermissions
    By banqueting and courtship 'twixt the acts
    Will keep back the catastrophe of your play   5
    Until the morning light.
Letoy.   All shall be short.
Joyless. And then in midst of scenes
    You interrupt your actors, and tie them
    To lengthen time in silence, while you hold
    Discourse by th' by.
Letoy.   Pox o' thy jealousy.   10
    Because I give thy wife a look or word
    Sometimes! What if I kiss (thus); I'll not eat her.
Joyless. So, so, his banquet works with him.
Letoy. And for my actors, they shall speak or not speak
    As much, or more, or less, and when I please.   15
    It is my way of pleasure, and I'll use it.

Flourish.

So, sit. They enter.

Enter Lawyer *and* Poet.

Lawyer. Your case is clear; I understand it fully,
    And need no more instructions. This shall serve
    To firk your adversary from court to court.   20
    If he stand out upon rebellious legs
    But till *Octavus Michaelis* next,
    I'll bring him on submissive knees.
Diana.   What's he?

ACT III] Act 3.Scene 1. *Q.*   17.1.] *Act 3.Scene 2. Q (before SD).*

    5. *catastrophe*] denouement.
    8–9. *tie . . . silence*] freeze them in a tableau. Letoy has probably done this at
123–6 and 138–146 in the previous scene.
    20. *firk*] drive.
    22. Octavus Michaelis] 7 October, eight days after Michaelmas Day; one of the
times for returning writs (Baker).

Letoy. A lawyer, and his client there, a poet.
Diana. Goes law so torn, and poetry so brave?   25
Joyless. Will you but give the actors leave to speak,
    They may have done the sooner!
Lawyer.   Let me see.
    This is your bill of parcels?
Poet.   Yes, of all
    My several wares, according to the rates
    Deliverèd unto my debtor.
Diana.   Wares,   30
    Does he say?
Letoy.   Yes, poetry is good ware in
    The Antipodes, though there be some ill payers,
    As well as here; but law there rights the poets.
Lawyer. [*Reads.*] Delivered to and for the use of the right
        worshipful Master Alderman Humblebee, as followeth: 35
    Imprimis—
    Umh, I cannot read your hand; your character
    Is bad, and your orthography much worse.
    Read it yourself, pray.
Diana.   Do aldermen
    Love poetry in Antipodean London?   40
Letoy. Better than ours do custard; but the worst
    Paymasters living there, worse than our gallants,
    Partly for want of money, partly wit.
Diana. Can aldermen want wit and money, too?
    That's wonderful.
Poet.   *Imprimis*, sir, here is   45
    For three religious madrigals to be sung
    By th' holy vestals in Bridewell for the
    Conversion of our city wives and daughters,

---

24. client there, a poet] Q *(corr.)*; Clyent, there's a Poet Q *(uncorr.).*   30. debtor]
Debitor Q.

---

25. *torn . . . brave*] shabby . . . smart. The man of letters is proverbially threadbare.
28. *bill of parcels*] itemised account.
32–3. *ill . . . here*] A common complaint amongst writers, but Brome was nursing a
particular grievance: see Author's Note, 6 note.
37. *character*] handwriting.
41. *custard*] It was the custom at the Lord Mayor's feast in London for a jester to
leap into an enormous bowl of custard.
47. *holy . . . Bridewell*] Bridewell prison near the outlet of the Fleet Ditch was used
to intern prostitutes. Brome's joke relies on a familiar association (cf. Hamlet's pun on
'nunnery' meaning a brothel) and it lacks the Blakean bite of Jonson's 'decay'd vestals
of Picthatch' (*Alchemist*, II.i.62).

Ten groats apiece: it was his own agreement.
Lawyer. 'Tis very reasonable.
Poet.   *Item,* twelve hymns   50
    For the twelve sessions during his shrievalty,
    Sung by the choir of Newgate in the praise
    Of city clemency (for in that year
    No guiltless person suffered by their judgement),
    Ten groats apiece also.
Lawyer.   So, now it rises.   55
Diana. Why speaks your poet so demurely?
                                        O,
Letoy.
    'Tis a precise tone he has got among
    The sober sisterhood.
Diana.   O, I remember:
    The doctor said poets were all puritans
    In the Antipodes. But where's the doctor?   60
    And where's your son, my Joyless?
Letoy.   Do not mind him.
Poet. Item, a distich, graven in his thumb ring,
    Of all the wise speeches and sayings of all
    His alder predecessors and his brethren
    In two kings' reigns.
Lawyer.   There was a curious piece.   65
Poet. Two pieces he promised to me for it.
    Item, inscriptions in his hall and parlour,
    His gallery, and garden, round the walls,
    Of his own public acts between the time

---

49. *groats*] a groat was originally worth four (old) pence.

51. *shrievalty*] sheriff's term of office.

52. *choir of Newgate*] Newgate was one of the gates of the old city, and served as London's chief prison. In *Jests to Make You Merrie*, Dekker sketches 'Our Newgate-Bird (whose notes you have heard before)': 'What musicke hath he to cheere up his Spirites in this sadness? none but this, he heares wretches (equally miserable) breaking their heart-strings every night with grones, every day with sighes, every houre with cares' (*Non-Dramatic Works*, ed. A.B. Grosart (1885), II.341–3).

57. *precise*] restrained, puritanical.

62. *distich*] verse couplet.

64. *alder*] OED gives this only as an archaic or dialectal form of 'older', but here the word (capitalised in Q) refers to his predecessors as alderman (chief officer of a city ward).

65. *curious*] ingenious.

66. *pieces*] gold coins worth 22 shillings.

67–8. *inscriptions . . . walls*] satirising citizen pomposity: Baker compares Jonson's *Poetaster*, II.i.105–7: 'hang no pictures in the hall, nor in the dining-room chamber . . . but in the gallery only, for 'tis not courtly else'.

He was a common councilman and shrief,   70
One thousand lines put into wholesome verse.
Lawyer. Here's a sum towards indeed! A thousand verses?
Poet. They come to, at the known rate of the city,
That is to say at forty pence the score,
Eight pounds, six shillings, eightpence.
Lawyer.   Well, sir, on.   75
Poet. Item, an elegy for Mistress Alderwoman
Upon the death of one of her coach-mares
She prized above her daughter, being crooked—
Diana. The more beast she.
Martha.   Ha, ha, ha!
Barbara.   Enough, enough, sweetheart.
Martha. 'Tis true, for I should weep for that poor daughter,   80
'Tis like she'll have no children. Pray now, look:
Am not I crooked, too?
Barbara.   No, no, sit down.
Poet. Item, a love epistle for the aldermanikin his son,
And a book of the godly life and death
Of Mistress Katherine Stubbes, which I have turned   85
Into sweet metre, for the virtuous youth
To woo an ancient lady widow with.
Lawyer. Here's a large sum in all, for which I'll try
His strength in law till he *peccavi cry,*
When I shall sing, for all his present bigness   90
Jamque opus exegi, quod nec Jovis ira, nec ignis.
Diana. The lawyer speaks the poet's part.
Letoy.   He thinks
The more; the poets in th' Antipodes
Are slow of tongue, but nimble with the pen.

---

70. *shrief*] sheriff.
78. *crooked*] deformed.
79.] Diana's quip and Martha's hysterical laughter are simultaneous, divergent responses; Barbara's soothing words complete the verse line.
83. *aldermanikin*] little alderman (Brome's own coinage).
84–5. *book ... Stubbes*] *A Chrystall Glasse for Christian Women* (1591), the much-reprinted account by the Puritan Philip Stubbes of his wife's exemplary death at the age of twenty. Its main burden, that she 'obeyed the commandement of the Apostle, who biddeth women to be silent, and to learne of their husbands at home' (A2v), would be unlikely to impress an ancient lady widow, either in London or the Antipodes.
89. *peccavi*] lit. 'I have sinned'; an admission of guilt or liability.
91.] The ringing conclusion to the *Metamorphoses*: 'And now the worke is ended, which, *Jove's* rage,/Nor fire, nor Sword shall raze, nor eating Age' (XV.871–2; Sandys, *Ovid,* p. 510).

Poet. The counsel and the comfort you have given me   95
  Requires a double fee. (*Offers money.*)
Lawyer.   Will you abuse me therefore?
  I take no fees, double nor single, I.
  Retain your money; you retain not me else.
  Away, away; you'll hinder other clients.
Poet. Pray, give me leave to send then to your wife.   100
Lawyer. Not so much as a posy for her thimble,
  For fear I spoil your cause.
Poet.   Y'ave warned me, sir.   *Exit.*
Diana. What a poor honest lawyer's this?
Letoy.   They are
  All so in th' Antipodes.

              Enter a spruce young Captain.

Lawyer.   Y'are welcome, captain.
  In your two causes I have done my best.   105
Captain. And what's the issue, pray sir?
Lawyer.   Truly, sir,
  Our best course is not to proceed to trial.
Captain. Your reason? I shall then recover nothing.
Lawyer. Yes, more by composition than the court
  Can lawfully adjudge you, as I have laboured;   110
  And, sir, my course is, where I can compound
  A difference, I'll not toss nor bandy it
  Into the hazard of a judgement.
Diana.   Still
  An honest lawyer, and though poor, no marvel.
Letoy. A kiss for thy conceit. [*Kisses her.*]
Joyless.   A sweet occasion!   115
Captain. How have you done, sir?
Lawyer.   First, you understand
  Your several actions, and your adversaries:
  The first, a battery against a coachman

104.] *Act 3.Scene 3. Q (before SD).*

    101. *posy*] inscription.
    111. *compound*] settle.
    112–13. *toss...judgement*] risk putting it to the test in court. The lawyer's terms are all drawn from tennis.
    114. *no marvel*] because after all he spins out negotiations just like a London lawyer.
    115. *occasion*] pretext.
    118. *battery*] i.e. a charge of assault.

That beat you sorely.
Diana.   What hard-hearted fellow
　Could beat so spruce a gentleman, and a captain?   120
Captain. By this fair hilt, he did, sir, and so bruised
　My arms, so crushed my ribs, and stitched my sides,
　That I have had no heart to draw my sword since.
　And shall I put it up, and not his purse
　Be made to pay for't?
Lawyer.   It is up already, sir,   125
　If you can be advised. Observe, I pray,
　Your other actions 'gainst your feathermaker,
　And that of trespass for th'incessant trouble
　He puts you to by importunate requests
　To pay him no money, but take longer day.   130
Captain. Against all human reason, for although
　I have bought feathers of him these four years
　And never paid him a penny, yet he duns me
　So desperately to keep my money still,
　As if I owed him nothing; he haunts and breaks my sleeps!   135
　I swear, sir, by the motion of this I wear now,

　　　　　　　　　　He shakes his hat.

　I have had twenty better feathers of him,
　And as ill paid for.
　Yet still he duns me to forbear my payment
　And to take longer day! I ha' not said my prayers   140
　In mine own lodging, sir, this twelvemonth's day
　For sight or thought of him; and how can you
　Compound this action, or the other of
　That ruffian coachman that durst lift a hand
　'Gainst a commander?
Lawyer.   Very easily, thus: 145
　The coachman's poor, and scarce his twelvemonth's

　　　　　　　　　　　　　　　　　　　　wages,

---

132. years] *Q corr.*; yea *Q uncorr.* 135. owed] ought *Q.* 136.1. *He . . . hat*]
Shakes it. Q. 137–40. I . . . day!] I . . . for,/Yet . . . payment,/And . . . day. *most
copies of Q. Some (apparently uncorrected) copies of Q place a colon after day and
follow it (on the next line) with the words* More then at first.

---

122. *stitched*] stabbed.
124. *put it up*] endure it.
125. *It is up*] The case has been brought.
133. *duns*] importunes.
136. *this*] i.e. the feather in his hat.

Though't be five marks a year, will satisfy.
Captain. Pray name no sum in marks; I have had too many
  Of's marks already.
Lawyer.   So you owe the other
  A debt of twenty pound, the coachman now   150
  Shall for your satisfaction beat you out
  Of debt.
Captain.   Beat me again?
Lawyer.   No, sir, he shall beat
  For you your featherman, till he take his money.
Captain. So I'll be satisfied, and help him to
  More customers of my rank.
Lawyer.   Leave it to me then.   155
  It shall be by posterity repeaten
  That soldiers ought not to be dunned or beaten.
  Away and keep your money.
Captain.   Thank you, sir.   *Exit.*
Diana. An honest lawyer still! How he considers
  The weak estate of a young gentleman   160
  At arms.

                Enter Buff Woman.

            But who comes here? a woman?
Letoy. Yes, that has taken up the newest fashion
  Of the town militasters.
Diana.   Is it buff,
  Or calfskin, trow? She looks as she could beat
  Out a whole tavern garrison before her   165
  Of—mill tasters, call you 'em? If her husband
  Be an old, jealous man now, and can please her
  No better than most ancient husbands can,
  I warrant she makes herself good upon him.
Joyless. 'Tis very good; the play begins to please me. 170

          The Lawyer *reads on papers.*

---

158. *Exit*] *not in* Q.   161.] *Act.3.Sce.4.* Q (*before* SD).   170.1.] *next to* 167–8 *in*
Q.

---

147. *marks*] A mark was worth two-thirds of a pound.
  151. *for . . . satisfaction*] i.e. to make proper amends for his treatment of you.
  161.SD *Buff*] i.e. dressed in a jerkin made of buff leather, ox-hide dressed with oil
and with a velvety finish (Linthicum). It was commonly worn by soldiers; the
following lines make it clear that the military look was fashionable.
  163. *militasters*] spare-time soldiers.

Buff Woman. [*To Lawyer*] I wait to speak w' ye, sir, but must
                                                          I stand
   Your const'ring and piercing of your scribblings?
Lawyer. Cry mercy, lady.
Diana.   'Lady' does he call her?
Lawyer. Thus far I have proceeded in your cause
   I'th' marshal's court.
Buff Woman.   But shall I have the combat?   175
Lawyer. Pray observe the passages of my proceedings, and
   The pros and contras in the windings, workings,
   And carriage of the cause.
Buff Woman.   Fah on your passages,
   Your windy workings, and your fizzlings at
   The bar. Come me to th' point. Is it decreed   180
   A combat?
Lawyer.   Well, it is; and here's your order.
Buff Woman. Now thou hast spoken like a lawyer,
   And here's thy fee.
Lawyer.   By no means, gentle lady.
Buff Woman. Take it, or I will beat thy carcass thinner
   Than thou hast worn thy gown here.
Lawyer.   Pardon me.   185
Buff Woman. Must I then take you in hand?
Lawyer.   Hold, hold! I take it.
Diana. Alas, poor man! He will take money yet
   Rather than blows; and so far he agrees
   With our rich lawyers, that sometimes give blows,
   And shrewd ones, for their money.
Buff Woman.   Now victory   190
   Afford me, Fate, or bravely let me die.   *Exit.*
Letoy. Very well acted, that.
Diana.   Goes she to fight now?
Letoy. You shall see that anon.

         Enter a Beggar *and a* Gallant.

Diana.   What's here, what's here?
   A courtier, or some gallant, practising
   The beggar's trade, who teaches him, I think.   195

193.] *Act.3.Scene.5. Q (before SD).*

---

  172. *const'ring*] deciphering.
  179. *fizzlings*] silent farts; here implying a lame conclusion to so much legal effort.
  190. *shrewd*] vicious.

Letoy. Y'are something near the subject.
Beggar.   Sir, excuse me; I have
     From time to time supplied you, without hope
     Or purpose to receive least retribution
     From you; no, not so much as thanks or bare
     Acknowledgement of the free benefits   200
     I have conferred upon you.
Gallant.   Yet, good uncle—
Beggar. Yet do you now, when that my present store
     Responds not my occasions, seek to oppress me
     With vain petitionary breath for what I may not
     Give without fear of dangerous detriment?   205
Diana. In what a phrase the ragged orator
     Displays himself!
Letoy.   The beggars are the
     Most absolute courtiers in th' Antipodes.
Gallant. If not a piece, yet spare me half a piece
     For goodness sake, good sir; did you but know   210
     My instant want, and to what virtuous use
     I would distribute it, I know you would not
     Hold back your charity.
Diana.   And how feelingly
     He begs. Then as the beggars are the best
     Courtiers, it seems the courtiers are best beggars   215
     In the Antipodes; how contrary in all
     Are they to us!
Beggar.   Pray, to what virtuous uses
     Would you put money to now, if you had it?
Gallant. I would bestow a crown in ballads,
     Love pamphlets, and such poetical rarities   220
     To send down to my lady grandmother.
     She's very old, you know, and given much
     To contemplation. I know she'll send me for 'em
     In puddings, bacon, souse, and pot-butter
     Enough to keep my chamber all this winter.   225

---

198. *retribution*] recompense.
203. *Responds . . . occasions*] doesn't answer my present needs.
215. *courtiers . . . beggars*] an allusion to the practice of scheming to be granted the reversion of forfeited estates, usually by informing on the owner. Jonson refers to it in *Poetaster*, V.iii.41–2, and *Staple of News*, IV.Int.50–1, and it is central to the action of Brome's *Court Begger* (1632), where Mendicant seeks to 'raise [his] state by Court-suits, begging as some call it' (I.i; *Works* 1873, I.187).
224. *souse*] pickled trotters (or pigs' ears).
pot-butter] salted butter in jars.

So shall I save my father's whole allowance
To lay upon my back, and not be forced
To shift out from my study for my victuals.
Diana. Belike he is some student.
Beggar.   There's a crown.
Gallant. I would bestow another crown in   230
Hobbyhorses and rattles for my grandfather,
Whose legs and hearing fail him very much.
Then, to preserve his sight, a Jack-a-lent
In a green sarc'net suit; he'll make my father
To send me one of scarlet, or he'll cry   235
His eyes out for't.
Diana.   O politic young student.
Beggar. I have but just a fee left for my lawyer;
If he exact not that, I'll give it thee.
Diana. He'll take no fee, that's sure enough, young man,
Of beggars, I know that.
Letoy.   You are deceived.   240
Diana. I'll speak to him myself else, to remit it.
Joyless. You will not, sure; will you turn actor, too?
Pray do, be put in for a share amongst 'em!
Diana. How must I be put in?
Joyless.   The players will quickly
Show you, if you perform your part; perhaps   245
They may want one to act the whore amongst 'em.
Letoy. Fie, Master Joyless, y'are too foul.
Joyless.   My lord,
She is too fair, it seems in your opinion,
For me; therefore, if you can find it lawful,
Keep her; I will be gone.
Letoy.   Now I protest   250
Sit, and sit civilly, till the play be done!
I'll lock thee up else, as I am true Letoy.
Joyless. Nay, I ha' done. (*Whistles 'Fortune my foe'.*)

---

227. *lay . . . back*] spend on clothes.
231. *Hobbyhorses*] lightweight models of horses worn around the waist.
233. *Jack-a-Lent*] gaudily dressed puppet set up during Lent for children to pelt with stones. There may be an antipodean implication that its ritual scapegoat function will invert the effects of old age, but the simple idea is that the grandfather will *preserve his sight* by taking aim.
234. *sarc'net*] sarcenet was an expensive soft silk fabric.
243. *be . . . 'em*] Principal actors were often shareholders in a theatrical company.
253. 'Fortune my foe'] popularly known as the 'hanging tune', to which numerous dying speeches both real and fictional were set. It is frequently alluded to by dramatists; see W. Chappell, *Old English Popular Music* (1893), I.76–9.

Lawyer. Give me my fee; I cannot hear you else.
Beggar. Sir, I am poor, and all I get is at   255
    The hands of charitable givers; pray, sir—
Lawyer. You understand me, sir: your cause is to be
    Pleaded today, or you are quite o'erthrown in't.
    The judge by this time is about to sit.
    Keep fast your money, and forgo your wit.   *Exit.* 260
Beggar. Then I must follow, and entreat him to it;
    Poor men in law must not disdain to do it.   *Exit.*
Gallant. Do it then; I'll follow you and hear the cause.   *Exit.*
Diana. True Antipodeans still; for as with us
    The gallants follow lawyers, and the beggars them,   265
    The lawyer here is followed by the beggar,
    While the gentleman follows him.
Letoy. The moral is, the lawyers here prove beggars,
    And beggars only thrive by going to law.
Diana. How takes the lawyers, then, the beggars' money,   270
    And none else by their wills?
Letoy.   They send it all
    Up to our lawyers, to stop their mouths
    That curse poor clients that are put upon 'em
    In forma pauperis.
Diana.   In truth, most charitable,
    But sure that money's lost by th' way sometimes.   275
    Yet, sweet my lord, whom do these beggars beg of
    That they can get aforehand so for law?
    Who are their benefactors?
Letoy.   Usurers, usurers.
Diana. Then they have usurers in th' Antipodes, too?
Letoy. Yes, usury goes round the world, and will do   280
    Till the general conversion of the Jews.
Diana. But ours are not so charitable, I fear.
    Who be their usurers?
Letoy.   Soldiers and courtiers chiefly,

   268–9.] A moral that plays against numerous familiar proverbs about lawyers and
beggars, e.g. B240, 242, 245, L125, 127.
   270. *How*] Why; how comes it.
   271. *none else*] nobody else's. As Diana has already noticed (114), lawyers are only
partially transformed by the Antipodes, and demonstrate their incorrigible rapacity by
'begging' only from the poorest in society.
   274. In forma pauperis] Under this rubric the poor could sue or defend themselves
in a court of law without paying costs.

And some that pass for grave and pious churchmen.
Diana. How finely contrary th'are still to ours!   285
Letoy. [*Calls.*] Why do you not enter? What, are you asleep?

Enter BYPLAY.

Byplay. My lord, the mad young gentleman—
Joyless.   What of him?
Byplay. He has got into our tiring-house amongst us,
    And ta'en a strict survey of all our properties:
    Our statues and our images of gods,   290
    Our planets and our constellations,
    Our giants, monsters, furies, beasts, and bugbears,
    Our helmets, shields, and vizors, hairs, and beards,
    Our pasteboard marchpanes, and our wooden pies.
Letoy. Sirrah, be brief; be not you now as long in   295
    Telling what he saw as he surveying.
Byplay. Whether he thought 'twas some enchanted castle,
    Or temple hung and piled with monuments
    Of uncouth and of various aspects,
    I dive not to his thoughts. Wonder he did   300
    A while it seemed, but yet undaunted stood;
    When on the sudden, with thrice knightly force,
    And thrice thrice puissant arm he snatcheth down
    The sword and shield that I played Bevis with,
    Rusheth amongst the foresaid properties,   305

286.1.] *after 285 and preceded by Act.3.Scene.5. Q (this and remainder of scenes in Act III misnumbered).*

284.] In *Newes in the Antipodes* the satire on worldly clerics is less deadpan: 'The Bishops there bee all honest, preaching Bishops, not studying *Court* pollicy, but preferring sollid divinitie' (p. 6).

289. *properties*] The list that follows is the stock in trade of popular romantic theatre: cf. Henslowe's inventory in Gurr, pp. 187–8, and the list of small props at the Red Bull theatre (for which Brome wrote earlier in the 1630s) given by Reynolds, pp. 85–7.

291. *our . . . constellations*] Henslowe itemises 'the clothe of the Sone & Mone' (Gurr, p. 187).

294. *marchpanes*] decorative cakes and sweets. English cooks were famous for creating dishes in elaborate shapes like animals and castles, and banquet scenes in plays no doubt reproduced some of these.

295–6. *be . . . surveying*] Letoy guesses that Byplay sees an opportunity to extemporise the role of messenger delivering a tragic report; its mock-heroic is firmly in the quixotic tradition of Barbaroso's barber shop in Beaumont's *Knight*, III.iii.230 ff.

304. *Bevis*] Sir Bevis of Hampton, hero of an enormously popular romance whose fifteenth (extant) edition came out in 1639. There is no record of a theatrical version but it is unlikely that none was ever made.

Kills monster after monster, takes the puppets
Prisoners, knocks down the Cyclops, tumbles all
Our jigambobs and trinkets to the wall.
Spying at last the crown and royal robes
I'th' upper wardrobe, next to which by chance   310
The devils' vizors hung, and their flame-painted
Skin coats, those he removed with greater fury;
And, having cut the infernal ugly faces
All into mammocks, with a reverend hand
He takes the imperial diadem and crowns   315
Himself King of the Antipodes, and believes
He has justly gained the kingdom by his conquest.
Letoy. Let him enjoy his fancy.
Byplay.   Doctor Hughball
Hath soothed him in't, so that nothing can
Be said against it. He begins to govern   320
With purpose to reduce the manners
Of this country to his own. H' has constituted
The doctor his chief officer, whose secretary
I am to be; you'll see a court well ordered.
Letoy. I see th'event already, by the aim   325
The doctor takes. Proceed you with your play,
And let him see it in what state he pleases.
Byplay. I go, my lord.   *Exit.*

          LETOY *whispers with* BARBARA.

Diana.   Trust me, this same Extempore
(I know not's tother name) pleases me better
For absolute action than all the rest.   330
Joyless. You were best beg him of his lord.
Diana.   Say you so?
He's busy, or I'd move him.
Letoy.   Prithee do so,

---

328. LETOY . . . BARBARA] *next to* 325–6 *in* Q.

308. *jigambobs*] knick-knacks.
310. *upper wardrobe*] The wardrobe was housed at gallery level in the tiring-house, with the props being kept in the room below.
314. *mammocks*] shreds.
321. *reduce*] subdue, adapt. The term was commonly employed to describe the process of colonisation.
327. *state*] form: Byplay is to use his improvising skills to accommodate Peregrine's demands of the play. The word might also mean 'throne', since Peregrine has had a view of the stage furniture.
330. *For . . . action*] in terms of pure performance.

Good Mistress Blaze.——(*To Martha*) Go with her, gentle
lady.

Do as she bids you. You shall get a child by't.
Martha. I'll do as anybody bids me for a child.   335
Joyless. Diana, yet be wise; bear not the name
Of sober chastity to play the beast in.
Diana. Think not yourself, nor make yourself a beast
Before you are one; and when you appear so,
Then thank yourself. Your jealousy durst not trust me   340
Behind you in the country, and since I'm here,
I'll see and know and follow th' fashion; if
It be to cuckold you, I cannot help it.
Joyless. I now could wish my son had been as far
In the Antipodes as he thinks himself   345
Ere I had run this hazard.
Letoy. [*To Barbara*]   Y'are instructed.
Barbara. And I'll perform't, I warrant you, my lord.
Exeunt BARBARA *and* MARTHA.
Diana. Why should you wish so? Had you rather lose
Your son than please your wife? You show your love both
ways!

Letoy. Now what's the matter?
Joyless.   Nothing, nothing.

Flourish.

Letoy.   Sit,   350
The actors enter.

Enter BYPLAY *as the governor*, Macebearer, Swordbearer,
Officer; *the mace and sword laid on the table.*
The governor sits.

Diana. What's he, a king?
Letoy.   No, 'tis the city governor,
And the chief judge within their corporation.
Joyless. Here's a city like to be well governed then!

Enter PEREGRINE *and* Doctor HUGHBALL.

Letoy. Yonder's a king. Do you know him?
Diana.   'Tis your son,   355

351.1] *Act.3.Scene 6. Q (before SD).   as*] *not in Q.*

---

341. *Behind*] i.e. to stay behind.

My Joyless. Now y'are pleased.
Joyless.   Would you were pleased
    To cease your housewif'ry in spinning out
    The play at length thus.
Doctor.   Here, sir, you shall see
    A point of justice handled.
Byplay.   Officer.
Officer.   My lord.
Byplay. Call the defendant and the plaintiff in.   360
Swordbearer. Their counsel and their witnesses.
Byplay.   How now!
    How long ha' you been free o'th'pointmakers,
    Good Master hilt-and-scabbard carrier
    (Which is in my hands now)? Do you give order
    For counsel and for witnesses in a cause   365
    Fit for my hearing, or for me to judge, haw?
    I must be ruled and circumscribed by lawyers, must I,
    And witnesses, haw? No, you shall know
    I can give judgement, be it right or wrong,
    Without their needless proving and defending!   370
    So bid the lawyers go and shake their ears,
    If they have any, and the witnesses
    Preserve their breath to prophesy of dry summers.
    Bring me the plaintiff and defendant only,
    But the defendant first; I will not hear   375
    Any complaint before I understand
    What the defendant can say for himself.   *Exit* Officer.
Peregrine. I have not known such downright equity.
    If he proceeds as he begins, I'll grace him.

                Re-enter Officer *with* Gentleman.

Byplay. Now, sir, are you the plaintiff or defendant, haw?   380
Gentleman. Both, as the case requires, my lord.
Byplay.   I cannot
    Hear two at once; speak first as y'are defendant.

377.SD] *not in* Q.   379.1.] *Act.3.Sce.7 Enter Gentleman, and Officer. Q.*

---

357. *housewif'ry*] thriftiness—in making the play last so long.
362. *free ... pointmakers*] For free = member of a company or guild, cf. *Travels*, iii.12 note. Points were the tags or laces used to attach the hose to the doublet, or to lace a bodice; Byplay puns on the sense of 'legal point'.
364. *Which ... now*] Byplay takes up the sword of justice from the table.
379. *grace*] show favour to.

Gentleman. Mine adversary doth complain—
Byplay.   I will hear no
    Complaint; I say speak your defence.
Gentleman.   For silks
    And stuffs received by me—
Byplay.   A mercer is he, haw?   385
Gentleman. Yes, my good lord. He doth not now complain—
Byplay. That I like well.
Gentleman.   For money nor for wares
    Again; but he complains—
Byplay.   Complains again?
    Do you double with me, haw?
Gentleman.   In his wife's cause.
Byplay. Of his wife, does he, haw? That I must confess   390
    Is many a good man's case. You may proceed.
Gentleman. In money I tender him double satisfaction,
    With his own wares again unblemished, undishonoured.
Byplay. That is, unworn, unpawned.
Diana.   What an odd,
    Jeering judge is this?
Gentleman.   But unto me   395
    They were delivered, upon this condition
    That I should satisfy his wife.
Byplay.   He'll have
    Your body for her then, unless I empt
    My breast of mercy to appease her for you.
    Call in the plaintiff!   *Exit* Officer.
    [*To Gentleman*]   Sir, stand you aside.   400
Diana. O, 'tis the flinching gentleman that broke
    With the kind citizen's wife. I hope the judge
    Will make him an example.

Re-enter Officer *with* Citizen.

Byplay.   Come you forwards;
    Yet nearer, man. I know my face is terrible,
    And that a citizen had rather lose
    His debt, than that a judge should truly know   405

403.] *Act.3.Scene.8. Enter Citizen, and Officer. Q.*

394–5. *That . . . this*] Byplay's terse deflation of the gentleman's pompous language
is presumably seen as the opposite of customary legal rhetoric.

404. *my . . . terrible*] Haaker compares the 'reverend Magisterial frown' of the judge
about to pass sentence in Cartwright's *The Ordinary*, B3v.

His dealings with a gentleman. Yet speak,
Repeat without thy shopbook now, and without
Fear it may rise in judgement here against thee,
What is thy full demand? What satisfaction   410
Requirest thou of this gentleman?
Citizen.   And please you, sir—
Swordbearer. Sir? You forget yourself.
Byplay.   'Twas well said, Swordbearer;
Thou know'st thy place, which is to show correction.
Citizen. My lord, an't please you, if it like your honour—
Byplay. La! An intelligent citizen, and may grow   415
In time himself to sit in place of worship.
Citizen. I ask no satisfaction of the gentleman
But to content my wife; what her demand is,
'Tis best known to herself. Please her, please me,
An't please you, sir—my lord, an't like your honour.   420
But before he has given her satisfaction
I may not fall my suit, nor draw my action.
Byplay. You may not.
Citizen.   No, alack-a-day, I may not,
Nor find content, nor peace at home, an't please you,
My lord (an't like your honour, I would say).   425
An't please you, what's a tradesman that
Has a fair wife, without his wife, an't please you?
And she without content is no wife. Considering
We tradesmen live by gentlemen, an't please you,
And our wives drive a half-trade with us: if the gentlemen 430
Break with our wives, our wives are no wives to us,
And we but broken tradesmen, an't please you,
An't like your honour, my good lord, an't please you.
Byplay. You argue honestly.
Citizen.   Yet gentlemen—
Alack-a-day, and please you, and like your honour—   435
Will not consider our necessities,
And our desire in general through the city
To have our sons all gentlemen like them.
Byplay. Nor though a gentleman consume
His whole estate among ye, yet his son   440

---

408. *shopbook*] account book.
416. *worship*] authority.
422. *fall . . . draw*] drop . . . withdraw.
430. *drive . . . half-trade*] share the business (with innuendo).
439. *consume*] waste, forfeit.

  May live t'inherit it?
Citizen.   Right, right, an't please you,
  Your honour, my good lord, an't please you.
Byplay.   Well,
  This has so little to be said against it,
  That you say nothing. Gentlemen, it seems
  Y'are obstinate, and will stand out—
Gentleman.   My lord,   445
  Rather than not to stand out with all men's wives
  Except mine own, I'll yield me into prison.
Citizen. Alack-a-day!
Diana.   If our young gentlemen
  Were like those of th' Antipodes, what decay
  Of trade would here be, and how full the prisons! 450
Gentleman. I offer him any other satisfaction;
  His wares again, or money twice the value.
Byplay. That's from the point.
Citizen.   Ay, ay, alack-a-day,
  Nor do I sue to have him up in prison.
  Alack-a-day, what good (good gentleman)
  Can I get by his body?   455
Byplay.   Peace. I should
  Now give my sentence; and for your contempt,
  Which is a great one, such as if let pass
  Unpunished, may spread forth a dangerous
  Example to the breach of city custom, 460
  By gentlemen's neglect of tradesmen's wives—
  I should say for this contempt commit you
  Prisoner from sight of any other woman
  Until you give this man's wife satisfaction,
  And she release you; justice so would have it. 465
  But as I am a citizen by nature
  (For education made it so), I'll use
  Urbanity in your behalf towards you.
  And as I am a gentleman by calling
  (For so my place must have it), I'll perform 470
  For you the office of a gentleman
  Towards his wife. I therefore order thus:
  That you bring me the wares here into court—
  I have a chest shall hold 'em as mine own—
  And you send me your wife; I'll satisfy her 475

---

446. *stand out*] avoid involvement.

Myself. I'll do't, and set all straight and right.
Justice is blind, but judges have their sight.
Diana. And feeling, too, in the Antipodes,
    Ha'n't they, my lord?
Joyless.   What's that to you, my lady?
Within. Dismiss the court.   480
Letoy. Dismiss the court; cannot you hear the prompter?
    Ha' you lost your ears, judge?
Byplay.   No. [*To Officer*] Dismiss the court.
    Embrace you, friends, and to shun further strife,
    See you send me your stuff and you your wife.
            Exeunt Officer, Citizen *and* Gentleman.
Peregrine. Most admirable justice.   485

               BYPLAY *removes his robes.*

Diana. Protest, Extempore played the judge! And I
    Knew him not all this while.
Joyless.   What oversight
    Was there!
Diana.   He is a properer man, methinks
    Now, than he was before; sure I shall love him.
Joyless. Sure, sure you shall not, shall you?
Diana.   And I warrant,   490
    By his judgement speech e'en now, he loves a woman well;
    For he said, if you noted him, that he
    Would satisfy the citizen's wife himself.
    Methinks a gentlewoman might please him better.
Joyless. How dare you talk so?   495

        BYPLAY *kneels, and kisses* PEREGRINE's *hand.*

Diana. What's he a-doing now, trow?
Peregrine.   Kneel down
    Again. Give me a sword, somebody.
Letoy. The king's about to knight him.
Byplay.   Let me pray
    Your majesty be pleased yet to withhold
    That undeservèd honour, till you first   500
    Vouchsafe to grace the city with your presence.

484.1.] *not in* Q.   485.1.] *not in* Q.

---

478. *feeling*] susceptibility to bribes; but Diana may also be teasing Joyless with a
pun on sexual impulses. Her humour seems to distract Byplay, who has to be
prompted in 480.

Accept one of our hall feasts, and a freedom,
And freely use our purse for what great sums
Your majesty will please.
Diana.   What subjects there are
In the Antipodes!
Letoy.   None in the world so loving.   505
Peregrine. Give me a sword, I say. Must I call thrice?
Letoy. No, no, take mine, my liege.
Peregrine.   Yours? What are you?
Doctor. A loyal lord, one of your subjects, too.
Peregrine. He may be loyal; he's a wondrous plain one.
Joyless. Prithee, Diana, yet let's slip away   510
Now while he's busy.
Diana.   But where's your daughter-in-law?
Joyless. Gone home, I warrant you, with Mistress Blaze.
Let them be our example.
Diana.   You are cozened.
Joyless. Y'are an impudent whore!
Diana.   I know not what I may
Be made by your jealousy.
Peregrine. [*Throws down Letoy's sword.*] I'll none o' this;   515
Give me that princely weapon. [*Points at sword of office.*]
Letoy.   Give it him.
Swordbearer. [*Aside to Letoy*] It is a property, you know, my
                                                        lord,
No blade, but a rich scabbard with a lath in't.
Letoy. So is the sword of justice, for aught he knows.
Peregrine. It is enchanted.
Byplay.   Yet on me let it fall,
Since 'tis your highness' will, scabbard and all.   520
Peregrine. Rise up, our trusty well-belovèd knight.
Byplay. Let me find favour in your gracious sight
To taste a banquet now, which is prepared,
And shall be by your followers quickly shared.   525
Peregrine. My followers, where are they?
Letoy. [*Calls.*]   Come, sirs, quickly.

Enter 5 or 6 Courtiers.

---

502. *freedom*] i.e. of the city.
518. *lath*] thin piece of wood; the usual term for a theatrical sword or dagger.
519.] The theatrical in-joke encloses a neat political satire.
520. *enchanted*] Peregrine is pulling at the sword handle, which in this case is just a painted fixture.

Peregrine. 'Tis well; lead on the way.

                         Exeunt PEREGRINE *and* Courtiers.

Diana.   And must not we

    Go to the banquet, too?

Letoy.   He must not see

    You yet. I have provided otherwise

    For both you in my chamber, and from thence   530

    We'll at a window see the rest o'th' play;

    Or if you needs, sir, will stay here, you may.

Joyless. Was ever man betrayed thus into torment?   *Exeunt.*

527.SD] *not in* Q.

ACT IV

Enter DOCTOR *and* PEREGRINE.

Doctor. Now, sir, be pleased to cloud your princely raiment
With this disguise.

            PEREGRINE *puts on a cloak and hat.*

            Great kings have done the like
To make discovery of passages
Among the people; thus you shall perceive
What to approve, and what correct among 'em.   5
Peregrine. And so I'll cherish, or severely punish.

    Enter an Old Woman *reading a handbill; to her,*
         a young Maid *with a book.*

Doctor. Stand close, sir, and observe.
Old Woman. [*Reads.*] 'Royal pastime in a great match between
the tanners and the butchers, six dogs of a side, to play
single at the game bear for fifty pound, and a ten-pound   10
supper for their dogs and themselves. Also you shall see
two ten-dog courses at the great bear.'
Maid. Fie, Granny, fie! Can no persuasions,
Threat'nings, nor blows prevail, but you'll persist
In these profane and diabolical courses?   15
To follow bearbaitings, when you can scarce
Spell out their bills with spectacles?
Old Woman.   What though
My sight be gone beyond the reach of spectacles
In any print but this, and though I cannot—
No, no, I cannot read your meditations—   20

         Strikes down her book.

Yet I can see the royal game played over and over,

ACT IV] Act 4.Scene I. Q.   2.SD PEREGRINE] *not in Q (rest of SD next to 3−4).* 6.1.
a handbill] *not in Q.* 6.2. *with a book*] *not in Q.*

---

  3. *passages*] goings-on.
  10. *single*] one at a time.
  12. *two . . . courses*] two rounds of ten dogs making a combined attack, as a finale.
Presumably their victim was an especially large bear kept for the purpose, as distinct
from the *game bear* used in single combat.

And tell which dog does best, without my spectacles.
And though I could not, yet I love the noise;
The noise revives me, and the Bear-garden scent
Refresheth much my smelling.
Maid.   Let me entreat you   25
Forbear such beastly pastimes; th'are satanical.
Old Woman. Take heed, child, what you say; 'tis the king's
                                                        game.
Peregrine. What is my game?
Doctor.   Bear-baiting, sir, she means.
Old Woman. 'A bear's a princely beast, and one side venison',
Writ a good author once; you yet want years,   30
And are with baubles pleased. I'll see the bears.   *Exit.*
Maid. And I must bear with it. She's full of wine,
And for the present wilful; but in due
Season I'll humble her. But we are all
Too subject to infirmity.

         Enter a young Gentleman, *and an old* Servingman.

Gentleman.   Boy. Boy.   35
Servingman. Sir.
Gentleman.   Here, take my cloak.
Peregrine. Boy, did he say?
Doctor.   Yes, sir. Old servants are
But boys to masters, be they ne'er so young.
Gentleman. 'Tis heavy, and I sweat.
Servingman.   Take mine and keep
You warm then; I'll wear yours.

35.] *Act 4.Scene 2. (before SD). Q.*

21. *royal game*] Bear-baiting had been a favourite pastime of Tudor monarchs and
of James I (who even experimented with the baiting of lions!), but there is no evidence
of it being patronised by the Caroline court.

23. *though*] even if.

24. *Bear-garden scent*] See note to II.i.83. In the Induction to Jonson's
Bartholomew Fair, performed at the Hope in 1614, the theatre is said to be an
appropriate venue for the play since it is 'as dirty as Smithfield, and as stinking every
whit' (161–2). Brome had reason to remember this Induction as in it he is referred to
as Jonson's 'man', and may have been an actor in the play.

29. *venison*] heart (punning on hart). Haaker compares Jonson, *Magnetic Lady*,
Induction, 28–30: 'which side of the people?/The Venison side, if you know it,
Boy./That's the left side'; but Jonson does not appear to be the author in question.

37–8.] The paradox anticipates colonial modes of address to men servants. Cf. the
'fine contrarietie' in *Newes in the Antipodes*, where 'a young Boy that hath no hope
of beard, will keep an old servant whom hee cals Boy, and abuse him at his pleasure'
(p. 4).

They exchange cloaks.

Gentleman.   Out, you varlet!   40
    Dost thou obscure it as thou meant'st to pawn it?
    Is this a cloak unworthy of the light?
    Publish it, sirrah.—O, presumptuous slave,
    Display it on one arm.—O ignorance!
Servingman. Pray load your ass yourself as you would have it.   45
Gentleman. Nay, prithee be not angry. [*Arranges cloak.*]
                Thus; and now
    Be sure you bear't at no such distance but
    As't may be known appendix to this book.
Peregrine. This custom I have seen with us.
Doctor.   Yes, but
    It was derived from the Antipodes.   50
Maid. It is a dainty creature, and my blood
    Rebels against the spirit: I must speak to him.
Servingman. Sir, here's a gentlewoman makes towards you.
Gentleman. Me? She's deceived; I am not for her mowing.
Maid. Fair sir, may you vouchsafe my company?   55
Gentleman. No truly, I am none of those you look for.
    The way is broad enough; unhand me, pray you.
Maid. Pray sir, be kinder to a lass that loves you.
Gentleman. Some such there are, but I am none of those.
Maid. Come, this is but a copy of your countenance.   60
    I ha' known you better than you think I do.
Gentleman. What ha' you known me for?
Maid.   I knew you once
    For half a piece, I take it.
Gentleman.   You are deceived
    The whole breadth of your nose. I scorn it!

40.SD] *not in* Q.

---

43. *Publish*] display. Cloaks were often richly lined and embroidered, and after 1620 the fashion was to wear them draped over one shoulder or across the chest in such a way as to show off their velvet or silk linings (Linthicum).
    45. *ass*] i.e. beast of burden, servant.
    48. *this book*] i.e. myself.
    51. *dainty*] pleasing, choice.
    54. *mowing*] cropping. The assumption is that she is a prostitute; alternatively, in view of the maid's earlier manner, he may at first think that she is a religious nut, uncharitably dismissing her smile of welcome as a 'mow' or grimace.
    60. *copy . . . countenance*] mere outward show.
    63. *piece*] i.e. of gold or silver—probably half a sovereign.
    64. *The . . . nose*] Cf. to be nosed (= duped), led by the nose; Brome's emphatic version was presumably a familiar expression.

Maid. Come, be not coy, but send away your servant,   65
 And let me gi' you a pint of wine.
Gentleman.   Pray keep
 Your courtesy; I can bestow the wine
 Upon myself if I were so disposed
 To drink in taverns. Fah!
Maid.   Let me bestow't
 Upon you at your lodging then; and there   70
 Be civilly merry.
Gentleman.   Which if you do,
 My wife shall thank you for it. But your better
 Course is to seek one fitter for your turn;
 You'll lose your aim in me, and I befriend you
 To tell you so.
Maid.   Gip gaffer shotten, fagh!   75
 Take that for your coy counsel. (*Kicks.*)
Gentleman.   Help! O, help!
Servingman. What mean you, gentlewoman?
Maid.   That to you, sir. (*Kicks.*)
Gentleman. O murder, murder!
Servingman.   Peace, good master,
 And come away. Some cowardly jade, I warrant,
 That durst not strike a woman.

Enter Constable *and* Watch.

Constable.   What's the matter?   80
Servingman. But and we were your match—
Watch.   What would you do?
 Come, come afore the constable. Now, if
 You were her match, what would you do, sir?
Maid.   Do?
 They have done too much already, sir. (*Weeps.*) A virgin
 Shall not pass shortly for these streetwalkers,   85
 If some judicious order be not taken.

80.] *Act* 4.*Scene* 3. *(before SD). Q.*

---

 73. *turn*] romp (in bed).
 75. *Gip ... fagh!*] Get lost, grandad! (Warwickshire dialect).
 80. *That ... woman*] i.e. but will hit a man: another antipodean inversion.
 81. *and*] if.
 85. *pass*] be able to come and go.
 streetwalkers] The inverted situation fully exploits the pun on 'prostitutes' and
'strutting gallants'.

Gentleman. Hear me the truth.
Constable.   Sir, speak to your companions.
   I have a wife and daughters, and am bound
   By hourly precepts to hear women first,
   Be't truth, or no truth. Therefore, virgin, speak,   90
   And fear no bugbears. I will do thee justice.
Maid. Sir, they assailed me, and with violent hands,
   When words could not prevail, they would have drawn me
   Aside unto their lust, till I cried murder.
Gentleman. 'Protest, sir, as I am a gentleman,   95
   And as my man's a man, she beat us both
   Till I cried murder.
Servingman.   That's the woeful truth on't.
Constable. You are a party, and no witness, sir;
   Besides y'are two, and one is easier
   To be believed. Moreover as you have the odds   100
   In number, what were justice if it should not support
   The weaker side? Away with them to the Counter.
Peregrine. Call you this justice?
Doctor.   In th' Antipodes.
Peregrine. Here's much to be reformed. Young man, thy virtue
   Hath won my favour; go, thou art at large.   105

           The Gentleman *hesitates.*

Doctor. [*Aside*] Be gone.
Gentleman. [*Aside*]   He puts me out; my part is now
   To bribe the constable.
Doctor. [*Aside*]   No matter; go.
           Exeunt Gentleman *and* Servingman.
Peregrine. [*To Constable*] And you, sir, take that sober-
                 seeming wanton
   And clap her up, till I hear better of her;
   I'll strip you of your office and your ears else.   110
Doctor. At first show mercy.
Peregrine.   They are an ignorant nation,
   And have my pity mingled with correction.
   And, therefore, damsel—for you are the first
   Offender I have noted here, and this

105.1.] *Haaker; not in* Q.   107.1. Servingman] Servant Q.

  91. *fear . . . bugbears*] don't be needlessly fearful.
  102. *Counter*] The name given to two debtors' prisons in London.
  110. *ears*] ear-cropping was a common punishment.

Your first offence, for aught I know—
Maid.   Yes, truly.   115
Doctor. [*Aside to Maid*] That was well said.
Peregrine.   Go and transgress no more;
      And as you find my mercy sweet, see that
      You be not cruel to your grandmother
      When she returns from bear-baiting.
Doctor. [*Aside*]   So, all be gone.
                        Exeunt all except PEREGRINE *and* DOCTOR.

      Enter Buff Woman, *her head and face bleeding, and many*
                  Women *as from a prize.*

Peregrine. And what are these?   120
Doctor. A woman fencer that has played a prize,
      It seems with loss of blood.
Peregrine.   It doth amaze me.
                        They pass over the stage, and exeunt.
      What can her husband be, when she's a fencer?
Doctor. He keeps a school, and teacheth needlework,
      Or some such arts which we call womanish.   125
Peregrine. 'Tis most miraculous and wonderful.
Man-Scold. (*Within*) Rogues, varlets, harlots, ha' you done
                                          your worst,
      Or would you drown me? Would you take my life?
Women. (*Within*) Duck him again; duck him again.
Peregrine.   What noise is this?
Doctor. Some man, it seems, that's ducked for scolding.   130
Peregrine. A man for scolding?
Doctor.   You shall see.

                  Enter Women *and* Man-scold.

1 *Woman.*   So, so;
      Enough, enough; he will be quiet now.
Man-Scold. How know you that, you devil-ridden witch you?
      How, quiet? why quiet? Has not the law passed on me,
      Over and over me, and must I be quiet?   135
2 *Woman.* Will you incur the law the second time?
Man-Scold. The law's the river, is't? Yes, 'tis a river,

119.1.] *Ex. Q (and no following scene-division).*   122.1.] *They passe over. Q.*
131. *Act.4.Scene 4. (before SD).*   1 *Woman] Wom. Q.*   136. 2 *Woman] 1 Wom. Q.*

---

   121. *prize*] a fencing bout—the *combat* of III.181.
   131, 136, 145.] *Q's* attribution of these lines is faulty: see collation.

Through which great men, and cunning, wade or swim;
But mean and ignorant must drown in't. No,
You hags and hellhounds, witches, bitches, all   140
That were the law, the judge, and executioners
To my vexation, I hope to see
More flames about your ears than all the water
You cast me in can quench.
3 *Woman.*   In with him again!
He calls us names.   .
Man-Scold.   No, no—I charge ye, no!   145
Was ever harmless creature so abused?
To be drenched under water, to learn dumbness
Amongst the fishes, as I were forbidden
To use the natural members I was born with,
And of them all the chief that man takes pleasure in,   150
The tongue! O me, accursed wretch! (*Weeps.*)
Peregrine.   Is this a man?
I ask not by his beard, but by his tears.
1 *Woman.* This shower will spend the fury of his tongue,
And so the tempest's over.
2 *Woman.*   I am sorry for't;
I would have had him ducked once more.   155
But somebody will shortly raise the storm
In him again, I hope, for us to make
More holiday-sport of him.
                          Exeunt Women *and* Man-scold.
Peregrine.   Sure these are dreams,
Nothing but dreams.
Doctor.   No, doubtless we are awake, sir.
Peregrine. Can men and women be so contrary   160
In all that we hold proper to each sex?
Doctor. [*Aside*] I'm glad he takes a taste of sense in that yet.
Peregrine. 'Twill ask long time and study to reduce
Their manners to our government.
Doctor.   These are
Low things and easy to be qualified.   165
But see, sir, here come courtiers; note their manners.

145. No...no!] *given to* 2 *Wom. in* Q.   158.SD] *Exit.* Q.   166.1.] *Act.4.Scene 5.*
Enter a Courtier. Q.

150–1. *And...tongue*] The same joke is found in Webster's *Duchess of Malfi*,
I.i.336–8: 'women like that part which.../Hath ne'er a bone in't...I mean the
tongue'; but here it is turned against the speaker, who has lost his manhood and
acquired instead the female vice of loquacity.
    165. *qualified*] regulated.

Enter a Courtier *examining his purse.*

1 *Courtier.* This was three shillings yesterday. How now!
  All gone but this? Sixpence for leather soles
  To my new green silk stockings, and a groat
  My ordinary in pompions baked with onions.   170
Peregrine. Do such eat pompions?
Doctor.   Yes, and clowns musk-melons.

Enter second Courtier *behind the first.*

1 *Courtier.* Threepence I lost at ninepins; but I got
  Six tokens towards that at pigeon-holes.
  'Snails, where's the rest? Is my poke bottom broke?
2 *Courtier.* What, Jack! A pox o'ertake thee not? How dost?   175
                          (*Kicks him.*)
1 *Courtier.* What with a vengeance ailst? Dost think my breech
  Is made of bell metal? Take that! (*Box o'th' ear*)
2 *Courtier.*   In earnest?
1 *Courtier.* Yes, till more comes. [*Grabs his hair.*]
2 *Courtier.* Pox rot your hold; let go my lock. D'ee think
  Y'are currying of your father's horse again?   180
1 *Courtier.* I'll teach you to abuse a man behind
  Was troubled too much afore. (*They buffet.*)

Enter third Courtier.

3 *Courtier.*   Hey, there boys, there.

p. 292 (5.4)

171.1.] *not in* Q. 175.1.] *kicke.* Q. 182.SD *Enter . . .* Courtier] *Act* 4.*Sc.*6.
*Ent.*3.*Court.* Q.

168–9. *soles . . . stockings*] soles for pumps which were worn with silk stockings by
fashion-conscious gallants.
  170. *My . . . pompions*] at my eating-house on pumpkins.
  171. *clowns*] poor country folk.
  musk-melons] a relatively recent import into England, and presumably expensive.
  173. *tokens*] small pieces of brass or copper issued by tradesmen.
  pigeon-holes] a game like bagatelle, with the arches for the balls resembling the
entrances to a dove-cote (Baker).
  174. *poke*] pocket.
  177–8. *In . . . comes*] The first courtier puns on *earnest* meaning foretaste or instal-
ment. His next move makes the joke a threat to pull out his hair.
  179. *lock*] of long hair.
  180. *currying*] grooming.
  182. *afore*] before you came along—but punning on 'in front'. Sodomy, like
women on top (I.iii.141), is an antipodean sexual act: cf. Richard Lovelace's poem
'Cupid Far Gone', where Cupid 'proffers *Jove* a back Caresse,/And all his Love in the
Antipodes' (*Poems*, ed. C. H. Wilkinson, 1925, I.242).

Good boys are good boys still. There, Will; there, Jack;
Not a blow!

       The second Courtier *knocks down the first.*

         Now he's down.
2 *Courtier.*   'Twere base; I scorn't.
1 *Courtier.* There's as proud fall, as stand in court or city.   185
3 *Courtier.* That's well said, Will. Troth, I commend you both.
   How fell you out? I hope in no great anger.
2 *Courtier.* For mine own part, I vow I was in jest.
1 *Courtier.* But I have told you twice and once, Will, jest not
   With me behind. I never could endure,   190
   Not of a boy, to put up things behind,
   And that my tutor knew—I had been a scholar else!
   Besides, you know my sword was nocked i'th' fashion,
   Just here behind, for my back-guard and all;
   And yet you would do't.   195
   I had as lief you would take a knife—
3 *Courtier.*   Come, come,
   Y'are friends. Shake hands. I'll give you half a dozen
   At the next ale house, to set all right and straight,
   And a new song, a dainty one; here 'tis.

         Shows them a printed ballad.

1 *Courtier.* O, thou art happy that canst read;   200
   I would buy ballads, too, had I thy learning.
3 *Courtier.* Come, we burn daylight, and the ale may sour.
                        Exeunt Courtiers.
Peregrine. Call you these courtiers? They are rude silken
                                clowns,
   As coarse within as watermen or carmen.
Doctor. Then look on these; here are of those conditions.   205

184.SD] *Baker; not in* Q. 199.1.] *a Ballad.* Q. 202.1.] *Ex.* Q. 205.1.] *Act
4.Scen.7. (before SD)* Q.

---

   189. *twice . . . once*] once and for all.
   191. *of*] since I was. The innuendo of what follows hints at general gossip about
Oxford and Cambridge tutors and abuse of their role *in loco parentis.*
   193. *nocked*] i.e. worn behind diagonally; Baker compares *The Court Begger,* III:
'Why dost thou weare a Sword? Only to hurt mens feet that kick thee?' (*Works* 1873,
III.230). Not in *OED* in this sense, but there is a sexual pun on 'notched', i.e. cleft
(like buttocks).
   202. *burn daylight*] are wasting time.
   204. *carmen*] carters.
   205. *of . . . conditions*] some members of those trades.

Enter Carman *and* Waterman.

Waterman. Sir, I am your servant.
Carman.   I am much obliged,
    Sir, by the plenteous favours your humanity
    And noble virtue have conferred upon me,
    To answer with my service your deservings.
Waterman. You speak what I should say. Be therefore pleased   210
    T'unload, and lay the weight of your commands
    Upon my care to serve you.
Carman.   Still your courtesies,
    Like waves of a spring tide, o'erflow the banks
    Of your abundant store; and from your channel
    Or stream of fair affections, you cast forth   215
    Those sweet refreshings on me that were else
    But sterile earth; which cause a gratitude
    To grow upon me, humble, yet ambitious
    In my devoir to do you best of service.
Waterman. I shall no more extend my utmost labour   220
    With oar and sail to gain the livelihood
    Of wife and children than to set ashore
    You and your faithful honourers at the haven
    Of your best wishes.
Carman.   Sir, I am no less
    Ambitious to be made the happy means,   225
    With whip and whistle, to draw up or drive
    All your detractors to the gallows.

Enter Sedanman.

Waterman.   See,

227.SD] *Act 4.Scene 8. (before SD).*

212–19. *Still . . . service*] parodying the obsequious courtly mode which writers felt
compelled to adopt in composing literary dedications. Brome's own Epistle for this
play is comparatively restrained and dignified.
    219. *devoir*] endeavour.
    226–7. *to . . . gallows*] The carters were responsible for transporting condemned
prisoners to the gallows at Tyburn.
    227–9. *See . . . virtues*] In reality, the providers of public transport in London were
in fierce competition. The sedan-chair was still a novelty: 'Mounsier *Sedan . . .* a
Greene-goose hatch'd but the other day; one that hath no leggs to stand upon, but is
faine to bee carried between two . . . a meere stranger, till of late in *England*'. A
waterman tells him that 'you conceale most of our delicate feminine fares, in your
boxes by land, that were woont to bee our best customers by water'; and Beere-Cart
grumbles: 'Sedan, you thinke your selfe so countenanced at the Court' (H. Peacham
(attrib.), *Coach and Sedan, pleasantly Disputing*, 1636, B2–F2).

Our noble friend.

Sedanman.   Right happily encountered;
I am the just admirer of your virtues.

Carman & Waterman. We are in all your servants.

Sedanman.   I was in quest 230
Of such elect society, to spend
A dinner time withal.

Carman & Waterman.   Sir, we are for you.

Sedanman. Three are the golden number in a tavern;
And at the next of best, with the best meat
And wine the house affords (if you so please)   235
We will be competently merry. I
Have received, lately, letters from beyond seas,
Importing much of the occurrences
And passages of foreign states. The knowledge
Of all I shall impart to you.

Waterman.   And I   240
Have all the new advertisements from both
Our universities of what has passed
The most remarkably of late.

Carman.   And from
The court I have the news at full, of all
That was observable this progress.   245

Peregrine. From court?

Doctor.   Yes, sir; they know not there they have
A new king here at home.

Sedanman.   'Tis excellent!
We want but now the news-collecting gallant
To fetch his dinner, and materials
For his this week's dispatches.

Waterman.   I dare think,   250
The meat and news being hot upon the table,
He'll smell his way to't.

Sedanman.   Please you to know yours, sir?

Carman. Sir, after you.

Sedanman.   Excuse me.

Waterman.   By no means, sir.

---

234. *next of best*] nearest and best tavern.

245. *progress*] royal journey. Progresses outside London were a prime means of stimulating public affection and respect for the monarch.

248–50. *the ... dispatches*] Taverns and ordinaries were prime centres of news gathering, and London residents composed newsletters which they sent to relatives and other correspondents in the country. Cf. Jonson, *Staple of News*, III.ii.182–3, and *Underwood* 47.27–8.

Carman. Sweet sir, lead on.
Sedanman.   It shall be as your servant
    Then, to prepare your dinner.   *Exit, leading the way.*
Waterman.   Pardon me.   255
Carman. In sooth, I'll follow you.
Waterman.   Yet 'tis my obedience.
                    Exit Waterman *followed by* Carman.
Peregrine. Are these but labouring men, and t'other courtiers?
Doctor. 'Tis common here, sir, for your watermen
    To write most learnedly, when your courtier
    Has scarce ability to read.
Peregrine.   Before I reign   260
    A month among them, they shall change their notes,
    Or I'll ordain a course to change their coats.
    I shall have much to do in reformation.
Doctor. Patience and counsel will go through it, sir.
Peregrine. What if I craved a counsel from New England?   265
    The old will spare me none.
Doctor. [*Aside*]   Is this man mad?
    My cure goes fairly on.—Do you marvel that
    Poor men outshine the courtiers? Look you, sir:

        These persons pass over the stage in couples, according as
                        he describes them.

    A sick man giving counsel to a physician;
    And there's a puritan tradesman teaching a   270
    Great traveller to lie; that ballad-woman

255.SD] Baker (subst.).   256.1.]   Ex. Q.   268.1–2.] next to 272–7 in Q.

258–9. *your . . . learnedly*] A hit at John Taylor the Water-Poet: see note on 'To Censuring Critics', 5.

259–60. *when . . . read*] Brome inherits a literary tradition of criticising high-born ignorance and philistinism, e.g. Jonson's epigrams 'To My Lord Ignorant' and 'To My Bookseller'. The latter surveys the potential audience for *Epigrams* and gets in a lethal stab after referring to the working man 'Who scarce can spell the hard names; whose knight less can' (HS VIII.28–9).

265–6. *What . . . none*] The British colonies from the start were administered by a Governor and Council, and New England had a relatively democratic polity which could be seen as being in sharp contrast to the regime of Charles I, who ruled without parliaments throughout the 1630s. But Brome's satire appears to be directed at pious reformation in Puritan America rather than at Charles' personal rule.

270–1. *there's . . . lie*] Travellers were said to 'lie by authority' because nobody could challenge their reports; but once again the irony is double-edged: John Earle's typical shopkeeper is a Puritan hypocrite who 'makes great use of honesty to professe upon. He tells you lyes by rote, and not minding, as the Phrase to sell in' (*Microcosmographie*, 1638, Character 70).

Gives light to the most learned antiquary
In all the kingdom.
Ballad-woman.   Buy new ballads, come.
Doctor. A natural fool, there, giving grave instructions
T'a lord ambassador; that's a schismatic,   275
Teaching a scrivener to keep his ears;
A parish clerk, there, gives the rudiments
Of military discipline to a general;
And there's a basket-maker confuting Bellarmine.
Peregrine. Will you make me mad?
Doctor.   We are sailed, I hope,   280
Beyond the line of madness. Now, sir, see
A statesman, studious for the commonwealth,
Solicited by projectors of the country.

Enter BYPLAY *like a stateman; and 3 or 4* Projectors *with
bundles of papers.*

Byplay. Your projects are all good; I like them well,
Especially these two: this for th'increase of wool,   285
And this for the destroying of mice. They're good,
And grounded on great reason.—As for yours,
For putting down the infinite use of jacks,
Whereby the education of young children
In turning spits is greatly hindered,   290

283.1–2.] *next to 279–84 in* Q (*preceded by Act 4.Sc.9.*).

274. *natural fool*] born idiot.
275–6. *schismatic . . . ears*] A Caroline audience would immediately think of the
lawyer William Prynne and *Histrio-mastix* (see note to I.iii.200). Because the book
seemed to cast aspersions on the queen acting in court dramas and compared
the Caroline court to Nero's theatre-loving one, he was convicted of sedition and
sentenced to have his ears cropped. The same penalty was meted out to dishonest
scriveners; presumably the schismatic mimes a secretive act of writing for his partner's
benefit.
279. *Bellarmine*] Cardinal Bellarmine (1542–1621), Catholic theologian who
became famous through his disputes with James I over the temporal authority of the
Pope. A number of his writings were reissued in 1638. The basket-maker obviously
represents working-class nonconformity.
282. *studious for*] attentive to the needs of.
283. *projectors*] entrepreneurs. There was a flood of new enterprises and development schemes in the early seventeenth century, many of which were perceived to
enhance the wealth of courtiers, often through monopolies. See Brome's satire in *The
Court Begger* (*Works* 1873, I.192), where the projectors gloat over 'the certainty
o'th'propounded profits' to be had from 'The Monopoly/Of making all the Perrukes
male and female,/Through Court and Kingdome'.
288–90. *jacks . . . spits*] 'Jack . . . was frequently bestowed upon . . . a . . . servant.
Thus, roasting jacks were so named from performing the office of a man, who acted as
turnspit, before that office devolved upon dogs' (Nares, *Glossary*, 1888, I.444).

It may be looked into.—And yours against
The multiplicity of pocket watches,
Whereby much neighbourly familiarity,
By asking, 'What d'ye guess it is o'clock?'
Is lost when every puny clerk can carry   295
The time o'th' day in's breeches: this and these
Hereafter may be looked into. For present,
This for the increase of wool—that is to say,
By flaying of live horses and new covering them
With sheepskins—I do like exceedingly.   300
And this for keeping of tame owls in cities
To kill up rats and mice, whereby all cats
May be destroyed, as an especial means
To prevent witchcraft and contagion.
Peregrine. Here's a wise business!
1 *Projector.*   Will your honour now   305
Be pleased to take into consideration
The poor men's suits for briefs to get relief
By common charity throughout the kingdom,
Towards recovery of their lost estates?
Byplay. What are they? Let me hear.   310
2 *Projector.* First, here's a gamester, that sold house and land
To the known value of five thousand pounds,
And by misfortune of the dice lost all,
To his extreme undoing, having neither
A wife or child to succour him.
Byplay.   A bachelor?   315
2 *Projector.* Yes, my good lord.
Byplay.   And young and healthful?
2 *Projector.*   Yes.
Byplay. Alas, 'tis lamentable; he deserves much pity.
Peregrine. How's this?
Doctor.   Observe him further, pray sir.
3 *Projector.* Then, here's a bawd, of sixty-odd years standing.
Byplay. How old was she when she set up?
3 *Projector.*   But four   320
And twenty, my good lord. She was both ware
And merchant, flesh and butcher (as they say)
For the first twelve years of her housekeeping.
She's now upon fourscore, and has made markets

305.SP 1 *Projector*] *Pro. Q.*

305.SP. *1* Projector] *Q* does not differentiate the speakers of the projectors' lines.

Of twice four thousand choice virginities,   325
And twice their number of indifferent gear.
(No riff-raff was she ever known to cope for.)
Her life is certified here by the justices
Adjacent to her dwelling—
Byplay.   She is decayed?
3 *Projector.* Quite trade-fallen, my good lord, now in
                                                 her dotage, 330
And desperately undone by riot.
Byplay.   'Las, good woman.
3 *Projector.* She has consumed in prodigal feasts and fiddlers,
And lavish lendings to debauched comrades
That sucked her purse, in jewels, plate, and money
To the full value of six thousand pounds.   335
Byplay. She shall have a collection, and deserves it.
Peregrine. 'Tis monstrous, this.
1 *Projector.*   Then here are divers more,
Of panders, cheaters, house and highway robbers,
That have got great estates in youth and strength,
And wasted all as fast in wine and harlots   340
Till age o'ertook 'em, and disabled them
For getting more.
Byplay.   For such the law provides
Relief within those counties where they practised.
Peregrine. Ha! What, for thieves?
Doctor.   Yes, their law punisheth
The robbed, and not the thief, for surer warning   345
And the more safe prevention. I have seen
Folks whipped for losing of their goods and money,
And the pickpockets cherished.
Byplay.   The weal public,
As it severely punisheth their neglect
(Undone by fire-ruins, shipwreck, and the like)   350
With whips, with brands, and loss of careless ears,
Imprisonment, banishment, and sometimes death;
And carefully maintaineth houses of correction

---

326. *indifferent gear*] the ordinary sort.
328. *Her. . . . certified*] her good character is attested. But Brome points the irony of
the inversion by his use of *certified*, referring to the monthly certificate of vagrants and
miscreants required to be drawn up by constables in each parish and submitted to JPs.
In Caroline London the old bawd's activities would have come under the jurisdiction
of petty sessions.
329. *decayed*] fallen on hard times.

For decayed scholars and maimed soldiers;
So doth it find relief and almshouses   355
For such as lived by rapine and by cozenage.
Peregrine. Still worse and worse! Abominable, horrid!
4 Projector. Yet here is one, my lord, 'bove all the rest,
   Whose services have generally been known,
   Though now he be a spectacle of pity.
Byplay.   Who's that?   360
4 Projector. The captain of the cutpurses, my lord,
   That was the best at's art that ever was,
   Is fallen to great decay by the dead palsy
   In both his hands, and craves a large collection.
Byplay. I'll get it him.
Peregrine.   You shall not get it him!   365
   Do you provide whips, brands, and ordain death
   For men that suffer under fire or shipwreck
   The loss of all their honest gotten wealth,
   And find relief for cheaters, bawds, and thieves?
   I'll hang ye all.
Byplay.   Mercy, great King.
Omnes.   O mercy!   370
Byplay. Let not our ignorance suffer in your wrath
   Before we understand your highness' laws.
   We went by custom, and the warrant which
   We had in your late predecessor's reign.
   But let us know your pleasure, you shall find   375
   The State and commonwealth in all obedient
   To alter custom, law, religion, all,
   To be conformable to your commands.
Peregrine. 'Tis a fair protestation, and my mercy
   Meets your submission. See you merit it   380
   In your conformity.
Byplay.   Great sir, we shall.

   LETOY, DIANA *and* JOYLESS *appear above.*

In sign whereof we lacerate these papers,
And lay our necks beneath your kingly feet.

---

354. *decayed ... soldiers*] Two groups notoriously neglected and unemployable in England at this time.

373–4.] A clear allusion to the reign of James I, when the court was a place of licence and excess and was perceived to set a bad example to the country.

381.1. above] i.e. in the gallery—the 'window' of III.531.

382–3.] Diana's reaction (385) indicates that Byplay seizes this opportunity for extravagant clowning.

BYPLAY *tears the documents and prostrates himself, and the*
Projectors *follow suit.*

Peregrine. Stand up; you have our favour.

                             Exeunt Projectors.

Diana.   And mine, too!

  Never was such an actor as Extempore!   385

Joyless. You were best to fly out of the window to him.

Diana. Methinks I am even light enough to do it.

Joyless. I could find in my heart to quoit thee at him.

Diana. So he would catch me in his arms, I cared not.

Letoy. Peace, both of you, or you'll spoil all.

Byplay. [*To Peregrine*]   Your grace   390

  Abounds—abounds—your grace—I say, abounds—

Letoy. Pox o' your mumbling chops. Is your brain dry?

  Do you pump?

Diana.   He has done much, my lord, and may

  Hold out a little.

Letoy.   Would you could hold your peace

  So long.

Diana.   Do you sneap me, too, my lord?

Joyless.   Ha, ha, ha!   395

Letoy. Blockhead!

Joyless.   I hope his hotter zeal to's actors

  Will drive out my wife's love heat.

Diana.   I

  Had no need to come hither to be sneaped.

Letoy. Hoyday! The rest will all be lost. We now

  Give over the play, and do all by extempore   400

  For your son's good, to soothe him into's wits.

  If you'll mar all, you may. [*Aside to Byplay*] Come nearer,

                                 cockscomb;

  Ha' you forgotten, puppy, my instructions

  Touching his subjects and his marriage?

Byplay. [*Aside*] I have all now, my lord.

Flourish.

Peregrine.   What voice was that?   405

383.1–2.] *not in* Q.   384.SD] *not in* Q.   405.SD] *not in* Q.

---

387. *light*] with a pun on 'wanton'.
388. *quoit*] throw.
393. *Do . . . pump?*] Have you exhausted yourself?
395. *sneap*] chide.

Byplay. A voice out of the clouds, that doth applaud
    Your highness' welcome to your subjects' loves.
Letoy. So, now he's in. [*To Joyless and Diana*] Sit still, I must
                                                    go down
    And set out things in order.   *Exit.*
Byplay. A voice that doth inform me of the tidings   410
    Spread through your kingdom of your great arrival,
    And of the general joy your people bring
    To celebrate the welcome of their king. (*Shouts within*)
    Hark how the country shouts with joyful votes,
    Rending the air with music of their throats.   415

Drum & Trumpets.

    Hark how the soldier with his martial noise
    Threatens your foes, to fill your crown with joys.

Hautboys.

    Hark how the city with loud harmony
    Chants a free welcome to your majesty.

Soft music.

    Hark how the court prepares your grace to meet   420
    With solemn music, state, and beauty sweet.

> *The soft music playing, enter by two and two divers*
> *courtiers;* MARTHA *after them like a queen, between*
> *two boys in robes, her train borne up by* BARBARA.
> *All the lords kneel and kiss* PEREGRINE'S *hand.*
> MARTHA *approaching, he starts back, but is drawn on*
> *by* BYPLAY *and the* DOCTOR. LETOY *enters and mingles*
> *with the rest, and seems to instruct them all.*

Diana. O, here's a stately show! Look, Master Joyless:
    Your daughter-in-law presented like a queen
    Unto your son; I warrant now he'll love her.
Joyless. A queen?
Diana.   Yes, yes, and Mistress Blaze is made   425
    The mother of her maids—if she have any;
    Perhaps the Antipodean court has none!

421.] *Act.4.Sce.10 Q (right-hand margin).*

408. *in*] i.e. back on track.
414. *votes*] voices of support.
426. *mother . . . maids*] i.e. chief bridesmaid.

See, see, with what a majesty he receives 'em.

SONG

> Health, wealth, and joy our wishes bring,
> All in a welcome to our king.
>   May no delight be found,
>   Wherewith he be not crowned.
>   Apollo with the Muses,
>   Who arts divine infuses,
> With their choice garlands deck his head;
> Love and the graces make his bed.
> And to crown all, let Hymen to his side
> Plant a delicious, chaste, and fruitful bride.

Byplay. Now, sir, be happy in a marriage choice
  That shall secure your title of a king.
  See, sir, your state presents to you the daughter,
  The only child and heir apparent of
  Our late deposed and deceased sovereign,
  Who with his dying breath bequeathed her to you.
Peregrine. A crown secures not an unlawful marriage.
  I have a wife already.
Doctor.   No, you had, sir;
  But she's deceased.
Peregrine.   How know you that?
Doctor. By sure advertisement; and that her fleeting spirit
  Is flown into and animates this princess.
Peregrine. Indeed, she's wondrous like her.
Doctor.   Be not slack
  T'embrace and kiss her, sir.

He kisses her and retires.

Martha.   He kisses sweetly;
  And that is more than e'er my husband did.
  But more belongs than kissing to child-getting;
  And he's so like my husband, if you note him,
  That I shall but lose time and wishes by him.
  No, no, I'll none of him.
Barbara. I'll warrant you he shall fulfil your wishes.
Martha. O, but try him you first, and then tell me.
Barbara. There's a new way, indeed, to choose a husband!
  Yet 'twere a good one to bar fool-getting.

430

435

440

445

450

455

460

---

437. *Hymen*] god of marriage.

Doctor. Why do you stand aloof, sir?
Peregrine.   Mandeville writes
    Of people near the Antipodes called Gadlibriens,
    Where on the wedding night the husband hires
    Another man to couple with his bride,
    To clear the dangerous passage of a maidenhead.   465
Doctor. 'Slid, he falls back again to Mandeville madness.
Peregrine. She may be of that serpentine generation
    That stings oft-times to death (as Mandeville writes).
Doctor. She's no Gadlibrien, sir, upon my knowledge.
    You may as safely lodge with her as with   470
    A maid of our own nation. Besides,
    You shall have ample counsel. For the present
    Receive her, and entreat her to your chapel.
Byplay. For safety of your kingdom, you must do it.

            Hautboys. Exeunt in state as LETOY *directs.*
            LETOY *remains on-stage, gesticulating.*

Letoy. So, so, so, so; this yet may prove a cure.   475
Diana. [*Above*] See, my lord now is acting by himself.
Letoy. And Letoy's wit cried up triumphant, ho!
    Come, Master Joyless and your wife, come down
    Quickly; your parts are next. I had almost
    Forgot to send my chaplain after them.   480
    You, Domine, where are you?
                    Exeunt above JOYLESS *and* DIANA.

            Enter QUAILPIPE *in a fantastical shape.*

Quailpipe.   Here, my lord.
Letoy. What, in that shape?
Quailpipe.   'Tis for my part, my lord,
    Which is not all performed.
Letoy. It is, sir, and the play for this time. We
    Have other work in hand.
Quailpipe.   Then have you lost   485

474.2] *this ed.; Manet Letoy. Q.*   479.] *Act.4.Sce.11 Q (right-hand margin).*
481.SD] *not in Q.*

461–8. *Mandeville . . . writes*] Mandeville explains: 'I asked what was the cause
why they had that custome, and they said, heretofore men lay with their wives first &
no other, and their wives had serpents in their bodies, and stung their husbands in the
yard [penis], or on their bodies, and so were many men slaine' (S3).
    481–3. fantastical . . . *performed*] Having been unfairly rebuked at the start (II.i.56)
for not being ready, poor Quailpipe is now deprived of his last and (in his eyes) best
turn.

Action—I dare be bold to speak it!—that
Most of my coat could hardly imitate.
Letoy. Go, shift your coat, sir, or for expedition
Cover it with your own, due to your function.
Follies, as well as vices, may be hid so;   490
Your virtue is the same. Dispatch, and do
As Doctor Hughball shall direct you. Go.   *Exit* QUAILPIPE.

Enter JOYLESS *and* DIANA.

Letoy. Now, Master Joyless, do you note the progress
And the fair issue likely to ensue
In your son's cure? Observe the doctor's art.   495
First, he has shifted your son's known disease
Of madness into folly, and has wrought him
As far short of a competent reason as
He was of late beyond it. As a man
Infected by some foul disease is drawn   500
By physic into an anatomy,
Before flesh fit for health can grow to rear him,
So is a madman made a fool, before
Art can take hold of him to wind him up
Into his proper centre, or the medium   505
From which he flew beyond himself. The doctor
Assures me now, by what he has collected
As well from learned authors as his practice,
That his much troubled and confusèd brain
Will by the real knowledge of a woman   510
Now opportunely ta'en, be by degrees
Settled and rectified, with the helps beside
Of rest and diet, which he'll administer.

492.] *Act.4.Sce.12. Exit.Qua. Q.*

487. *coat*] profession.
488. *for expedition*] to save time.
489. *your . . . function*] i.e. your servant's livery—the *bravery* Letoy refers to at
I.ii.62.
500–1. *drawn . . . anatomy*] turned into a skeleton by treatment.
508. *learned authors*] Burton cites numerous authorities on the consequences
of sexual abstinence, which '*sends up poysoned vapours to the Braine and Heart*'
(I.2.ii.4); though he also warns against the dangers of over-indulgence. But the belief
in the specific therapeutic value of 'real knowledge of a woman' belongs more to folk-
lore, of the kind invoked by Mosca when he claims that to save Volpone 'some young
woman must be straight sought out,/Lusty, and full of juice, to sleep by him' (Jonson,
Volpone, II.vi.34–5). Cf. the related idea of the virgin Helena's curing of the King in
All's Well.

Diana. But 'tis the real knowledge of the woman
  (Carnal, I think you mean) that carries it.   515
Letoy. Right, right.
Diana.   Nay, right or wrong, I could even wish
  If he were not my husband's son, the doctor
  Had made myself his recipe, to be the means
  Of such a cure.
Joyless.   How, how?
Diana. Perhaps that course might cure your madness too   520
  Of jealousy, and set all right on all sides.
  Sure, if I could but make him such a fool
  He would forgo his madness, and be brought
  To Christian sense again.
Joyless.   Heaven grant me patience,
  And send us to my country home again!   525
Diana. Besides, the young man's wife's as mad as he.
  What wise work will they make!
Letoy.   The better, fear't not:
  Bab Blaze shall give her counsel, and the youth
  Will give her royal satisfaction,
  Now, in this kingly humour.—[*Aside to Diana*] I have a
              way   530
  To cure your husband's jealousy myself.
Diana. [*Aside*] Then I am friends again; even now I was not
  When you sneaped me, my lord.
Letoy. [*Aside to Diana*]   That you must pardon.—
  Come, Master Joyless. The new-married pair
  Are towards bed by this time; we'll not trouble them,   535
  But keep a house-side to ourselves. Your lodging
  Is decently appointed.
Joyless.   Sure your lordship
  Means not to make your house our prison?
Letoy.   By
  My lordship, but I will for this one night.
  See, sir, the keys are in my hand. Y'are up,   540
  As I am true Letoy. Consider, sir,
  The strict necessity that ties you to't,
  As you expect a cure upon your son.

---

 522. *make . . . fool*] i.e. by cuckolding him. Diana speaks this aside to Letoy but
makes sure Joyless hears it.
 535. *we'll . . . them*] a departure from the custom of accompanying newly-weds to
the door of their bedchamber (see V.i.71–2).
 540. *Y'are up*] You're trapped.

    Come, lady, see your chamber.
Diana.   I do wait
    Upon your lordship.
Joyless.   I both wait, and watch;   545
    Never was man so mastered by his match. *Exeunt omnes.*

---

546. *match*] wife.

ACT V

SCENE i

Enter JOYLESS *with a light in his hand.*

Joyless. Diana! Ho! Where are you? She is lost.
  [*Tries the doors.*] Here is no further passage. All's made
                                                            fast.
  This was the bawdy way by which she 'scaped
  My narrow watching. Have you privy posterns
  Behind the hangings in your strangers' chambers?   5
  She's lost from me forever. Why then seek I?
  O my dull eyes, to let her slip so from ye,
  To let her have her lustful will upon me!
  Is this the hospitality of lords?
  Why, rather, if he did intend my shame   10
  And her dishonour, did he not betray me
  From her out of his house, to travail in
  The bare suspicion of their filthiness,
  But hold me a nose witness to its rankness?
  No! This is sure the lordlier way, and makes   15
  The act more glorious in my sufferings. [*Kneels.*] O!
  May my hot curses on their melting pleasures
  Cement them so together in their lust
  That they may never part, but grow one monster.

Enter BARBARA.

Barbara. [*Aside*] Good gentleman! He is at his prayers now,   20
  For his mad son's good night-work with his bride.—
  Well fare your heart, sir; you have prayed to purpose,
  But not all night, I hope.—Yet sure he has;
  He looks so wild for lack of sleep.—Y'are happy, sir.
  Your prayers are heard, no doubt, for I'm persuaded   25

19.1.] *Act 5.Scene 2. Q (before SD).*

4. *privy posterns*] secret entrances.
11. *betray*] divert.
12. *travail*] labour.
14. *But*] rather than.

You have a child got you tonight.

Joyless.   Is't gone

So far, do you think?

Barbara.   I cannot say how far.

Not fathom deep, I think; but to the scantling

Of a child-getting, I dare well imagine.

For which, as you have prayed, forget not, sir,   30

To thank the lord o'th' house.

Joyless.   For getting me

A child? Why, I am none of his great lordship's tenants,

Nor of his followers, to keep his bastards.

Barbara turns to leave.

Pray stay a little.

Barbara.   I should go tell my lord

The news. He longs to know how things do pass.   35

Joyless. Tell him I take it well, and thank him.

I did before despair of children, I.

But I'll go wi' ye, and thank him.

Barbara. [*Aside*]   Sure his joy

Has madded him; here's more work for the doctor!

Joyless. [*Drawing a knife*] But tell me first: were you their

                                    bawd that speak this?   40

Barbara. What mean you with that dagger?

Joyless.   Nothing; I

But play with't. Did you see the passages

Of things? I ask, were you their bawd?

Barbara.   Their bawd?

I trust she is no bawd that sees, and helps

If need require, an ignorant lawful pair   45

To do their best.

Joyless.   Lords' actions all are lawful!

And how? And how?

Barbara. [*Aside*]   These old folks love to hear.—

I'll tell you, sir—and yet I will not neither.

Joyless. Nay, pray thee out with't.

Barbara.   Sir, they went to bed.

Joyless. To bed! Well, on.

Barbara.   On? They were off sir, yet;   50

33.1.] *not in* Q.

28–9. *to . . . Of*] close enough for. In archery a *scantling* is the distance from the
mark within which a shot counts as a hit (*OED*).

And yet a good while after. They were both
So simple that they knew not what nor how,
For she's, sir, a pure maid.
Joyless.   Who dost thou speak of?
Barbara. I'll speak no more, 'less you can look more tamely.
Joyless. Go, bring me to 'em then. Bawd, will you go?   55

He threatens her with his dagger.

Barbara. Ah—

Enter BYPLAY *and holds* JOYLESS.

Byplay. What ail you, sir? Why bawd? Whose bawd is she?
Joyless. Your lord's bawd, and my wife's.
                                    You are jealous mad.
Byplay. Suppose your wife be missing at your chamber,
And lord, too, at his; they may be honest.   60
If not, what's that to her, or you, I pray,
Here in my lord's own house?
Joyless.   Brave, brave, and monstrous!
Byplay. She has not seen them. I heard all your talk.
The child she intimated is your grandchild
In posse, sir, and of your son's begetting.   65
Barbara. Ay, I'll be sworn I meant and said so, too!
Joyless. Where is my wife?
Byplay.   I can give no account.
If she be with my lord I dare not trouble 'em,
Nor must you offer at it. No, nor stab yourself—

BYPLAY *takes away his dagger.*

But come with me. I'll counsel, or at least   70
Govern you better. She may be, perhaps,
About the bride-chamber to hear some sport,
For you can make her none, 'las, good old man—
Joyless. I'm most insufferably abused.
Byplay.   —Unless
The killing of yourself may do't, and that   75
I would forbear, because perhaps 'twould please her.
Joyless. If fire or water, poison, cord or steel

55.1.] *Baker; not in* Q.   56.1.] *Act 5.Scene 3.* Q *(before SD).*

62. *Brave*] impudent.
65. In posse] potentially, in the making.
69. *offer at*] try.

Or any means be found to do it, I'll do it;
Not to please her, but rid me of my torment.
Byplay. I have more care and charge of you than so.   80
                              Exeunt JOYLESS *and* BYPLAY.
Barbara. What an old desperate man is this, to make
Away yourself for fear of being a cuckold!
If every man that is, or that but knows
Himself to be o'th'order, should do so,
How many desolate widows would here be;   85
They are not all of that mind. Here's my husband.

         Enter BLAZE *with a habit in his hand.*

Blaze. Bab! Art thou here?
                        Look well. How thinkst thou,
Barbara.   Tony?
Hast not thou neither slept tonight?
Blaze.   Yes, yes.
I lay with the butler. Who was thy bedfellow?
Barbara. You know I was appointed to sit up.   90
Blaze. Yes, with the doctor in the bride-chamber.
But had you two no waggery? Ha!
Barbara.   Why,
How now, Tony?
Blaze.   Nay, facks, I am not jealous.
Thou know'st I was cured long since, and how.
I jealous! I an ass. A man shan't ask   95
His wife shortly how such a gentleman does,
Or how such a gentleman did, or which did best,
But she must think him jealous.
Barbara.   You need not; for
If I were now to die on't, nor the doctor
Nor I came in a bed tonight. I mean   100
Within a bed.
Blaze.   Within, or without, or over, or under,
I have no time to think o' such poor things.
Barbara. What's that thou carriest, Tony?
Blaze.   O ho, Bab.

86.1.] *Act 5.Scene 4. (before SD) Q.*

85. *here*] in the theatre audience.
92. *But...waggery?*] remembering Hughball's zeal for 'undertaking' women
(I.i.166, see note).
93. *facks*] 'faith.

This is a shape.
Barbara.   A shape? What shape, I prithee, Tony?
Blaze. Thou'lt see me in't anon, but shalt not know me   105
From the stark'st fool i'th' town. And I must dance
Naked in't, Bab.
Barbara.   Will here be dancing, Tony?
Blaze. Yes, Bab. My lord gave order for't last night.
It should ha' been i'th' play; but because that
Was broke off, he will ha't today.
Barbara.   O Tony,   110
I did not see thee act i'th' play.
Blaze.   O, but
I did though, Bab, two mutes.
Barbara.   What, in those breeches?
Blaze. Fie, fool; thou understandst not what a mute is.
A mute is a dumb speaker in the play.
Barbara. Dumb speaker! That's a bull. Thou wert the bull   115
Then, in the play? Would I had seen thee roar.
Blaze. That's a bull, too, as wise as you are, Bab.
A mute is one that acteth speakingly,
And yet says nothing. I did two of them,
The sage man-midwife, and the basket-maker.   120
Barbara. Well, Tony, I will see thee in this thing,
And 'tis a pretty thing.
Blaze.   Prithee, good Bab,
Come in and help me on with't in our tiring-house,
And help the gentlemen, my fellow dancers,
And thou shalt then see all our things, and all   125
Our properties, and practice to the music.
Barbara. O, Tony, come; I long to be at that.   *Exeunt.*

---

104. *shape*] costume. It is described in detail at V.ii.331–3.
107. *Naked*] without inhibition.
112. *mutes . . . breeches*] Barbara takes 'mute' in its obsolete sense of 'excreta'.
115. *bull*] contradiction in terms. Barbara next takes the word in its sense of 'theatrical blunder'.
118. *speakingly*] expressively.
120. *man-midwife*] Blaze remembers the phrase from I.i.177, where Barbara used it in conjunction with traveller's tales. The mimed episodes at IV.269–79 probably involved some doubling by pairs of actors, and as well as playing the basket-maker Blaze might have portrayed the tradesman (270) who gets the traveller to produce his strange reports.
126. *practice to*] rehearsal of.

ACT V   SCENE ii

Enter LETOY *and* DIANA.

A table set forth, covered with treasure.

Diana. My lord, your strength and violence prevail not.
    There is a providence above my virtue
    That guards me from the fury of your lust.
Letoy. Yet, yet, I prithee yield. Is it my person
    That thou despisest? See, here's wealthy treasure,   5
    Jewels that Cleopatra would have left
    Her Marcus for.
Diana.   My lord, 'tis possible
    That she who leaves a husband may be bought
    Out of a second friendship.
Letoy.   Had stout Tarquin
    Made such an offer, he had done no rape,   10
    For Lucrece had consented, saved her own,
    And all those lives that followed in her cause.
Diana. Yet then she had been a loser.
Letoy.   Wouldst have gold?
    Mammon nor Pluto's self should overbid me,
    For I'd give all. First, let me rain a shower   15
    To outvie that which overwhelmed Danaë;
    And after that another. A full river
    Shall from my chests perpetually flow
    Into thy store.
Diana.   I have not much loved wealth,
    But have not loathed the sight of it till now   20

0.2.] *next to* 5–7 *in Q.*

0.2.] Q has the SD next to 5–7, but its wording suggests that the table is on stage from the beginning of the scene. If Letoy 'discovers' the treasure at 5 he probably removes a cloth or carpet covering it.

5. *See . . . treasure*] The ensuing episode is modelled on the attempted seduction of Celia in Jonson's *Volpone*, III.vii.

9. *friendship*] relationship.

9–12. *Had . . . cause*] The rape of Lucrece by Sextus Tarquinius is one of the founding myths of the Roman Republic: see Shakespeare's *Lucrece*, Argument.

15–16. *let . . . Danaë*] The myth of Zeus visiting Danaë in a shower of gold and fathering the hero Perseus is alluded to several times in Ovid. George Sandys drew the moral: 'In a golden showre, which is, with gifts, he corrupted *Danae*' (Sandys, *Ovid*, p. 220); and Thomas Wilson thought that by the story 'is none other thynge elles signified, but that women have bene, and wyll be overcome with money' (*Arte of rhetoricke*, 1585, p. 199).

That you have soiled it, with that foul opinion
Of being the price of virtue. Though the metal
Be pure and innocent in itself, such use
Of it is odious, indeed damnable,
Both to the seller and the purchaser.   25
Pity it should be so abused. It bears
A stamp upon't, which but to clip is treason.
'Tis ill used there, where law the life controls;
Worse, where 'tis made a salary for souls.

Letoy. Deny'st thou wealth? Wilt thou have pleasure then   30
Given, and ta'en freely, without all condition?
I'll give thee such as shall, if not exceed,
Be at the least comparative with those
Which Jupiter got the demigods with; and
Juno was mad she missed.

Diana.   My lord, you may   35
Gloss o'er and gild the vice, which you call pleasure,
With god-like attributes, when it is at best
A sensuality so far below
Dishonourable that it is mere beastly,
Which reason ought to abhor; and I detest it   40
More than your former hated offers.

Letoy.   Lastly,
Wilt thou have honour? I'll come closer to thee,
For now the flames of love grow higher in me,
And I must perish in them, or enjoy thee.
Suppose I find by power, or law, or both,   45
A means to make thee mine, by freeing
Thee from thy present husband.

Diana.   Hold, stay there.
Now, should you utter volumes of persuasions,
Lay the whole world of riches, pleasures, honours
Before me in full grant, that one last word   50
'Husband', and from your own mouth spoke, confutes
And vilifies even all. The very name
Of husband, rightly weighed and well remembered,

---

48. you] *Baker;* I *Q.*

27. *clip*] (1) to deface current coin by paring its edges (2) embrace.
29. *salary*] payment.
33–4. *those ... with*] Zeus' amorous exploits on earth produced many semi-divine characters in Greek mythology.
52. *vilifies*] discredits.

Without more law or discipline, is enough
To govern womankind in due obedience,   55
Master all loose affections, and remove
Those idols which too much, too many love,
And you have set before me to beguile
Me of the faith I owe him. But remember
You grant I have a husband; urge no more;   60
I seek his love. 'Tis fit he loves no whore.
Letoy. [*Aside*] This is not yet the way.— You have seen, lady,
My ardent love, which you do seem to slight,
Though to my death, pretending zeal to your husband.
My person nor my proffers are so despicable   65
But that they might, had I not vowed affection
Entirely to yourself, have met with th'embraces
Of greater persons, no less fair; that can
Too (if they please) put on formality
And talk in as divine a strain as you.   70
This is not earnest! Make my word but good
Now with a smile, I'll give thee a thousand pound.
Look o' my face. Come! Prithee, look and laugh not.
Yes, laugh, and dar'st. Dimple this cheek a little;
I'll nip it else.
Diana.   I pray forbear, my lord.   75
I'm past a child, and will be made no wanton.
Letoy. How can this be? So young, so vigorous,
And so devoted to an old man's bed!
Diana. That is already answered. He's my husband.
You are old too, my lord.
Letoy.   Yes, but of better mettle.   80
A jealous old man, too, whose disposition
Of injury to beauty and young blood
Cannot but kindle fire of just revenge
In you, if you be woman, to requite
With your own pleasure his unnatural spite.   85
You cannot be worse to him than he thinks you,
Considering all the open scorns and jeers
You cast upon him, to a flat defiance.
Then the affronts I gave to choke his anger;
And lastly your stol'n absence from his chamber.   90

---

64. *zeal*] devotion.
65. *My*] i.e. neither my.
71. *This . . . earnest!*] You can't mean this!
81. *disposition*] tendency.

All which confirms—we have as good as told him—
That he's a cuckold. Yet you trifle time
As 'twere not worth the doing.
Diana.   Are you a lord?
Dare you boast honour, and be so ignoble?
Did not you warrant me upon that pawn   95
Which can take up no money, your blank honour,
That you would cure his jealousy, which affects him
Like a sharp sore, if I to ripen it
Would set that counterfeit face of scorn upon him
Only in show of disobedience?—which   100
You won me to upon your protestation
To render me unstained to his opinion,
And quit me of his jealousy forever.
Letoy. No, not unstained, by your leave, if you call
Unchastity a stain. But for his yellows,   105
Let me but lie with you, and let him know it,
His jealousy is gone, all doubts are cleared,
And for his love and good opinion
He shall not dare deny't. Come, be wise,
And this is all; all is as good as done   110
To him already. Let't be so with us;
And trust to me, my power, and your own
To make all good with him. If not—now mark,
To be revenged for my lost hopes (which yet
I pray thee save), I'll put thee in his hands,   115
Now in his heat of fury, and not spare
To boast thou art my prostitute, and thrust ye
Out of my gates, to try't out by yourselves.
Diana. This you may do, and yet be still a lord;
This can I bear, and still be the same woman!   120
I am not troubled now. Your wooing oratory,
Your violent hands (made stronger by your lust),
Your tempting gifts, and larger promises
Of honour and advancements were all frivolous;
But this last way of threats, ridiculous   125
To a safe mind that bears no guilty grudge.

---

96. *blank*] very—with a suggestion of 'spotless'.
101–2. *protestation/To render*] promise to restore.
105. *yellows*] jealousy.
118. *try't out*] settle it.
126. *grudge*] misgiving, insecurity.

My peace dwells here, while yonder sits my judge,
And in that faith I'll die.

Enter JOYLESS *and* BYPLAY.

Letoy. [*Aside*] She is invincible!
Come, I'll relate you to your husband.
Joyless. No,
I'll meet her with more joy than I received 130
Upon our marriage day. My better soul,
Let me again embrace thee.
Byplay. Take your dudgeon, sir,
I ha' done you simple service.
Joyless. O, my lord,
My lord, you have cured my jealousy, I thank you;
And more, your man for the discovery; 135
But most the constant means, my virtuous wife,
Your medicine, my sweet lord.
Letoy. She has ta'en all
I mean to give her, sir. [*To Byplay*] Now, sirrah, speak.
Byplay. I brought you to the stand from whence you saw
How the game went.
Joyless. O my dear, dear Diana. 140
Byplay. I seemed to do it against my will, by which I gained
Your bribe of twenty pieces.
Joyless. Much good do thee.
Byplay. But I assure you, my lord give me order
To place you there after it seems he had
Well put her to't within.
Joyless. Stay, stay, stay, stay! 145
Why may not this be then a counterfeit action,
Or a false mist to blind me with more error?
The ill I feared may have been done before,
And all this but deceit to daub it o'er.
Diana. Do you fall back again?

---

128. *Act.5.Sce. (before SD) Q.* 143. give] *Q; gave Baker.*

132. *dudgeon*] dagger with wooden handle.
139. *stand*] vantage point. The audience's response to Letoy's temptation of Diana
will obviously be affected if it has observed Joyless' concealment; and a director who
decides to control the emotional temperature of the scene in this way will have to
decide at what point he begins to eavesdrop.
142. *do thee*] may it do thee.
143–5. *But ... within*] Is this provocative remark part of Letoy's planned testing of
Joyless, or a mischievous improvisation?

Joyless. [*Fumbles in pocket.*] Shugh, give me leave—   150
Byplay. I must take charge, I see, o'th' dagger again.

                    He takes the dagger from him.

Letoy. Come, Joyless, I have pity on thee; hear me.
    I swear upon mine honour she is chaste.
Joyless. Honour! An oath of glass!
Letoy.   I prithee, hear me.
    I tried and tempted her for mine own ends,   155
    More than for thine.
Joyless.   That's easily believed!
Letoy. And had she yielded, I not only had
    Rejected her—for it was ne'er my purpose,
    Heaven I call thee to witness, to commit
    A sin with her—but laid a punishment   160
    Upon her greater than thou couldst inflict.
Joyless. But how can this appear?
Letoy.   Do you know
    Your father, lady?
Diana. I hope I am so wise a child.
Letoy. [*To Byplay*]   Go call
    In my friend Truelock.
Byplay. [*To Joyless*]   Take your dagger, sir;   165
    Now I dare trust you.
Letoy.   Sirrah, dare you fool
    When I am serious? Send in Master Truelock.

                                        Exit BYPLAY.

Diana. That is my father's name.
Joyless.   Can he be here?
Letoy. Sir, I am neither conjurer nor witch,
    But a great fortune-teller that you'll find   170
    You are happy in a wife, sir, happier—yes,
    Happier by a hundred thousand pound
    Than you were yesterday.
Joyless.   So, so, now he's mad.
Letoy. I mean in possibilities, provided that
    You use her well, and never more be jealous.   175
Joyless. Must it come that way?
Letoy.   Look you this way, sir,

151.1.] *not in* Q.

164. *I . . . child*] 'It is a wise child that knows its own father' (C309).
170. *that*] who says that (Baker).

When I speak to you; I'll cross your fortune else,
    As I am true Letoy.
Joyless.   Mad, mad, he's mad.
    Would we were quickly out on's fingers yet.
Letoy. When saw you your wife's father? Answer me?   180
Joyless. He came for London four days before us.
Letoy. 'Tis possible he's here then. Do you know him?

Enter TRUELOCK.

Diana. O, I am happy in his sight. (*She kneels.*) Dear sir.
Letoy. 'Tis but so much knee-labour lost. Stand up,
    Stand up, and mind me.
Truelock.   You are well met, son Joyless.   185
Joyless. How have you been concealed, and in this house?
    Here's mystery in this.
Truelock.   My good lord's pleasure.
Letoy. Know, sir, that I sent for him, and for you,
    Instructing your friend Blaze, my instrument,
    To draw you to my doctor with your son.   190
    Your wife, I knew, must follow. What my end
    Was in't shall quickly be discovered to you
    In a few words of your supposèd father.
Diana. Supposèd father!
Letoy.   Yes. Come, Master Truelock,
    My constant friend of thirty years' acquaintance,   195
    Freely declare with your best knowledge now
    Whose child this is.
Truelock.   Your honour does as freely
    Release me of my vow, then, in the secret
    I locked up in this breast these seventeen years
    Since she was three days old.
Letoy.   True, Master Truelock.   200
    I do release you of your vow; now speak.
Truelock. Now she is yours, my lord, your only daughter.
    And know you, Master Joyless, for some reason
    Known to my lord, and large reward to me,
    She has been from the third day of her life   205
    Reputed mine, and that so covertly,
    That not her lady mother nor my wife

181.] *Act.5.Sc.6. Q (right-hand margin)*   186. in] *Baker; om. Q.*

179. *on's fingers*] of his clutches.

Knew to their deaths the change of my dead infant,
Nor this sweet lady. 'Tis most true we had
A trusty nurse's help and secrecy,   210
Well paid for, in the carriage of our plot.
Letoy. Now shall you know what moved me, sir. I was
A thing beyond a madman, like yourself
Jealous; and had that strong distrust, and fancied
Such proofs unto myself against my wife   215
That I conceived the child was not mine own,
And scorned to father it. Yet I gave to breed her
And marry her as the daughter of this gentleman—
Two thousand pound I guess you had with her.
But since your match, my wife upon her death-bed   220
So cleared herself of all my foul suspicions
(Blest be her memory) that I then resolved
By some quaint way (for I am still Letoy)
To see and try her throughly; and so much
To make her mine, as I should find her worthy.   225
And now thou art my daughter, [*To Joyless*] and mine heir,
Provided still (for I am still Letoy)
You honourably love her, and defy
The cuckold-making fiend, foul jealousy.
Joyless. My lord, 'tis not her birth and fortune, which   230
Do jointly claim a privilege to live
Above my reach of jealousy, shall restrain
That passion in me, but her well-tried virtue;
In the true faith of which I am confirmed,
And throughly cured.
Letoy.   As I am true Letoy,   235
Well said. I hope thy son is cured by this, too.

Enter BARBARA.

Letoy. Now Mistress Blaze! Here is a woman now!
I cured her husband's jealousy, and twenty more
I'th' town, by means I and my doctor wrought.
Barbara. Truly, my lord, my husband has ta'en bread   240
And drunk upon't, that under heaven he thinks
You were the means to make me an honest woman,
Or (at the least) him a contented man.

236.] *Acts.5.Sce.7. Q (right-hand margin).*

---

208. *the change*] about the swapping.
241. *drunk*] taken an oath.

Letoy. Ha' done, ha' done—
Barbara.   Yes, I believe you have done!
  And if your husband, lady, be cured, as he should be,   245
  And as all foolish jealous husbands ought to be,
  I know what was done first, if my lord took
  That course with you as me—
Letoy.   Prithee, what cam'st thou for?
Barbara. My lord, to tell you (as the doctor tells me)
  The bride and bridegroom, both, are coming on   250
  The sweetliest to their wits again.
Letoy.   I told you.
Barbara. Now you are a happy man, sir, and I hope
  A quiet man.
Joyless.   Full of content and joy.
Barbara. Content! So was my husband when he knew
  The worst he could by his wife. Now you'll live quiet, lady. 255
Letoy. Why flyest thou off thus, woman, from the subject
  Thou wert upon?
Barbara.   I beg your honour's pardon.
  And now I'll tell you. Be it by skill or chance,
  Or both, was never such a cure as is
  Upon that couple! Now they strive which most   260
  Shall love the other.
Letoy.   Are they up and ready?
Barbara. Up! Up, and ready to lie down again:
  There is no ho with them!
  They have been in th' Antipodes to some purpose,
  And now are risen and returned themselves.   265
  He's her dear 'Per', and she is his sweet 'Mat'.
  His kingship and her queenship are forgotten,
  And all their melancholy and his travels passed,
  And but supposed their dreams.
Letoy.   'Tis excellent.
Barbara. Now, sir, the doctor—for he is become   270
  An utter stranger to your son, and so
  Are all about 'em—craves your presence,
  And such as he's acquainted with.
Letoy. [*To Joyless*]   Go, sir.

---

244. *done!*] For the bawdy, cf. *Measure for Measure*: 'What has he done?/A woman' (I.ii.80–1, Arden ed.).
261. *ready*] dressed.
263. *no . . . with*] no stopping.
273. *he's*] i.e. Peregrine.

> And go you, daughter.
Barbara. [*Aside*]   Daughter! That's the true trick
> Of all old whoremasters, to call their wenches   275
> Daughters.
Letoy.   Has he known you, friend Truelock, too?
Truelock. Yes, from his childhood.
Letoy.   Go, then, and possess him,
> Now he is sensible, how things have gone,
> What art, what means, what friends have been employed
> In his rare cure; and win him, by degrees,   280
> To sense of where he is. Bring him to me;
> And I have yet an entertainment for him
> Of better settle-brain than drunkard's porridge
> To set him right. As I am true Letoy,
> I have one toy left. Go.
>   *Exeunt* TRUELOCK, JOYLESS *and* DIANA.
>   And go you; why stay'st thou?   285
Barbara. If I had been a gentlewoman born,
> I should have been your daughter too, my lord.
Letoy. But never as she is. You'll know anon.
Barbara. Neat city wives' flesh yet may be as good
> As your coarse country gentlewoman's blood.   290
>   *Exit* BARBARA.
Letoy. Go with thy flesh to Turnbull shambles! Ho,
> Within there!

Enter QUAILPIPE.

Quailpipe.   Here, my lord.
Letoy.   The music, songs,
> And dance I gave command for, are they ready?
Quailpipe. All, my lord; and in good sooth I cannot
> Enough applaud your honour's quaint conceit   295

278–82.] *as Baker; prose in* Q. 285.SD] *Exe.Ioy.* Q (*at end of line*). 292.]
Act.5.Sce.8. (before SD) Q. 294–302.] *as Haaker; prose in* Q. 305.] *Act* 5.*Sce.9.*
Q (*right-hand margin*).

---

283. *drunkard's porridge*] porridge was regarded as 'grosse fare' which induces a
'thick braine' (Jonson, *Every Man Out*, II.iii.71–3), and therefore perhaps as
a suitable cure for a hangover.

286–7.] i.e. you weren't prepared to use that one on me. Letoy's answer
acknowledges that he is not above such a ploy.

291. *Turnbull*] Turnbull Street, running south from Clerkenwell, was a notorious
centre of prostitution.

In the design, so apt, so regular,
So pregnant, so acute, and so withal
Poetice legitimate, as I may say
Justly with Plautus—
Letoy.   Prithee say no more,
But see upon my signal given they act   300
As well as I designed.
Quailpipe.   Nay not so well,
My exact lord, but as they may, they shall.   *Exit.*
Letoy. I know no flatterer in my house but this,
But for his custom I must bear with him.
'Sprecious, they come already. Now begin.   305

> *A solemn lesson upon the recorders. Enter* TRUELOCK,
> JOYLESS *and* DIANA, PEREGRINE *and* MARTHA,
> Doctor HUGHBALL *and* BARBARA; LETOY *meets them.*
> TRUELOCK *presents* PEREGRINE *and* MARTHA *to him;*
> *he salutes them. They seem to make some short discourse.*
> *Then* LETOY *appoints them to sit.* PEREGRINE *seems*
> *something amazed. The music ceases.*

Letoy. Again you are welcome, sir, and welcome all.
Peregrine. I am what you are pleased to make me; but
Withal so ignorant of mine own condition—
Whether I sleep, or wake, or talk, or dream;
Whether I be, or be not; or if I am,   310
Whether I do, or do not anything.
For I have had (if now I wake) such dreams,
And been so far transported in a long
And tedious voyage of sleep, that I may fear
My manners can acquire no welcome where   315
Men understand themselves.
Letoy.   This is music, sir!
You are welcome, and I give full power unto
Your father and my daughter here, your mother,
To make you welcome. (JOYLESS *whispers to* PEREGRINE.)
Peregrine.   How! Your daughter, sir?

306–27.] *prose in Q.*   319.SD *to*] *not in Q.*

296–9. *so . . . Plautus*] Ben Jonson thought that 'in *Plautus*, wee shall see the
Oeconomy, and disposition of *Poems*, better observed then in *Terence*' (*Discoveries*,
1816–18, HS VIII.618).
    298. *Poetice*] poetically.
    304. *for . . . custom*] because it is his customary manner.
    305.1. *lesson*] piece.

Doctor. [*Aside*] My lord, you'll put him back again if you   320
Trouble his brain with new discoveries.
Letoy. [*Aside*] Fetch him you on again then; pray, are you
Letoy or I?
Joyless.   Indeed it is so, son.
Doctor. [*Aside*] I fear your show will but perplex him too.
Letoy. [*Aside*] I care not, sir; I'll have it to delay   325
Your cure a while, that he recover soundly.—
Come, sit again; again you are most welcome.

A most untuneable flourish. Enter Discord *attended by* Folly,
Jealousy, Melancholy *and* Madness.

Letoy. There's an unwelcome guest, uncivil Discord, that trains
into my house her followers: Folly and Jealousy, Melancholy and Madness.   330
Barbara. My husband presents Jealousy in the black and
yellow jaundied suit there, half like man and t'other half
like woman, with one horn and ass ear upon his head.
Letoy. Peace, woman. [*To* PEREGRINE] Mark what they do;
but by the way,
Conceive me this but show, sir, and device.   335
Peregrine. I think so.
Letoy. [*Aside*] How goes he back again now, doctor? Sheugh!

Song in untuneable notes.

Discord.   Come forth my darlings, you that breed
The common strifes that discord feed.
Come in the first place, my dear Folly,   340
Jealousy next, then Melancholy.
And last come Madness, thou art he
That bear'st th' effects of all those three.
Lend me your aids, so Discord shall you crown,
And make this place a kingdom of our own.   345

327.1.] *Act* 5.*Sce.*10. *Q* (*before SD*).   328. *Letoy*] *not in Q*.   345.1.] *Act* 5.*Scene*
11. *Q* (*before SD*).

327.1. untuneable] discordant.
328. *trains*] lures.
333. *one horn*] signifying fear of cuckoldry.
335. *device*] dramatic artifice.
337.1–345.3. Song...down] Discord and her attendants form an anti-masque,
representing the evil and disorderly forces that will be vanquished in the main body of
the masque. Brome's mentor Jonson perfected this dramatic structure in his Jacobean
masques.

They dance. After a while they are broke off by a flourish,
and the approach of Harmony *followed by* Mercury, Cupid,
Bacchus *and* Apollo. Discord *and her faction fall down.*

Letoy. See, Harmony approaches, leading on
　　'Gainst Discord's factions four great deities:
　　Mercury, Cupid, Bacchus, and Apollo.
　　Wit against Folly, Love against Jealousy,
　　Wine against Melancholy, and 'gainst Madness, Health.　　350
　　Observe the matter and the method.
Peregrine.　　　　　　　　　　　　　　Yes.
Letoy. And how upon the approach of Harmony
　　Discord and her disorders are confounded.

　　　　　　　　　　　　Song.

Harmony. Come Wit, come Love, come Wine, come Health,
　　　　　Maintainers of my commonwealth,　　　　　　355
　　　　　'Tis you make Harmony complete,
　　　　　And from the spheres, her proper seat,
　　　　　You give her power to reign on earth
　　　　　Where Discord claims a right by birth.
　　　　　Then let us revel it while we are here,　　　360
　　　　　And keep possession of this hemisphere.

After a strain or two, Discord *cheers up her faction.*
They all rise and mingle in the dance with Harmony
　　　　　and the rest. Dance.

Letoy. Note there how Discord cheers up her disorders,
　　To mingle in defiance with the virtues.
　　　　　　　　　　　　Exit Discord *and her followers.*
　　But soon they vanish; and the mansion quit
　　Unto the gods of health, love, wine and wit　　　365
　　Who triumph in their habitation new,
　　Which they have taken and assign to you.
　　In which they now salute you, bid you be
　　Of cheer, and for it lay the charge on me.
　　　　　　　　Harmony *and her followers salute and exeunt.*
　　And unto me y'are welcome, welcome all.　　　370
　　Meat, wine and mirth shall flow, and what I see
　　Yet wanting in your cure, supplied shall be.

---

347. four] feare Q.　363.1.] *Ex.Discord.* Q.　368. bid] *Baker;* bids Q.　369 lay]
Baker; lays Q.　369.1.] *as Baker; Salute Exe.* Q *(next to 368).*

Peregrine.   Indeed, I find me well.
Martha.   And so shall I
    After a few such nights more!
Barbara.   Are you there?
Martha.   [*To Diana*] Good madam, pardon errors of my
                                             tongue.   375
Diana.   I am too happy made to think of wrong.
Letoy.   We will want nothing for you that may please,
    Though we dive for it to th'Antipodes.

THE EPILOGUE

Doctor.   Whether my cure be perfect yet or no
    It lies not in my doctorship to know.   380
    Your approbation may more raise the man
    Than all the College of Physicians can,
    And more health from your fair hands may be won
    Than by the strokings of the seventh son.
Peregrine.   And from our travels in th'Antipodes   385
    We are not yet arrived from off the seas;
    But on the waves of desp'rate fears we roam
    Until your gentler hands do waft us home.

FINIS

375.] Editors give this line to Barbara, but her words in 374 seem to be an interjection (in *Q* they are printed well to the right of Martha's *After . . . more*, thus obviating the need for a new speech-prefix for Martha in 375). It is the latter's immodesty rather than Barbara's abruptness that requires a conventional apology.

384. *by . . . son*] Seven symbolically denoted completion or perfection; the seventh son in the family was supposedly endowed with supernatural powers (Haaker, citing *OED*).

INDEX TO THE COMMENTARY

This index lists words and phrases which receive some discussion in a note; those which are simply glossed or paraphrased are not included unless they are of unusual interest or of particular relevance to the book's theme. Characters' names are included only if they are discussed in commentary other than that on cast-lists.

An asterisk before a word indicates that the note contains information about meaning, usage or date which supplements that given in the *OED*.

Initial lower-case roman numerals followed by an arabic number (e.g. vii.43) always refer to *Travels*; references to *Sea Voyage* and *Antipodes* are distinguished by prefatory S/ and A/ respectively, eg. S/IV.iii.25, A/III.67. Other abbreviations used are Epist.*Trav*.=Epistle to *Travels*; Prol.*Trav*.=Prologue to *Travels*; Ep.*Trav*.=Epilogue to *Travels*; A/C.C.=prefatory poem To Censuring Critics.